The Java™ Web Services Tutorial

12/7/2002 B+N 44.99

The Java™ Series

Lisa Friendly, Series Editor
Tim Lindholm, Technical Editor
Ken Arnold, Technical Editor of The Jini™ Technology Series
Jim Inscore, Technical Editor of The Java™ Series, Enterprise Edition

---

Ken Arnold, James Gosling, David Holmes
The Java™ Programming Language, Third Edition

Joshua Bloch
Effective Java™ Programming Language Guide

Greg Bollella, James Gosling, Ben Brosgol, Peter Dibble, Steve Furr, David Hardin, Mark Turnbull
The Real-Time Specification for Java™

Mary Campione, Kathy Walrath, Alison Huml
The Java™ Tutorial, Third Edition: A Short Course on the Basics

Mary Campione, Kathy Walrath, Alison Huml, Tutorial Team
The Java™ Tutorial Continued: The Rest of the JDK™

Patrick Chan
The Java™ Developers Almanac 2000

Patrick Chan, Rosanna Lee
The Java™ Class Libraries, Second Edition, Volume 2: java.applet, java.awt, java.beans

Patrick Chan, Rosanna Lee, Doug Kramer
The Java™ Class Libraries, Second Edition, Volume 1: java.io, java.lang, java.math, java.net, java.text, java.util

Patrick Chan, Rosanna Lee, Doug Kramer
The Java™ Class Libraries, Second Edition, Volume 1: Supplement for the Java™ 2 Platform, Standard Edition, v1.2

Kirk Chen, Li Gong
Programming Open Service Gateways with Java™ Embedded Server

Zhiqun Chen
Java Card™ Technology for Smart Cards: Architecture and Programmer's Guide

Li Gong
Inside Java™ 2 Platform Security: Architecture, API Design, and Implementation

James Gosling, Bill Joy, Guy Steele, Gilad Bracha
The Java™ Language Specification, Second Edition

Doug Lea
Concurrent Programming in Java™, Second Edition: Design Principles and Patterns

Rosanna Lee, Scott Seligman
JNDI API Tutorial and Reference: Building Directory-Enabled Java™ Applications

Sheng Liang
The Java™ Native Interface: Programmer's Guide and Specification

Tim Lindholm, Frank Yellin
The Java™ Virtual Machine Specification, Second Edition

Roger Riggs, Antero Taivalsaari, Mark VandenBrink
Programming Wireless Devices with the Java™ 2 Platform, Micro Edition

Henry Sowizral, Kevin Rushforth, Michael Deering
The Java 3D™ API Specification, Second Edition

Sun Microsystems, Inc.
Java™ Look and Feel Design Guidelines: Advanced Topics

Kathy Walrath, Mary Campione
The JFC Swing Tutorial: A Guide to Constructing GUIs

Seth White, Maydene Fisher, Rick Cattell, Graham Hamilton, Mark Hapner
JDBC™ API Tutorial and Reference, Second Edition: Universal Data Access for the Java™ 2 Platform

Steve Wilson, Jeff Kesselman
Java™ Platform Performance: Strategies and Tactics

The Jini™ Technology Series

Eric Freeman, Susanne Hupfer, Ken Arnold
JavaSpaces™ Principles, Patterns, and Practice

Jim Waldo/Jini™ Technology Team
The Jini™ Specifications, Second Edition, edited by Ken Arnold

The Java™ Series, Enterprise Edition

Stephanie Bodoff, Dale Green, Kim Haase, Eric Jendrock, Monica Pawlan, Beth Stearns
The J2EE™ Tutorial

Rick Cattell, Jim Inscore, Enterprise Partners
J2EE™ Technology in Practice: Building Business Applications with the Java™ 2 Platform, Enterprise Edition

Mark Hapner, Rich Burridge, Rahul Sharma, Joseph Fialli, Kim Haase
Java™ Message Service API Tutorial and Reference: Messaging for the J2EE™ Platform

Nicholas Kassem, Enterprise Team
Designing Enterprise Applications with the Java™ 2 Platform, Enterprise Edition

Vlada Matena and Beth Stearns
Applying Enterprise JavaBeans™: Component-Based Development for the J2EE™ Platform

Bill Shannon, Mark Hapner, Vlada Matena, James Davidson, Eduardo Pelegri-Llopart, Larry Cable, Enterprise Team
Java™ 2 Platform, Enterprise Edition: Platform and Component Specifications

Rahul Sharma, Beth Stearns, Tony Ng
J2EE™ Connector Architecture and Enterprise Application Integration

http://www.javaseries.com

The Java™ Web Services Tutorial

Eric Armstrong
Stephanie Bodoff
Debbie Carson
Maydene Fisher
Dale Green
Kim Haase

Addison-Wesley

Boston • San Francisco • New York • Toronto • Montreal
London • Munich • Paris • Madrid
Capetown • Sydney • Tokyo • Singapore • Mexico City

Duke™ designed by Joe Palrang

Pearson Education Corporate Sales Division

201 W. 103rd Street
Indianapolis, IN 46290
(800) 428-5331
corpsales@pearsoned.com

Visit AW on the Web: www.aw.com/cseng/

Library of Congress Control Number: 2002102590

ISBN 0-201-76811-9

Text printed on recycled paper

1 2 3 4 5 6 7 8 9 10—MA—0605040302

First printing, March 2002

Contents

Foreword

BACK in the fall of 1996 the buzz on Java technology was exploding, but our team at Sun Microsystems was still very small. There were about 25 of us and we took turns responding to the email that started pouring in.

Even in 1996 so many developers were asking us, "What are the best books to read on this stuff?" Many would write in and say, "We love the online *Java Tutorial* by Campione and Walrath. When can we buy it as a book?"

It made us realize that while we were pioneering the idea of publishing technical documentation online, our team also needed to be a beacon in the explosion of books on this new technology. So along with James Gosling and Bill Joy, I started the Java Series; books directly from our engineering team, published on our behalf by Addison-Wesley. Developers would still have a great selection of books to choose from, and when they needed to, they could come directly to the source.

That same explosion of interest is happening now with Web Services technology. Our email makes it clear that developers need the tutorial on this stuff today. Especially with early access technology, developers want to hear "from the Source." Because we've been writing the definitive tutorials on Java technology for seven years now, you can rely on the fact that our authors, editors, and technical reviewers know how to apply the same high standards to a book on Web Services that we apply to our other outstanding Java tutorials.

By releasing this Early Access Edition of the *Web Services Tutorial* in time for the JavaOne Developers Conference 2002, we're getting the information to you that you need to be successful with Web Services technology now. We've included a CD loaded with all the downloads, tutorials, demos, and sample code you can use to get up to speed very quickly.

There's an email alias (webservicestutorial@sun.com) where you can send us your feedback. Please do. As we did in 1996, and have ever since, we read and respond to every piece of email that comes in regarding the Java Series. Write to us and you'll definitely hear back from us.

Until then,

Lisa Friendly
Java Series Managing Editor, Sun Microsystems, Inc.
Santa Clara, CA
February, 2002

Preface

THE Java™ Web Services Tutorial is a beginner's guide to developing Web services and Web applications using the Java Web Services Developer Pack (Java WSDP). The Java WSDP is an all-in-one download containing key technologies to simplify building of Web services using the Java 2 Platform. The technologies available on the Java WSDP are:

- Java Servlets
- JavaServer Pages (JSP)
- JSP Standard Tag Library (JSTL)
- Java XML Pack, which includes:
    - Java API for XML Messaging (JAXM)
    - Java API for XML Processing (JAXP)
    - Java API for XML Registries (JAXR)
    - Java API for XML-based RPC (JAX-RPC)

To provide a development and deployment environment, the Java WSDP includes the:

- Tomcat servlet and JSP container
- Ant build tool
- Java WSDP Registry Server

Here we cover all the things you need to know to make the best use of *The Java™ Web Services Tutorial.*

Who Should Use This Tutorial

This tutorial is intended for programmers interested in developing and deploying Web services and Web applications on the Java WSDP.

About the Examples

This tutorial includes many complete, working examples.

Prerequisites for the Examples

To understand the examples you will need a good knowledge of the Java programming language, SQL, and relational database concepts. The following topics in the Java Tutorial are particularly relevant:

Topic	Java Tutorial
JDBC	`http://java.sun.com/docs/books/tutorial/jdbc`
Threads	`http://java.sun.com/docs/books/tutorial/essential/threads`
JavaBeans	`http://java.sun.com/docs/books/tutorial/javabeans`
Security	`http://java.sun.com/docs/books/tutorial/security1.2`

Running the Examples

This section tells you everything you need to know to obtain, build, deploy, and run the examples.

Required Software

If you are viewing this online, you need to download *The Java Web™ Services Tutorial* from:

```
http://java.sun.com/webservices/downloads/webservicestutorial.html
```

Once you have installed the tutorial bundle, the example source code is in the `<JWSDP_HOME>/docs/tutorial/examples` directory, with subdirectories for each of the technologies included in the pack.

This tutorial documents the Java WSDP EA1. To build, deploy, and run the examples you need a copy of the Java WSDP and the Java 2 Platform, Standard Edition (J2SE™) SDK 1.3.1 or 1.4. You can download the Java WSDP from:

```
http://java.sun.com/webservices/downloads/webservicespack.html
```

the J2SE 1.3.1 SDK from:

```
http://java.sun.com/j2se/1.3/
```

or the J2SE 1.4 SDK from:

```
http://java.sun.com/j2se/1.4/
```

Set the environment variables to the values noted in Table 1.

Table 1 Required Environment Variables

Environment Variable	Value
JAVA_HOME	The location of the J2SE SDK installation.
JWSDP_HOME	The location of the Java WSDP installation. This variable is used by the example build files.
PATH	Add the bin directories of the Java WSDP and J2SE SDK installations to the front. The Java WSDP bin directory contains the startup scripts for Tomcat, ant, and the registry server as well as other tools.

Building the Examples

Most of the examples are distributed with a configuration file for version 1.4.1 of ant, a portable build tool contained in the Java WSDP. Directions for building the examples are provided in each chapter.

Deploying the Examples

Most of the Java WSDP examples run on Tomcat. Before you can run an example you must first deploy it on Tomcat. To deploy an application execute `ant deploy`. The deploy task usually copies some files into the `<JWSDP_HOME>/webapps` directory. Some things you need to keep in mind:

- For this release of the Java WSDP you must be running Tomcat on the same machine that you are developing on.
- The first time an application is deployed you must start or restart Tomcat (see next section). Thereafter, when you modify an application, you can build, deploy, and then reload the example, as described in the next section.

Running Tomcat

You run Tomcat by executing the `startup` script in a terminal window.

Reloading the Examples

You reload an application with the command:

```
http://localhost:8080/manager/reload?path=/target
```

This command invokes the `manager` Web application. Before you can use this application you must add your user name and password combination and associate the role name `manager` with it to `<JWSDP_HOME>/conf/tomcat-users.xml`, which can be edited with any text editor. This file contains an element `<user>` for each individual user, which might look something like this:

```
<user name="adeveloper" password="secret" roles="manager" />
```

The Tomcat reference documentation distributed with the Java WSDP contains information about the manager application.

Related Information

For further information on the technologies discussed in this tutorial see the reference documentation contained in the Java WSDP (`<JWSDP_HOME>/docs/index.html`) and the Web sites listed in Table 2. References to individual technology homes listed in some chapters map as follows:

- `JAXM-HOME` to `JWSDP_HOME/docs/jaxm/index.html`
- `JAXP-HOME` to `JWSDP_HOME/docs/jaxp/index.html`
- `JAXR-HOME` to `JWSDP_HOME/docs/jaxr/index.html`
- `JAXRPC-HOME` to `JWSDP_HOME/docs/jaxrpc/index.html`

Table 2 Related Information

Technology	Web Site
Java Servlets	`http://java.sun.com/products/servlet/index.html`
JavaServer Pages	`http://java.sun.com/products/jsp/index.html`
JSP Standard Tag Library	`http://java.sun.com/products/jsp/taglibraries.html#jstl`
JAXM	`http://java.sun.com/xml/jaxm/index.html`
JAXP	`http://java.sun.com/xml/jaxp/index.html`
JAXR	`http://java.sun.com/xml/jaxr/index.html`
JAX-RPC	`http://java.sun.com/xml/jaxrpc/index.html`
Tomcat	`http://jakarta.apache.org/tomcat/index.html`
ant	`http://jakarta.apache.org/ant/index.html`

How to Print This Tutorial

To print this tutorial, follow these steps:

- Ensure that Adobe Acrobat Reader is installed on your system.
- Open the PDF version of this book.
- Click the printer icon in Adobe Acrobat Reader.

Typographical Conventions

The following table lists the typographical conventions used in this tutorial.

Table 3 Typographical Conventions

Font Style	Uses
italic	Emphasis, titles, first occurrence of terms
`monospace`	URLs, code examples, file names, command names, programming language keywords
`italic monospace`	Programming variables, variable file names

CHAPTER 1

Introduction to Web Services

Maydene Fisher

IN THIS CHAPTER

WEB services, as the name implies, are services offered via the Web. In a typical Web services scenario, a business application sends a request to a service at a given URL using the SOAP protocol over HTTP. The service receives the request, processes it, and returns a response. An often-cited example of a Web service is that of a stock quote service, in which the request asks for the current price of a specified stock, and the response gives the stock price. This is one of the simplest forms of a Web service in that the request is filled almost immediately, with the request and response being parts of the same method call.

Another example could be a service that maps out an efficient route for the delivery of goods. In this case, a business sends a request containing the delivery destinations, which the service processes to determine the most cost-effective delivery route. The time it takes to return the response depends on the complexity of the routing, but the response will probably be sent as an operation that is separate from the request.

Web services and consumers of Web services are typically businesses, making Web services predominantly business-to-business (B-to-B) transactions. An enterprise can be the provider of Web services and also the consumer of other Web services. For example, a wholesale distributor of spices could be in the consumer role when it uses a Web service to check on the availability of vanilla beans and in the provider role when it supplies prospective customers with different vendors' prices for vanilla beans.

1.1 The Role of XML and the Java Platform

Web services depend on the ability of parties to communicate with each other even if they are using different information systems and different data formats. XML, a markup language that makes data portable, is a key technology in addressing this need. Enterprises have discovered the benefits of using XML for the integration of data both internally for sharing legacy data among departments and externally for sharing data with other enterprises. As a result, XML is increasingly being used for enterprise integration applications, both in tightly coupled and loosely coupled systems. Because of this data integration ability, XML has become the underpinning for Web-related computing.

Web services also depend on the ability of enterprises using different computing platforms to communicate with each other. This requirement makes the Java platform, which makes code portable, the natural choice for developing Web services. This choice is even more attractive as the new Java APIs for XML become available, making it easier and easier to use XML from the Java programming language. These APIs are summarized later in this introduction and explained in detail in the tutorials for each API.

In addition to data portability and code portability, Web services need to be scalable, secure, and efficient, especially as they grow. The Java 2 Platform, Enterprise Edition (J2EE), is specifically designed to fill just such needs. It facilitates the really hard part of developing Web services, which is programming the infrastructure, or "plumbing." This infrastructure includes features such as security, distributed transaction management, and connection pool management, all of which are essential for industrial strength Web services. And because components are reusable, development time is substantially reduced.

XML and the Java platform, being such an ideal combination, have come to play a central role in Web services. In fact, the advantages offered by the Java APIs for XML and the J2EE platform make them the ideal combination for deploying Web services.

The APIs described in this tutorial complement and layer on top of the J2EE APIs. These APIs enable the Java community, developers, tool and container vendors, to start developing Web services applications and products using standard Java APIs that maintain the fundamental Write Once, Run Anywhere proposition of Java technology. The Java Web Services Developer Pack (Java WSDP) makes all these APIs available in a single bundle. The Java WSDP includes JAR files implementing these APIs as well as documentation and examples. The examples in the Java WSDP will run in the Tomcat container (included in the Java WSDP to help with ease of use), as well as in a J2EE container once the Java WSDP JAR files are installed in the J2EE SDK. Instructions on how to install the JAR files on the J2EE SDK will be available with the 1.3.1 release of the J2EE SDK.

The remainder of this introduction first gives a quick look at XML and how it makes data portable. Then it gives an overview of the Java APIs for XML, explaining what they do and how they make writing Web applications easier. It describes each of the APIs individually and then presents a scenario that illustrates how they can work together.

The tutorials that follow give more detailed explanations and walk you through how to use the Java APIs for XML to build applications for Web services. They also provide sample applications that you can run.

1.2 What Is XML?

The chapter Understanding XML (page 29) includes a more thorough and detailed explanation of XML and how to process it. The goal of this section is to give you a quick introduction to what XML is and how it makes data portable so that you have some background for reading the summaries of the Java APIs for XML that follow.

XML (Extensible Markup Language) is an industry-standard, system-independent way of representing data. Like HTML (HyperText Markup Language), XML encloses data in tags, but there are significant differences between the two markup languages. First, XML tags relate to the meaning of the enclosed text, whereas HTML tags specify how to display the enclosed text. The following XML example shows a price list with the name and price of two coffees.

```
<priceList>
    <coffee>
        <name>Mocha Java</name>
        <price>11.95</price>
    </coffee>
```

```
    <coffee>
        <name>Sumatra</name>
        <price>12.50</price>
    </coffee>
</priceList>
```

The <coffee> and </coffee> tags tell a parser that the information between them is about a coffee. The two other tags inside the <coffee> tags specify that the enclosed information is the coffee's name and its price per pound. Because XML tags indicate the content and structure of the data they enclose, they make it possible to do things like archiving and searching.

A second major difference between XML and HTML is that XML tags are extensible, allowing you to write your own XML tags to describe your content. With HTML, you are limited to using only those tags that have been predefined in the HTML specification.

With the extensibility that XML provides, you can create the tags you need for a particular type of document. You define the tags using an XML schema language. A schema describes the structure of a set of XML documents and can be used to constrain the contents of the XML documents. Probably the most widely used schema language is still the Document Type Definition schema language because it is an integral part of the XML 1.0 specification. A schema written in this language is called a DTD. The DTD that follows defines the tags used in the price list XML document. It specifies four tags (elements) and further specifies which tags may occur (or are required to occur) in other tags. The DTD also defines the hierarchical structure of an XML document, including the order in which the tags must occur.

```
<!ELEMENT priceList (coffee)+>
<!ELEMENT coffee (name, price) >
<!ELEMENT name (#PCDATA) >
<!ELEMENT price (#PCDATA) >
```

The first line in the example gives the highest level element, priceList, which means that all the other tags in the document will come between the <priceList> and </priceList> tags. The first line also says that the priceList element must contain one or more coffee elements (indicated by the plus sign). The second line specifies that each coffee element must contain both a name element and a price element, in that order. The third and fourth lines specify that the data between the tags <name> and </name> and between <price> and </price> is character data that should be parsed. The name and price of each coffee are the actual text that makes up the price list.

Another popular schema language is XML schema, which is being developed by the World Wide Web (W3C) consortium. XML Schema is a significantly more powerful language than DTD, and with its passage into a W3C Recommendation in May of 2001, its use and implementations have increased. The community of developers using the Java platform has recognized this, and the expert group for the Java API for XML Processing (JAXP) has been working on adding support for XML Schema to the JAXP 1.2 specification. This release of the Java Web Services Developer Pack (Java WSDP) includes support for XML Schema.

1.2.1 What Makes XML Portable?

A schema gives XML data its portability. The `priceList` DTD, discussed previously, is a simple example of a schema. If an application is sent a `priceList` document in XML format and has the `priceList` DTD, it can process the document according to the rules specified in the DTD. For example, given the `priceList` DTD, a parser will know the structure and type of content for any XML document based on that DTD. If the parser is a validating parser, it will know that the document is not valid if it contains an element not included in the DTD, such as the element `<tea>`, or if the elements are not in the prescribed order, such as having the `price` element precede the `name` element.

Other features also contribute to the popularity of XML as a method for data interchange. For one thing, it is written in a text format, which is readable by both human beings and text-editing software. Applications can parse and process XML documents, and human beings can also read them in case there is an error in processing. Another feature is that because an XML document does not include formatting instructions, it can be displayed in various ways. Keeping data separate from formatting instructions means that the same data can be published to different media.

XML enables document portability, but it cannot do the job in a vacuum; that is, parties who use XML must agree to certain conditions. For example, in addition to agreeing to use XML for communicating, two applications must agree to what set of elements they will use and what those elements mean. For them to use Web services, they must also agree on what Web services methods they will use, what those methods do, and when more than one method is needed, the order in which they are invoked.

Enterprises have several technologies available to help satisfy these requirements. They can use DTDs and XML schemas to describe the valid terms and XML documents they will use in communicating with each other. Registries provide a means for describing Web services and their methods. For higher level concepts, enterprises can use partner agreements and workflow charts and choreographies. There will be more about schemas and registries later in this document.

1.3 Overview of the Java APIs for XML

The Java APIs for XML let you write your Web applications entirely in the Java programming language. They fall into two broad categories: those that deal directly with processing XML documents and those that deal with procedures.

- Document-oriented
    - Java API for XML Processing (JAXP)—processes XML documents using various parsers
- Procedure-oriented
    - Java API for XML Messaging (JAXM)—sends SOAP messages over the Internet in a standard way
    - Java API for XML Registries (JAXR)—provides a standard way to access business registries and share information
    - Java API for XML-based RPC (JAX-RPC)—sends SOAP method calls to remote parties over the Internet and receives the results

Perhaps the most important feature of the Java APIs for XML is that they all support industry standards, thus ensuring interoperability. Various network interoperability standards groups, such as the World Wide Web Consortium (W3C) and the Organization for the Advancement of Structured Information Standards (OASIS), have been defining standard ways of doing things so that businesses who follow these standards can make their data and applications work together.

Another feature of the Java APIs for XML is that they allow a great deal of flexibility. Users have flexibility in how they use the APIs. For example, JAXP code can use various tools for processing an XML document, and JAXM code can use various messaging protocols on top of SOAP. Implementers have flexibility as well. The Java APIs for XML define strict compatibility requirements to ensure that all implementations deliver the standard functionality, but they also give developers a great deal of freedom to provide implementations tailored to specific uses.

The following sections discuss each of these APIs, giving an overview and a feel for how to use them.

1.4 JAXP

The Java API for XML Processing (page 67) (JAXP) makes it easy to process XML data using applications written in the Java programming language. JAXP leverages the parser standards SAX (Simple API for XML Parsing) and DOM (Document Object Model) so that you can choose to parse your data as a stream of events or to build an object representation of it. The latest versions of JAXP also supports the XSLT (XML Stylesheet Language Transformations) standard, giving you control over the presentation of the data and enabling you to convert the data to other XML documents or to other formats, such as HTML. JAXP also provides namespace support, allowing you to work with XML Schemas that might otherwise have naming conflicts.

Designed to be flexible, JAXP allows you to use any XML-compliant parser from within your application. It does this with what is called a pluggability layer, which allows you to plug in an implementation of the SAX or DOM APIs. The pluggability layer also allows you to plug in an XSL processor, letting you control how your XML data is displayed.

The latest version of JAXP is JAXP 1.2, a maintenance release that adds support for XML Schema. This version is currently being finalized through the Java Community Process℠ (JSR-63). An early access version of JAXP 1.2 is included in this Java WSDP release and is also available in the Java XML Pack.

1.4.1 The SAX API

The Simple API for XML (page 77) defines an API for an event-based parser. Being event-based means that the parser reads an XML document from beginning to end, and each time it recognizes a syntax construction, it notifies the application that is running it. The SAX parser notifies the application by calling methods from the `ContentHandler` interface. For example, when the parser comes to a less than symbol (<), it calls the `startElement` method; when it comes to character data, it calls the `characters` method; when it comes to the less than symbol followed by a slash (</), it calls the `endElement` method, and so on. To illustrate, let's look at part of the example XML document from the first section and walk through what the parser does for each line. (For simplicity, calls to the method `ignorableWhiteSpace` are not included.)

```
<priceList>[parser calls startElement]
    <coffee>    [parser calls startElement]
        <name>Mocha Java</name>   [parser calls startElement,
                                  characters, and endElement]
```

```
        <price>11.95</price>     [parser calls startElement,
                                  characters, and endElement]
    </coffee>    [parser calls endElement]
```

The default implementations of the methods that the parser calls do nothing, so you need to write a subclass implementing the appropriate methods to get the functionality you want. For example, suppose you want to get the price per pound for Mocha Java. You would write a class extending `DefaultHandler` (the default implementation of `ContentHandler`) in which you write your own implementations of the methods `startElement` and `characters`.

You first need to create a `SAXParser` object from a `SAXParserFactory` object. You would call the method `parse` on it, passing it the price list and an instance of your new handler class (with its new implementations of the methods `startElement` and `characters`). In this example, the price list is a file, but the `parse` method can also take a variety of other input sources, including an `InputStream` object, a URL, and an `InputSource` object.

```
SAXParserFactory factory = SAXParserFactory.newInstance();
SAXParser saxParser = factory.newSAXParser();
saxParser.parse("priceList.xml", handler);
```

The result of calling the method `parse` depends, of course, on how the methods in *`handler`* were implemented. The SAX parser will go through the file `priceList.xml` line by line, calling the appropriate methods. In addition to the methods already mentioned, the parser will call other methods such as `startDocument`, `endDocument`, `ignorableWhiteSpace`, and `processingInstructions`, but these methods still have their default implementations and thus do nothing.

The following method definitions show one way to implement the methods `characters` and `startElement` so that they find the price for Mocha Java and print it out. Because of the way the SAX parser works, these two methods work together to look for the `name` element, the characters "Mocha Java", and the `price` element immediately following Mocha Java. These methods use three flags to keep track of which conditions have been met. Note that the SAX parser will have to invoke both methods more than once before the conditions for printing the price are met.

```
public void startElement(..., String elementName, ...){
    if(elementName.equals("name")){
        inName = true;
    } else if(elementName.equals("price") && inMochaJava ){
        inPrice = true;
```

```
            inName = false;
        }
    }
    public void characters(char [] buf, int offset, int len) {
        String s = new String(buf, offset, len);
        if (inName && s.equals("Mocha Java")) {
            inMochaJava = true;
            inName = false;
        } else if (inPrice) {
            System.out.println("The price of Mocha Java is: " + s);
            inMochaJava = false;
            inPrice = false;
            }
        }
    }
```

Once the parser has come to the Mocha Java coffee element, here is the relevant state after the following method calls:

next invocation of `startElement` -- `inName` is `true`
next invocation of `characters` -- `inMochaJava` is `true`
next invocation of `startElement` -- `inPrice` is `true`
next invocation of `characters` -- prints price

The SAX parser can perform validation while it is parsing XML data, which means that it checks that the data follows the rules specified in the XML document's DTD. A SAX parser will be validating if it is created by a `SAXParserFactory` object that has had validation turned on. This is done for the `SAXParserFactory` object `factory` in the following line of code.

```
factory.setValidating(true);
```

So that the parser knows which DTD to use for validation, the XML document must refer to the DTD in its `DOCTYPE` declaration. The `DOCTYPE` declaration should be similar to this:

```
<!DOCTYPE PriceList SYSTEM "priceList.DTD">
```

1.4.2 The DOM API

The Document Object Model (page 149), defined by the W3C DOM Working Group, is a set of interfaces for building an object representation, in the form of a tree, of a parsed XML document. Once you build the DOM, you can manipulate it with DOM methods such as `insert` and `remove`, just as you would manipulate any other tree data structure. Thus, unlike a SAX parser, a DOM parser allows random access to particular pieces of data in an XML document. Another difference is that with a SAX parser, you can only read an XML document, but with a DOM parser, you can build an object representation of the document and manipulate it in memory, adding a new element or deleting an existing one.

In the previous example, we used a SAX parser to look for just one piece of data in a document. Using a DOM parser would have required having the whole document object model in memory, which is generally less efficient for searches involving just a few items, especially if the document is large. In the next example, we add a new coffee to the price list using a DOM parser. We cannot use a SAX parser for modifying the price list because it only reads data.

Let's suppose that you want to add Kona coffee to the price list. You would read the XML price list file into a DOM and then insert the new coffee element, with its name and price. The following code fragment creates a `DocumentBuilderFactory` object, which is then used to create the `DocumentBuilder` object *`builder`*. The code then calls the `parse` method on *`builder`*, passing it the file `priceList.xml`.

```
DocumentBuilderFactory factory =
                        DocumentBuilderFactory.newInstance();
DocumentBuilder builder = factory.newDocumentBuilder();
Document document = builder.parse("priceList.xml");
```

At this point, *`document`* is a DOM representation of the price list sitting in memory. The following code fragment adds a new coffee (with the name "Kona" and the price 13.50) to the price list document. Because we want to add the new coffee right before the coffee whose name is "Mocha Java", the first step is to get a list of the name elements and iterate through the list to find "Mocha Java". Using the `Node` interface included in the `org.w3c.dom` package, the code then creates a `Node` object for the new coffee element and also new nodes for the name and price elements. The name and price elements contain character data, so the code creates a `TextNode` object for each of them and appends the text nodes to the nodes representing the `name` and `price` elements.

```
NodeList list = document.getElementsByTagName("name");
Node thisNode = list.item(0);
    // loop through list
```

```
Node thisChild = thisNode.getChildNode();
if (thisNode.getFirstChild() instanceof org.w3c.dom.TextNode) {
    String data = thisNode.getFirstChild().getData();
}
if (data.equals("Mocha Java")) {
    // new node will be inserted before Mocha Java
    Node newNode = document.createElement("coffee");
    Node nameNode = document.createElement("name");
    TextNode textNode = document.createTextNode("Kona");
    nameNode.appendChild(textNode);

Node priceNode = document.createElement("price");
    TextNode tpNode = document.createTextNode("13.50");
    priceNode.appendChild(tpNode);

newNode.appendChild(nameNode);
    newNode.appendChild(priceNode);
    thisNode.insertBefore(newNode, thisNode);
}
```

You get a DOM parser that is validating the same way you get a SAX parser that is validating: You call `setValidating(true)` on a DOM parser factory before using it to create your DOM parser, and you make sure that the XML document being parsed refers to its DTD in the `DOCTYPE` declaration.

XML Namespaces

All the names in a DTD are unique, thus avoiding ambiguity. However, if a particular XML document references more than one DTD, there is a possibility that two or more DTDs contain the same name. Therefore, the document needs to specify a namespace for each DTD so that the parser knows which definition to use when it is parsing an instance of a particular DTD.

There is a standard notation for declaring an XML Namespace, which is usually done in the root element of an XML document. In the following example namespace declaration, the notation `xmlns` identifies `nsName` as a namespace, and `nsName` is set to the URL of the actual namespace:

```
<priceList xmlns:nsName="myDTD.dtd"
            xmlns:otherNsName="myOtherDTD.dtd">
...
</priceList>
```

Within the document, you can specify which namespace an element belongs to as follows:

```
<nsName:price> ...
```

To make your SAX or DOM parser able to recognize namespaces, you call the method `setNamespaceAware(true)` on your `ParserFactory` instance. After this method call, any parser that the parser factory creates will be namespace aware.

1.4.3 The XSLT API

XML Stylesheet Language for Transformations (page 203), defined by the W3C XSL Working Group, describes a language for transforming XML documents into other XML documents or into other formats. To perform the transformation, you usually need to supply a stylesheet, which is written in the XML Stylesheet Language (XSL). The XSL stylesheet specifies how the XML data will be displayed. XSLT uses the formatting instructions in the stylesheet to perform the transformation. The converted document can be another XML document or a document in another format, such as HTML.

JAXP supports XSLT with the `javax.xml.transform` package, which allows you to plug in an XSLT transformer to perform transformations. The subpackages have SAX-, DOM-, and stream-specific APIs that allow you to perform transformations directly from DOM trees and SAX events. The following two examples illustrate how to create an XML document from a DOM tree and how to transform the resulting XML document into HTML using an XSL stylesheet.

Transforming a DOM Tree to an XML Document

To transform the DOM tree created in the previous section to an XML document, the following code fragment first creates a `Transformer` object that will perform the transformation.

```
TransformerFactory transFactory =
               TransformerFactory.newInstance();
Transformer transformer = transFactory.newTransformer();
```

Using the DOM tree root node, the following line of code constructs a `DOMSource` object as the source of the transformation.

```
DOMSource source = new DOMSource(document);
```

The following code fragment creates a StreamResult object to take the results of the transformation and transforms the tree to XML.

```
File newXML = new File("newXML.xml");
FileOutputStream os = new FileOutputStream(newXML);
StreamResult result = new StreamResult(os);
transformer.transform(source, result);
```

Transforming an XML Document to an HTML Document

You can also use XSLT to convert the new XML document, newXML.xml, to HTML using a stylesheet. When writing a stylesheet, you use XML Namespaces to reference the XSL constructs. For example, each stylesheet has a root element identifying the stylesheet language, as shown in the following line of code.

```
<xsl:stylesheet version="1.0" xmlns:xsl=
                    "http://www.w3.org/1999/XSL/Transform">
```

When referring to a particular construct in the stylesheet language, you use the namespace prefix followed by a colon and the particular construct to apply. For example, the following piece of stylesheet indicates that the name data must be inserted into a row of an HTML table.

```
<xsl:template match="name">
    <tr><td>
        <xsl:apply-templates/>
    </td></tr>
</xsl:template>
```

The following stylesheet specifies that the XML data is converted to HTML and that the coffee entries are inserted into a row in a table.

```
<xsl:stylesheet version="1.0"
        xmlns:xsl="http://www.w3.org/1999/XSL/Transform">
    <xsl:template match="priceList">
        <html><head>Coffee Prices</head>
            <body>
                <table>
                    <xsl:apply-templates />
                </table>
            </body>
        </html>
    </xsl:template>
```

```
        <xsl:template match="name">
            <tr><td>
                <xsl:apply-templates />
            </td></tr>
        </xsl:template>
        <xsl:template match="price">
            <tr><td>
                <xsl:apply-templates />
            </td></tr>
        </xsl:template>
    </xsl:stylesheet>
```

To perform the transformation, you need to obtain an XSLT transformer and use it to apply the stylesheet to the XML data. The following code fragment obtains a transformer by instantiating a `TransformerFactory` object, reading in the stylesheet and XML files, creating a file for the HTML output, and then finally obtaining the `Transformer` object *`transformer`* from the `TransformerFactory` object *`tFactory`*.

```
TransformerFactory tFactory =
                    TransformerFactory.newInstance();
String stylesheet = "prices.xsl";
String sourceId = "newXML.xml";
File pricesHTML = new File("pricesHTML.html");
FileOutputStream os = new FileOutputStream(pricesHTML);
Transformer transformer =
    tFactory.newTransformer(new StreamSource(stylesheet));
```

The transformation is accomplished by invoking the `transform` method, passing it the data and the output stream.

```
transformer.transform(
        new StreamSource(sourceId), new StreamResult(os));
```

1.5 JAX-RPC

The Java API for XML-based RPC (page 305) (JAX-RPC) makes it possible to write an application in the Java programming language that uses SOAP to make a remote procedure call (RPC). JAX-RPC can also be used to send request-response messages and, in some cases, one-way messages. In addition to these conventional uses, JAX-RPC makes it possible for an application to define its own XML schema and to use that schema to send XML documents and XML fragments. The result of this combination of JAX-RPC and XML Schema is a powerful computing tool.

The Java programming language already has two other APIs for making remote procedure calls, Java IDL and Remote Method Invocation (RMI). All three have an API for marshalling and unmarshalling arguments and for transmitting and receiving procedure calls. The difference is that JAX-RPC is based on SOAP and is geared to Web services. Java IDL is based on the Common Object Request Broker Architecture (CORBA) and uses the Object Management Group's Interface Definition Language (OMG IDL). RMI is based on RPC where both the method calls and the methods being invoked are in the Java programming language—although with RMI over IIOP, the methods being invoked may be in another language. Sun will continue its support of CORBA and RMI in addition to developing JAX-RPC, as each serves a distinct need and has its own set of users.

All varieties of RPC are fairly complex underneath, involving the mapping and reverse mapping of data types and the marshalling and unmarshalling of arguments. However, these take place behind the scenes and are not visible to the user. JAX-RPC continues this model, which means that a client using XML-based RPC can invoke remote procedures or do SOAP messaging by simply making Java method calls.

1.5.1 Using JAX-RPC

JAX-RPC makes using a Web service easier, and it also makes developing a Web service easier, especially if you use the J2EE platform. An RPC-based Web service is basically a collection of procedures that can be called by a remote client over the Internet. The service itself is a server application deployed on a server-side container that implements the procedures that are available for clients to call. For example, a typical RPC-based Web service is a stock quote service that takes a SOAP request for the price of a specified stock and returns the price via SOAP.

A Web service needs to make itself available to potential clients, which it can do, for instance, by describing itself using the Web Services Description Language (WSDL). A consumer (Web client) can then do a lookup of the WSDL document to access the service.

Interoperability across clients and servers that have been described using WSDL is key to JAX-RPC. A consumer using the Java programming language can use JAX-RPC to send its request to a service that may or may not have been defined and deployed on a Java platform. The converse is also possible, that is, a client using another programming language can send its request to a service that has been defined and deployed on a Java platform. This interoperability is a primary strength of JAX-RPC.

Although JAX-RPC implements a remote procedure call as a request-response SOAP message, a user of JAX-RPC is shielded from this level of detail. So, underneath the covers, JAX-RPC is based on SOAP messaging.

JAX-RPC is the main client and server Web services API, largely because of its simplicity. The JAX-RPC API is simple to use and requires no set up. Also, JAX-RPC focuses on point-to-point SOAP messaging, the basic mechanism that most Web services clients use. Although it can provide asynchronous messaging and can be extended to provide higher quality support, JAX-RPC concentrates on being easy to use for the most common tasks. Thus, JAX-RPC is a good choice for applications that wish to avoid the more complex aspects of SOAP messaging and for those that find communication using the RPC model a good fit.

JAX-RPC is not yet final. The specification is still being fine tuned, and the latest draft includes features such as interceptors and Servlet JAX-RPC endpoints. In future releases of the Java WSDP, this introductory overview will be expanded to reflect JAX-RPC more fully.

1.6 JAXM

The Java API for XML Messaging (page 265) (JAXM) provides a standard way to send XML documents over the Internet from the Java platform. It is based on the SOAP 1.1 and SOAP with Attachments specifications and can be extended to work with higher level messaging protocols such as ebXML Transport, Routing, and Packaging that are built on top of SOAP.

Typically, a business uses a messaging provider service, which does the behind-the-scenes work required to transport and route messages. When a messaging provider is used, all JAXM messages go through it, so when a business sends a message, the message first goes to the sender's messaging provider, then to the recipient's messaging provider, and finally to the intended recipient. It is also possible to route a message to go to intermediate recipients before it goes to the ultimate destination.

Because messages go through it, a messaging provider can take care of housekeeping details like assigning message identifiers, storing messages, and keeping track of whether a message has been delivered before. A messaging provider can also try resending a message that did not reach its destination on the first attempt at delivery. The beauty of a messaging provider is that the client using JAXM technology (JAXM client) is totally unaware of what the provider is doing in the background. The JAXM client simply makes Java method calls, and the messaging provider in conjunction with the messaging infrastructure makes everything happen behind the scenes.

Though in the typical scenario a business uses a messaging provider, it is also possible to do JAXM messaging without using a messaging provider. In this case, the JAXM client (called a *standalone* client) is limited to sending point-to-point messages directly to a Web service that is implemented for request-response messaging. Request-response messaging is synchronous, meaning that a request is sent and its response is received in the same operation. A request-response message is sent over a `SOAPConnection` object via the method `SOAPConnection.call`, which sends the message and blocks until it receives a response. A standalone client can operate only in a client role, that is, it can only send requests and receive their responses. In contrast, a JAXM client that uses a messaging provider may act in either the client or server (service) role. In the client role, it can send requests; in the server role, it can receive requests, process them, and send responses.

Though it is not required, JAXM messaging usually takes place within a container, generally a servlet or a J2EE container. A Web service that uses a messaging provider and is deployed in a container has the capability of doing one-way messaging, meaning that it can receive a request as a one-way message and can return a response some time later as another one-way message.

Because of the features that a messaging provider can supply, JAXM can sometimes be a better choice for SOAP messaging than JAX-RPC. The following list includes features that JAXM can provide and that RPC, including JAX-RPC, does not generally provide:

- One-way (asynchronous) messaging
- Routing of a message to more than one party
- Reliable messaging with features such as guaranteed delivery

A JAXM message is made up of two parts, a required SOAP part and an optional attachment part. The SOAP part, which consists of a `SOAPEnvelope` object containing a `SOAPHeader` object and a `SOAPBody` object. The `SOAPBody` object can hold XML fragments as the content of the message being sent. If you want to send content that is not in XML format or that is an entire XML document, your message will need to contain an attachment part in addition to the SOAP part. There is no limitation on the content in the attachment part, so it can include images or any other kind of content, including XML fragments and documents.

1.6.1 Getting a Connection

The first thing a JAXM client needs to do is get a connection, either a SOAP-Connection object or a ProviderConnection object.

Getting a Point-to-Point Connection

A standalone client is limited to using a SOAPConnection object, which is a point-to-point connection that goes directly from the sender to the recipient. All JAXM connections are created by a connection factory. In the case of a SOAP-Connection object, the factory is a SOAPConnectionFactory object. A client obtains the default implementation for SOAPConnectionFactory by calling the following line of code.

```
SOAPConnectionFactory factory =
                SOAPConnectionFactory.newInstance();
```

The client can use *factory* to create a SOAPConnection object.

```
SOAPConnection con = factory.createConnection();
```

Getting a Connection to the Messaging Provider

In order to use a messaging provider, an application must obtain a Provider-Connection object, which is a connection to the messaging provider rather than to a specified recipient. There are two ways to get a ProviderConnection object, the first being similar to the way a standalone client gets a SOAPConnection object. This way involves obtaining an instance of the default implementation for ProviderConnectionFactory, which is then used to create the connection.

```
ProviderConnectionFactory pcFactory =
            ProviderConnectionFactory.newInstance();
ProviderConnection pcCon = pcFactory.createConnection();
```

The variable *pcCon* represents a connection to the default implementation of a JAXM messaging provider.

The second way to create a ProviderConnection object is to retrieve a ProviderConnectionFactory object that is implemented to create connections to a specific messaging provider. The following code demonstrates getting such a ProviderConnectionFactory object and using it to create a connection. The first two lines use the JNDI API to retrieve the appropriate ProviderConnection-Factory object from the naming service where it has been registered with the name "CoffeeBreakProvider". When this logical name is passed as an argument, the method `lookup` returns the `ProviderConnectionFactory` object to which the logical name was bound. The value returned is a Java `Object`, which must be narrowed to a `ProviderConnectionFactory` object so that it can be used to create a connection. The third line uses a JAXM method to actually get the connection.

```
Context ctx = getInitialContext();
ProviderConnectionFactory pcFactory =
(ProviderConnectionFactory)ctx.lookup("CoffeeBreakProvider");
ProviderConnection con = pcFactory.createConnection();
```

The `ProviderConnection` instance *con* represents a connection to The Coffee Break's messaging provider.

1.6.2 Creating a Message

As is true with connections, messages are created by a factory. And similar to the case with connection factories, `MessageFactory` objects can be obtained in two ways. The first way is to get an instance of the default implementation for the `MessageFactory` class. This instance can then be used to create a basic `SOAPMessage` object.

```
MessageFactory messageFactory = MessageFactory.newInstance();
SOAPMessage m = messageFactory.createMessage();
```

All of the `SOAPMessage` objects that *messageFactory* creates, including *m* in the previous line of code, will be basic SOAP messages. This means that they will have no predefined headers.

Part of the flexibility of the JAXM API is that it allows a specific usage of a SOAP header. For example, protocols such as ebXML can be built on top of SOAP messaging. This usage of SOAP by a given standards group or industry is called a *profile*. In the second way to create a `MessageFactory` object, you use the `ProviderConnection` method `createMessageFactory` and give it a profile. The `SOAPMessage` objects produced by the resulting `MessageFactory` object will support the specified profile. For example, in the following code fragment, in which *schemaURI* is the URI of the schema for the desired profile, *m2* will support the messaging profile that is supplied to `createMessageFactory`.

```
MessageFactory messageFactory2 =
                    con.createMessageFactory(<schemaURI>);
SOAPMessage m2 = messageFactory2.createMessage();
```

Each of the new SOAPMessage objects *m* and *m2* automatically contains the required elements SOAPPart, SOAPEnvelope, and SOAPBody, plus the optional element SOAPHeader (which is included for convenience). The SOAPHeader and SOAPBody objects are initially empty, and the following sections will illustrate some of the typical ways to add content.

1.6.3 Populating a Message

Content can be added to the SOAPPart object, to one or more AttachmentPart objects, or to both parts of a message.

Populating the SOAP Part of a Message

As stated earlier, all messages have a SOAPPart object, which has a SOAP-Envelope object containing a SOAPHeader object and a SOAPBody object. One way to add content to the SOAP part of a message is to create a SOAPHeader-Element object or a SOAPBodyElement object and add an XML document that you build with the method SOAPElement.addTextNode. The first three lines of the following code fragment access the SOAPBody object *body*, which is used to create a new SOAPBodyElement object and add it to *body*. The argument passed to the createName method is a Name object identifying the SOAPBodyElement being added. The last line adds the XML string passed to the method addText-Node.

```
SOAPPart sp = m.getSOAPPart();
SOAPEnvelope envelope = sp.getSOAPEnvelope();
SOAPBody body = envelope.getSOAPBody();
SOAPBodyElement bodyElement = body.addBodyElement(
                envelope.createName("text", "hotitems",
                "http://hotitems.com/products/gizmo");
bodyElement.addTextNode("some-xml-text");
```

Another way is to add content to the SOAPPart object by passing it a javax.xml.transform.Source object, which may be a SAXSource, DOMSource, or StreamSource object. The Source object contains content for the SOAP part of the message and also the information needed for it to act as source input. A StreamSource object will contain the content as an XML document; the SAXSource or DOMSource object will contain content and instructions for transforming it into an XML document.

The following code fragments illustrates adding content as a DOMSource object. The first step is to get the SOAPPart object from the SOAPMessage object.

Next the code uses methods from the Java API for XML Processing (JAXP) to build the XML document to be added. It uses a `DocumentBuilderFactory` object to get a `DocumentBuilder` object. Then it parses the given file to produce the document that will be used to initialize a new `DOMSource` object. Finally, the code passes the `DOMSource` object *`domSource`* to the method `SOAPPart.setContent`.

```
SOAPPart soapPart = message.getSOAPPart();

DocumentBuilderFactory dbf=
            DocumentBuilderFactory.newInstance();
DocumentBuilder db = dbf.newDocumentBuilder();
Document doc = db.parse("file:///foo.bar/soap.xml");
DOMSource domSource = new DOMSource(doc);

soapPart.setContent(domSource);
```

Populating the Attachment Part of a Message

A `Message` object may have no attachment parts, but if it is to contain anything that is not in XML format, that content must be contained in an attachment part. There may be any number of attachment parts, and they may contain anything from plain text to image files. In the following code fragment, the content is an image in a JPEG file, whose URL is used to initialize the `javax.activation.DataHandler` object *`dh`*. The `Message` object *`m`* creates the `AttachmentPart` object *`attachPart`*, which is initialized with the data handler containing the URL for the image. Finally, the message adds `attachPart` to itself.

```
URL url = new URL("http://foo.bar/img.jpg");
DataHandler dh = new DataHandler(url);
AttachmentPart attachPart = m.createAttachmentPart(dh);
m.addAttachmentPart(attachPart);
```

A `SOAPMessage` object can also give content to an `AttachmentPart` object by passing an `Object` and its content type to the method `createAttachmentPart`.

```
AttachmentPart attachPart =
    m.createAttachmentPart("content-string", "text/plain");
m.addAttachmentPart(attachPart);
```

A third alternative is to create an empty `AttachmentPart` object and then to pass the `AttachmentPart.setContent` method an `Object` and its content type.

In this code fragment, the Object is a ByteArrayInputStream initialized with a jpeg image.

```
AttachmentPart ap = m.createAttachmentPart();
byte[] jpegData =  ...;
ap.setContent(new ByteArrayInputStream(jpegData),
                                        "image/jpeg");
m.addAttachmentPart(ap);
```

1.6.4 Sending a Message

Once you have populated a SOAPMessage object, you are ready to send it. A standalone client uses the SOAPConnection method call to send a message. This method sends the message and then blocks until it gets back a response. The arguments to the method call are the message being sent and an Endpoint object that contains the URL of the receiver.

```
SOAPMessage response =
                soapConnection.call(message, urlEndpoint);
```

An application that is using a messaging provider uses the ProviderConnection method send to send a message. This method sends the message asynchronously, meaning that it sends the message and returns immediately. The response, if any, will be sent as a separate operation at a later time. Note that this method takes only one parameter, the message being sent. The messaging provider will use header information to determine the destination.

```
providerConnection.send(message);
```

1.7 JAXR

The Java API for XML Registries (page 323) (JAXR) provides a convenient way to access standard business registries over the Internet. Business registries are often described as electronic yellow pages because they contain listings of businesses and the products or services the businesses offer. JAXR gives developers writing applications in the Java programming language a uniform way to use business registries that are based on open standards (such as ebXML) or industry consortium-led specifications (such as UDDI).

Businesses can register themselves with a registry or discover other businesses with which they might want to do business. In addition, they can submit material to be shared and search for material that others have submitted. Standards groups have developed DTDs for particular kinds of XML documents, and two businesses might, for example, agree to use the DTD for their industry's standard purchase order form. Because the DTD is stored in a standard business registry, both parties can use JAXR to access it.

Registries are becoming an increasingly important component of Web services because they allow businesses to collaborate with each other dynamically in a loosely coupled way. Accordingly, the need for JAXR, which enables enterprises to access standard business registries from the Java programming language, is also growing.

1.7.1 Using JAXR

The following sections give examples of two of the typical ways a business registry is used. They are meant to give you an idea of how to use JAXR rather than to be complete or exhaustive.

Registering a Business

An organization that uses the Java platform for its electronic business would use JAXR to register itself in a standard registry. It would supply its name, a description of itself, and some classification concepts to facilitate searching for it. This is shown in the following code fragment, which first creates the `RegistryService` object *`rs`* and then uses it to create the `BusinessLifeCycleManager` object *`lcm`*. The business, a chain of coffee houses called The Coffee Break, is represented by the `Organization` object *`org`*, to which The Coffee Break adds its name, a description of itself, and its classification within the North American Industry Classification System (NAICS). Then *`org`*, which now contains the properties and classifications for The Coffee Break, is added to the `Collection` object *`orgs`*. Finally, *`orgs`* is saved by *`lcm`*, which will manage the life cycle of the `Organization` objects contained in *`orgs`*.

```
RegistryService rs = connection.getRegistryService();

BusinessLifeCycleManager lcm =
                    rs.getBusinessLifeCycleManager();

Organization org = lcm.createOrganization("The Coffee Break");
org.setDescription(
    "Purveyor of only the finest coffees. Established 1895");
```

```
ClassificationScheme cScheme =
            lcm.createClassificationScheme("ntis-gov:naics",
           "North American Industry Classification System");
javax.xml.registry.infomodel.Key cKey = lcm.createKey(
                "uuid:C0B9FE13-179F-413D-8A5B-5004DB8E5BB2");
cScheme.setKey(cKey);
Classification classification =
        (Classification)lcm.createClassification(cScheme,
        "Snack and Nonalcoholic Beverage Bars", "722213");

Collection classifications = new ArrayList();
classifications.add(classification);

org.addClassifications(classifications);
Collection orgs = new ArrayList();
orgs.add(org);
lcm.saveOrganizations(orgs);
```

Searching a Registry

A business can also use JAXR to search a registry for other businesses. The following code fragment uses the `BusinessQueryManager` object *bqm* to search for The Coffee Break. Before *bqm* can invoke the method `findOrganizations`, the code needs to define the search criteria to be used. In this case, three of the possible six search parameters are supplied to `findOrganizations`; because `null` is supplied for the third, fifth, and sixth parameters, those criteria are not used to limit the search. The first, second, and fourth arguments are all `Collection` objects, with *findQualifiers* and *namePatterns* being defined here. The only element in *findQualifiers* is a `String` specifying that no organization be returned unless its name is a case-sensitive match to one of the names in the *namePatterns* parameter. This parameter, which is also a `Collection` object with only one element, says that businesses with "Coffee" in their names are a match. The other `Collection` object is *classifications*, which was defined when The Coffee Break registered itself. The previous code fragment, in which the industry for The Coffee Break was provided, is an example of defining classifications.

```
BusinessQueryManager bqm = rs.getBusinessQueryManager();

//Define find qualifiers
Collection findQualifiers = new ArrayList();
findQualifiers.add(FindQualifier.CASE_SENSITIVE_MATCH);
```

```
Collection namePatterns = new ArrayList();
namePatterns.add("%Coffee%"); // Find orgs with name containing
"//" 'Coffee'

//Find using only the name and the classifications
BulkResponse response = bqm.findOrganizations(findQualifiers,
        namePatterns, null, classifications, null, null);
Collection orgs = response.getCollection();
```

JAXR also supports using an SQL query to search a registry. This is done using a `DeclarativeQueryManager` object, as the following code fragment demonstrates.

```
DeclarativeQueryManager dqm = rs.getDeclarativeQueryManager();
Query query = dqm.createQuery(Query.QUERY_TYPE_SQL,
"SELECT id FROM RegistryEntry WHERE name LIKE %Coffee% " +
    "AND majorVersion >= 1 AND " +
    "(majorVersion >= 2 OR minorVersion >= 3)");
BulkResponse response2 = dqm.executeQuery(query);
```

The `BulkResponse` object *`response2`* will contain a value for `id` (a uuid) for each entry in `RegistryEntry` that has "Coffee" in its name and that also has a version number of 1.3 or greater.

To ensure interoperable communication between a JAXR client and a registry implementation, the messaging is done using JAXM. This is done completely behind the scenes, so as a user of JAXR, you are not even aware of it.

1.8 Sample Scenario

The following scenario is an example of how the Java APIs for XML might be used and how they work together. Part of the richness of the Java APIs for XML is that in many cases they offer alternate ways of doing something and thus let you tailor your code to meet individual needs. This section will point out some instances in which an alternate API could have been used and will also give the reasons why one API or the other might be a better choice.

1.8.1 Scenario

Suppose that the owner of a chain of coffee houses, called The Coffee Break, wants to expand the line of coffees that he sells. He instructs his business manager to find some new coffee suppliers, get their wholesale prices, and then arrange for orders to be placed as the need arises. The Coffee Break can analyze the prices and decide which new coffees it wants to carry and which companies it wants to buy them from. The business manager assigns the task to the company's software engineer, who decides that the best way to locate new coffee suppliers is to search a Universal Description, Discovery, and Integration (UDDI) registry, where The Coffee Break has already registered itself.

The engineer uses JAXR to send a query searching for wholesale coffee suppliers. JAXR sends messages using JAXM in the background, which ensures that the registry will be able to receive and understand it.

The UDDI registry will receive the query and apply the search criteria transmitted in the JAXR code to the information it has about the organizations registered with it. When the search is completed, the registry will send back information on how to contact the wholesale coffee distributors that met the specified criteria.

The engineer's next step is to draft a request for price lists and send it to each of the coffee distributors using JAXM. She writes an application that gets a connection to the company's messaging service so that she can send the requests. She then creates a JAXM message, adds the request, and sends it.

Each coffee distributor receives the request, and before sending out current prices, checks with its stock quote service using JAX-RPC to get the latest quotes for the relevant coffee futures. Based on the figures they get back, the distributors send The Coffee Break their newly revised prices in an XML price sheet. The vendors use an agreed upon XML schema for their price sheets because that way they can use a format that is convenient for them and that their buyers can process easily.

Compare Prices and Order Coffees

The engineer processes the price lists using SAX. After her application gets the prices quoted by the different vendors, it compares them and displays the results.

When the owner and business manager decide which suppliers to do business with, based on the engineer's price comparisons, they are ready to send orders to the suppliers. The orders are sent via JAXM, and each supplier will acknowledge receipt of the order via JAXM.

Selling Coffees on the Internet

Meanwhile, The Coffee Break has been preparing for its expanded coffee line. It will need to publish a new price list/order form in HTML for its Web site. But before that can be done, the company needs to determine what prices it will charge. The engineer writes an application that will multiply each price by 125 percent to arrive at the price that The Coffee Break will charge. With a few modifications, the list of retail prices will become the online order form.

The engineer uses JavaServer Pages (JSP) technology to create an HTML order form that customers can use to order coffee online. From the JSP page, she uses SAX to access the name and the price of each coffee, and then she inserts them into an HTML table on the JSP page. The customer enters the quantity of each coffee he or she wants to order and clicks the Submit button to send the order.

1.8.2 Conclusion

Although this scenario is simplified for the sake of brevity, it illustrates how pervasive XML technologies are becoming in the world of Web services. And now, with the Java APIs for XML and the J2EE platform, it keeps getting easier to implement Web services and to write applications that are the consumers of Web services.

CHAPTER 2

Understanding XML

Eric Armstrong

In This Chapter

THIS chapter describes the Extensible Markup Language (XML) and its related specifications.

2.1 Introduction to XML

This section covers the basics of XML. The goal is to give you just enough information to get started, so you understand what XML is all about. (You'll learn about XML in later sections of the tutorial.) We then outline the major features that make XML great for information storage and interchange, and give you a general idea of how XML can be used.

2.1.1 What Is XML?

XML is a text-based markup language that is fast becoming the standard for data interchange on the Web. As with HTML, you identify data using tags (identifiers enclosed in angle brackets, like this: <...>). Collectively, the tags are known as "markup."

But unlike HTML, XML tags *identify* the data, rather than specifying how to display it. Where an HTML tag says something like "display this data in bold font" (`<b>...</b>`), an XML tag acts like a field name in your program. It puts a label on a piece of data that identifies it (for example: `<message>...</message>`).

Note: Since identifying the data gives you some sense of what it *means* (how to interpret it, what you should do with it), XML is sometimes described as a mechanism for specifying the *semantics* (meaning) of the data.

In the same way that you define the field names for a data structure, you are free to use any XML tags that make sense for a given application. Naturally, though, for multiple applications to use the same XML data, they have to agree on the tag names they intend to use.

Here is an example of some XML data you might use for a messaging application:

```
<message>
    <to>you@yourAddress.com</to>
    <from>me@myAddress.com</from>
    <subject>XML Is Really Cool</subject>
    <text>
        How many ways is XML cool? Let me count the ways...
    </text>
</message>
```

Note: Throughout this tutorial, we use boldface text to highlight things we want to bring to your attention. XML does not require anything to be in bold!

The tags in this example identify the message as a whole, the destination and sender addresses, the subject, and the text of the message. As in HTML, the `<to>` tag has a matching end tag: `</to>`. The data between the tag and its matching end tag defines an element of the XML data. Note, too, that the content of the `<to>` tag is entirely contained within the scope of the `<message>..</message>` tag. It is this ability for one tag to contain others that gives XML its ability to represent hierarchical data structures.

Once again, as with HTML, whitespace is essentially irrelevant, so you can format the data for readability and yet still process it easily with a program. Unlike HTML, however, in XML you could easily search a data set for messages containing "cool" in the subject, because the XML tags identify the content of the data, rather than specifying its representation.

Tags and Attributes

Tags can also contain attributes—additional information included as part of the tag itself, within the tag's angle brackets. The following example shows an e-mail message structure that uses attributes for the "`to`," "`from`," and "`subject`" fields:

```
<message to="you@yourAddress.com" from="me@myAddress.com"
        subject="XML Is Really Cool">
    <text>
        How many ways is XML cool? Let me count the ways...
    </text>
</message>
```

As in HTML, the attribute name is followed by an equal sign and the attribute value, and multiple attributes are separated by spaces. Unlike HTML, however, in XML commas between attributes are not ignored—if present, they generate an error.

Since you could design a data structure like `<message>` equally well using either attributes or tags, it can take a considerable amount of thought to figure out which design is best for your purposes. Designing an XML Data Structure (page 48), includes ideas to help you decide when to use attributes and when to use tags.

Empty Tags

One really big difference between XML and HTML is that an XML document is always constrained to be well formed. There are several rules that determine when a document is well-formed, but one of the most important is that every tag has a closing tag. So, in XML, the `</to>` tag is not optional. The `<to>` element is never terminated by any tag other than `</to>`.

Note: Another important aspect of a well-formed document is that all tags are completely nested. So you can have `<message>..<to>..</to>..</message>`, but never `<message>..<to>..</message>..</to>`. A complete list of requirements is contained in the list of XML Frequently Asked Questions (FAQ) at `http://www.ucc.ie/xml/#FAQ-VALIDWF`. (This FAQ is on the w3c Recommended Reading list at `http://www.w3.org/XML/`.)

Sometimes, though, it makes sense to have a tag that stands by itself. For example, you might want to add a "`flag`" tag that marks the message as important. A tag like that doesn't enclose any content, so it's known as an "empty tag." You can create an empty tag by ending it with `/>` instead of `>`. For example, the following message contains such a tag:

```
<message to="you@yourAddress.com" from="me@myAddress.com"
        subject="XML Is Really Cool">
    <flag/>
    <text>
        How many ways is XML cool? Let me count the ways...
    </text>
</message>
```

Note: The empty tag saves you from having to code `<flag></flag>` in order to have a well-formed document. You can control which tags are allowed to be empty by creating a Document Type Definition, or DTD. We'll talk about that in a few moments. If there is no DTD, then the document can contain any kinds of tags you want, as long as the document is well-formed.

Comments in XML Files

XML comments look just like HTML comments:

```
<message to="you@yourAddress.com" from="me@myAddress.com"
        subject="XML Is Really Cool">
    <!-- This is a comment -->
    <text>
        How many ways is XML cool? Let me count the ways...
    </text>
</message>
```

The XML Prolog

To complete this journeyman's introduction to XML, note that an XML file always starts with a prolog. The minimal prolog contains a declaration that identifies the document as an XML document, like this:

```
<?xml version="1.0"?>
```

The declaration may also contain additional information, like this:

```
<?xml version="1.0" encoding="ISO-8859-1" standalone="yes"?>
```

The XML declaration is essentially the same as the HTML header, `<html>`, except that it uses `<?..?>` and it may contain the following attributes:

version

Identifies the version of the XML markup language used in the data. This attribute is not optional.

encoding

Identifies the character set used to encode the data. "ISO-8859-1" is "Latin-1" in the Western European and English language character set. (The default is compressed Unicode: UTF-8.)

standalone

Tells whether or not this document references an external entity or an external data type specification (see below). If there are no external references, then "yes" is appropriate

The prolog can also contain definitions of entities (items that are inserted when you reference them from within the document) and specifications that tell which tags are valid in the document, both declared in a Document Type Definition (DTD) that can be defined directly within the prolog, as well as with pointers to external specification files. But those are the subject of later tutorials. For more information on these and many other aspects of XML, see the Recommended Reading list of the w3c XML page at `http://www.w3.org/XML/`.

Note: The declaration is actually optional. But it's a good idea to include it whenever you create an XML file. The declaration should have the version number, at a minimum, and ideally the encoding as well. That standard simplifies things if the XML standard is extended in the future, and if the data ever needs to be localized for different geographical regions.

Everything that comes after the XML prolog constitutes the document's *content.*

Processing Instructions

An XML file can also contain *processing instructions* that give commands or information to an application that is processing the XML data. Processing instructions have the following format:

```
<?target instructions?>
```

where the *target* is the name of the application that is expected to do the processing, and *instructions* is a string of characters that embodies the information or commands for the application to process.

Since the instructions are application specific, an XML file could have multiple processing instructions that tell different applications to do similar things, though in different ways. The XML file for a slideshow, for example, could have processing instructions that let the speaker specify a technical or executive-level version of the presentation. If multiple presentation programs were used, the program might need multiple versions of the processing instructions (although it would be nicer if such applications recognized standard instructions).

Note: The target name "xml" (in any combination of uppercase or lowercase letters) is reserved for XML standards. In one sense, the declaration is a processing instruction that fits that standard. (However, when you're working with the parser later, you'll see that the method for handling processing instructions never sees the declaration.)

2.1.2 Why Is XML Important?

There are a number of reasons for XML's surging acceptance. This section lists a few of the most prominent.

Plain Text

Since XML is not a binary format, you can create and edit files with anything from a standard text editor to a visual development environment. That makes it easy to debug your programs, and makes it useful for storing small amounts of data. At the other end of the spectrum, an XML front end to a database makes it possible to efficiently store large amounts of XML data as well. So XML provides scalability for anything from small configuration files to a company-wide data repository.

Data Identification

XML tells you what kind of data you have, not how to display it. Because the markup tags identify the information and break up the data into parts, an email program can process it, a search program can look for messages sent to particular people, and an address book can extract the address information from the rest of the message. In short, because the different parts of the information have been identified, they can be used in different ways by different applications.

Stylability

When display is important, the stylesheet standard, XSL (page 41), lets you dictate how to portray the data. For example, the stylesheet for:

```
<to>you@yourAddress.com</to>
```

can say:

1. Start a new line.
2. Display "To:" in bold, followed by a space
3. Display the destination data.

Which produces:

```
To: you@yourAddress
```

Of course, you could have done the same thing in HTML, but you wouldn't be able to process the data with search programs and address-extraction programs and the like. More importantly, since XML is inherently style-free, you can use a completely different stylesheet to produce output in postscript, TEX, PDF, or some new format that hasn't even been invented yet. That flexibility amounts to what one author described as "future-proofing" your information. The XML documents you author today can be used in future document-delivery systems that haven't even been imagined yet.

Inline Reusability

One of the nicer aspects of XML documents is that they can be composed from separate entities. You can do that with HTML, but only by linking to other documents. Unlike HTML, XML entities can be included "in line" in a document. The included sections look like a normal part of the document—you can search the whole document at one time or download it in one piece. That lets you modularize your documents without resorting to links. You can single-source a section so that an edit to it is reflected everywhere the section is used, and yet a document composed from such pieces looks for all the world like a one-piece document.

Linkability

Thanks to HTML, the ability to define links between documents is now regarded as a necessity. The next section of this tutorial, XML and Related Specs: Digesting the Alphabet Soup (page 39), discusses the link-specification initiative. This initiative lets you define two-way links, multiple-target links, "expanding" links (where clicking a link causes the targeted information to appear inline), and links between two existing documents that are defined in a third.

Easily Processed

As mentioned earlier, regular and consistent notation makes it easier to build a program to process XML data. For example, in HTML a `<dt>` tag can be delimited by `</dt>`, another `<dt>`, `<dd>`, or `</dl>`. That makes for some difficult programming. But in XML, the `<dt>` tag must always have a `</dt>` terminator, or else it will be defined as a `<dt/>` tag. That restriction is a critical part of the constraints that make an XML document well-formed. (Otherwise, the XML parser won't be able to read the data.) And since XML is a vendor-neutral standard, you can choose among several XML parsers, any one of which takes the work out of processing XML data.

Hierarchical

Finally, XML documents benefit from their hierarchical structure. Hierarchical document structures are, in general, faster to access because you can drill down to the part you need, like stepping through a table of contents. They are also easier to rearrange, because each piece is delimited. In a document, for example, you could move a heading to a new location and drag everything under it along with the heading, instead of having to page down to make a selection, cut, and then paste the selection into a new location.

2.1.3 How Can You Use XML?

There are several basic ways to make use of XML:

- Traditional data processing, where XML encodes the data for a program to process
- Document-driven programming, where XML documents are containers that build interfaces and applications from existing components
- Archiving—the foundation for document-driven programming, where the customized version of a component is saved (archived) so it can be used later
- Binding, where the DTD or schema that defines an XML data structure is used to automatically generate a significant portion of the application that will eventually process that data

Traditional Data Processing

XML is fast becoming the data representation of choice for the Web. It's terrific when used in conjunction with network-centric Java-platform programs that send and retrieve information. So a client/server application, for example, could transmit XML-encoded data back and forth between the client and the server.

In the future, XML is potentially the answer for data interchange in all sorts of transactions, as long as both sides agree on the markup to use. (For example, should an e-mail program expect to see tags named `<FIRST>` and `<LAST>`, or `<FIRSTNAME>` and `<LASTNAME>`) The need for common standards will generate a lot of industry-specific standardization efforts in the years ahead. In the meantime, mechanisms that let you "translate" the tags in an XML document will be important. Such mechanisms include projects like the RDF (page 46) initiative, which defines "meat tags," and the XSL (page 41) specification, which lets you translate XML tags into other XML tags.

Document-Driven Programming (DDP)

The newest approach to using XML is to construct a document that describes how an application page should look. The document, rather than simply being displayed, consists of references to user interface components and business-logic components that are "hooked together" to create an application on the fly.

Of course, it makes sense to utilize the Java platform for such components. Both Java Beans for interfaces and Enterprise Java Beans for business logic can be used to construct such applications. Although none of the efforts undertaken so far are ready for commercial use, much preliminary work has already been done.

Note: The Java programming language is also excellent for writing XML-processing tools that are as portable as XML. Several Visual XML editors have been written for the Java platform. For a listing of editors, processing tools, and other XML resources, see the "Software" section of Robin Cover's SGML/XML Web Page at `http://www.oasis-open.org/cover/`.

Binding

Once you have defined the structure of XML data using either a DTD or the one of the schema standards, a large part of the processing you need to do has already been defined. For example, if the schema says that the text data in a `<date>` element must follow one of the recognized date formats, then one aspect of the validation criteria for the data has been defined—it only remains to write the code. Although a DTD specification cannot go the same level of detail, a DTD (like a schema) provides a grammar that tells which data structures can occur, in what sequences. That specification tells you how to write the high-level code that processes the data elements.

But when the data structure (and possibly format) is fully specified, the code you need to process it can just as easily be generated automatically. That process is known as *binding*—creating classes that recognize and process different data elements by processing the specification that defines those elements. As time goes on, you should find that you are using the data specification to generate significant chunks of code, so you can focus on the programming that is unique to your application.

Archiving

The Holy Grail of programming is the construction of reusable, modular components. Ideally, you'd like to take them off the shelf, customize them, and plug them together to construct an application, with a bare minimum of additional coding and additional compilation.

The basic mechanism for saving information is called *archiving*. You archive a component by writing it to an output stream in a form that you can reuse later. You can then read it in and instantiate it using its saved parameters. (For example, if you saved a table component, its parameters might be the number of rows and columns to display.) Archived components can also be shuffled around the Web and used in a variety of ways.

When components are archived in binary form, however, there are some limitations on the kinds of changes you can make to the underlying classes if you want to retain compatibility with previously saved versions. If you could modify the archived version to reflect the change, that would solve the problem. But that's hard to do with a binary object. Such considerations have prompted a number of investigations into using XML for archiving. But if an object's state were archived in text form using XML, then anything and everything in it could be changed as easily as you can say, "search and replace."

XML's text-based format could also make it easier to transfer objects between applications written in different languages. For all of these reasons, XML-based archiving is likely to become an important force in the not-too-distant future.

Summary

XML is pretty simple, and very flexible. It has many uses yet to be discovered—we are just beginning to scratch the surface of its potential. It is the foundation for a great many standards yet to come, providing a common language that different computer systems can use to exchange data with one another. As each industry-group comes up with standards for what they want to say, computers will begin to link to each other in ways previously unimaginable.

For more information on the background and motivation of XML, see this great article in *Scientific American* at

```
http://www.sciam.com/1999/0599issue/0599bosak.html.
```

2.2 XML and Related Specs: Digesting the Alphabet Soup

Now that you have a basic understanding of XML, it makes sense to get a high-level overview of the various XML-related acronyms and what they mean. There is a lot of work going on around XML, so there is a lot to learn.

The current APIs for accessing XML documents either serially or in random access mode are, respectively, SAX (page 40) and DOM (page 40). The specifications for ensuring the validity of XML documents are DTD (page 41) (the original mechanism, defined as part of the XML specification) and various Schema Standards (page 42) proposals (newer mechanisms that use XML syntax to do the job of describing validation criteria).

Other future standards that are nearing completion include the XSL (page 41) standard—a mechanism for setting up translations of XML documents (for example to HTML or other XML) and for dictating how the document is rendered. The transformation part of that standard, XSLT (+XPATH) (page 42), is completed and covered in this tutorial. Another effort nearing completion is the XML Link Language specification (XML Linking (page 44)), which enables links between XML documents.

Those are the major initiatives you will want to be familiar with. This section also surveys a number of other interesting proposals, including the HTML-lookalike standard, XHTML (page 45), and the meta-standard for describing the information an XML document contains, RDF (page 46). There are also standards efforts that aim to extend XML, including XLink, and XPointer.

Finally, there are a number of interesting standards and standards-proposals that build on XML, including Synchronized Multimedia Integration Language (SMIL (page 47)), Mathematical Markup Language (MathML (page 47)), Scalable Vector Graphics (SVG (page 47)), and DrawML (page 47), as well as a number of eCommerce standards.

The remainder of this section gives you a more detailed description of these initiatives. To help keep things straight, it's divided into:

- Basic Standards (page 40)
- Schema Standards (page 42)
- Linking and Presentation Standards (page 44)
- Knowledge Standards (page 46)

- Standards That Build on XML (page 47)

Skim the terms once, so you know what's here, and keep a copy of this document handy so you can refer to it whenever you see one of these terms in something you're reading. Pretty soon, you'll have them all committed to memory, and you'll be at least "conversant" with XML!

2.2.1 Basic Standards

These are the basic standards you need to be familiar with. They come up in pretty much any discussion of XML.

SAX

Simple API for XML

This API was actually a product of collaboration on the XML-DEV mailing list, rather than a product of the W3C. It's included here because it has the same "final" characteristics as a W3C recommendation.

You can also think of this standard as the "serial access" protocol for XML. This is the fast-to-execute mechanism you would use to read and write XML data in a server, for example. This is also called an event-driven protocol, because the technique is to register your handler with a SAX parser, after which the parser invokes your callback methods whenever it sees a new XML tag (or encounters an error, or wants to tell you anything else).

For more information on the SAX protocol, see Simple API for XML (page 77).

DOM

Document Object Model

The Document Object Model protocol converts an XML document into a collection of objects in your program. You can then manipulate the object model in any way that makes sense. This mechanism is also known as the "random access" protocol, because you can visit any part of the data at any time. You can then modify the data, remove it, or insert new data. For more information on the DOM specification, see Document Object Model (page 149).

DTD

Document Type Definition

The DTD specification is actually part of the XML specification, rather than a separate entity. On the other hand, it is optional—you can write an XML document without it. And there are a number of Schema Standards (page 42) proposals that offer more flexible alternatives. So it is treated here as though it were a separate specification.

A DTD specifies the kinds of tags that can be included in your XML document, and the valid arrangements of those tags. You can use the DTD to make sure you don't create an invalid XML structure. You can also use it to make sure that the XML structure you are reading (or that got sent over the net) is indeed valid.

Unfortunately, it is difficult to specify a DTD for a complex document in such a way that it prevents all invalid combinations and allows all the valid ones. So constructing a DTD is something of an art. The DTD can exist at the front of the document, as part of the prolog. It can also exist as a separate entity, or it can be split between the document prolog and one or more additional entities.

However, while the DTD mechanism was the first method defined for specifying valid document structure, it was not the last. Several newer schema specifications have been devised. You'll learn about those momentarily.

For more information, see Creating a Document Type Definition (DTD) (page 114).

Namespaces

The namespace standard lets you write an XML document that uses two or more sets of XML tags in modular fashion. Suppose, for example, that you created an XML-based parts list that uses XML descriptions of parts supplied by other manufacturers (online!). The "price" data supplied by the subcomponents would be amounts you want to total up, while the "price" data for the structure as a whole would be something you want to display. The namespace specification defines mechanisms for qualifying the names so as to eliminate ambiguity. That lets you write programs that use information from other sources and do the right things with it.

The latest information on namespaces can be found at `http://www.w3.org/TR/REC-xml-names`.

XSL

Extensible Stylesheet Language

The XML standard specifies how to identify data, not how to display it. HTML, on the other hand, told how things should be displayed without identifying what they were. The XSL standard has two parts, XSLT (the transformation standard, described next) and XSL-FO (the part that covers *formatting objects*, also known as *flow objects*). XSL-FO gives you the ability to define multiple areas on a page and then link them together. When a text stream is directed at the collection, it fills the first area and then "flows" into the second when the first area is filled. Such objects are used by newsletters, catalogs, and periodical publications.

The latest W3C work on XSL is at `http://www.w3.org/TR/WD-xsl`.

XSLT (+XPATH)

Extensible Stylesheet Language for Transformations

The XSLT transformation standard is essentially a translation mechanism that lets you specify what to convert an XML tag into so that it can be displayed—for example, in HTML. Different XSL formats can then be used to display the same data in different ways, for different uses. (The XPATH standard is an addressing mechanism that you use when constructing transformation instructions, in order to specify the parts of the XML structure you want to transform.)

For more information, see XML Stylesheet Language for Transformations (page 203).

2.2.2 Schema Standards

A DTD makes it possible to validate the structure of relatively simple XML documents, but that's as far as it goes.

A DTD can't restrict the content of elements, and it can't specify complex relationships. For example, it is impossible to specify with a DTD that a <heading> for a <book> must have both a <title> and an <author>, while a <heading> for a <chapter> only needs a <title>. In a DTD, once you only get to specify the structure of the <heading> element one time. There is no context-sensitivity.

This issue stems from the fact that a DTD specification is not hierarchical. For a mailing address that contained several "parsed character data" (PCDATA) elements, for example, the DTD might look something like this:

```
<!ELEMENT mailAddress (name, address, zipcode)>
<!ELEMENT name (#PCDATA)>
<!ELEMENT address (#PCDATA)>
<!ELEMENT zipcode (#PCDATA)>
```

As you can see, the specifications are linear. That fact forces you to come up with new names for similar elements in different settings. So if you wanted to add another "name" element to the DTD that contained the <firstname>, <middle-

Initial>, and <lastName>, then you would have to come up with another identifier. You could not simply call it "name" without conflicting with the <name> element defined for use in a <mailAddress>.

Another problem with the non-hierarchical nature of DTD specifications is that it is not clear what comments are meant to explain. A comment at the top like `<!-- Address used for mailing via the postal system -->` would apply to all of the elements that constitute a mailing address. But a comment like `<!-- Addressee -->` would apply to the `name` element only. On the other hand, a comment like `<!-- A 5-digit string -->` would apply specifically to the `#PCDATA` part of the `zipcode` element, to describe the valid formats. Finally, DTDs do not allow you to formally specify field-validation criteria, such as the 5-digit (or 5 and 4) limitation for the `zipcode` field.

Finally, a DTD uses syntax that is substantially different from XML, so it can't be processed with a standard XML parser. That means you can't read a DTD into a DOM, for example, modify it, and then write it back out again.

To remedy these shortcomings, a number of proposals have been made for a more database-like, hierarchical "schema" that specifies validation criteria. The major proposals are shown below.

XML Schema

This large, complex standard has two parts. One part specifies structure relationships. (This is the largest and most complex part.) The other part specifies mechanisms for validating the content of XML elements by specifying a (potentially very sophisticated) *datatype* for each element.

The good news is that XML Schema for Structures lets you specify any kind of relationship you can conceive of. The bad news is that it takes a lot of work to implement, and it takes a bit of learning to use. Most of the alternatives provide for simpler structure definitions, while incorporating the XML Schema datatype standard.

For more information on the XML Schema proposal, see the W3C specs XML Schema (Structures) and XML Schema (Datatypes).

RELAX

This is a Regular Language description for XML.

Simpler than XML Structure Schema, RELAX uses XML syntax to express the structure relationships that are present in a DTD, and adds the XML Datatype Schema mechanisms, as well. It includes a DTD to RELAX converter.

For more information on RELAX, see `http://www.xml.gr.jp/relax/`.

SOX

This is a Schema for Object-oriented XML.

SOX is a schema proposal that includes extensible data types, namespaces, and embedded documentation.

For more information on SOX, see `http://www.w3.org/TR/NOTE-SOX`.

TREX

This is a Tree Regular Expressions for XML.

This is a means of expressing validation criteria by describing a *pattern* for the structure and content of an XML document. It includes a RELAX to TREX converter.

For more information on TREX, see `http://www.thaiopensource.com/trex/`.

Schematron

This is a Schema for Object-oriented XML.

It is an assertion-based schema mechanism that allows for sophisticated validation.

For more information on Schematron, see `http://www.ascc.net/xml/resource/schematron/schematron.html`.

2.2.3 Linking and Presentation Standards

Arguably the two greatest benefits provided by HTML were the ability to link between documents, and the ability to create simple formatted documents (and, eventually, very complex formatted documents). The following standards aim at preserving the benefits of HTML in the XML arena, and to adding additional functionality, as well.

XML Linking

These specifications provide a variety of powerful linking mechanisms, and are sure to have a big impact on how XML documents are used.

XLink

The XLink protocol is a proposed specification to handle links between XML documents. This specification allows for some pretty sophisticated linking, including two-way links, links to multiple documents, "expanding" links that insert the linked information into your document rather than replacing your document with a new page, links between two documents that are created in a third, independent document, and indirect links (so you can point to an "address book" rather than directly to the target document—updating the address book then automatically changes any links that use it).

XML Base

This standard defines an attribute for XML documents that defines a "base" address, that is used when evaluating a relative address specified in the document. (So, for example, a simple file name would be found in the base-address directory.)

XPointer

In general, the XLink specification targets a document or document-segment using its ID. The XPointer specification defines mechanisms for "addressing into the internal structures of XML documents," without requiring the author of the document to have defined an ID for that segment. To quote the spec, it provides for "reference to elements, character strings, and other parts of XML documents, whether or not they bear an explicit ID attribute."

For more information on the XML Linking standards, see `http://www.w3.org/XML/Linking`.

XHTML

The XHTML specification is a way of making XML documents that look and act like HTML documents. Since an XML document can contain any tags you care to define, why not define a set of tags that look like HTML? That's the thinking behind the XHTML specification, at any rate. The result of this specification is a document that can be displayed in browsers and also treated as XML data. The data may not be quite as identifiable as "pure" XML, but it will be easier to manipulate than standard HTML, because XML specifies a good deal more regularity and consistency.

For example, every tag in a well-formed XML document must either have an end-tag associated with it or it must end in />. So you might see `<p>...</p>`, or you might see `<p/>`, but you will never see `<p>` standing by itself. The upshot of that requirement is that you never have to program for the weird kinds of cases you see in HTML where, for example, a `<dt>` tag might be terminated by `</DT>`, by another `<DT>`, by `<dd>`, or by `</dl>`. That makes it a lot easier to write code!

The XHTML specification is a reformulation of HTML 4.0 into XML. The latest information is at `http://www.w3.org/TR/xhtml1`.

2.2.4 Knowledge Standards

When you start looking down the road five or six years, you can visualize how the information on the Web will begin to turn into one huge knowledge base (the "semantic Web"). For the latest on the semantic Web, visit `http://www.w3.org/2001/sw/`.

In the meantime, here are the fundamental standards you'll want to know about:

RDF

Resource Description Framework

RDF is a proposed standard for defining data about data. Used in conjunction with the XHTML specification, for example, or with HTML pages, RDF could be used to describe the content of the pages. For example, if your browser stored your ID information as `FIRSTNAME`, `LASTNAME`, and `EMAIL`, an RDF description could make it possible to transfer data to an application that wanted `NAME` and `EMAILADDRESS`. Just think: One day you may not need to type your name and address at every Web site you visit!

For the latest information on RDF, see `http://www.w3.org/TR/REC-rdf-syntax`.

RDF Schema

The RDF Schema proposal allows the specification of consistency rules and additional information that describe how the statements in a Resource Description Framework (RDF) should be interpreted.

For more information on the RDF Schema recommendation, see `http://www.w3.org/TR/rdf-schema`.

XTM

XML Topic Maps

In many ways a simpler, more readily usable knowledge-representation than RDF, the Topic Maps Standard, is one worth watching. So far, RDF is the W3C standard for knowledge representation, but Topic Maps could possibly become the "developer's choice" among knowledge representation standards.

For more information on XML Topic Maps, `http://www.topicmaps.org/xtm/index.html`. For information on Topic Maps and the Web, see `http://www.topicmaps.org/`.

2.2.5 Standards That Build on XML

The following standards and proposals build on XML. Since XML is basically a language-definition tool, these specifications use it to define standardized languages for specialized purposes.

Extended Document Standards

These standards define mechanisms for producing extremely complex documents—books, journals, magazines, and the like—using XML.

SMIL. Synchronized Multimedia Integration Language

SMIL is a W3C recommendation that covers audio, video, and animations. It also addresses the difficult issue of synchronizing the playback of such elements.

For more information on SMIL, see `http://www.w3.org/TR/REC-smil`.

MathML. Mathematical Markup Language

MathML is a W3C recommendation that deals with the representation of mathematical formulas.

For more information on MathML, see `http://www.w3.org/TR/REC-MathML`.

SVG. Scalable Vector Graphics

SVG is a W3C working draft that covers the representation of vector graphic images (vector graphic images that are built from commands that say things like "draw a line (square, circle) from point xi to point m,n" rather than encoding the image as a series of bits. Such images are more easily scalable, although they typically require more processing time to render).

For more information on SVG, see `http://www.w3.org/TR/WD-SVG`.

DrawML. Drawing Meta Language

DrawML is a W3C note that covers 2D images for technical illustrations. It also addresses the problem of updating and refining such images.

For more information on DrawML, see `http://www.w3.org/TR/NOTE-drawml`.

eCommerce Standards

These standards are aimed at using XML in the world of business-to-business (B2B) and business-to-consumer (B2C) commerce.

ICE. Information and Content Exchange

ICE is a protocol for use by content syndicators and their subscribers. It focuses on "automating content exchange and reuse, both in traditional publishing contexts and in business-to-business relationships."

For more information on ICE, see `http://www.w3.org/TR/NOTE-ice`.

ebXML. Electronic Business with XML

This standard aims at creating a modular electronic business framework using XML. It is the product of a joint initiative by the United Nations (UN/CEFACT) and the Organization for the Advancement of Structured Information Systems (OASIS).

For more information on ebXML, see `http://www.ebxml.org/`.

cxml. Commerce XML

cxml is a RosettaNet (`www.rosettanet.org`) standard for setting up interactive online catalogs for different buyers, where the pricing and product offerings are company specific. It includes mechanisms to handle purchase orders, change orders, status updates, and shipping notifications.

For more information on cxml, see `http://www.cxml.org/`

CBL. Common Business Library

CBL is a library of element and attribute definitions maintained by CommerceNet (`www.commerce.net`).

For more information on CBL and a variety of other initiatives that work together to enable eCommerce applications, see `http://www.commerce.net/projects/currentprojects/eco/wg/eCo_Framework_Specifications.html`.

2.2.6 Summary

XML is becoming a widely-adopted standard that is being used in a dizzying variety of application areas.

2.3 Designing an XML Data Structure

This section covers some heuristics you can use when making XML design decisions.

2.3.1 Saving Yourself Some Work

Whenever possible, use an existing DTD. It's usually a lot easier to ignore the things you don't need than to design your own from scratch. In addition, using a standard DTD makes data interchange possible, and may make it possible to use data-aware tools developed by others.

So, if an industry standard exists, consider referencing that DTD with an external parameter entity. One place to look for industry-standard DTDs is at the repository created by the Organization for the Advancement of Structured Information Standards (OASIS) at `http://www.XML.org`. Another place to check is

CommerceOne's XML Exchange at `http://www.xmlx.com`, which is described as "a repository for creating and sharing document type definitions."

Note: Many more good thoughts on the design of XML structures are at the OASIS page, `http://www.oasis-open.org/cover/elementsAndAttrs.html`.

2.3.2 Attributes and Elements

One of the issues you will encounter frequently when designing an XML structure is whether to model a given data item as a subelement or as an attribute of an existing element. For example, you could model the title of a slide either as:

```
<slide>
    <title>This is the title</title>
</slide>
```

or as:

```
<slide title="This is the title">...</slide>
```

In some cases, the different characteristics of attributes and elements make it easy to choose. Let's consider those cases first, and then move on to the cases where the choice is more ambiguous.

Forced Choices

Sometimes, the choice between an attribute and an element is forced on you by the nature of attributes and elements. Let's look at a few of those considerations:

The data contains substructures

In this case, the data item must be modeled as an *element*. It can't be modeled as an attribute, because attributes take only simple strings. So if the title can contain emphasized text like this: `The <em>Best</em> Choice`, then the title must be an element.

The data contains multiple lines

Here, it also makes sense to use an *element*. Attributes need to be simple, short strings or else they become unreadable, if not unusable.

The data changes frequently

When the data will be frequently modified, especially by the end user, then it makes sense to model it as an *element*. XML-aware editors tend to make it very easy to find and modify element data. Attributes can be somewhat harder to get to, and therefore somewhat more difficult to modify.

The data is a small, simple string that rarely if ever changes

This is data that can be modeled as an *attribute*. However, just because you *can* does not mean that you should. Check the "Stylistic Choices" section next, to be sure.

The data is confined to a small number of fixed choices

Here is one time when it really makes sense to use an *attribute*. Using the DTD, the attribute can be prevented from taking on any value that is not in the pre-approved list. An XML-aware editor can even provide those choices in a drop-down list. Note, though, that the gain in validity restriction comes at a cost in extensibility. The author of the XML document cannot use any value that is not part of the DTD. If another value becomes useful in the future, the DTD will have to be modified before the document author can make use of it.

Stylistic Choices

As often as not, the choices are not as cut and dried as those shown above. When the choice is not forced, you need a sense of "style" to guide your thinking. The question to answer, then, is what makes good XML style, and why.

Defining a sense of style for XML is, unfortunately, as nebulous a business as defining "style" when it comes to art or music. There are a few ways to approach it, however. The goal of this section is to give you some useful thoughts on the subject of "XML style."

Visibility

The first heuristic for thinking about XML elements and attributes uses the concept of *visibility*. If the data is intended to be shown—to be displayed to some end user—then it should be modeled as an element. On the other hand, if the information guides XML processing but is never displayed, then it may be better to model it as an attribute. For example, in order-entry data for shoes, shoe size would definitely be an element. On the other hand, a manufacturer's code number would be reasonably modeled as an attribute.

Consumer / Provider

Another way of thinking about the visibility heuristic is to ask who is the consumer and/or provider of the information. The shoe size is entered by a human sales clerk, so it's an element. The manufacturer's code number for a given shoe model, on the other hand, may be wired into the application or stored in a database, so that would be an attribute. (If it were entered by the clerk, though, it should perhaps be an element.) You can also think in terms of who or what is processing the information. Things can get a bit murky at that end of the process, however. If the information "consumers" are order-filling clerks, will they need to see the manufacturer's code number? Or, if an order-filling program is doing all the processing, which data items should be elements in that case? Such philosophical distinctions leave a lot of room for differences in style.

Container vs. Contents

Another way of thinking about elements and attributes is to think of an element as a *container*. To reason by analogy, the *contents* of the container (water or milk) correspond to XML data modeled as elements. On the other hand, *characteristics* of the container (blue or white, pitcher or can) correspond to XML data modeled as attributes. Good XML style will, in some consistent way, separate each container's contents from its characteristics.

To show these heuristics at work: In a slideshow the type of the slide (executive or technical) is best modeled as an attribute. It is a characteristic of the slide that lets it be selected or rejected for a particular audience. The title of the slide, on the other hand, is part of its contents. The visibility heuristic is also satisfied here. When the slide is displayed, the title is shown but the type of the slide isn't. Finally, in this example, the consumer of the title information is the presentation audience, while the consumer of the type information is the presentation program.

2.3.3 Normalizing Data

The section Designing an XML Data Structure (page 48) shows how to create an external entity that you can reference in an XML document. Such an entity has all the advantages of a modularized routine—changing that one copy affects every document that references it. The process of eliminating redundancies is known as *normalizing*, so defining entities is one good way to normalize your data.

In an HTML file, the only way to achieve that kind of modularity is with HTML links—but of course the document is then fragmented, rather than whole.

XML entities, on the other hand, suffer no such fragmentation. The entity reference acts like a macro—the entity's contents are expanded in place, producing a whole document, rather than a fragmented one. And when the entity is defined in an external file, multiple documents can reference it.

The considerations for defining an entity reference, then, are pretty much the same as those you would apply to modularized program code:

- Whenever you find yourself writing the same thing more than once, think entity. That lets you write it in one place and reference it multiple places.
- If the information is likely to change, especially if it is used in more than one place, definitely think in terms of defining an entity. An example is defining `productName` as an entity so that you can easily change the documents when the product name changes.
- If the entity will never be referenced anywhere except in the current file, define it in the local_subset of the document's DTD, much as you would define a method or inner class in a program.
- If the entity will be referenced from multiple documents, define it as an external entity, the same way that would define any generally usable class as an external class.

External entities produce modular XML that is smaller, easier to update and maintain. They can also make the resulting document somewhat more difficult to visualize, much as a good OO design can be easy to change, once you understand it, but harder to wrap your head around at first.

You can also go overboard with entities. At an extreme, you could make an entity reference for the word "the"—it wouldn't buy you much, but you could do it.

Note: The larger an entity, the less likely that changing it will have unintended effects. When you define an external entity that covers a whole section on installation instructions, for example, making changes to the section is unlikely to make any of the documents that depend on it come out wrong. Small inline substitutions can be more problematic, though. For example, if `productName` is defined as an entity, the name change can be to a different part of speech, and that can kill you! Suppose the product name is something like "HtmlEdit." That's a verb. So you write, "You can HtmlEdit your file...." Then, when the official name is decided, it's "Killer." After substitution, that becomes "You can Killer your file...." Argh. Still, even if such simple substitutions can sometimes get you in trouble, they can also save a lot of work. To be totally safe, though, you could set up entities named `productNoun`, `productVerb`, `productAdj`, and `productAdverb`!

2.3.4 Normalizing DTDs

Just as you can normalize your XML document, you can also normalize your DTD declarations by factoring out common pieces and referencing them with a parameter entity. This process is described in the SAX tutorial in Defining Parameter Entities and Conditional Sections (page 134). Factoring out the DTDs (also known as modularizing or normalizing) gives the same advantages and disadvantages as normalized XML—easier to change, somewhat more difficult to follow.

You can also set up conditionalized DTDs, as described in the SAX tutorial section Conditional Sections (page 136). If the number and size of the conditional sections is small relative to the size of the DTD as a whole, that can let you "single source" a DTD that you can use for multiple purposes. If the number of conditional sections gets large, though, the result can be a complex document that is difficult to edit.

CHAPTER 3

Getting Started with Tomcat

Debbie Carson

In This Chapter

THIS chapter shows you how to develop, deploy, and run a simple Web application that consists of a currency conversion class and a Web page client created with JavaServer Pages technology (JSP). This application will be deployed to and run on Tomcat, the Java Servlet and JSP container included with the Java Web Services Developer Pack (Java WSDP). This chapter is intended as an introduction to using Tomcat to deploy Web services and Web applications. The material in this chapter provides a basis for other chapters in this tutorial.

3.1 Setting Up

Before you start developing the example application, you should follow the instructions in this section and in About the Examples (page xx).

3.1.1 Getting the Example Code

The source code for the example is in *<JWDSP_HOME>*/docs/tutorial/examples/gs/, a directory that is created when you unzip the tutorial bundle. If you are viewing this tutorial online, you can download the tutorial bundle from:

```
http://java.sun.com/webservices/downloads/webservicestutorial.html
```

The example application at *<JWDSP_HOME>*/docs/tutorial/examples/gs/ consists of the following files.

- `Converter.java` - The Java class that contains the methods `dollarToYen` and `yenToEuro`. These methods are used to convert U.S. dollars to Yen, then convert Yen to Euros.
- `index.jsp` - The Web client, which is a JavaServer Pages page that accepts the value to be converted, the buttons to submit the value, and the result of the conversion.
- `build.xml` - The build file that uses the `ant` tool to build and deploy the Web application.

The rest of this document shows how this example application was created, built, deployed, and run. If you would like to skip the information on creating the example application, you can go directly to the sections describing how to build, deploy, and run the example application, starting with Building and Deploying the Getting Started Application Using Ant (page 59).

3.1.2 Checking the Environment Variables

The installation instructions for the Java Web Services Developer Pack explain how to set the required environment variables. Please verify that the environment variables have been set to the values noted in Table 3.1.

Table 3.1 Required Environment Variables

Environment Variable	Value
`JAVA_HOME`	The location of the Java 2 Platform, Standard Edition (J2SE) installation.
`JWSDP_HOME`	The location of the Java Web Services Developer Pack installation.
`PATH`	Should include the `bin` directories of the Java Web Services Developer Pack and J2SE installations. Make sure that these directories are located at the **front** of your path statement.

3.2 Creating the Getting Started Application

The example application contains a `Converter` class and a Web component. For this example, we will create a top-level *project source directory* named `gs/`. All of the files in this example application are created in this directory.

3.2.1 The Converter Class

The `Converter` class used in the example application is used in conjunction with a JavaServer Pages page. The resulting application is a form that enables you to convert American dollars to Euros or Yen. The source code for the `Converter` class is in the *<JWDSP_HOME>*`/docs/examples/gs/` directory.

Coding the Converter Class

The `Converter` class for this example implements two methods, `dollarToYen` and `yenToEuro`. The source code for the `Converter` class follows.

```
import java.math.*;

public class Converter {

    static BigDecimal yenRate = new BigDecimal("138.7800");
    static BigDecimal euroRate = new BigDecimal("0.0084");

   public static BigDecimal dollarToYen(BigDecimal dollars) {
      BigDecimal result = dollars.multiply(yenRate);
      return result.setScale(2,BigDecimal.ROUND_UP);
   }

   public static BigDecimal yenToEuro(BigDecimal yen) {
      BigDecimal result = yen.multiply(euroRate);
      return result.setScale(2,BigDecimal.ROUND_UP);
   }

   public Converter() {}
}
```

3.2.2 The Web Client

The Web client is contained in the JSP page *<JWDSP_HOME>*/docs/tutorials/examples/gs/index.jsp. A JSP page is a text-based document that contains both static and dynamic content. The static content is the template data that can be expressed in any text-based format, such as HTML, WML, or XML. JSP elements construct the dynamic content.

Coding the Web Client

The JSP page, index.jsp, is used to create the form that will appear in the Web browser when the application client is running. This JSP page is a typical mixture of static HTML markup and JSP elements. If you have developed Web pages, you are probably familiar with the HTML document structure statements (<head>, <body>, and so on) and the HTML statements that create a form <form> and a menu <select>. The highlighted lines in the example contain the following types of JSP constructs:

- Directives (**<%@page ... %>**) import classes in the Converter class, and set the content type returned by the page.
- Scriptlets (<% ... %>) retrieve the value of the amount request parameter, convert it to a BigDecimal, and convert the value to Yen or Euro.
- Expressions (<%= ... %>) insert the value of the amount into the response.

The source code for index.jsp follows.

```
<%@ page import="Converter,java.math.*" %>
<%@ page contentType="text/html; charset=ISO-8859-1" %>
<html>
<head>
    <title>Converter</title>
</head>

<body bgcolor="white">
<h1><center>Converter</center></h1>
<hr>
<p>Enter an amount to convert:</p>
<form method="get">
<input type="text" name="amount" size="25">
<br>
```

```
<p>
<input type="submit" value="Submit">
<input type="reset" value="Reset">
</form>
<%
     String amount = request.getParameter("amount");
    if ( amount != null && amount.length() > 0 ) {
        BigDecimal d = new BigDecimal (amount);
%>
    <p><%= amount %> dollars are
        <%= Converter.dollarToYen(d) %>  Yen.
    <p><%= amount %> Yen are
        <%= Converter.yenToEuro(d) %>  Euro.
<%
     }
%>
</body>
</html>
```

3.3 Building and Deploying the Getting Started Application Using Ant

Now the example Web application is ready to build and deploy.

3.3.1 Setting the CLASSPATH

To build and run the example code, you will need to set the CLASSPATH variable properly. Instructions for setting up the CLASSPATH can be found online at

```
http://java.sun.com/j2se/1.4/docs/tooldocs/solaris/classpath.html
```

For this example, the CLASSPATH, which will need to include the `<JWSDP_HOME>/webapps/gs/WEB-INF/classes` directory, is set in the build file described in the next section. Information on what directories need to be included in the CLASSPATH can be found at "Managing Files" in the Java Tutorial, which can be viewed from:

```
http://java.sun.com/docs/books/tutorial/java/interpack/
managingfiles.html
```

3.3.2 Creating the Build File for Ant

This release of the Java Web Services Developer Pack includes `ant`, a make tool that is portable across platforms. Documentation for the `ant` tool can be found in the file `index.html` from the *<JWDSP_HOME>*`/docs/ant/` directory of your Java WSDP installation.

To use `ant` for this example, create the file `build.xml` in the `gs/` directory. The code for this file follows:

```
<!-- Setting up the Getting Started example to prepare to build
     and deploy -->
<project name="wspack-getting-started-example" default=""
 basedir=".">
    <target name="init">
        <tstamp/>
    </target>

<!-- This section sets properties used in the rest of this
     build file -->
<property name="build" value="build" />
<property environment="myenv" />

<!-- These libraries need to be included in the CLASSPATH -->
<path id="classpath">
<fileset dir="${myenv.JWSDP_HOME}/common/lib">
<include name="*.jar"/>
</fileset>
</path>

<!-- This section prepares the directory structure needed
     for Web applications -->
<target name="prepare" depends="init"
 description="Create build directories.">
    <mkdir dir="${build}/WEB-INF/classes" />
</target>

<!-- This section compiles the Java files and copies the
     HTML and JSP pages to the appropriate locations -->
<target name="build" depends="prepare"
 description="Compile app Java files and copy HTML and JSP
 pages" >
```

```
    <javac srcdir="." destdir="${build}/WEB-INF/classes">
        <include name="**/*.java" />
        <classpath refid="classpath"/>
    </javac>
    <copy todir="${build}">
        <fileset dir=".">
            <include name="*.html" />
            <include name="*.jsp" />
        </fileset>
    </copy>
</target>

<!-- This section deploys the application by copying the
     appropriate files to the webapps/ directory -->
<target name="deploy" depends="build"
 description="Deploy app to webapps.">
    <copy todir="${myenv.JWSDP_HOME}/webapps/gs">
        <fileset dir="${build}" />
    </copy>
</target>

</project>
```

3.3.3 Compiling the Source Files

Tomcat automatically compiles JSP pages. The steps for compiling the Java class (`Converter.java`) follows.

1. In a terminal window, go to the `gs/` directory if you are creating the application on your own, or go to the *<JWDSP_HOME>*`/docs/tutorial/examples/gs/` directory if you are compiling the example files downloaded with the tutorial.
2. Type the following command to build the Java files:

   ```
   ant build
   ```

   This command compiles the source files for the `Converter` class. It places the resulting class files in the `gs/build/WEB-INF/classes/` directory as specified in the build target in `build.xml`.

3.3.4 Deploying the Application

A Web application is defined as a hierarchy of directories and files in a standard layout. In this example, the hierarchy is accessed in an “unpacked” form, where each directory and file exists in the file system separately. In later releases of the Java Web Services Developer Pack, this chapter will discuss creating a Web ARchive (WAR) file for deploying your application and handling security issues. This section includes information for deploying your application. For information on handling security issues in this release, read *Security Manager How-To* in `<JWDSP_HOME>/docs/tomcat/security-manager-howto.html`.

The `build.xml` file includes commands for deploying the Web application. The steps for deploying this Web application follow.

1. In a terminal window, go to the `gs/` directory.
2. Type the following command to deploy the Web application files:

```
ant deploy
```

This command copies the Web client file, `index.jsp`, to `<JWSDP_HOME>/webapps/gs/` and copies the Java class file, `Converter.class`, to `<JWSDP_HOME>/webapps/gs/WEB-INF/classes/`.

3.4 Running the Getting Started Application

To run the application, you need to start Tomcat, then run the JSP page from a Web browser. Documentation for Tomcat can be found at `<JWDSP_HOME>/docs/tomcat/index.html`.

3.4.1 Starting Tomcat

To start Tomcat, type the following command in a terminal window. This command uses the environment variable `JWSDP_HOME`.

```
$JWSDP_HOME/bin/startup.sh          (UNIX platform)
%JWSDP_HOME%\bin\startup            (Microsoft Windows)
```

The startup script starts the task in the background and then returns the user to the command line prompt immediately. Even though you are returned to the command line, the startup script may not have completely started Tomcat. If the Web client does not run immediately, wait up to a minute and then retry to load the Web client.

3.4.2 Running the Web Client

After Tomcat is started, you can run the Web client by pointing your browser at the following URL. Replace *<host>* with the name or IP address of the host running Tomcat. If your browser is running on the same host as Tomcat, you may replace *<host>* with `localhost`.

```
http://<host>:8080/gs
```

You should see the following after entering `100` in the input field and clicking Submit:

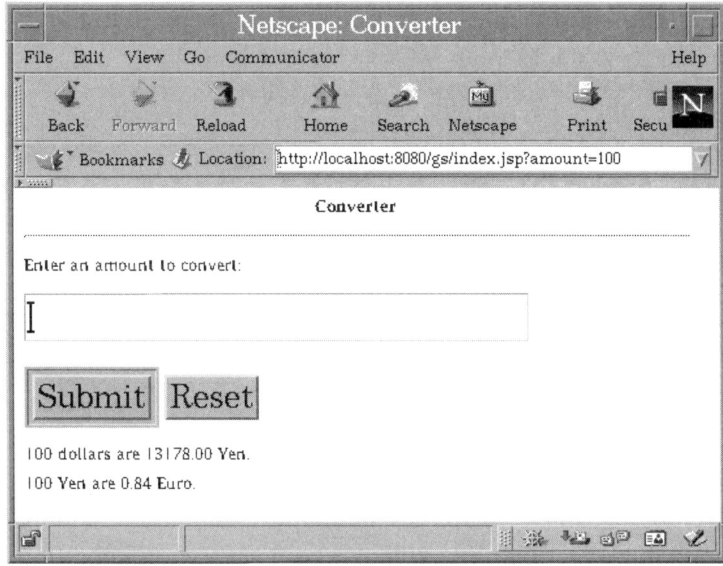

Figure 3.1 Converter Web client

3.4.3 Shutting Down Tomcat

When you are finished testing and developing your application, you should shut down Tomcat.

```
$JWSDP_HOME/bin/shutdown.sh        (UNIX platform)
%JWSDP_HOME%\bin\shutdown          (Microsoft Windows)
```

3.5 Modifying the Application

Since the Java Web Services Developer Pack is intended for experimentation, it supports iterative development. Whenever you make a change to an application, you must redeploy and reload the application.

3.5.1 Modifying a Class File

To modify a class file in a Java component, you change the source code, recompile it, and redeploy the application. For example, suppose that you want to change the exchange rate in the `dollarToYen` method of the `Converter` class:

1. Edit `Converter.java` in the source directory.
2. Recompile `Converter.java` by typing `ant build`.
3. Redeploy `Converter.java` by typing `ant deploy`.
4. Restart the Web application.
5. Reload the JSP page in the Web browser.

3.5.2 Modifying the Web Client

To modify the Web client:

1. Edit `index.jsp` in the source directory.
2. Redeploy `index.jsp` by typing `ant deploy`.
3. Reload the Web application.
4. Reload the application in the Web browser.

3.5.3 Reloading the Application

You reload an application with the command:

```
http://localhost:8080/manager/reload?path=/target
```

This command invokes the `manager` Web application. Before you can use this application you must add your user name/password combination and associate the role name `manager` with it to `<JWSDP_HOME>/conf/tomcat-users.xml`, which can be edited with any text editor. This file contains an element `<user>` for each individual user, which might look something like this:

```
<user name="adeveloper" password="secret" roles="manager" />
```

The Tomcat reference documentation distributed with the Java WSDP contains information about the manager application.

3.6 Common Problems and Their Solutions

3.6.1 Cannot Start the Tomcat Server

"Out of Environment Space" Error. Symptom: An "out of environment space" error when running the startup and shutdown batch files in Microsoft Windows 9X/ME-based operating systems.

Solution: In the Microsoft Windows Explorer, right-click on the `startup.bat` and `shutdown.bat` files. Select Properties, then select the Memory tab. Increase the Initial Environment field to something like 4096. Select Apply.

After you select Apply, shortcuts will be created in the directory you use to start and stop the container.

3.6.2 Compilation Errors

Ant Cannot Locate the Build File. Symptom: When you type `ant build`, these messages appear:

```
Buildfile: build.xml does not exist!
Build failed.
```

Solution: Start `ant` from the *<JWSDP_HOME>*`/docs/tutorial/examples/gs/` directory, or from the directory where you created the application. If you want to run `ant` from your current directory, then you must specify the build file on the command line. For example, on Microsoft Windows operating systems, you would type this command on a single line:

```
ant -buildfile C:\wspack1.0\docs\examples\src\gs\build.xml
build
```

The Compiler Cannot Resolve Symbols. Symptom: When you type `ant build`, the compiler reports many errors, including these:

```
cannot resolve symbol
. . .
```

```
BUILD FAILED
. . .
Compile failed, messages should have been provided
```

Solution: Make sure that you've set the JWSDP_HOME environment variable correctly. See Checking the Environment Variables (page 56).

3.6.3 Deployment Errors

Failure to Run Client Application. Symptom: The browser reports that the page cannot be found (HTTP 404).

Solution: The startup script starts the task in the background and then returns the user to the command line prompt immediately. Even though you are returned to the command line, the startup script may not have completely started Tomcat. If the Web client does not run immediately, wait up to a minute and then retry to load the Web client.

The localhost Machine Is Not Found. Symptom: The browser reports that the page cannot be found (HTTP 404).

Solution: Sometimes when you are behind a proxy and the firewall does not let you access the `localhost` machine. To fix this, change the proxy setting so that it does not use the proxy to access `localhost`.

To do this in the Netscape Navigator browser, select Edit -> Preferences -> Advanced -> Proxies and select `No Proxy for: localhost`. In Internet Explorer, select Tools -> Internet Options -> Connections -> LAN Settings.

The Application Has Not Been Deployed. Symptom: The browser reports that the page cannot be found (HTTP 404).

Solution: Deploy the application. For more detail, see Deploying the Application (page 62).

CHAPTER 4

Java API for XML Processing

Eric Armstrong

In This Chapter

THE Java API for XML Processing ("JAXP") is for processing XML data using applications written in the Java programming language. JAXP leverages the parser standards SAX (Simple API for XML Parsing) and DOM (Document Object Model) so that you can choose to parse your data as a stream of events or to build an object representation of it. JAXP also supports the XSLT (XML Stylesheet Language Transformations) standard, giving you control over the presentation of the data and enabling you to convert the data to other XML documents or to other formats, such as HTML. JAXP also provides namespace support, allowing you to work with DTDs that might otherwise have naming conflicts.

Designed to be flexible, JAXP allows you to use any XML-compliant parser from within your application. It does this with what is called a pluggability layer, which allows you to plug in an implementation of the SAX or DOM APIs. The pluggability layer also allows you to plug in an XSL processor, letting you control how your XML data is displayed.

4.1 The JAXP APIs

The main JAXP APIs are defined in the `javax.xml.parsers` package. That package contains two vendor-neutral factory classes: `SAXParserFactory` and `DocumentBuilderFactory` that give you a `SAXParser` and a `DocumentBuilder`, respectively. The `DocumentBuilder`, in turn, creates DOM-compliant `Document` object.

The factory APIs give you the ability to plug in an XML implementation offered by another vendor without changing your source code. The implementation you get depends on the setting of the `javax.xml.parsers.SAXParserFactory` and `javax.xml.parsers.DocumentBuilderFactory` system properties. The default values (unless overridden at runtime) point to the reference implementation.

The remainder of this section shows how the different JAXP APIs work when you write an application.

4.2 An Overview of the Packages

The SAX and DOM APIs are defined by XML-DEV group and by the W3C, respectively. The libraries that define those APIs are:

`javax.xml.parsers`

The JAXP APIs, which provide a common interface for different vendors' SAX and DOM parsers.

`org.w3c.dom`

Defines the `Document` class (a DOM), as well as classes for all of the components of a DOM.

`org.xml.sax`

Defines the basic SAX APIs.

`javax.xml.transform`

Defines the XSLT APIs that let you transform XML into other forms.

The "Simple API" for XML (SAX) is the event-driven, serial-access mechanism that does element-by-element processing. The API for this level reads and writes XML to a data repository or the Web. For server-side and high-performance apps, you will want to fully understand this level. But for many applications, a minimal understanding will suffice.

The DOM API is generally an easier API to use. It provides a relatively familiar tree structure of objects. You can use the DOM API to manipulate the hierarchy of application objects it encapsulates. The DOM API is ideal for interactive applications because the entire object model is present in memory, where it can be accessed and manipulated by the user.

On the other hand, constructing the DOM requires reading the entire XML structure and holding the object tree in memory, so it is much more CPU and memory intensive. For that reason, the SAX API will tend to be preferred for server-side applications and data filters that do not require an in-memory representation of the data.

Finally, the XSLT APIs defined in `javax.xml.transform` let you write XML data to a file or convert it into other forms. And, as you'll see in the XSLT section, of this tutorial, you can even use it in conjunction with the SAX APIs to convert legacy data to XML.

4.3 The Simple API for XML (SAX) APIs

The basic outline of the SAX parsing APIs are shown at right. To start the process, an instance of the `SAXParserFactory` classed is used to generate an instance of the parser.

The parser wraps a `SAXReader` object. When the parser's `parse()` method is invoked, the reader invokes one of several callback methods implemented in the application. Those methods are defined by the interfaces `ContentHandler`, `ErrorHandler`, `DTDHandler`, and `EntityResolver`.

Here is a summary of the key SAX APIs:

`SAXParserFactory`

A `SAXParserFactory` object creates an instance of the parser determined by the system property, `javax.xml.parsers.SAXParserFactory`.

`SAXParser`

The `SAXParser` interface defines several kinds of `parse()` methods. In general, you pass an XML data source and a `DefaultHandler` object to the parser, which processes the XML and invokes the appropriate methods in the handler object.

`SAXReader`

The `SAXParser` wraps a `SAXReader`. Typically, you don't care about that, but every once in a while you need to get hold of it using `SAXParser`'s

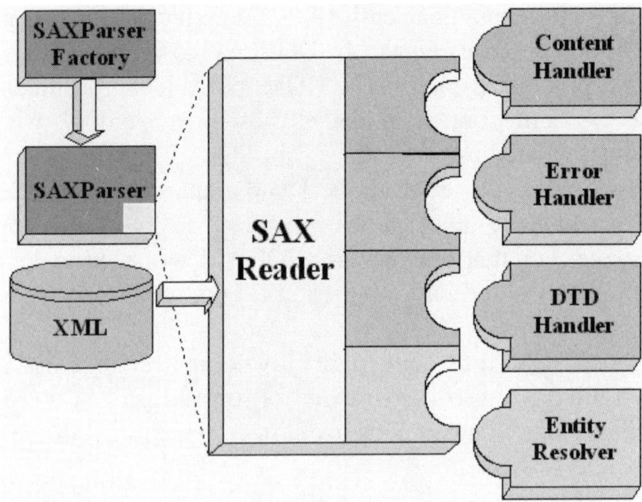

Figure 4.1 SAX APIs

`getXMLReader()`, so you can configure it. It is the `SAXReader` which carries on the conversation with the SAX event handlers you define.

`DefaultHandler`

Not shown in the diagram, a `DefaultHandler` implements the `ContentHandler`, `ErrorHandler`, `DTDHandler`, and `EntityResolver` interfaces (with null methods), so you can override only the ones you're interested in.

`ContentHandler`

Methods like `startDocument`, `endDocument`, `startElement`, and `endElement` are invoked when an XML tag is recognized. This interface also defines methods `characters` and `processingInstruction`, which are invoked when the parser encounters the text in an XML element or an inline processing instruction, respectively.

`ErrorHandler`

Methods `error`, `fatalError`, and `warning` are invoked in response to various parsing errors. The default error handler throws an exception for fatal errors and ignores other errors (including validation errors). That's one reason you need to know something about the SAX parser, even if you are using the DOM. Sometimes, the application may be able to recover from a validation error.

Other times, it may need to generate an exception. To ensure the correct handling, you'll need to supply your own error handler to the parser.

`DTDHandler`

Defines methods you will generally never be called upon to use. Used when processing a DTD to recognize and act on declarations for an *unparsed entity*.

`EntityResolver`

The `resolveEntity` method is invoked when the parser must identify data identified by a URI. In most cases, a URI is simply a URL, which specifies the location of a document, but in some cases the document may be identified by a URN—a *public identifier*, or name, that is unique in the Web space. The public identifier may be specified in addition to the URL. The `EntityResolver` can then use the public identifier instead of the URL to find the document, for example to access a local copy of the document if one exists.

A typical application implements most of the `ContentHandler` methods, at a minimum. Since the default implementations of the interfaces ignore all inputs except for fatal errors, a robust implementation may want to implement the `ErrorHandler` methods, as well.

4.3.1 The SAX Packages

The SAX parser is defined in the following packages listed in Table 4.1.

Table 4.1 SAX Packages

Package	Description
`org.xml.sax`	Defines the SAX interfaces. The name `org.xml` is the package prefix that was settled on by the group that defined the SAX API.
`org.xml.sax.ext`	Defines SAX extensions that are used when doing more sophisticated SAX processing; for example, to process a document type definitions (DTD) or to see the detailed syntax for a file.
`org.xml.sax.helpers`	Contains helper classes that make it easier to use SAX—for example, by defining a default handler that has null-methods for all of the interfaces, so you only need to override the ones you actually want to implement.
`javax.xml.parsers`	Defines the `SAXParserFactory` class which returns the `SAXParser`. Also defines exception classes for reporting errors.

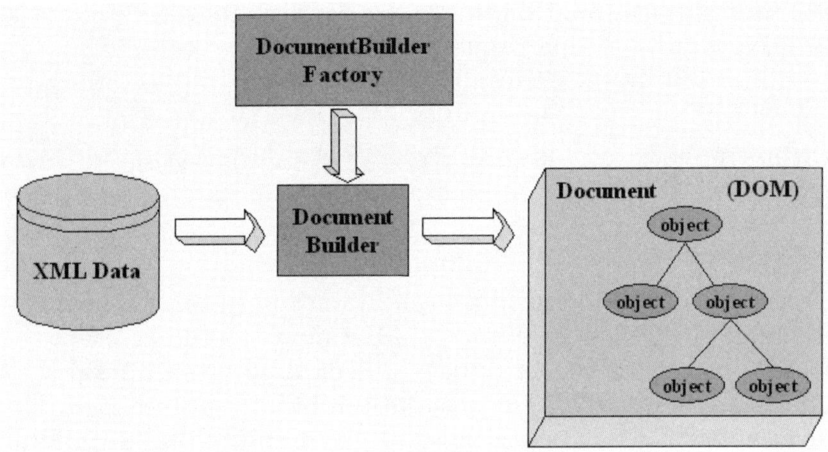

Figure 4.2 DOM APIs

4.4 The Document Object Model (DOM) APIs

Figure 4.2 shows the JAXP APIs in action.

You use the `javax.xml.parsers.DocumentBuilderFactory` class to get a `DocumentBuilder` instance, and use that to produce a `Document` (a DOM) that conforms to the DOM specification. The builder you get, in fact, is determined by the System property, `javax.xml.parsers.DocumentBuilderFactory`, which selects the factory implementation that is used to produce the builder. (The platform's default value can be overridden from the command line.)

You can also use the `DocumentBuilder` `newDocument()` method to create an empty `Document` that implements the `org.w3c.dom.Document` interface. Alternatively, you can use one of the builder's parse methods to create a `Document` from existing XML data. The result is a DOM tree like that shown in the diagram.

Note: Although they are called objects, the entries in the DOM tree are actually fairly low-level data structures. For example, under every *element node* (which corresponds to an XML element) there is a *text node* which contains the name of the element tag! This issue will be explored at length in the DOM section of the tutorial, but users who are expecting objects are usually surprised to find that invoking the `text()` method on an element object returns nothing! For a truly object-oriented tree, see the JDOM API at `http://www.jdom.org`.

Table 4.2 DOM Packages

Package	Description
`org.w3c.dom`	Defines the DOM programming interfaces for XML (and, optionally, HTML) documents, as specified by the W3C.
`javax.xml.parsers`	Defines the `DocumentBuilderFactory` class and the `DocumentBuilder` class, which returns an object that implements the W3C Document interface. The factory that is used to create the builder is determined by the `javax.xml.parsers` system property, which can be set from the command line or overridden when invoking the `new Instance` method. This package also defines the `ParserConfigurationException` class for reporting errors.

4.4.1 The DOM Packages

The Document Object Model implementation is defined in the following packages in Table 4.2.

4.5 The XML Stylesheet Language for Transformation (XSLT) APIs

Figure 4.3 shows the XSLT APIs in action.

A `TransformerFactory` object is instantiated, and used to create a `Transformer`. The source object is the input to the transformation process. A source object can be created from SAX reader, from a DOM, or from an input stream.

Similarly, the result object is the result of the transformation process. That object can be a SAX event handler, a DOM, or an output stream.

When the transformer is created, it may be created from a set of transformation instructions, in which case the specified transformations are carried out. If it is created without any specific instructions, then the transformer object simply copies the source to the result.

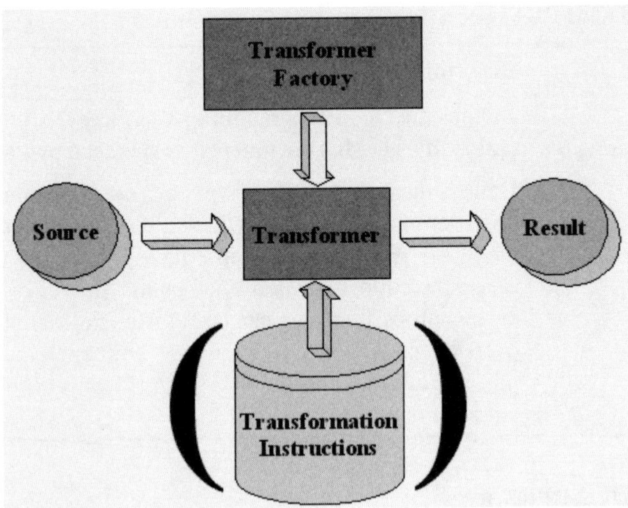

Figure 4.3 XSLT APIs

4.5.1 The XSLT Packages

The XSLT APIs are defined in the following packages:

Table 4.3 XSLT Packages

Package	Description
`javax.xml.transform`	Defines the `TransformerFactory` and `Transformer` classes, which you use to get a object capable of doing transformations. After creating a transformer object, you invoke its `transform()` method, providing it with an input (source) and output (result).
`javax.xml.transform.dom`	Classes to create input (source) and output (result) objects from a DOM.
`javax.xml.transform.sax`	Classes to create input (source) from a SAX parser and output (result) objects from a SAX event handler.
`javax.xml.transform.stream`	Classes to create input (source) and output (result) objects from an I/O stream.

4.6 Compiling and Running the Programs

In the Java WSDP, the JAXP libraries are distributed in the directory `<JWSDP_HOME>/common/lib`. To compile and run the sample programs, you'll first need to install the JAXP libraries in the appropriate location. (The location depends on which version of the JVM you are using.) See the JAXP release notes at `<JWSDP_HOME>/docs/jaxp/ReleaseNotes.html` for details.

4.7 Where Do You Go from Here?

At this point, you have enough information to begin picking your own way through the JAXP libraries. Your next step from here depends on what you want to accomplish. You might want to go to:

The XML Thread

If you want to learn more about XML, spend as little time as possible on the Java APIs. You will see all of the XML sections in the normal course of the tutorial. Follow this thread if you want to bypass the API programming steps:

- Introduction to XML (page 29)
- Writing a Simple XML File (page 78)
- Substituting and Inserting Text (page 110)
- Creating a Document Type Definition (DTD) (page 114)
- Defining Attributes and Entities in the DTD (page 122)
- Referencing Binary Entities (page 128)
- Defining Parameter Entities and Conditional Sections (page 134)

Designing an XML Data Structure (page 48)

If you are creating XML data structures for an application and want some tips on how to proceed. (This is the next step in the XML overview.)

Simple API for XML (page 77)

If the data structures have already been determined, and you are writing a server application or an XML filter that needs to do the fastest possible processing. This section also takes you step by step through the process of constructing an XML document.

Document Object Model (page 149)

If you need to build an object tree from XML data so you can manipulate it in an application, or convert an in-memory tree of objects to XML. This part of the tutorial ends with a section on namespaces.

XML Stylesheet Language for Transformations (page 203)

If you need to transform XML tags into some other form, if you want to generate XML output, or if you want to convert legacy data structures to XML.

CHAPTER 5

Simple API for XML

Eric Armstrong

IN THIS CHAPTER

IN this chapter we focus on the Simple API for XML (SAX), an event-driven, serial-access mechanism for accessing XML documents. This is the protocol that most servlets and network-oriented programs will want to use to transmit and receive XML documents, because it's the fastest and least memory-intensive mechanism that is currently available for dealing with XML documents.

The SAX protocol requires a lot more programming than the Document Object Model (DOM). It's an event-driven model (you provide the callback methods, and the parser invokes them as it reads the XML data), which makes it harder to visualize. Finally, you can't "back up" to an earlier part of the document, or rearrange it, any more than you can back up a serial data stream or rearrange characters you have read from that stream.

For those reasons, developers who are writing a user-oriented application that displays an XML document and possibly modifies it will want to use the DOM mechanism described in the next part of the tutorial, Document Object Model (page 149).

However, even if you plan to do build DOM apps exclusively, there are several important reasons for familiarizing yourself with the SAX model:

- Same Error Handling

  When parsing a document for a DOM, the same kinds of exceptions are generated, so the error handling for JAXP SAX and DOM apps are identical.

- Handling Validation Errors

  By default, the specifications require that validation errors (which you'll be learning more about in this part of the tutorial) are ignored. If you want to throw an exception in the event of a validation error (and you probably do), then you need to understand how the SAX error handling works.

- Converting Existing Data

  As you'll see in the DOM section of the tutorial, Sun's reference implementation provides a mechanism you can use to convert an existing data set to XML—however, taking advantage of that mechanism requires an understanding the SAX model.

5.1 Writing a Simple XML File

Let's start out by writing up a simple version of the kind of XML data you could use for a slide presentation. In this exercise, you'll use your text editor to create the data in order to become comfortable with the basic format of an XML file. You'll be using this file and extending it in later exercises.

Note: The examples in this chapter can be found in `docs/tutorial/examples/jaxp/sax/samples`.

5.1.1 Creating the File

Using a standard text editor, create a file called `slideSample.xml`.

Note: Here is a version of it that already exists: `slideSample01.xml`. (The browsable version is `slideSample01-xml.html`.) You can use this version to compare your work, or just review it as you read this guide.

5.1.2 Writing the Declaration

Next, write the declaration, which identifies the file as an XML document. The declaration starts with the characters "<?", which is the standard XML identifier for a *processor instruction*. (You'll see other processor instructions later on in this tutorial.)

```
<?xml version='1.0' encoding='utf-8'?>
```

This line identifies the document as an XML document that conforms to version 1.0 of the XML specification, and says that it uses the 8-bit Unicode character-encoding scheme. (For information on encoding schemes, see Java Encoding Schemes (page 493).)

Since the document has not been specified as *standalone*, the parser assumes that it may contain references to other documents. To see how to specify a document as *standalone*, see The XML Prolog (page 32).

5.1.3 Adding a Comment

Comments are ignored by XML parsers. You never see them in fact, unless you activate special settings in the parser. You'll see how to do that later on in the tutorial, when we discuss Handling Lexical Events (page 140). For now, add the text highlighted below to put a comment into the file.

```
<?xml version='1.0' encoding='utf-8'?>

<!-- A SAMPLE set of slides -->
```

5.2 Defining the Root Element

After the declaration, every XML file defines exactly one element, known as the root element. Any other elements in the file are contained within that element.

Enter the text highlighted below to define the root element for this file, `slideshow`:

```
<?xml version='1.0' encoding='utf-8'?>

<!-- A SAMPLE set of slides -->

<slideshow>

</slideshow>
```

Note: XML element names are case-sensitive. The end-tag must exactly match the start-tag.

Adding Attributes to an Element

A slide presentation has a number of associated data items, none of which require any structure. So it is natural to define them as attributes of the `slideshow` element. Add the text highlighted below to set up some attributes:

```
...
    <slideshow
        title="Sample Slide Show"
        date="Date of publication"
        author="Yours Truly"
        >
    </slideshow>
```

When you create a name for a tag or an attribute, you can use hyphens ("`-`"), underscores ("`_`"), colons ("`:`"), and periods ("`.`") in addition to characters and numbers. Unlike HTML, values for XML attributes are always in quotation marks, and multiple attributes are never separated by commas.

Note: Colons should be used with care or avoided altogether, because they are used when defining the namespace for an XML document.

5.2.1 Adding Nested Elements

XML allows for hierarchically structured data, which means that an element can contain other elements. Add the text highlighted below to define a slide element and a title element contained within it:

```
<slideshow
    ...
    >

     <!-- TITLE SLIDE -->
    <slide type="all">
        <title>Wake up to WonderWidgets!</title>
    </slide>
</slideshow>
```

Here you have also added a *type* attribute to the slide. The idea of this attribute is that slides could be earmarked for a mostly technical or mostly executive audience with `type="tech"` or `type="exec"`, or identified as suitable for both with `type="all"`.

More importantly, though, this example illustrates the difference between things that are more usefully defined as elements (the *title* element) and things that are more suitable as attributes (the *type* attribute). The visibility heuristic is primarily at work here. The title is something the audience will see. So it is an element. The type, on the other hand, is something that never gets presented, so it is an attribute. Another way to think about that distinction is that an element is a container, like a bottle. The type is a characteristic of the *container* (is it tall or short, wide or narrow). The title is a characteristic of the *contents* (water, milk, or tea). These are not hard and fast rules, of course, but they can help when you design your own XML structures.

5.2.2 Adding HTML-Style Text

Since XML lets you define any tags you want, it makes sense to define a set of tags that look like HTML. The XHTML standard does exactly that, in fact. You'll see more about that towards the end of the SAX tutorial. For now, type the text highlighted below to define a slide with a couple of list item entries that use an HTML-style <em> tag for emphasis (usually rendered as italicized text):

```
    ...
    <!-- TITLE SLIDE -->
    <slide type="all">
        <title>Wake up to WonderWidgets!</title>
    </slide>
```

```
<!-- OVERVIEW -->
<slide type="all">
    <title>Overview</title>
        <item>Why <em>WonderWidgets</em> are great</item>
        <item>Who <em>buys</em> WonderWidgets</item>
</slide>

</slideshow>
```

We'll see later that defining a *title* element conflicts with the XHTML element that uses the same name. We'll discuss the mechanism that produces the conflict (the DTD) and several possible solutions when we cover Parsing the Parameterized DTD (page 137).

5.2.3 Adding an Empty Element

One major difference between HTML and XML, though, is that all XML must be *well-formed*—which means that every tag must have an ending tag or be an empty tag. You're getting pretty comfortable with ending tags, by now. Add the text highlighted below to define an empty list item element with no contents:

```
...
<!-- OVERVIEW -->
<slide type="all">
    <title>Overview</title>
    <item>Why <em>WonderWidgets</em> are great</item>
    <item/>
    <item>Who <em>buys</em> WonderWidgets</item>
</slide>

</slideshow>
```

Note that any element can be empty element. All it takes is ending the tag with "/>" instead of ">." You could do the same thing by entering `<item></item>`, which is equivalent.

Note: Another factor that makes an XML file *well-formed* is proper nesting. So `<b><i>some_text</i></b>` is well-formed, because the `<i>...</i>` sequence is completely nested within the `<b>..</b>` tag. This sequence, on the other hand, is not well-formed: `<b><i>some_text</b></i>`.

5.2.4 The Finished Product

Here is the completed version of the XML file:

```
<?xml version='1.0' encoding='utf-8'?>

<!--  A SAMPLE set of slides  -->
<slideshow
    title="Sample Slide Show"
    date="Date of publication"
    author="Yours Truly"
    >

    <!-- TITLE SLIDE -->
    <slide type="all">
        <title>Wake up to WonderWidgets!</title>
    </slide>

    <!-- OVERVIEW -->
    <slide type="all">
        <title>Overview</title>
        <item>Why <em>WonderWidgets</em> are great</item>
        <item/>
        <item>Who <em>buys</em> WonderWidgets</item>
    </slide
</slideshow>
```

Now that you've created a file to work with, you're ready to write a program to echo it using the SAX parser. You'll do that in the next section.

5.3 Echoing an XML File with the SAX Parser

In real life, you are going to have little need to echo an XML file with a SAX parser. Usually, you'll want to process the data in some way in order to do something useful with it. (If you want to echo it, it's easier to build a DOM tree and use that for output.) But echoing an XML structure is a great way to see the SAX parser in action, and it can be useful for debugging.

In this exercise, you'll echo SAX parser events to `System.out`. Consider it the "Hello World" version of an XML-processing program. It shows you how to use the SAX parser to get at the data, and then echoes it to show you what you've got.

Note: The code discussed in this section is in `Echo01.java`. The file it operates on is `slideSample01.xml`. (The browsable version is `slideSample01-xml.html`.)

5.3.1 Creating the Skeleton

Start by creating a file named `Echo.java` and enter the skeleton for the application:

```
public class Echo
{
    public static void main(String argv[])
    {
        }
}
```

Since we're going to run it standalone, we need a main method. And we need command-line arguments so we can tell the app which file to echo.

5.3.2 Importing Classes

Next, add the import statements for the classes the app will use:

```
import java.io.*;
import org.xml.sax.*;
import org.xml.sax.helpers.DefaultHandler;
import javax.xml.parsers.SAXParserFactory;
import javax.xml.parsers.ParserConfigurationException;
import javax.xml.parsers.SAXParser;
public class Echo
{
    ...
```

The classes in `java.io`, of course, are needed to do output. The `org.xml.sax` package defines all the interfaces we use for the SAX parser. The `SAXParserFactory` class creates the instance we use. It throws a `ParserConfigurationException` if it is unable to produce a parser that matches the specified configuration of options. (You'll see more about the configuration options later.) The `SAXParser` is what the factory returns for parsing, and the `DefaultHandler` defines the class that will handle the SAX events that the parser generates.

5.3.3 Setting up for I/O

The first order of business is to process the command line argument, get the name of the file to echo, and set up the output stream. Add the text highlighted below to take care of those tasks and do a bit of additional housekeeping:

```
public static void main(String argv[])

{
    if (argv.length != 1) {
        System.err.println("Usage: cmd filename");
        System.exit(1);
    }
    try {
        // Set up output stream
        out = new OutputStreamWriter(System.out, "UTF8");

        } catch (Throwable t) {
        t.printStackTrace();
    }
    System.exit(0);
}

static private Writer out;
```

When we create the output stream writer, we are selecting the UTF-8 character encoding. We could also have chosen US-ASCII, or UTF-16, which the Java platform also supports. For more information on these character sets, see Java Encoding Schemes (page 493).

5.3.4 Implementing the ContentHandler Interface

The most important interface for our current purposes is the `ContentHandler` interface. That interface requires a number of methods that the SAX parser invokes in response to different parsing events. The major event handling methods are: `startDocument`, `endDocument`, `startElement`, `endElement`, and `characters`.

The easiest way to implement that interface is to extend the DefaultHandler class, defined in the org.xml.sax.helpers package. That class provides do-nothing methods for all of the ContentHandler events. Enter the code highlighted below to extend that class:

```
public class Echo extends DefaultHandler
{
    ...
}
```

Note: DefaultHandler also defines do-nothing methods for the other major events, defined in the DTDHandler, EntityResolver, and ErrorHandler interfaces. You'll learn more about those methods as we go along.

Each of these methods is required by the interface to throw a SAXException. An exception thrown here is sent back to the parser, which sends it on to the code that invoked the parser. In the current program, that means it winds up back at the Throwable exception handler at the bottom of the main method.

When a start tag or end tag is encountered, the name of the tag is passed as a String to the startElement or endElement method, as appropriate. When a start tag is encountered, any attributes it defines are also passed in an Attributes list. Characters found within the element are passed as an array of characters, along with the number of characters (length) and an offset into the array that points to the first character.

5.3.5 Setting up the Parser

Now (at last) you're ready to set up the parser. Add the text highlighted below to set it up and get it started:

```
public static void main(String argv[])
{
    if (argv.length != 1) {
        System.err.println("Usage: cmd filename");
        System.exit(1);
    }
        // Use an instance of ourselves as the SAX event handler
    DefaultHandler handler = new Echo();

        // Use the default (non-validating) parser
    SAXParserFactory factory = SAXParserFactory.newInstance();
```

```
    try {
        // Set up output stream

        out = new OutputStreamWriter(System.out, "UTF8");

         // Parse the input
        SAXParser saxParser = factory.newSAXParser();
        saxParser.parse( new File(argv[0]), handler );

        } catch (Throwable t) {
        t.printStackTrace();
    }
    System.exit(0);
}
```

With these lines of code, you created a `SAXParserFactory` instance, as determined by the setting of the `javax.xml.parsers.SAXParserFactory` system property. You then got a parser from the factory and gave the parser an instance of this class to handle the parsing events, telling it which input file to process.

Note: The `javax.xml.parsers.SAXParser` class is a wrapper that defines a number of convenience methods. It wraps the (somewhat-less friendly) `org.xml.sax.Parser` object. If needed, you can obtain that parser using the `SAXParser`'s `getParser()` method.

For now, you are simply catching any exception that the parser might throw. You'll learn more about error processing in a later section of the tutorial, Handling Errors with the Nonvalidating Parser (page 101).

5.3.6 Writing the Output

The `ContentHandler` methods throw `SAXExceptions` but not `IOExceptions`, which can occur while writing. The `SAXException` can wrap another exception, though, so it makes sense to do the output in a method that takes care of the exception-handling details. Add the code highlighted below to define an `emit` method that does that:

```
static private Writer out;

private void emit(String s)
throws SAXException
```

```
{
    try {
        out.write(s);
        out.flush();
    } catch (IOException e) {
        throw new SAXException("I/O error", e);
    }
}
...
```

When emit is called, any I/O error is wrapped in `SAXException` along with a message that identifies it. That exception is then thrown back to the SAX parser. You'll learn more about SAX exceptions later on. For now, keep in mind that `emit` is a small method that handles the string output. (You'll see it called a lot in the code ahead.)

5.3.7 Spacing the Output

There is one last bit of infrastructure we need before doing some real processing. Add the code highlighted below to define a `nl()` method that writes the kind of line-ending character used by the current system:

```
private void emit(String s)
    ...
}

private void nl()
throws SAXException
{
    String lineEnd =  System.getProperty("line.separator");
    try {
        out.write(lineEnd);
    } catch (IOException e) {
        throw new SAXException("I/O error", e);
    }
}
```

Note: Although it seems like a bit of a nuisance, you will be invoking `nl()` many times in the code ahead. Defining it now will simplify the code later on. It also provides a place to indent the output when we get to that section of the tutorial.

5.3.8 Handling Content Events

Finally, let's write some code that actually processes the `ContentHandler` events. Add the code highlighted below to handle the start-document and end-document events:

```
static private Writer out;

public void startDocument()
throws SAXException
{
    emit("<?xml version='1.0' encoding='UTF-8'?>");
    nl();
}

public void endDocument()
throws SAXException
{
    try {
        nl();
        out.flush();
    } catch (IOException e) {
        throw new SAXException("I/O error", e);
    }
}

private void emit(String s)
...
```

Here, you are echoing an XML declaration when the parser encounters the start of the document. Since you set up the `OutputStreamWriter` using the UTF-8 encoding, you include that specification as part of the declaration.

Note: However, the IO classes don't understand the hyphenated encoding names, so you specified "UTF8" rather than "UTF-8".

At the end of the document, you simply put out a final newline and flush the output stream. There's not much going on there. Now for the interesting stuff. Add the code highlighted below to process the start-element and end-element events:

```
public void startElement(String namespaceURI,
                String sName, // simple name (localName)
                String qName, // qualified name
                Attributes attrs)
throws SAXException
{
    String eName = sName; // element name
    if ("".equals(eName)) eName = qName; // namespaceAware = false
    emit("<"+eName);
    if (attrs != null) {
        for (int i = 0; i < attrs.getLength(); i++) {
            String aName = attrs.getLocalName(i); // Attr name
            if ("".equals(aName)) aName = attrs.getQName(i);
            emit("");
            emit(aName+"=\"+attra.getvalue(i)+"\"");
        }
    }
    emit(">");
}}

public void endElement(String namespaceURI,
                String sName, // simple name
                String qName  // qualified name
                )

throws SAXException
{
    emit("</"+sName+">");
}

private void emit(String s)
...
```

With this code, you echoed the element tags, including any attributes defined in the start tag. Note that when the `startElement()` method is invoked, the simple name ("local name") for elements and attributes could turn out to be the empty string, if namespace processing was not enabled. The code handles that case by using the qualified name whenever the simple name is the empty string.

To finish this version of the program, add the code highlighted below to echo the characters the parser sees:

```
public void characters(char buf[], int offset, int len)
throws SAXException
{
    String s = new String(buf, offset, len);
    emit(s);
}

private void emit(String s)
...
```

Congratulations! You've just written a SAX parser application. The next step is to compile and run it.

Note: To be strictly accurate, the character handler should scan the buffer for ampersand characters ('&');and left-angle bracket characters ('<') and replace them with the strings "&" or "<", as appropriate. You'll find out more about that kind of processing when we discuss entity references in Substituting and Inserting Text (page 110).

5.3.9 Compiling and Running the Program

In the Java WSDP, the JAXP libraries are distributed in the directory *<JWSDP_HOME>*/common/lib. To compile the program you created, you'll first need to install the JAXP JAR files in the appropriate location. (The names of the JAR files and their location depends on which version of JAXP you are using. See the Java XML release notes at *<JWSDP_HOME>*/docs/jaxp/ReleaseNotes.html for details.) Then you can execute the following command:

```
javac -cp jaxp-jar-files Echo.java
```

where javac is a version 1.2 or later Java platform compiler.

To run the program, execute the command below:

```
java -cp jaxp-jar-files Echo slideSample.xml
```

5.3.10 Checking the Output

The program's output as shown in Echo01-01. Here is part of it, showing some of its weird-looking spacing:

```
...
<slideshow title="Sample Slide Show" date="Date of publication"
author="Yours Truly">


    <slide type="all">
        <title>Wake up to WonderWidgets!</title>
    </slide>
    ...
```

Looking at this output, a number of questions arise. Namely, where is the excess vertical whitespace coming from? And why is it that the elements are indented properly, when the code isn't doing it? We'll answer those questions in a moment. First, though, there are a few points to note about the output:

- The comment defined at the top of the file

  ```
  <!-- A SAMPLE set of slides -->
  ```

  does not appear in the listing. Comments are ignored by definition, unless you implement a LexicalHandler. You'll see more about that later on in this tutorial.
- Element attributes are listed all together on a single line. If your window isn't really wide, you won't see them all.
- The single-tag empty element you defined (<item/>) is treated exactly the same as a two-tag empty element (<item></item>). It is, for all intents and purposes, identical. (It's just easier to type and consumes less space.)

5.3.11 Identifying the Events

This version of the echo program might be useful for displaying an XML file, but it's not telling you much about what's going on in the parser. The next step is to modify the program so that you see where the spaces and vertical lines are coming from.

Note: The code discussed in this section is in Echo02.java. The output it produces is shown in Echo02-01.

Make the changes highlighted below to identify the events as they occur:

```
public void startDocument()
throws SAXException
{
    nl();
    nl();
    emit("START DOCUMENT");
    nl();
    emit("<?xml version='1.0' encoding='UTF-8'?>");
    nl();
}

public void endDocument()
throws SAXException
{
    nl(); emit("END DOCUMENT");
    try {
    ...
}

public void startElement(...)
throws SAXException
{
    nl(); emit("ELEMENT: ");
    emit("<"+sName);
    if (attrs != null) {
        for (int i = 0; i < attrs.getLength(); i++) {
            emit(" ");
            emit(attrs.getName(i)+"=\""+attrs.getValue(i)+"\"");
            nl();
            emit("   ATTR: ");
            emit(attrs.getLocalName(i));
            emit("\"");
            emit(attrs.getValue(i));
            emit("\"");
        }
    }
    if (attrs.getLength() > 0) nl();
    emit(">");
}
public void endElement(...)
throws SAXException
```

```
{
    nl();
    emit("END_ELM: ");
    emit("</"+sName+">");
}
public void characters(char buf[], int offset, int Len)
throws SAXException
{
    nl(); emit("CHARS: |");
    String s = new String(buf, offset, Len);
    emit(s);
    emit("|");
}
```

Compile and run this version of the program to produce a more informative output listing. The attributes are now shown one per line, which is nice. But, more importantly, output lines like this one:

```
CHARS: |
  |
```

show that the `characters` method is responsible for echoing both the spaces that create the indentation and the multiple newlines that separate the attributes.

Note: The XML specification requires all input line separators to be normalized to a single newline. The newline character is specified as in Java, C, and UNIX systems, but goes by the alias "linefeed" in Windows systems.

5.3.12 Compressing the Output

To make the output more readable, modify the program so that it only outputs characters containing something other than whitespace.

Note: The code discussed in this section is in `Echo03.java`.

Make the changes shown below to suppress output of characters that are all whitespace:

```
public void characters(char buf[], int offset, int Len)
throws SAXException
```

```
{
    nl(); emit("CHARS: |");
    nl(); emit("CHARS:   ");
    String s = new String(buf, offset, Len);
    emit(s);
    emit("|");
    if (!s.trim().equals("")) emit(s);
}
```

If you run the program now, you will see that you have eliminated the indentation as well, because the indent space is part of the whitespace that precedes the start of an element. Add the code highlighted below to manage the indentation:

```
static private Writer out;
private String indentString = "    "; // Amount to indent
private int indentLevel = 0;

...

public void startElement(...)
throws SAXException
{
    indentLevel++;
    nl(); emit("ELEMENT: ");
    ...
}

public void endElement(...)
throws SAXException
{
    nl();
    emit("END_ELM: ");
    emit("</"+sName+">");
    indentLevel--;
}
...
private void nl()
throws SAXException
{
    ...
    try {
        out.write(lineEnd);
```

```
            for (int i=0; i < indentLevel; i++) out.write(indentString);
            } catch (IOException e) {
        ...
    }
```

This code sets up an indent string, keeps track of the current indent level, and outputs the indent string whenever the `nl` method is called. If you set the indent string to "", the output will be un-indented (Try it. You'll see why it's worth the work to add the indentation).

You'll be happy to know that you have reached the end of the "mechanical" code you have to add to the Echo program. From here on, you'll be doing things that give you more insight into how the parser works. The steps you've taken so far, though, have given you a lot of insight into how the parser sees the XML data it processes. It's also given you a helpful debugging tool you can use to see what the parser sees.

5.3.13 Inspecting the Output

The complete output for this version of the program is shown in `Echo03-01`. Part of that output is shown here:

```
ELEMENT: <slideshow
...
CHARS:
CHARS:
    ELEMENT: <slide
    ...
    END_ELM: </slide>
CHARS:
CHARS:
```

Note that the `characters` method was invoked twice in a row. Inspecting the source file `slideSample01.xml` shows that there is a comment before the first slide. The first call to `characters` comes before that comment. The second call comes after. (Later on, you'll see how to be notified when the parser encounters a comment, although in most cases you won't need such notifications.)

Note, too, that the `characters` method is invoked after the first slide element, as well as before. When you are thinking in terms of hierarchically structured data, that seems odd. After all, you intended for the `slideshow` element to contain `slide` elements, not text. Later on, you'll see how to restrict the `slideshow` element using a DTD. When you do that, the `characters` method will no longer be invoked.

In the absence of a DTD, though, the parser must assume that any element it sees contains text like that in the first item element of the overview slide:

```
<item>Why <em>WonderWidgets</em> are great</item>
```

Here, the hierarchical structure looks like this:

```
ELEMENT: <item>
CHARS:   Why
    ELEMENT: <em>
    CHARS:   WonderWidgets
    END_ELM: </em>
CHARS:    are great
END_ELM: </item>
```

5.3.14 Documents and Data

In this example, it's clear that there are characters intermixed with the hierarchical structure of the elements. The fact that text can surround elements (or be prevented from doing so with a DTD or schema) helps to explain why you sometimes hear talk about "XML data" and other times hear about "XML documents." XML comfortably handles both structured data and text documents that include markup. The only difference between the two is whether or not text is allowed between the elements.

Note: In an upcoming section of this tutorial, you will work with the `ignorableWhitespace` method in the `ContentHandler` interface. This method can only be invoked when a DTD is present. If a DTD specifies that `slideshow` does not contain text, then all of the whitespace surrounding the `slide` elements is by definition ignorable. On the other hand, if `slideshow` can contain text (which must be assumed to be true in the absence of a DTD), then the parser must assume that spaces and lines it sees between the `slide` elements are significant parts of the document.

5.4 Adding Additional Event Handlers

Besides `ignorableWhitespace`, there are two other `ContentHandler` methods that can find uses in even simple applications: `setDocumentLocator` and `processingInstruction`. In this section of the tutorial, you'll implement those two event handlers.

5.4.1 Identifying the Document's Location

A *locator* is an object that contains the information necessary to find the document. The `Locator` class encapsulates a system ID (URL) or a public identifier (URN), or both. You would need that information if you wanted to find something relative to the current document—in the same way, for example, that an HTML browser processes an `href="anotherFile"` attribute in an anchor tag—the browser uses the location of the current document to find `anotherFile`.

You could also use the locator to print out good diagnostic messages. In addition to the document's location and public identifier, the locator contains methods that give the column and line number of the most recently-processed event. The `setDocumentLocator` method is called only once at the beginning of the parse, though. To get the current line or column number, you would save the locator when `setDocumentLocator` is invoked and then use it in the other event-handling methods.

Note: The code discussed in this section is in `Echo04.java`. Its output is stored at `Echo04-01`.

Add the method below to the Echo program to get the document locator and use it to echo the document's system ID.

```
...
private String indentString = "    "; // Amount to indent
private int indentLevel = 0;

public void setDocumentLocator(Locator l)
{
    try {
        out.write("LOCATOR");
        out.write("SYS ID: " + l.getSystemId() );
        out.flush();
    } catch (IOException e) {
        // Ignore errors
    }
}

public void startDocument()
...
```

Note: This method, in contrast to every other ContentHandler method, does not return a SAXException. So, rather than using emit for output, this code writes directly to System.out. (This method is generally expected to simply save the Locator for later use, rather than do the kind of processing that generates an exception, as here.)

The spelling of these methods is "Id", not "ID". So you have getSystemId and getPublicId.

When you compile and run the program on slideSample01.xml, here is the significant part of the output:

```
LOCATOR
SYS ID: file:<path>/../samples/slideSample01.xml

START DOCUMENT
<?xml version='1.0' encoding='UTF-8'?>
...
```

Here, it is apparent that setDocumentLocator is called before startDocument. That can make a difference if you do any initialization in the event handling code.

5.4.2 Handling Processing Instructions

It sometimes makes sense to code application-specific processing instructions in the XML data. In this exercise, you'll add a processing instruction to your slideSample.xml file and then modify the Echo program to display it.

Note: The code discussed in this section is in Echo05.java. The file it operates on is slideSample02.xml. (The browsable version is slideSample02-xml.html.) The output is stored at Echo05-02.

As you saw in Introduction to XML (page 29), the format for a processing instruction is <?target data?>, where "target" is the target application that is expected to do the processing, and "data" is the instruction or information for it to process. Add the text highlighted below to add a processing instruction for a mythical slide presentation program that will query the user to find out which slides to display (technical, executive-level, or all):

```
<slideshow
    ...
    >

    <!-- PROCESSING INSTRUCTION -->
    <?my.presentation.Program QUERY="exec, tech, all"?>

    <!-- TITLE SLIDE -->
```

Note: The "data" portion of the processing instruction can contain spaces, or may even be null. But there cannot be any space between the initial <? and the target identifier.

The data begins after the first space.

Fully qualifying the target with the complete Web-unique package prefix makes sense, so as to preclude any conflict with other programs that might process the same data.

For readability, it seems like a good idea to include a colon (:) after the name of the application, like this:

```
<?my.presentation.Program: QUERY="..."?>
```

The colon makes the target name into a kind of "label" that identifies the intended recipient of the instruction. However, while the w3c spec allows ":" in a target name, some versions of IE5 consider it an error. For this tutorial, then, we avoid using a colon in the target name.

Now that you have a processing instruction to work with, add the code highlighted below to the Echo app:

```
public void characters(char buf[], int offset, int len)
...
}

public void processingInstruction(String target, String data)
throws SAXException
{
    nl();
    emit("PROCESS: ");
    emit("<?"+target+" "+data+"?>");
}
private void emit(String s)
...
```

When your edits are complete, compile and run the program. The relevant part of the output should look like this:

```
...
CHARS:
CHARS:
PROCESS: <?my.presentation.Program QUERY="exec, tech, all"?>
CHARS:
CHARS:
...
```

Now that you've had a chance to work with the processing instruction, you can remove that instruction from the XML file. You won't be needing it any more.

5.4.3 Summary

With the minor exception of `ignorableWhitespace`, you have used most of the `ContentHandler` methods that you need to handle the most commonly useful SAX events. You'll see `ignorableWhitespace` a little later on. Next, though, you'll get deeper insight into how you handle errors in the SAX parsing process.

5.5 Handling Errors with the Nonvalidating Parser

This version of the Echo program uses the nonvalidating parser. So it can't tell if the XML document contains the right tags, or if those tags are in the right sequence. In other words, it can't tell you if the document is valid. It can, however, tell whether or not the document is well-formed.

In this section of the tutorial, you'll modify the slideshow file to generate different kinds of errors and see how the parser handles them. You'll also find out which error conditions are ignored, by default, and see how to handle them.

Introducing an Error

The parser can generate one of three kinds of errors: fatal error, error, and warning. In this exercise, you'll make a simple modification to the XML file to introduce a fatal error. Then you'll see how it's handled in the Echo app.

Note: The XML structure you'll create in this exercise is in `slideSampleBad1.xml`. (The browsable version is `slideSampleBad1-xml.html`.) The output is in `Echo05-Bad1`.

One easy way to introduce a fatal error is to remove the final "/" from the empty `item` element to create a tag that does not have a corresponding end tag. That constitutes a fatal error, because all XML documents must, by definition, be well formed. Do the following:

1. Copy `slideSample.xml` to `badSample.xml`.
2. Edit `badSample.xml` and remove the character shown below:

```
...
<!-- OVERVIEW -->
<slide type="all">
    <title>Overview</title>
    <item>Why <em>WonderWidgets</em> are great</item>
    <item/>
    <item>Who <em>buys</em> WonderWidgets</item>
</slide>
...
```

   to produce:

```
...
<item>Why <em>WonderWidgets</em> are great</item>
<item>
<item>Who <em>buys</em> WonderWidgets</item>
...
```

3. Run the Echo program on the new file.

   The output you get now looks like this:

```
...
        ELEMENT: <item>
        CHARS:   The
            ELEMENT: <em>
            CHARS:   Only
            END_ELM: </em>
        CHARS:    Section
        END_ELM: </item>
    CHARS:
    END_ELM:
CHARS:   org.xml.sax.SAXParseException: Expected "</item>"
        to terminate element starting on line 20.
```

```
...
at javax.xml.parsers.SAXParser.parse(SAXParser.java:286)
at Echo05.main(Echo05.java:61)
```

When a fatal error occurs, the parser is unable to continue. So, if the application does not generate an exception (which you'll see how to do a moment), then the default error-event handler generates one. The stack trace is generated by the `Throwable` exception handler in your main method:

```
    ...
} catch (Throwable t) {
    t.printStackTrace();
}
```

That stack trace is not too useful, though. Next, you'll see how to generate better diagnostics when an error occurs.

Handling a SAXParseException

When the error was encountered, the parser generated a `SAXParseException`—a subclass of `SAXException` that identifies the file and location where the error occurred.

Note: The code you'll create in this exercise is in `Echo06.java`. The output is in `Echo06-Bad1`.

Add the code highlighted below to generate a better diagnostic message when the exception occurs:

```
...
} catch (SAXParseException spe) {
    // Error generated by the parser
    System.out.println("* Parsing error"
        + ", line " + spe.getLineNumber()
        + ", uri " + spe.getSystemId());
    System.out.println("   " + spe.getMessage() );

} catch (Throwable t) {
    t.printStackTrace();
}
```

Running the program now generates an error message which is a bit more helpful, like this:

```
** Parsing error, line 22, uri file:<path>/slideSampleBad1.xml
Next character must be...
```

Note: Catching all throwables like this is *not* a good idea for production applications. We're just doing it now so we can build up to full error handling gradually.

Handling a SAXException

A more general `SAXException` instance may sometimes be generated by the parser, but it more frequently occurs when an error originates in one of application's event handling methods. For example, the signature of the `startDocument` method in the `ContentHandler` interface is defined as returning a `SAXException`:

```
public void startDocument() throws SAXException
```

All of the `ContentHandler` methods (except for `setDocumentLocator`) have that signature declaration.

A `SAXException` can be constructed using a message, another exception, or both. So, for example, when `Echo.startDocument` outputs a string using the `emit` method, any I/O exception that occurs is wrapped in a `SAXException` and sent back to the parser:

```
private void emit(String s)
throws SAXException
{
    try {
        out.write(s);
        out.flush();
    } catch (IOException e) {
        throw new SAXException("I/O error", e);
    }
}
```

Note: If you saved the `Locator` object when `setDocumentLocator` was invoked, you could use it to generate a `SAXParseException`, identifying the document and location, instead of generating a `SAXException`.

When the parser delivers the exception back to the code that invoked the parser, it makes sense to use the original exception to generate the stack trace. Add the code highlighted below to do that:

```
    ...
} catch (SAXParseException err) {
    System.out.println("** Parsing error"
        + ", line " + err.getLineNumber()
        + ", uri " + err.getSystemId());
    System.out.println("   " + err.getMessage());

} catch (SAXException sxe) {
    // Error generated by this application
    // (or a parser-initialization error)
    Exception  x = sxe;
    if (sxe.getException() != null)
        x = sxe.getException();
    x.printStackTrace();

} catch (Throwable t) {
    t.printStackTrace();
}
```

This code tests to see if the SAXException is wrapping another exception. If so, it generates a stack trace originating from where that exception occurred to make it easier to pinpoint the code responsible for the error. If the exception contains only a message, the code prints the stack trace starting from the location where the exception was generated.

Improving the SAXParseException Handler

Since the SAXParseException can also wrap another exception, add the code highlighted below to use it for the stack trace:

```
    ...
} catch (SAXParseException err) {
    System.out.println("** Parsing error"
        + ", line " + err.getLineNumber()
        + ", uri " + err.getSystemId());
    System.out.println("   " + err.getMessage());
```

```
    // Unpack the delivered exception to get the exception it contains
     Exception  x = spe;
         if (spe.getException() != null)
             x = spe.getException();
         x.printStackTrace();

} catch (SAXException e) {
     // Error generated by this application
     // (or a parser-initialization error)
     Exception             x = e;
     if (e.getException() != null)
         x = e.getException();
     x.printStackTrace();

} catch (Throwable t) {
     t.printStackTrace();
}
```

The program is now ready to handle any SAX parsing exceptions it sees. You've seen that the parser generates exceptions for fatal errors. But for nonfatal errors and warnings, exceptions are never generated by the default error handler, and no messages are displayed. Next, you'll learn more about errors and warnings and find out how to supply an error handler to process them.

Handling a ParserConfigurationException

Finally, recall that the `SAXParserFactory` class could throw an exception if it were for unable to create a parser. Such an error might occur if the factory could not find the class needed to create the parser (class not found error), was not permitted to access it (illegal access exception), or could not instantiate it (instantiation error).

Add the code highlighted below to handle such errors:

```
} catch (SAXException e) {
     Exception             x = e;
     if (e.getException() != null)
         x = e.getException();
     x.printStackTrace();
```

```
} catch (ParserConfigurationException pce) {
    // Parser with specified options can't be built
    pce.printStackTrace();

} catch (Throwable t) {
    t.printStackTrace();
```

This code, like the SAXException handler, takes into account the possibility that the reported exception might be wrapping another exception. (Admittedly, there are quite a few error handlers here. But at least now you know the kinds of exceptions that can occur.)

Note: A javax.xml.parsers.FactoryConfigurationError could also be thrown if the factory class specified by the system property cannot be found or instantiated. That is a non-trappable error, since the program is not expected to be able to recover from it.

Handling an IOException

Finally, while we're at it, let's stop intercepting all Throwable objects and catch the only remaining exceptions there is to catch, IOExceptions:

```
} catch (ParserConfigurationException pce) {
    // Parser with specified options can't be built
    pce.printStackTrace();

} catch (Throwable t) {
    t.printStackTrace();
} catch (IOException ioe) {
    // I/O error
    ioe.printStackTrace();
}
```

Understanding Nonfatal Errors

In general, a nonfatal *error* occurs when an XML document fails a validity constraint. If the parser finds that the document is not valid (which means that it contains an invalid tag or a tag in location that is disallowed), then an error event is generated. In general, then, errors are generated by a validating parser, given a DTD that tells it which tags are valid. There is one kind of error, though, that is generated by some implementations of this nonvalidating parser.

Note: This example does not work in JAXP 1.2. Read this section for understanding only. The file described here is `slideSampleBad2.xml` (The browsable version is `slideSampleBad2-xml.html`.) The output that was produced using JAXP1.1 is in `Echo06-Bad2`. (Since some elements of error handling are implementation-specific, it may be possible to reproduce that output using another parser.)

The SAX specification requires an error event to be generated if the XML document uses a version of XML that the parser does not support. To generate such an error, make the changes shown below to alter your XML file so it specifies `version="1.2"`.

```
<?xml version='1.02' encoding='utf-8'?>
```

Now run your version of the Echo program on that file. What happens? (See below for the answer.)

Answer: Nothing happens! By default, the error is ignored. The output from the Echo program looks the same as if `version="1.0"` had been properly specified. To do something else, you need to supply your own error handler. You'll do that next.

Handling Nonfatal Errors

A standard treatment for "nonfatal" errors is to treat them as if they were fatal. After all, if a validation error occurs in a document you are processing, you probably don't want to continue processing it. In this exercise, you'll do exactly that.

Note: The code for the program you'll create in this exercise is in `Echo07.java`. The output is in `Echo07-Bad2`.

To take over error handling, you override the `DefaultHandler` methods that handle fatal errors, nonfatal errors, and warnings as part of the `ErrorHandler` interface. The SAX parser delivers a `SAXParseException` to each of these methods, so generating an exception when an error occurs is as simple as throwing it back.

Add the code highlighted below to override the handlers for errors:

```
public void processingInstruction(String target, String data)
throws SAXException
{
    nl();
    emit("PROCESS: ");
    emit("<?"+target+" "+data+"?>");
```

```
}
// treat validation errors as fatal
public void error(SAXParseException e)
throws SAXParseException
{
    throw e;
}
```

Now when you run your app on the file with the faulty version number, you get an exception, as shown here (but slightly reformatted for readability):

```
START DOCUMENT
<?xml version='1.0' encoding='UTF-8'?>
    ** Parsing error, line 1, uri file:/<path>/slideSampleBad2.xml
    XML version "1.0" is recognized, but not "1.2".
org.xml.sax.SAXParseException: XML version "1.0" is recognized, but
not "1.2".
...
at javax.xml.parsers.SAXParser.parse(SAXParser.java:286)
at Echo07.main(Echo07.java:61)
```

Note: The error actually occurs after the `startDocument` event has been generated. The document header that the program "echoes" is the one it creates on the assumption that everything is OK, rather than the one that is actually in the file.

Handling Warnings

Warnings, too, are ignored by default. Warnings are informative, and require a DTD. For example, if an element is defined twice in a DTD, a warning is generated—it's not illegal, and it doesn't cause problems, but it's something you might like to know about since it might not have been intentional.

Add the code highlighted below to generate a message when a warning occurs:

```
// treat validation errors as fatal
public void error(SAXParseException e)
throws SAXParseException
{
    throw e;
}
```

```
// dump warnings too
public void warning(SAXParseException err)
throws SAXParseException
{
    System.out.println("** Warning"
        + ", line " + err.getLineNumber()
        + ", uri " + err.getSystemId());
    System.out.println("   " + err.getMessage());
}
```

Since there is no good way to generate a warning without a DTD, you won't be seeing any just yet. But when one does occur, you're ready!

Note: By default, `DefaultHandler` throws an exception when a fatal error occurs. You could override the `fatalError` method to throw a different exception, if you like. But if your code doesn't, the reference implementation's SAX parser will.

5.6 Substituting and Inserting Text

The next thing we want to do with the parser is to customize it a bit, so you can see how to get information it usually ignores. But before we can do that, you're going to need to learn a few more important XML concepts. In this section, you'll learn about:

- Handling Special Characters ("<", "&", and so on)
- Handling Text with XML-style syntax

5.6.1 Handling Special Characters

In XML, an entity is an XML structure (or plain text) that has a name. Referencing the entity by name causes it to be inserted into the document in place of the entity reference. To create an entity reference, the entity name is surrounded by an ampersand and a semicolon, like this:

```
&entityName;
```

Later, when you learn how to write a DTD, you'll see that you can define your own entities, so that `&yourEntityName;` expands to all the text you defined for that entity. For now, though, we'll focus on the predefined entities and character references that don't require any special definitions.

Predefined Entities

An entity reference like `&` contains a name (in this case, "amp") between the start and end delimiters. The text it refers to (&) is substituted for the name, like a macro in a C or C++ program. Table 5.1 shows the predefined entities for special characters.

Table 5.1 Predefined Entities

Character	Reference
&	&
<	<
>	>
"	"
'	'

Character References

A character reference like `“` contains a hash mark (#) followed by a number. The number is the Unicode value for a single character, such as 65 for the letter "A", 147 for the left-curly quote, or 148 for the right-curly quote. In this case, the "name" of the entity is the hash mark followed by the digits that identify the character.

5.6.2 Using an Entity Reference in an XML Document

Suppose you wanted to insert a line like this in your XML document:

```
Market Size < predicted
```

The problem with putting that line into an XML file directly is that when the parser sees the left-angle bracket (<), it starts looking for a tag name, which throws off the parse. To get around that problem, you put `<` in the file, instead of "<".

Note: The results of the modifications below are contained in `slideSample03.xml`. (The browsable version is `slideSample03-xml.html`.) The results of processing it are shown in Echo07-03.

If you are following the programming tutorial, add the text highlighted below to your `slideSample.xml` file:

```
    <!-- OVERVIEW -->
    <slide type="all">
        <title>Overview</title>
        ...
    </slide>

    <slide type="exec">
        <title>Financial Forecast</title>
        <item>Market Size &lt; predicted</item>
        <item>Anticipated Penetration</item>
        <item>Expected Revenues</item>
        <item>Profit Margin </item>
    </slide>
</slideshow>
```

When you run the Echo program on your XML file, you see the following output:

```
ELEMENT: <item>
CHARS:   Market Size
CHARS:   <
CHARS:    predicted
END_ELM: </item>
```

The parser converted the reference into the entity it represents, and passed the entity to the application.

5.6.3 Handling Text with XML-Style Syntax

When you are handling large blocks of XML or HTML that include many of the special characters, it would be inconvenient to replace each of them with the appropriate entity reference. For those situations, you can use a CDATA section.

Note: The results of the modifications below are contained in `slideSample04.xml`. (The browsable version is `slideSample04-xml.html`.) The results of processing it are shown in `Echo07-04`.

A `CDATA` section works like `<pre>...</pre>` in HTML, only more so—all whitespace in a `CDATA` section is significant, and characters in it are not interpreted as XML. A `CDATA` section starts with `<![CDATA[` and ends with `]]>`. Add the text highlighted below to your `slideSample.xml` file to define a `CDATA` section for a fictitious technical slide:

```
  ...
<slide type="tech">
    <title>How it Works</title>
    <item>First we fozzle the frobmorten</item>
    <item>Then we framboze the staten</item>
    <item>Finally, we frenzle the fuznaten</item>
    <item><![CDATA[Diagram:
        frobmorten <--------------------------- fuznaten
            |         <3>          ^
            | <1>                   |      <1> = fozzle
         V                                |      <2> = framboze
            Staten+     <3> = frenzle
                          <2>
    ]]></item>
</slide>
</slideshow>
```

When you run the Echo program on the new file, you see the following output:

```
    ELEMENT: <item>
  CHARS:   Diagram:

frobmorten <------------ -------fuznaten
    |                  <3>          ^
    | <1>                   |    <1> = fozzle
    V                   |    <2> = framboze
    Staten+    <3> = frenzle
               <2>
END_ELM: </item>
```

You can see here that the text in the `CDATA` section arrived as one entirely uninterpreted character string.

5.6.4 Handling CDATA and Other Characters

The existence of CDATA makes the proper echoing of XML a bit tricky. If the text to be output is *not* in a CDATA section, then any angle brackets, ampersands, and other special characters in the text should be replaced with the appropriate entity reference. (Replacing left angle brackets and ampersands is most important; other characters will be interpreted properly without misleading the parser.)

But if the output text *is* in a CDATA section, then the substitutions should not occur to produce text like that in the example above. In a simple program like our Echo application, it's not a big deal. But many XML-filtering applications will want to keep track of whether the text appears in a CDATA section, in order to treat special characters properly.

One other area to watch for is attributes. The text of an attribute value could also contain angle brackets and semicolons that need to be replaced by entity references. (Attribute text can never be in a CDATA section, though, so there is never any question about doing that substitution.)

Later in this tutorial, you will see how to use a `LexicalHandler` to find out whether or not you are processing a CDATA section. Next, though, you will see how to define a DTD.

5.7 Creating a Document Type Definition (DTD)

After the XML declaration, the document prolog can include a DTD, which lets you specify the kinds of tags that can be included in your XML document. In addition to telling a validating parser which tags are valid, and in what arrangements, a DTD tells both validating and nonvalidating parsers where text is expected, which lets the parser determine whether the whitespace it sees is significant or ignorable.

5.7.1 Basic DTD Definitions

When you were parsing the slideshow, for example, you saw that the `characters` method was invoked multiple times before and after comments and slide elements. In those cases, the whitespace consisted of the line endings and indentation surrounding the markup. The goal was to make the XML document readable—the whitespace was not in any way part of the document contents. To begin learning about DTD definitions, let's start by telling the parser where whitespace is ignorable.

Note: The DTD defined in this section is contained in `slideshow1a.dtd`. (The browsable version is `slideshow1a-dtd.html`.)

Start by creating a file named `slideshow.dtd`. Enter an XML declaration and a comment to identify the file, as shown below:

```
<?xml version='1.0' encoding='utf-8'?>
<!-- DTD for a simple "slide show". -->
```

Next, add the text highlighted below to specify that a `slideshow` element contains `slide` elements and nothing else:

```
<!-- DTD for a simple "slide show". -->
<!ELEMENT slideshow (slide+)>
```

As you can see, the DTD tag starts with `<!` followed by the tag name (`ELEMENT`). After the tag name comes the name of the element that is being defined (`slideshow`) and, in parentheses, one or more items that indicate the valid contents for that element. In this case, the notation says that a `slideshow` consists of one or more `slide` elements.

Without the plus sign, the definition would be saying that a `slideshow` consists of a single `slide` element. The qualifiers you can add to an element definition are shown in Table 5.2.

Table 5.2 DTD Element Qualifiers

Qualifier	Name	Meaning
?	Question Mark	Optional (zero or one)
*	Asterisk	Zero or more
+	Plus Sign	One or more

You can include multiple elements inside the parentheses in a comma separated list, and use a qualifier on each element to indicate how many instances of that element may occur. The comma-separated list tells which elements are valid and the order they can occur in.

You can also nest parentheses to group multiple items. For an example, after defining an `image` element (coming up shortly), you could declare that every `image` element must be paired with a `title` element in a slide by specifying `((image, title)+)`. Here, the plus sign applies to the `image/title` pair to indicate that one or more pairs of the specified items can occur.

5.7.2 Defining Text and Nested Elements

Now that you have told the parser something about where *not* to expect text, let's see how to tell it where text *can* occur. Add the text highlighted below to define the `slide`, `title`, `item`, and `list` elements:

```
<!ELEMENT slideshow (slide+)>
<!ELEMENT slide (title, item*)>
<!ELEMENT title (#PCDATA)>
<!ELEMENT item (#PCDATA | item)* >
```

The first line you added says that a slide consists of a `title` followed by zero or more `item` elements. Nothing new there. The next line says that a title consists entirely of *parsed character data* (PCDATA). That's known as "text" in most parts of the country, but in XML-speak it's called "parsed character data". (That distinguishes it from CDATA sections, which contain character data that is not parsed.) The "#" that precedes PCDATA indicates that what follows is a special word, rather than an element name.

The last line introduces the vertical bar (|), which indicates an *or* condition. In this case, either PCDATA or an `item` can occur. The asterisk at the end says that either one can occur zero or more times in succession. The result of this specification is known as a mixed-content model, because any number of `item` elements can be interspersed with the text. Such models must always be defined with #PCDATA specified first, some number of alternate items divided by vertical bars (|), and an asterisk (*) at the end.

5.7.3 Limitations of DTDs

It would be nice if we could specify that an `item` contains either text, or text followed by one or more list items. But that kind of specification turns out to be hard to achieve in a DTD. For example, you might be tempted to define an `item` like this:

```
<!ELEMENT item (#PCDATA | (#PCDATA, item+)) >
```

That would certainly be accurate, but as soon as the parser sees #PCDATA and the vertical bar, it requires the remaining definition to conform to the mixed-content model. This specification doesn't, so you can get an error that says: `Illegal mixed content model for 'item'. Found ( ...`, where the hex character 28 is the angle bracket that ends the definition.

Trying to double-define the item element doesn't work, either. A specification like this:

```
<!ELEMENT item (#PCDATA) >
<!ELEMENT item (#PCDATA, item+) >
```

produces a "duplicate definition" warning when the validating parser runs. The second definition is, in fact, ignored. So it seems that defining a mixed content model (which allows `item` elements to be interspersed in text) is about as good as we can do.

In addition to the limitations of the mixed content model mentioned above, there is no way to further qualify the kind of text that can occur where `PCDATA` has been specified. Should it contain only numbers? Should be in a date format, or possibly a monetary format? There is no way to say in the context of a DTD.

Finally, note that the DTD offers no sense of hierarchy. The definition for the `title` element applies equally to a `slide` title and to an `item` title. When we expand the DTD to allow HTML-style markup in addition to plain text, it would make sense to restrict the size of an `item` title compared to a `slide` title, for example. But the only way to do that would be to give one of them a different name, such as "`item-title`". The bottom line is that the lack of hierarchy in the DTD forces you to introduce a "hyphenation hierarchy" (or its equivalent) in your namespace. All of these limitations are fundamental motivations behind the development of schema-specification standards.

5.7.4 Special Element Values in the DTD

Rather than specifying a parenthesized list of elements, the element definition could use one of two special values: `ANY` or `EMPTY`. The `ANY` specification says that the element may contain any other defined element, or `PCDATA`. Such a specification is usually used for the root element of a general-purpose XML document such as you might create with a word processor. Textual elements could occur in any order in such a document, so specifying `ANY` makes sense.

The `EMPTY` specification says that the element contains no contents. So the DTD for e-mail messages that let you "flag" the message with `<flag/>` might have a line like this in the DTD:

```
<!ELEMENT flag EMPTY>
```

5.7.5 Referencing the DTD

In this case, the DTD definition is in a separate file from the XML document. That means you have to reference it from the XML document, which makes the DTD file part of the external subset of the full Document Type Definition (DTD) for the XML file. As you'll see later on, you can also include parts of the DTD within the document. Such definitions constitute the local subset of the DTD.

Note: The XML written in this section is contained in `slideSample05.xml`. (The browsable version is `slideSample05-xml.html`.)

To reference the DTD file you just created, add the line highlighted below to your `slideSample.xml` file:

```
<!--  A SAMPLE set of slides  -->
<!DOCTYPE slideshow SYSTEM "slideshow.dtd">
<slideshow
```

Again, the DTD tag starts with "`<!`". In this case, the tag name, `DOCTYPE`, says that the document is a `slideshow`, which means that the document consists of the `slideshow` element and everything within it:

```
<slideshow>
...
</slideshow>
```

This tag defines the `slideshow` element as the root element for the document. An XML document must have exactly one root element. This is where that element is specified. In other words, this tag identifies the document *content* as a `slideshow`.

The `DOCTYPE` tag occurs after the XML declaration and before the root element. The `SYSTEM` identifier specifies the location of the DTD file. Since it does not start with a prefix like `http:/` or `file:/`, the path is relative to the location of the XML document. Remember the `setDocumentLocator` method? The parser is using that information to find the DTD file, just as your application would to find a file relative to the XML document. A `PUBLIC` identifier could also be used to specify the DTD file using a unique name—but the parser would have to be able to resolve it.

The `DOCTYPE` specification could also contain DTD definitions within the XML document, rather than referring to an external DTD file. Such definitions would be contained in square brackets, like this:

```
<!DOCTYPE slideshow SYSTEM "slideshow1.dtd" [
    ...local subset definitions here...
]>
```

You'll take advantage of that facility later on to define some entities that can be used in the document.

5.8 DTD's Effect on the Nonvalidating Parser

In the last section, you defined a rudimentary document type and used it in your XML file. In this section, you'll use the Echo program to see how the data appears to the SAX parser when the DTD is included.

Note: The output shown in this section is contained in `Echo07-05`.

Running the Echo program on your latest version of `slideSample.xml` shows that many of the superfluous calls to the `characters` method have now disappeared:

```
ELEMENT: <slideshow
    ATTR: ...
>
PROCESS: ...
    ELEMENT: <slide
        ATTR: ...
    >
            ELEMENT: <title>
            CHARS:   Wake up to ...
            END_ELM: </title>
    END_ELM: </slide>
    ELEMENT: <slide
        ATTR: ...
    >
    ...
```

It is evident here that the whitespace characters which were formerly being echoed around the `slide` elements are no longer appearing, because the DTD declares that `slideshow` consists solely of `slide` elements:

```
<!ELEMENT slideshow (slide+)>
```

5.8.1 Tracking Ignorable Whitespace

Now that the DTD is present, the parser is no longer the `characters` method with whitespace that it knows to be irrelevant. From the standpoint of an application that is only interested in processing the XML data, that is great. The application is never bothered with whitespace that exists purely to make the XML file readable.

On the other hand, if you were writing an application that was filtering an XML data file, and you wanted to output an equally readable version of the file, then that whitespace would no longer be irrelevant—it would be essential. To get those characters, you need to add the `ignorableWhitespace` method to your application. You'll do that next.

Note: The code written in this section is contained in `Echo08.java`. The output is in `Echo08-05`.

To process the (generally) ignorable whitespace that the parser is seeing, add the code highlighted below to implement the `ignorableWhitespace` event handler in your version of the Echo program:

```
public void characters (char buf[], int offset, int len)
...
}
public void ignorableWhitespace(char buf[], int offset, int Len)
throws SAXException
{
    nl(); emit("IGNORABLE");
}
public void processingInstruction(String target, String data)
```

This code simply generates a message to let you know that ignorable whitespace was seen.

Note: Again, not all parsers are created equal. The SAX specification does not require this method to be invoked. The Java XML implementation does so whenever the DTD makes it possible.

When you run the Echo application now, your output looks like this:

```
ELEMENT: <slideshow
    ATTR: ...
>
IGNORABLE
IGNORABLE
PROCESS: ...
IGNORABLE
```

```
IGNORABLE
    ELEMENT: <slide
        ATTR: ...
    >
    IGNORABLE
        ELEMENT: <title>
        CHARS:   Wake up to ...
        END_ELM: </title>
    IGNORABLE
    END_ELM: </slide>
IGNORABLE
IGNORABLE
    ELEMENT: <slide
        ATTR: ...
    >
    ...
```

Here, it is apparent that the ignorable whitespace is being invoked before and after comments and slide elements, where characters was being invoked before there was a DTD.

5.8.2 Cleanup

Now that you have seen ignorable whitespace echoed, remove that code from your version of the Echo program—you won't be needing it any more in the exercises ahead.

Note: That change has been made in `Echo09.java`.

5.8.3 Documents and Data

Earlier, you learned that one reason you hear about XML *documents*, on the one hand, and XML *data*, on the other, is that XML handles both comfortably, depending on whether text is or is not allowed between elements in the structure.

In the sample file you have been working with, the `slideshow` element is an example of a *data element*—it contains only subelements with no intervening text. The `item` element, on the other hand, might be termed a *document element*, because it is defined to include both text and subelements.

As you work through this tutorial, you will see how to expand the definition of the title element to include HTML-style markup, which will turn it into a document element as well.

5.8.4 Empty Elements, Revisited

Now that you understand how certain instances of whitespace can be ignorable, it is time to revise the definition of an "empty" element. That definition can now be expanded to include

```
<foo>   </foo>
```

where there is whitespace between the tags and the DTD defines that whitespace as ignorable.

5.9 Defining Attributes and Entities in the DTD

The DTD you've defined so far is fine for use with the nonvalidating parser. It tells where text is expected and where it isn't, which is all the nonvalidating parser is going to pay attention to. But for use with the validating parser, the DTD needs to specify the valid attributes for the different elements. You'll do that in this section, after which you'll define one internal entity and one external entity that you can reference in your XML file.

5.9.1 Defining Attributes in the DTD

Let's start by defining the attributes for the elements in the slide presentation.

Note: The XML written in this section is contained in `slideshow1b.dtd`. (The browsable version is `slideshow1b-dtd.html`.)

Add the text highlighted below to define the attributes for the `slideshow` element:

```
<!ELEMENT slideshow (slide+)>
<!ATTLIST slideshow
        title    CDATA    #REQUIRED
        date     CDATA    #IMPLIED
        author   CDATA    "unknown"
>
<!ELEMENT slide (title, item*)>
```

The DTD tag `ATTLIST` begins the series of attribute definitions. The name that follows `ATTLIST` specifies the element for which the attributes are being defined. In this case, the element is the `slideshow` element. (Note once again the lack of hierarchy in DTD specifications.)

Each attribute is defined by a series of three space-separated values. Commas and other separators are not allowed, so formatting the definitions as shown above is helpful for readability. The first element in each line is the name of the attribute: `title`, `date`, or `author`, in this case. The second element indicates the type of the data: `CDATA` is character data—unparsed data, once again, in which a left-angle bracket (<) will never be construed as part of an XML tag. Table 5.3 presents the valid choices for the attribute type.

Table 5.3 Attribute Types

Attribute Type	Specifies...
`(value1 | value2 | ...)`	A list of values separated by vertical bars. (Example below)
`CDATA`	"Unparsed character data". (For normal people, a text string.)
`ID`	A name that no other ID attribute shares.
`IDREF`	A reference to an ID defined elsewhere in the document.
`IDREFS`	A space-separated list containing one or more ID references.
`ENTITY`	The name of an entity defined in the DTD.
`ENTITIES`	A space-separated list of entities.
`NMTOKEN`	A valid XML name composed of letters, numbers, hyphens, underscores, and colons.
`NMTOKENS`	A space-separated list of names.
`NOTATION`	The name of a DTD-specified notation, which describes a non-XML data format, such as those used for image files.*

*This is a rapidly obsolescing specification which will be discussed in greater length towards the end of this section.

When the attribute type consists of a parenthesized list of choices separated by vertical bars, the attribute must use one of the specified values. For an example, add the text highlighted below to the DTD:

```
<!ELEMENT slide (title, item*)>
<!ATTLIST slide
        type   (tech | exec | all) #IMPLIED
```

```
>
<!ELEMENT title (#PCDATA)>
<!ELEMENT item (#PCDATA | item)* >
```

This specification says that the `slide` element's `type` attribute must be given as `type="tech"`, `type="exec"`, or `type="all"`. No other values are acceptable. (DTD-aware XML editors can use such specifications to present a pop-up list of choices.)

The last entry in the attribute specification determines the attributes default value, if any, and tells whether or not the attribute is required. Table 5.4 shows the possible choices.

Table 5.4 Attribute-Specification Parameters

Specification	Specifies...
`#REQUIRED`	The attribute value must be specified in the document.
`#IMPLIED`	The value need not be specified in the document. If it isn't, the application will have a default value it uses.
"defaultValue"	The default value to use, if a value is not specified in the document.
`#FIXED` "fixedValue"	The value to use. If the document specifies any value at all, it must be the same.

5.9.2 Defining Entities in the DTD

So far, you've seen predefined entities like `&` and you've seen that an attribute can reference an entity. It's time now for you to learn how to define entities of your own.

> **Note:** The XML defined here is contained in `slideSample06.xml`. (The browsable version is `slideSample06-xml.html`.) The output is shown in `Echo09-06`.

Add the text highlighted below to the `DOCTYPE` tag in your XML file:

```
<!DOCTYPE slideshow SYSTEM "slideshow1.dtd" [
    <!ENTITY product  "WonderWidget">
    <!ENTITY products "WonderWidgets">
]>
```

The `ENTITY` tag name says that you are defining an entity. Next comes the name of the entity and its definition. In this case, you are defining an entity named "product" that will take the place of the product name. Later when the product name changes (as it most certainly will), you will only have to change the name one place, and all your slides will reflect the new value.

The last part is the substitution string that replaces the entity name whenever it is referenced in the XML document. The substitution string is defined in quotes, which are not included when the text is inserted into the document.

Just for good measure, we defined two versions, one singular and one plural, so that when the marketing mavens come up with "Wally" for a product name, you will be prepared to enter the plural as "Wallies" and have it substituted correctly.

Note: Truth be told, this is the kind of thing that really belongs in an external DTD. That way, all your documents can reference the new name when it changes. But, hey, this is an example...

Now that you have the entities defined, the next step is to reference them in the slide show. Make the changes highlighted below to do that:

```
<slideshow
    title="WonderWidget&product; Slide Show"
    ...
    <!-- TITLE SLIDE -->
    <slide type="all">
        <title>Wake up to WonderWidgets&products;!</title>
    </slide>
     <!-- OVERVIEW -->
    <slide type="all">
        <title>Overview</title>
        <item>Why <em>WonderWidgets&products;</em> are great</item>
        <item/>
        <item>Who <em>buys</em> WonderWidgets&products;</item>
    </slide>
```

The points to notice here are that entities you define are referenced with the same syntax (`&entityName;`) that you use for predefined entities, and that the entity can be referenced in an attribute value as well as in an element's contents.

5.9.3 Echoing the Entity References

When you run the Echo program on this version of the file, here is the kind of thing you see:

```
ELEMENT: <title>
CHARS:   Wake up to
CHARS:   WonderWidgets
CHARS:   !
END_ELM: </title>
```

Note that the existence of the entity reference generates an extra call to the `characters` method, and that the text you see is what results from the substitution.

5.9.4 Additional Useful Entities

Here are several other examples for entity definitions that you might find useful when you write an XML document:

```
<!ENTITY ldquo  "&#147;"> <!-- Left Double Quote -->
<!ENTITY rdquo  "&#148;"> <!-- Right Double Quote -->
<!ENTITY trade  "&#153;"> <!-- Trademark Symbol (TM) -->
<!ENTITY rtrade "&#174;"> <!-- Registered Trademark (R) -->
<!ENTITY copyr  "&#169;"> <!-- Copyright Symbol -->
```

5.9.5 Referencing External Entities

You can also use the `SYSTEM` or `PUBLIC` identifier to name an entity that is defined in an external file. You'll do that now.

Note: The XML defined here is contained in `slideSample07.xml` and in `copyright.xml`. (The browsable versions are `slideSample07-xml.html` and `copyright-xml.html`.) The Echo output is shown in `Echo09-07`.

To reference an external entity, add the text highlighted below to the `DOCTYPE` statement in your XML file:

```
<!DOCTYPE slideshow SYSTEM "slideshow.dtd" [
    <!ENTITY product  "WonderWidget">
    <!ENTITY products "WonderWidgets">
    <!ENTITY copyright SYSTEM "copyright.xml">
]>
```

This definition references a copyright message contained in a file named copyright.xml. Create that file and put some interesting text in it, perhaps something like this:

```
  <!--  A SAMPLE copyright  -->
This is the standard copyright message that our lawyers
make us put everywhere so we don't have to shell out a
million bucks every time someone spills hot coffee in his or her
lap...
```

Finally, add the text highlighted below to your slideSample.xml file to reference the external entity:

```
<!-- TITLE SLIDE -->
    ...
</slide>
<!-- COPYRIGHT SLIDE -->
<slide type="all">
    <item>&copyright;</item>
</slide>
```

You could also use an external entity declaration to access a servlet that produces the current date using a definition something like this:

```
<!ENTITY currentDate SYSTEM
    "http://www.example.com/servlet/CurrentDate?fmt=dd-MMM-yyyy">
```

You would then reference that entity the same as any other entity:

```
  Today's date is &currentDate;.
```

5.9.6 Echoing the External Entity

When you run the Echo program on your latest version of the slide presentation, here is what you see:

```
...
END_ELM: </slide>
ELEMENT: <slide
    ATTR: type                  "all"
>
    ELEMENT: <item>
    CHARS:
```

```
This is the standard copyright message that our lawyers
make us put everywhere so we don't have to shell out a
million bucks every time someone spills hot coffee in their
lap...
    END_ELM: </item>
END_ELM: </slide>
...
```

Note that the newline which follows the comment in the file is echoed as a character, but that the comment itself is ignored. That is the reason that the copyright message appears to start on the next line after the `CHARS:` label, instead of immediately after the label—the first character echoed is actually the newline that follows the comment.

5.9.7 Summarizing Entities

An entity that is referenced in the document content, whether internal or external, is termed a general entity. An entity that contains DTD specifications that are referenced from within the DTD is termed a parameter entity. (More on that later.)

An entity which contains XML (text and markup), and which is therefore parsed, is known as a parsed entity. An entity which contains binary data (like images) is known as an unparsed entity. (By its very nature, it must be external.) We'll be discussing references to unparsed entities in the next section of this tutorial.

5.10 Referencing Binary Entities

This section contains no programming exercises. Instead, it discusses the options for referencing binary files like image files and multimedia data files.

5.10.1 Using a MIME Data Type

There are two ways to go about referencing an unparsed entity like a binary image file. One is to use the DTD's `NOTATION`-specification mechanism. However, that mechanism is a complex, non-intuitive holdover that mostly exists for compatibility with SGML documents. We will have occasion to discuss it in a bit more depth when we look at the `DTDHandler` API, but for now suffice it to say that the combination of the recently defined XML namespaces standard in conjunction with the MIME data types defined for electronic messaging attachments, together provide a much more useful, understandable, and extensible mechanism for referencing unparsed external entities.

Note: The XML described here is in `slideshow1b.dtd`. We won't actually be echoing any images. That's beyond the scope of this tutorial's Echo program. This section is simply for understanding how such references can be made. It assumes that the application which will be processing the XML data knows how to handle such references.

To set up the slideshow to use image files, add the text highlighted below to your `slideshow.dtd` file:

```
<!ELEMENT slide (image?, title, item*)>
<!ATTLIST slide
        type   (tech | exec | all) #IMPLIED
>
<!ELEMENT title (#PCDATA)>
<!ELEMENT item (#PCDATA | item)* >
<!ELEMENT image EMPTY>
<!ATTLIST image
        alt    CDATA    #IMPLIED
        src    CDATA    #REQUIRED
        type   CDATA    "image/gif"
>
```

These modifications declare `image` as an optional element in a `slide`, define it as empty element, and define the attributes it requires. The `image` tag is patterned after the HTML 4.0 tag, `img`, with the addition of an image-type specifier, `type`. (The `img` tag is defined in the HTML 4.0 Specification.)

The `image` tag's attributes are defined by the `ATTLIST` entry. The `alt` attribute, which defines alternate text to display in case the image can't be found, accepts character data (`CDATA`). It has an "implied" value, which means that it is optional, and that the program processing the data knows enough to substitute something like "Image not found". On the other hand, the `src` attribute, which names the image to display, is required.

The `type` attribute is intended for the specification of a MIME data type, as defined at `ftp://ftp.isi.edu/in-notes/iana/assignments/media-types/`. It has a default value: `image/gif`.

Note: It is understood here that the character data (`CDATA`) used for the type attribute will be one of the MIME data types. The two most common formats are: `image/gif`, and `image/jpeg`. Given that fact, it might be nice to specify an attribute list here, using something like:

```
type ("image/gif", "image/jpeg")
```

That won't work, however, because attribute lists are restricted to name tokens. The forward slash isn't part of the valid set of name-token characters, so this declaration fails. Besides that, creating an attribute list in the DTD would limit the valid MIME types to those defined today. Leaving it as CDATA leaves things more open ended, so that the declaration will continue to be valid as additional types are defined.

In the document, a reference to an image named "intro-pic" might look something like this:

```
<image src="image/intro-pic.gif", alt="Intro Pic", type="image/gif" />
```

5.10.2 The Alternative: Using Entity References

Using a MIME data type as an attribute of an element is a mechanism that is flexible and expandable. To create an external `ENTITY` reference using the notation mechanism, you need DTD `NOTATION` elements for jpeg and gif data. Those can of course be obtained from some central repository. But then you need to define a different `ENTITY` element for each image you intend to reference! In other words, adding a new image to your document always requires both a new entity definition in the DTD and a reference to it in the document. Given the anticipated ubiquity of the HTML 4.0 specification, the newer standard is to use the MIME data types and a declaration like `image`, which assumes the application knows how to process such elements.

5.11 Using the Validating Parser

By now, you have done a lot of experimenting with the nonvalidating parser. It's time to have a look at the validating parser and find out what happens when you use it to parse the sample presentation.

Two things to understand about the validating parser at the outset are:

- The DTD is required.
- Since the DTD is present, the `ignorableWhitespace` method is invoked whenever the DTD makes that possible.

5.11.1 Configuring the Factory

The first step is modify the Echo program so that it uses the validating parser instead of the nonvalidating parser.

Note: The code in this section is contained in Echo10.java.

To use the validating parser, make the changes highlighted below:

```
public static void main(String argv[])
{
    if (argv.length != 1) {
        ...
    }
    // Use the default (non-validating) parser
    // Use the validating parser
    SAXParserFactory factory = SAXParserFactory.newInstance();
    factory.setValidating(true);
    try {
        ...
```

Here, you configured the factory so that it will produce a validating parser when newSAXParser is invoked. You can also configure it to return a namespace-aware parser using setNamespaceAware(true). The reference implementation supports any combination of configuration options.

5.11.2 Changing the Environment Variable

If no other factory class is specified, the default SAXParserFactory class is used. To use a different manufacturer's parser, you can change the value of the environment variable that points to it. You can do that from the command line, like this:

```
java -Djavax.xml.parsers.SAXParserFactory=yourFactoryHere ...
```

The factory name you specify must be a fully qualified class name (all package prefixes included). For more information, see the documentation in the newInstance() method of the SAXParserFactory class.

5.11.3 Experimenting with Validation Errors

To see what happens when the XML document does not specify a DTD, remove the DOCTYPE statement from the XML file and run the Echo program on it.

Note: The output shown here is contained in Echo10-01.

The result you see looks like this:

```
<?xml version='1.0' encoding='UTF-8'?>
** Warning, line 5, uri file: ...
   Valid documents must have a <!DOCTYPE declaration.
** Parsing error, line 5, uri file: ...
   Element type "slideshow" is not declared.
```

So now you know that a DTD is a requirement for a valid document. That makes sense. (Note, though, that the lack of a type declaration only generates a warning, as specified in the standard. On the other hand, any attempt to actually parse the document is immediately greeted with an error! Oh well...)

So what happens when you run the parser on your current version of the slide presentation, with the DTD specified?

Note: The output shown here is contained in `Echo10-07`.

This time, the parser gives the following error message:

```
** Parsing error, line 28, uri file:...
  Element "slide" does not allow "item" here.
```

This error occurs because the definition of the `slide` element requires a `title`. That element is not optional, and the copyright slide does not have one. To fix the problem, add the question mark highlighted below to make `title` an optional element:

```
<!ELEMENT slide (image?, title?, item*)>
```

Now what happens when you run the program?

Note: You could also remove the copyright slide, which produces the same result shown below, as reflected in Echo10-06.

The answer is that everything runs fine, until the parser runs into the <em> tag contained in the overview slide. Since that tag was not defined in the DTD, the attempt to validate the document fails. The output looks like this:

```
...
  ELEMENT: <title>
  CHARS:   Overview
```

```
    END_ELM: </title>
    ELEMENT: <item>
    CHARS:   Why ** Parsing error, line 24, uri file:...
Element "item" does not allow "em" -- (#PCDATA|item)
org.xml.sax.SAXParseException: Element "item" does not allow
"em" -- (#PCDATA|item)
        at com.sun.xml.parser.Parser.error(Parser.java:2798)
...
```

The error message identifies the part of the DTD that caused validation to fail. In this case it is the line that defines an `item` element as `(#PCDATA | item)`.

Exercise: Make a copy of the file and remove all occurrences of <em> from it. Can the file be validated now? (In the next section, you'll learn how to define parameter entries so that we can use XHTML in the elements we are defining as part of the slide presentation.)

5.11.4 Error Handling in the Validating Parser

It is important to recognize that the only reason an exception is thrown when the file fails validation is as a result of the error-handling code you entered in the early stages of this tutorial. That code is reproduced below:

```
public void error(SAXParseException e)
throws SAXParseException
{
    throw e;
}
```

If that exception is not thrown, the validation errors are simply ignored.

Exercise: Try commenting out the line that throws the exception. What happens when you run the parser now?

In general, a SAX parsing *error* is a validation error, although we have seen that it can also be generated if the file specifies a version of XML that the parser is not prepared to handle. The thing to remember is that your application will not generate a validation exception unless you supply an error handler like the one above.

5.12 Defining Parameter Entities and Conditional Sections

Just as a general entity lets you reuse XML data in multiple places, a parameter entity lets you reuse parts of a DTD in multiple places. In this section of the tutorial, you'll see how to define and use parameter entities. You'll also see how to use parameter entities with conditional sections in a DTD.

5.12.1 Creating and Referencing a Parameter Entity

Recall that the existing version of the slide presentation could not be validated because the document used <em> tags, and those are not part of the DTD. In general, we'd like to use a whole variety of HTML-style tags in the text of a slide, not just one or two, so it makes more sense to use an existing DTD for XHTML than it does to define all the tags we might ever need. A parameter entity is intended for exactly that kind of purpose.

Note: The DTD specifications shown here are contained in `slideshow2.dtd`. The XML file that references it is `slideSample08.xml`. (The browsable versions are `slideshow2-dtd.html` and `slideSample08-xml.html`.)

Open your DTD file for the slide presentation and add the text highlighted below to define a parameter entity that references an external DTD file:

```
<!ELEMENT slide (image?, title?, item*)>
<!ATTLIST slide
          ...
>
<!ENTITY % xhtml SYSTEM "xhtml.dtd">
%xhtml;
<!ELEMENT title ...
```

Here, you used an `<!ENTITY>` tag to define a parameter entity, just as for a general entity, but using a somewhat different syntax. You included a percent sign (%) before the entity name when you defined the entity, and you used the percent sign instead of an ampersand when you referenced it.

Also, note that there are always two steps for using a parameter entity. The first is to define the entity name. The second is to reference the entity name, which actually does the work of including the external definitions in the current DTD. Since the URI for an external entity could contain slashes (/) or other characters that are not valid in an XML name, the definition step allows a valid XML name to be associated with an actual document. (This same technique is used in the definition of namespaces, and anywhere else that XML constructs need to reference external documents.)

Note: The DTD file referenced by this definition is `xhtml.dtd`. You can either copy that file to your system or modify the `SYSTEM` identifier in the `<!ENTITY>` tag to point to the correct URL.

This file is a small subset of the XHTML specification, loosely modeled after the Modularized XHTML draft, which aims at breaking up the DTD for XHTML into bite-sized chunks, which can then be combined to create different XHTML subsets for different purposes. When work on the modularized XHTML draft has been completed, this version of the DTD should be replaced with something better. For now, this version will suffice for our purposes.

The whole point of using an XHTML-based DTD was to gain access to an entity it defines that covers HTML-style tags like `<em>` and `<b>`. Looking through `xhtml.dtd` reveals the following entity, which does exactly what we want:

```
<!ENTITY % inline "#PCDATA|em|b|a|img|br">
```

This entity is a simpler version of those defined in the Modularized XHTML draft. It defines the HTML-style tags we are most likely to want to use—emphasis, bold, and break, plus a couple of others for images and anchors that we may or may not use in a slide presentation. To use the `inline` entity, make the changes highlighted below in your DTD file:

```
<!ELEMENT title (#PCDATA %inline;)*>
<!ELEMENT item (#PCDATA %inline; | item)* >
```

These changes replaced the simple `#PCDATA` item with the `inline` entity. It is important to notice that `#PCDATA` is first in the `inline` entity, and that inline is first wherever we use it. That is required by XML's definition of a mixed-content model. To be in accord with that model, you also had to add an asterisk at the end of the `title` definition. (In the next two sections, you'll see that our definition of the `title` element actually conflicts with a version defined in `xhtml.dtd`, and see different ways to resolve the problem.)

Note: The Modularized XHTML DTD defines both `inline` and `Inline` entities, and does so somewhat differently. Rather than specifying `#PCDATA|em|b|a|img|Br`, their definitions are more like `(#PCDATA|em|b|a|img|Br)*`. Using one of those definitions, therefore, looks more like this:

```
<!ELEMENT title %Inline; >
```

5.12.2 Conditional Sections

Before we proceed with the next programming exercise, it is worth mentioning the use of parameter entities to control *conditional sections*. Although you cannot conditionalize the content of an XML document, you can define conditional sections in a DTD that become part of the DTD only if you specify `include`. If you specify `ignore`, on the other hand, then the conditional section is not included.

Suppose, for example, that you wanted to use slightly different versions of a DTD, depending on whether you were treating the document as an XML document or as a SGML document. You could do that with DTD definitions like the following:

```
someExternal.dtd:
    <![ INCLUDE [
        ... XML-only definitions
    ]]>
    <![ IGNORE [
        ... SGML-only definitions
    ]]>
    ... common definitions
```

The conditional sections are introduced by "`<![`", followed by the `INCLUDE` or `IGNORE` keyword and another "`[`". After that comes the contents of the conditional section, followed by the terminator: "`]]>`". In this case, the XML definitions are included, and the SGML definitions are excluded. That's fine for XML documents, but you can't use the DTD for SGML documents. You could change the keywords, of course, but that only reverses the problem.

The solution is to use references to parameter entities in place of the `INCLUDE` and `IGNORE` keywords:

```
someExternal.dtd:
    <![ %XML; [
        ... XML-only definitions
    ]]>
    <![ %SGML; [
        ... SGML-only definitions
    ]]>
    ... common definitions
```

Then each document that uses the DTD can set up the appropriate entity definitions:

```
<!DOCTYPE foo SYSTEM "someExternal.dtd" [
    <!ENTITY % XML  "INCLUDE" >
    <!ENTITY % SGML "IGNORE" >
]>
<foo>
    ...
</foo>
```

This procedure puts each document in control of the DTD. It also replaces the `INCLUDE` and `IGNORE` keywords with variable names that more accurately reflect the purpose of the conditional section, producing a more readable, self-documenting version of the DTD.

5.13 Parsing the Parameterized DTD

This section uses the Echo program to see what happens when you reference `xhtml.dtd` in `slideshow.dtd`. It also covers the kinds of warnings that are generated by the SAX parser when a DTD is present.

Note: The output described in this section is contained in `Echo10-08`.

When you try to echo the slide presentation, you find that it now contains a new error. The relevant part of the output is shown here (formatted for readability):

```
<?xml version='1.0' encoding='UTF-8'?>
** Parsing error, line 22,
    uri file:.../slideshow.dtd
Element "title" was already declared.
org.xml.sax.SAXParseException: ...
```

It seems that `xhtml.dtd` defines a `title` element that is entirely different from the `title` element defined in the slideshow DTD. Because there is no hierarchy in the DTD, these two definitions conflict.

Note: The Modularized XHTML DTD also defines a `title` element that is intended to be the document title, so we can't avoid the conflict by changing `xhtml.dtd`—the problem would only come back to haunt us later.

You could also use XML namespaces to resolve the conflict, or use one of the more hierarchical schema proposals described in Schema Standards (page 42). For now, though, let's simply rename the `title` element in `slideshow.dtd`.

Note: The XML shown here is contained in `slideshow3.dtd` and `slideSample09.xml`, which references `copyright.xml` and `xhtml.dtd`. (The browsable versions are `slideshow3-dtd.html`, `slideSample09-xml.html`, `copyright-xml.html`, and `xhtml-dtd.html`.) The results of processing are shown in `Echo10-09`.

To keep the two title elements separate, we'll resort to a "hyphenation hierarchy". Make the changes highlighted below to change the name of the `title` element in `slideshow.dtd` to `slide-title`:

```
<!ELEMENT slide (image?, slide-title?, item*)>
<!ATTLIST slide
            type   (tech | exec | all) #IMPLIED
>
<!-- Defines the %inline; declaration -->
<!ENTITY % xhtml SYSTEM "xhtml.dtd">
%xhtml;

<!ELEMENT slide-title (%inline;)*>
```

The next step is to modify the XML file to use the new element name. To do that, make the changes highlighted below:

```
...
<slide type="all">
<slide-title>Wake up to ... </slide-title>
</slide>

...

<!-- OVERVIEW -->
<slide type="all">
<slide-title>Overview</slide-title>
<item>...
```

Now run the Echo program on this version of the slide presentation. It should run to completion and display output like that shown in `Echo10-09`.

Congratulations! You have now read a fully validated XML document. The changes you made had the effect of putting your DTD's `title` element into a slideshow "namespace" that you artificially constructed by hyphenating the name. Now the `title` element in the "slideshow namespace" (`slide-title`, really) no longer conflicts with the `title` element in `xhtml.dtd`. In the next section of the tutorial, you'll see how to do that without renaming the definition. To finish off this section, we'll take a look at the kinds of warnings that the validating parser can produce when processing the DTD.

5.13.1 DTD Warnings

As mentioned earlier in this tutorial, warnings are generated only when the SAX parser is processing a DTD. Some warnings are generated only by the validating parser. The nonvalidating parser's main goal is operate as rapidly as possible, but it too generates some warnings. (The explanations that follow tell which does what.)

The XML specification suggests that warnings should be generated as result of:

- Providing additional declarations for entities, attributes, or notations.

  (Such declarations are ignored. Only the first is used. Also, note that duplicate definitions of *elements* always produce a fatal error when validating, as you saw earlier.)

- Referencing an undeclared element type.

  (A validity error occurs only if the undeclared type is actually used in the XML document. A warning results when the undeclared element is referenced in the DTD.)

- Declaring attributes for undeclared element types.

The Java XML SAX parser also emits warnings in other cases, such as:

- No <!DOCTYPE ...> when validating.
- Referencing an undefined parameter entity when not validating.

  (When validating, an error results. Although nonvalidating parsers are not required to read parameter entities, the Java XML parser does so. Since it is not a requirement, the Java XML parser generates a warning, rather than an error.)

- Certain cases where the character-encoding declaration does not look right.

At this point, you have digested many XML concepts, including DTDs, external entities. You have also learned your way around the SAX parser. The remainder of the SAX tutorial covers advanced topics that you will only need to understand if you are writing SAX-based applications. If your primary goal is to write DOM-based apps, you can skip ahead to Document Object Model (page 149).

5.14 Handling Lexical Events

You saw earlier that if you are writing text out as XML, you need to know if you are in a `CDATA` section. If you are, then angle brackets (<) and ampersands (&) should be output unchanged. But if you're not in a `CDATA` section, they should be replaced by the predefined entities `<` and `&`. But how do you know if you're processing a `CDATA` section?

Then again, if you are filtering XML in some way, you would want to pass comments along. Normally the parser ignores comments. How can you get comments so that you can echo them?

Finally, there are the parsed entity definitions. If an XML-filtering app sees `&myEntity;` it needs to echo the same string—not the text that is inserted in its place. How do you go about doing that?

This section of the tutorial answers those questions. It shows you how to use `org.xml.sax.ext.LexicalHandler` to identify comments, `CDATA` sections, and references to parsed entities.

Comments, `CDATA` tags, and references to parsed entities constitute *lexical* information—that is, information that concerns the text of the XML itself, rather than the XML's information content. Most applications, of course, are concerned only with the *content* of an XML document. Such apps will not use the `LexicalEventListener` API. But apps that output XML text will find it invaluable.

Note: Lexical event handling is a optional parser feature. Parser implementations are not required to support it. (The reference implementation does so.) This discussion assumes that the parser you are using does so, as well.

5.14.1 How the LexicalHandler Works

To be informed when the SAX parser sees lexical information, you configure the `XmlReader` that underlies the parser with a `LexicalHandler`. The `LexicalHandler` interface defines these even-handling methods:

`comment(String comment)`

Passes comments to the application.

`startCDATA(), endCDATA()`

Tells when a CDATA section is starting and ending, which tells your application what kind of characters to expect the next time `characters()` is called.

`startEntity(String name), endEntity(String name)`

Gives the name of a parsed entity.

`startDTD(String name, String publicId, String systemId), endDTD()`

Tells when a DTD is being processed, and identifies it.

5.14.2 Working with a LexicalHandler

In the remainder of this section, you'll convert the Echo app into a lexical handler and play with its features.

Note: The code shown in this section is in `Echo11.java`. The output is shown in `Echo11-09`.

To start, add the code highlighted below to implement the `LexicalHandler` interface and add the appropriate methods.

```
import org.xml.sax.ext.LexicalHandler;

public class Echo extends HandlerBase
    implements LexicalHandler
{
    public static void main(String argv[])
        {
            ...
            // Use an instance of ourselves as the SAX event handler
            DefaultHandler handler = new Echo11();
            Echo handler = new Echo();
            ...
```

At this point, the Echo class extends one class and implements an additional interface. You changed the class of the handler variable accordingly, so you can use the same instance as either a DefaultHandler or a LexicalHandler, as appropriate.

Next, add the code highlighted below to get the `XMLReader` that the parser delegates to, and configure it to send lexical events to your lexical handler:

```
public static void main(String argv[])
{
    ...
    try {
        ...
        // Parse the input
        SAXParser saxParser = factory.newSAXParser();
        XMLReader xmlReader = saxParser.getXMLReader();
        xmlReader.setProperty(
            "http://xml.org/sax/properties/lexical-handler",
            handler
            );
        saxParser.parse( new File(argv[0]), handler);
    } catch (SAXParseException spe) {
        ...
```

Here, you configured the `XMLReader` using the `setProperty()` method defined in the XMLReader class. The property name, defined as part of the SAX standard, is the URL, `http://xml.org/sax/properties/lexical-handler`.

Finally, add the code highlighted below to define the appropriate methods that implement the interface.

```
public void processingInstruction(String target, String data)
    ...
}

public void comment(char[] ch, int start, int length)throws
SAXException

{
}

public void startCDATA()
throws SAXException
{
}
```

```
public void endCDATA()
throws SAXException
{
}

public void startEntity(String name)
throws SAXException
{
}

public void endEntity(String name)
throws SAXException
{
}

public void startDTD(String name, String publicId, String systemId)
throws SAXException
{
}

public void endDTD()
throws SAXException
{
}

private void emit(String s)
    ...
```

You have now turned the `Echo` class into a lexical handler. In the next section, you'll start experimenting with lexical events.

Echoing Comments

The next step is to do something with one of the new methods. Add the code highlighted below to echo comments in the XML file:

```
public void comment(char[] ch, int start, int length)
    throws SAXException
{
    String text = new String(ch, start, length);
    nl(); emit("COMMENT: "+text);
}
```

When you compile the Echo program and run it on your XML file, the result looks something like this:

```
COMMENT:   A SAMPLE set of slides
COMMENT:  FOR WALLY / WALLIES
COMMENT:
    DTD for a simple "slide show".

COMMENT:  Defines the %inline; declaration
COMMENT:  ...
```

The line endings in the comments are passed as part of the comment string, once again normalized to newlines (). You can also see that comments in the DTD are echoed along with comments from the file. (That can pose problems when you want to echo only comments that are in the data file. To get around that problem, you can use the `startDTD` and `endDTD` methods.)

Echoing Other Lexical Information

To finish up this section, you'll exercise the remaining `LexicalHandler` methods.

Note: The code shown in this section is in `Echo12.java`. The file it operates on is `slideSample10.xml`. (The browsable version is `slideSample10-xml.html`.) The results of processing are in `Echo12-10`.

Make the changes highlighted below to remove the comment echo (you don't need that any more) and echo the other events:

```
public void comment(char[] ch, int start, int length)
throws SAXException
{
    String text = new String(ch, start, length);
    nl(); emit("COMMENT: "+text);
}
public void startCDATA()
throws SAXException
{
    nl(); emit("START CDATA SECTION");
}
public void endCDATA()
throws SAXException
```

```
{
    nl(); emit("END CDATA SECTION");
}
public void startEntity(String name)
throws SAXException
{
    nl(); emit("START ENTITY: "+name);
}
public void endEntity(String name)
throws SAXException
{
    nl(); emit("END ENTITY: "+name);
}
public void startDTD(String name, String publicId, String systemId)
throws SAXException
{
    nl(); emit("START DTD: "+name
        +"          publicId=" + publicId
        +"          systemId=" + systemId);
}

public void endDTD()
throws SAXException
{
    nl(); emit("END DTD");
}
```

Here is what you see when the DTD is processed:

```
START DTD: slideshow
           publicId=null
           systemId=file:/..../samples/slideshow3.dtd
END DTD
```

Note: To see events that occur while the DTD is being processed, use `org.xml.sax.ext.DeclHandler`.

Here is what happens when the internally defined `products` entity is processed with the latest version of the program:

```
ELEMENT: <slide-title>

CHARS:   Wake up to
START ENTITY: products
CHARS:   WonderWidgets
END ENTITY: products, INCLUDED=true
CHARS:   !
END_ELM: </slide-title>
```

And here is the result of processing the external copyright entity:

```
    START ENTITY: copyright
    CHARS:
This is the standard copyright message ...
    END ENTITY: copyright
```

Finally, you get output like this for the CDATA section:

```
START CDATA SECTION
CHARS:   Diagram:
         frobmorten <------------ fuznaten

   |             <3>        ^
   | <1>                    |   <1> = fozzle

   V                        |   <2> = framboze

staten --------------------+   <3> = frenzle

              <2>

END CDATA SECTION
```

In summary, the LexicalHandler gives you the event-notifications you need to produce an accurate reflection of the original XML text.

5.15 Using the DTDHandler and EntityResolver

In this section of the tutorial, we'll carry on a short discussion of the two remaining SAX event handlers: `DTDHandler` and `EntityResolver`. The `DTDHandler` is invoked when the DTD encounters an unparsed entity or a notation declaration. The `EntityResolver` comes into play when a URN (public ID) must be resolved to a URL (system ID).

5.15.1 The DTDHandler API

In the section Referencing Binary Entities (page 128) you saw a method for referencing a file that contains binary data, like an image file, using MIME data types. That is the simplest, most extensible mechanism to use. For compatibility with older SGML-style data, though, it is also possible to define an unparsed entity.

The `NDATA` keyword defines an unparsed entity, like this:

```
<!ENTITY myEntity SYSTEM "..URL.." NDATA gif>
```

The `NDATA` keyword says that the data in this entity is not parsable XML data, but is instead data that uses some other notation. In this case, the notation is named "gif". The DTD must then include a declaration for that notation, which would look something like this:

```
<!NOTATION gif SYSTEM "..URL..">
```

When the parser sees an unparsed entity or a notation declaration, it does nothing with the information except to pass it along to the application using the `DTDHandler` interface. That interface defines two methods:

```
notationDecl(String name, String publicId, String systemId)

unparsedEntityDecl(String name, String publicId,
    String systemId, String notationName)
```

The `notationDecl` method is passed the name of the notation and either the public or system identifier, or both, depending on which is declared in the DTD. The `unparsedEntityDecl` method is passed the name of the entity, the appropriate identifiers, and the name of the notation it uses.

Note: The DTDHandler interface is implemented by the `DefaultHandler` class.

Notations can also be used in attribute declarations. For example, the following declaration requires notations for the GIF and PNG image-file formats:

```
<!ENTITY image EMPTY>
<!ATTLIST image
        ...
        type  NOTATION  (gif | png) "gif"
>
```

Here, the `type` is declared as being either `gif`, or `png`. The default, if neither is specified, is `gif`.

Whether the notation reference is used to describe an unparsed entity or an attribute, it is up to the application to do the appropriate processing. The parser knows nothing at all about the semantics of the notations. It only passes on the declarations.

5.15.2 The EntityResolver API

The `EntityResolver` API lets you convert a public ID (URN) into a system ID (URL). Your application may need to do that, for example, to convert something like `href="urn:/someName"` into `"http://someURL"`.

The `EntityResolver` interface defines a single method:

```
resolveEntity(String publicId, String systemId)
```

This method returns an `InputSource` object, which can be used to access the entity's contents. Converting an URL into an `InputSource` is easy enough. But the URL that is passed as the system ID will be the location of the original document which is, as likely as not, somewhere out on the Web. To access a local copy, if there is one, you must maintain a catalog somewhere on the system that maps names (public IDs) into local URLs.

CHAPTER 6

Document Object Model

Eric Armstrong

IN THIS CHAPTER

IN the SAX chapter, you wrote an XML file that contains slides for a presentation. You then used the SAX API to echo the XML to your display.

In this chapter, you'll use the Document Object Model (DOM) to build a small Slideshow application. You'll start by constructing a DOM and inspecting it, then see how to write a DOM as an XML structure, display it in a GUI, and manipulate the tree structure.

A Document Object Model is a garden-variety tree structure, where each node contains one of the components from an XML structure. The two most common types of nodes are *element nodes* and *text nodes*. Using DOM functions lets you create nodes, remove nodes, change their contents, and traverse the node hierarchy.

In this chapter, you'll parse an existing XML file to construct a DOM, display and inspect the DOM hierarchy, convert the DOM into a user-friendly `JTree`, and explore the syntax of namespaces. You'll also create a DOM from scratch, and see how to use some of the implementation-specific features in Sun's JAXP reference implementation to convert an existing data set to XML.

Note: The examples in this chapter can be found in `docs/tutorial/examples/jaxp/dom/samples`.

6.1 Reading XML Data into a DOM

In this section of the tutorial, you'll construct a Document Object Model (DOM) by reading in an existing XML file. In the following sections, you'll see how to display the XML in a Swing tree component and practice manipulating the DOM.

Note: In the next part of the tutorial, XML Stylesheet Language for Transformations (page 203), you'll see how to write out a DOM as an XML file. (You'll also see how to convert an existing data file into XML with relative ease.)

6.1.1 Creating the Program

The Document Object Model (DOM) provides APIs that let you create nodes, modify them, delete and rearrange them. So it is relatively easy to create a DOM, as you'll see in later in this tutorial, Creating and Manipulating a DOM (page 193).

Before you try to create a DOM, however, it is helpful to understand how a DOM is structured. This series of exercises will make DOM internals visible by displaying them in a Swing `JTree`.

Create the Skeleton

Now that you've had a quick overview of how to create a DOM, let's build a simple program to read an XML document into a DOM, then write it back out again.

Note: The code discussed in this section is in `DomEcho01.java`. The file it operates on is `slideSample01.xml`. (The browsable version is `slideSample01-xml.html`.)

Start with a normal basic logic for an app, and check to make sure that an argument has been supplied on the command line:

```
public class DomEcho {
    public static void main(String argv[])
```

```
    {
        if (argv.length != 1) {
            System.err.println("Usage: java DomEcho filename");
            System.exit(1);
        }
    }// main
}// DomEcho
```

Import the Required Classes

In this section, you're going to see all the classes individually named. That's so you can see where each class comes from when you want to reference the API documentation. In your own apps, you may well want to replace import statements like those below with the shorter form: `javax.xml.parsers.*`.

Add these lines to import the JAXP APIs you'll be using:

```
import javax.xml.parsers.DocumentBuilder;
import javax.xml.parsers.DocumentBuilderFactory;
import javax.xml.parsers.FactoryConfigurationError;
import javax.xml.parsers.ParserConfigurationException;
```

Add these lines for the exceptions that can be thrown when the XML document is parsed:

```
import org.xml.sax.SAXException;
import org.xml.sax.SAXParseException;
```

Add these lines to read the sample XML file and identify errors:

```
import java.io.File;
import java.io.IOException;
```

Finally, import the W3C definition for a DOM and DOM exceptions:

```
import org.w3c.dom.Document;
import org.w3c.dom.DOMException;
```

Note: A `DOMException` is only thrown when traversing or manipulating a DOM. Errors that occur during parsing are reporting using a different mechanism that is covered next.

Declare the DOM

The `org.w3c.dom.Document` class is the W3C name for a Document Object Model (DOM). Whether you parse an XML document or create one, a Document instance will result. We'll want to reference that object from another method later on in the tutorial, so define it as a global object here:

```
public class DomEcho
{
    static Document document;

    public static void main(String argv[])
    {
```

It needs to be `static`, because you're going to generate its contents from the `main` method in a few minutes.

Handle Errors

Next, put in the error handling logic. This code is very similar to the logic you saw in Handling Errors with the Nonvalidating Parser (page 101) in the SAX tutorial, so we won't go into it in detail here. The major point worth noting is that a JAXP-conformant document builder is required to report SAX exceptions when it has trouble parsing the XML document. The DOM parser does not have to actually use a SAX parser internally, but since the SAX standard was already there, it seemed to make sense to use it for reporting errors. As a result, the error-handling code for DOM and SAX applications are very similar:

```
public static void main(String argv[])
{
    if (argv.length != 1) {
        ...
    }

    try {

    } catch (SAXException sxe) {
        // Error generated during parsing
        Exception  x = sxe;
        if (sxe.getException() != null)
            x = sxe.getException();
        x.printStackTrace();
```

```
    } catch (ParserConfigurationException pce) {
        // Parser with specified options can't be built
        pce.printStackTrace();

    } catch (IOException ioe) {
        // I/O error
        ioe.printStackTrace();
    }
}// main
```

The major difference between this code and the SAX error-handling code is that the DOM parser does not throw `SAXParseExceptions`, but only `SAXExceptions`.

Instantiate the Factory

Next, add the code highlighted below to obtain an instance of a factory that can give us a document builder:

```
public static void main(String argv[])
{
    if (argv.length != 1) {
        ...
    }
    DocumentBuilderFactory factory =
        DocumentBuilderFactory.newInstance();
    try {
```

Get a Parser and Parse the File

Now, add the code highlighted below to get a instance of a builder, and use it to parse the specified file:

```
try {
    DocumentBuilder builder = factory.newDocumentBuilder();
    document = builder.parse( new File(argv[0]) );
} catch (SAXParseException spe) {
```

Save This File!

By now, you should be getting the idea that every JAXP application starts pretty much the same way. You're right! Save this version of the file as a template. You'll use it later on as the basis for XSLT transformation app.

Run the Program

Throughout most of the DOM tutorial, you'll be using the sample slideshows you created in the SAX section. In particular, you'll use `slideSample01.xml`, a simple XML file with nothing much in it, and `slideSample10.xml`, a more complex example that includes a DTD, processing instructions, entity references, and a CDATA section.

For instructions on how to compile and run your program, see Compiling and Running the Program (page 91) and Run the Program, from the SAX tutorial. Substitute "DomEcho" for "Echo" as the name of the program, and you're ready to roll.

For now, just run the program on `slideSample01.xml`. If it ran without error, you have successfully parsed an XML document and constructed a DOM. Congratulations!

Note: You'll have to take my word for it, for the moment, because at this point you don't have any way to display the results. But that feature is coming shortly...

6.1.2 Additional Information

Now that you have successfully read in a DOM, there are one or two more things you need to know in order to use `DocumentBuilder` effectively. Namely, you need to know about:

- Configuring the Factory
- Handling Validation Errors

Configuring the Factory

By default, the factory returns a nonvalidating parser that knows nothing about namespaces. To get a validating parser, and/or one that understands namespaces, you configure the factory to set either or both of those options using the command(s) highlighted below:

```
public static void main(String argv[])
{
    if (argv.length != 1) {
        ...
    }
```

```
DocumentBuilderFactory factory =
    DocumentBuilderFactory.newInstance();
factory.setValidating(true);
factory.setNamespaceAware(true);
try {
    ...
```

Note: JAXP-conformant parsers are not required to support all combinations of those options, even though the reference parser does. If you specify an invalid combination of options, the factory generates a `ParserConfigurationException` when you attempt to obtain a parser instance.

You'll be learning more about how to use namespaces in the last section of the DOM tutorial, Using Namespaces (page 199). To complete this section, though, you'll want to learn something about...

Handling Validation Errors

Remember when you were wading through the SAX tutorial, and all you really wanted to do was construct a DOM? Well, here's when that information begins to pay off.

Recall that the default response to a validation error, as dictated by the SAX standard, is to do nothing. The JAXP standard requires throwing SAX exceptions, so you exactly the same error handling mechanisms as you used for a SAX app. In particular, you need to use the `DocumentBuilder`'s `setErrorHandler` method to supply it with an object that implements the SAX `ErrorHandler` interface.

Note: `DocumentBuilder` also has a `setEntityResolver` method you can use.

The code below uses an anonymous inner class adapter to provide that `ErrorHandler`. The highlighted code is the part that makes sure validation errors generate an exception.

```
builder.setErrorHandler(
    new org.xml.sax.ErrorHandler() {
        // ignore fatal errors (an exception is guaranteed)
        public void fatalError(SAXParseException exception)
        throws SAXException {
        }
        // treat validation errors as fatal
        public void error(SAXParseException e)
```

```
            throws SAXParseException
            {
                throw e;
            }

            // dump warnings too
            public void warning(SAXParseException err)
            throws SAXParseException
            {
                System.out.println("** Warning"
                    + ", line " + err.getLineNumber()
                    + ", uri " + err.getSystemId());
                System.out.println("   " + err.getMessage());
            }
        }
    );
```

This code uses an anonymous inner class to generate an instance of an object that implements the `ErrorHandler` interface. Since it has no class name, it's "anonymous". You can think of it as an "ErrorHandler" instance, although technically it's a no-name instance that implements the specified interface. The code is substantially the same as that described the Handling Errors with the Nonvalidating Parser (page 101) section of the SAX tutorial. For a more background on validation issues, refer to Using the Validating Parser (page 130) in that part of the tutorial.

6.1.3 Looking Ahead

In the next section, you'll display the DOM structure in a JTree and begin explore its structure. For example, you'll see how entity references and CDATA sections appear in the DOM. And perhaps most importantly, you'll see how text nodes (which contain the actual data) reside *under* element nodes in a DOM.

6.2 Displaying a DOM Hierarchy

To create a Document Object Hierarchy (DOM) or manipulate one, it helps to have a clear idea of how nodes in a DOM are structured. In this section of the tutorial, you'll expose the internal structure of a DOM.

6.2.1 Echoing Tree Nodes

What you need at this point is a way to expose the nodes in a DOM so can see what it contains. To do that, you'll convert a DOM into a `JTreeModel` and display the full DOM in a `JTree`. It's going to take a bit of work, but the end result will be a diagnostic tool you can use in the future, as well as something you can use to learn about DOM structure now.

6.2.2 Convert DomEcho to a GUI App

Since the DOM is a tree, and the Swing `JTree` component is all about displaying trees, it makes sense to stuff the DOM into a `JTree`, so you can look it. The first step in that process is to hack up the `DomEcho` program so it becomes a GUI application.

Note: The code discussed in this section is in `DomEcho02.java`.

Add Import Statements

Start by importing the GUI components you're going to need to set up the application and display a `JTree`:

```
// GUI components and layouts
import javax.swing.JFrame;
import javax.swing.JPanel;
import javax.swing.JScrollPane;
import javax.swing.JTree;
```

Later on in the DOM tutorial, we'll going to tailor the DOM display to generate a user-friendly version of the `JTree` display. When the user selects an element in that tree, you'll be displaying subelements in an adjacent editor pane. So, while we're doing the setup work here, import the components you need to set up a divided view (`JSplitPane`) and to display the text of the subelements (`JEditorPane`):

```
import javax.swing.JSplitPane;
import javax.swing.JEditorPane;
```

Add a few support classes you're going to need to get this thing off the ground:

```
// GUI support classes
import java.awt.BorderLayout;
import java.awt.Dimension;
import java.awt.Toolkit;
import java.awt.event.WindowEvent;
import java.awt.event.WindowAdapter;
```

Finally, import some classes to make a fancy border:

```
// For creating borders
import javax.swing.border.EmptyBorder;
import javax.swing.border.BevelBorder;
import javax.swing.border.CompoundBorder;
```

(These are optional. You can skip them and the code that depends on them if you want to simplify things.)

Create the GUI Framework

The next step is to convert the app into a GUI application. To do that, the static main method will create an instance of the main class, which will have become a GUI pane.

Start by converting the class into a GUI pane by extending the Swing `JPanel` class:

```
public class DomEcho02 extends JPanel
{
    // Global value so it can be ref'd by the tree-adapter
    static Document document;
    ...
```

While you're there, define a few constants you'll use to control window sizes:

```
public class DomEcho02 extends JPanel
{
    // Global value so it can be ref'd by the tree-adapter
    static Document document;

        static final int windowHeight = 460;
    static final int leftWidth = 300;
    static final int rightWidth = 340;
    static final int windowWidth = leftWidth + rightWidth;
```

Now, in the main method, invoke a method that will create the outer frame that the GUI pane will sit in:

```
public static void main(String argv[])
{
    ...
    DocumentBuilderFactory factory ...
    try {
        DocumentBuilder builder = factory.newDocumentBuilder();
        document = builder.parse( new File(argv[0]) );
        makeFrame();

     } catch (SAXParseException spe) {
        ...
```

Next, you'll need to define the `makeFrame` method itself. It contains the standard code to create a frame, handle the exit condition gracefully, give it an instance of the main panel, size it, locate it on the screen, and make it visible:

```
     ...
} // main

public static void makeFrame()
{
    // Set up a GUI framework
    JFrame frame = new JFrame("DOM Echo");
    frame.addWindowListener(new WindowAdapter() {
        public void windowClosing(WindowEvent e) {System.exit(0);}
    });

     // Set up the tree, the views, and display it all
    final DomEcho02 echoPanel = new DomEcho02();
    frame.getContentPane().add("Center", echoPanel );
    frame.pack();
    Dimension screenSize =
Toolkit.getDefaultToolkit().getScreenSize();
    int w = windowWidth + 10;
    int h = windowHeight + 10;
    frame.setLocation(screenSize.width/3 - w/2,
screenSize.height/2 - h/2);
    frame.setSize(w, h);
    frame.setVisible(true)
} // makeFrame
```

Add the Display Components

The only thing left in the effort to convert the program to a GUI app is create the class constructor and make it create the panel's contents. Here is the constructor:

```
public class DomEcho02 extends JPane
{
    ...
    static final int windowWidth = leftWidth + rightWidth;

    public DomEcho02()
    {
    } // Constructor
```

Here, you make use of the border classes you imported earlier to make a regal border (optional):

```
public DomEcho02()
{
    // Make a nice border
    EmptyBorder eb = new EmptyBorder(5,5,5,5);
    BevelBorder bb = new BevelBorder(BevelBorder.LOWERED);
    CompoundBorder cb = new CompoundBorder(eb,bb);
    this.setBorder(new CompoundBorder(cb,eb));
} // Constructor
```

Next, create an empty tree and put it a `JScrollPane` so users can see its contents as it gets large:

```
public DomEcho02(
{
    ...
    // Set up the tree
    JTree tree = new JTree();

     // Build left-side view
    JScrollPane treeView = new JScrollPane(tree);
    treeView.setPreferredSize(
        new Dimension( leftWidth, windowHeight ));

} // Constructor
```

Now create a non-editable `JEditPane` that will eventually hold the contents pointed to by selected `JTree` nodes:

```
public DomEcho02(
{
    ....

    // Build right-side view
    JEditorPane htmlPane = new JEditorPane("text/html","");
    htmlPane.setEditable(false);
    JScrollPane htmlView = new JScrollPane(htmlPane);
    htmlView.setPreferredSize(
        new Dimension( rightWidth, windowHeight ));

} // Constructor
```

With the left-side `JTree` and the right-side `JEditorPane` constructed, create a `JSplitPane` to hold them:

```
public DomEcho02()
{
    ....

     // Build split-pane view
    JSplitPane splitPane = new JSplitPane(
JSplitPane.HORIZONTAL_SPLIT,
                        treeView, htmlView );
    splitPane.setContinuousLayout( true );
    splitPane.setDividerLocation( leftWidth );
    splitPane.setPreferredSize(
        new Dimension( windowWidth + 10, windowHeight+10 ));

} // Constructor
```

With this code, you set up the `JSplitPane` so with a vertical divider. That produces a "horizontal split" between the tree and the editor pane. (More of a horizontal layout, really.) You also set the location of the divider so that the tree got the width it prefers, with the remainder of the window width allocated to the editor pane.

Finally, specify the layout for the panel and add the split pane:

```
public DomEcho02()
{
    ...
    // Add GUI components
    this.setLayout(new BorderLayout());
    this.add("Center", splitPane );
} // Constructor
```

Congratulations! The program is now a GUI app. You can run it now to see what the general layout will look like on screen. For reference, here is the completed constructor:

```
public DomEcho02()
{
    // Make a nice border
    EmptyBorder eb = new EmptyBorder(5,5,5,5);
    BevelBorder bb = new BevelBorder(BevelBorder.LOWERED);
    CompoundBorder CB = new CompoundBorder(eb,bb);
    this.setBorder(new CompoundBorder(CB,eb));
    // Set up the tree
    JTree tree = new JTree();
    // Build left-side view
    JScrollPane treeView = new JScrollPane(tree);
    treeView.setPreferredSize(
        new Dimension( leftWidth, windowHeight ));
    // Build right-side view
    JEditorPane htmlPane = new JEditorPane("text/html","");
    htmlPane.setEditable(false);
    JScrollPane htmlView = new JScrollPane(htmlPane);
    htmlView.setPreferredSize(
        new Dimension( rightWidth, windowHeight ));
    // Build split-pane view
    JSplitPane splitPane = new JSplitPane(
        JSplitPane.HORIZONTAL_SPLIT,
                        treeView, htmlView )
    splitPane.setContinuousLayout( true );
    splitPane.setDividerLocation( leftWidth );
    splitPane.setPreferredSize(
        new Dimension( windowWidth + 10, windowHeight+10 ));
```

```
        // Add GUI components
        this.setLayout(new BorderLayout());
        this.add("Center", splitPane );
    } // Constructor
```

6.2.3 Create Adapters to Display the DOM in a JTree

Now that you have a GUI framework to display a `JTree` in, the next step is get the `JTree` to display the DOM. But a JTree wants to display a `TreeModel`. A DOM is a tree, but it's not a `TreeModel`. So you'll need to create an adapter class that makes the DOM look like a `TreeModel` to a `JTree`.

Now, when the `TreeModel` passes nodes to the `JTree`, `JTree` uses the `toString` function of those nodes to get the text to display in the tree. The standard `toString` function isn't going to be very pretty, so you'll need to wrap the DOM nodes in an `AdapterNode` that returns the text we want. What the `TreeModel` gives to the `JTree`, then, will in fact be `AdapterNode` objects that wrap DOM nodes.

Note: The classes that follow are defined as inner classes. If you are coding for the 1.1 platform, you will need to define these class as external classes.

Define the AdapterNode Class

Start by importing the tree, event, and utility classes you're going to need to make this work:

```
// For creating a TreeModel
import javax.swing.tree.*;
import javax.swing.event.*;
import java.util.*;

public class DomEcho extends JPanel
{
```

Moving back down to the end of the program, define a set of strings for the node element types:

```
        ...
    } // makeFrame

    // An array of names for DOM node-types
    // (Array indexes = nodeType() values.)
```

```
static final String[] typeName = {
    "none",
    "Element",
    "Attr",
    "Text",
    "CDATA",
    "EntityRef",
    "Entity",
    "ProcInstr",
    "Comment",
    "Document",
    "DocType",
    "DocFragment",
    "Notation",
};

} // DomEcho
```

These are the strings that will be displayed in the `JTree`. The specification of these nodes types can be found in the Document Object Model (DOM) Level 2 Core Specification at `http://www.w3.org/TR/2000/REC-DOM/Level-2-Core-20001113`, under the specification for Node. Table 6.1 is reproduced below, with the headings modified for clarity, and with the `nodeType()` column added:

Table 6.1 Node Types

Node	nodeName()	nodeValue()	attributes	nodeType()
Attr	name of attribute	value of attribute	null	2
CDATASection	#cdata-section	content of the CDATA Section	null	4
Comment	#comment	content of the comment	null	8
Document	#document	null	null	9
DocumentFragment	#document-fragment	null	null	11
DocumentType	document type name	null	null	10
Element	tag name	null	NamedNodeMap	1
Entity	entity name	null	null	6

Table 6.1 Node Types *(Continued)*

Node	nodeName()	nodeValue()	attributes	nodeType()
EntityReference	name of entity referenced	null	null	5
Notation	notation name	null	null	12
Processing-Instruction	target	entire content excluding the target	null	7
Text	#text	content of the text node	null	3

Suggestion:

Print this table and keep it handy. You need it when working with the DOM, because all of these types are intermixed in a DOM tree. So your code is forever asking, "Is this the kind of node I'm interested in?"

Next, define the `AdapterNode` wrapper for DOM nodes:

```
static final String[] typeName = {
    ...
};

public class AdapterNode
{
    org.w3c.dom.Node domNode;

    // Construct an Adapter node from a DOM node
    public AdapterNode(org.w3c.dom.Node node) {
        domNode = node;
    }

    // Return a string that identifies this node in the tree
    // *** Refer to table at top of org.w3c.dom.Node ***
    public String toString() {
        String s = typeName[domNode.getNodeType()];
        String nodeName = domNode.getNodeName();
        if (! nodeName.startsWith("#")) {
            s += ": " + nodeName;
        }
```

```
        if (domNode.getNodeValue() != null) {
            if (s.startsWith("ProcInstr"))
                s += ", ";
            else
                s += ": ";
            // Trim the value to get rid of NL's at the front
            String t = domNode.getNodeValue().trim();
            int x = t.indexOf(");
            if (x >= 0) t = t.substring(0, x);
            s += t;
        }
        return s;
    }
    } // AdapterNode

} // DomEcho
```

This class declares a variable to hold the DOM node, and requires it to be specified as a constructor argument. It then defines the `toString` operation, which returns the node type from the `String` array, and then adds to that additional information from the node, to further identify it.

As you can see in the table of node types in `org.w3c.dom.Node`, every node has a type, and name, and a value, which may or may not be empty. In those cases where the node name starts with "#", that field duplicates the node type, so there is in point in including it. That explains the lines that read:

```
if (! nodeName.startsWith("#")) {
    s += ": " + nodeName;
}
```

The remainder of the `toString` method deserves a couple of notes, as well. For instance, these lines:

```
if (s.startsWith("ProcInstr"))
    s += ", ";
else
    s += ": ";
```

merely provide a little "syntactic sugar". The type field for a Processing Instructions end with a colon (:) anyway, so those codes keep from doubling the colon.

The other interesting lines are:

```
String t = domNode.getNodeValue().trim();
int x = t.indexOf(");
if (x >= 0) t = t.substring(0, x);
s += t;
```

Those lines trim the value field down to the first newline (linefeed) character in the field. If you leave those lines out, you will see some funny characters (square boxes, typically) in the `JTree`.

Note: Recall that XML stipulates that all line endings are normalized to newlines, regardless of the system the data comes from. That makes programming quite a bit simpler.

Wrapping a `DomNode` and returning the desired string are the `AdapterNode`'s major functions. But since the `TreeModel` adapter will need to answer questions like "How many children does this node have?" and satisfy commands like "Give me this node's Nth child," it will be helpful to define a few additional utility methods. (The adapter could always access the DOM node and get that information for itself, but this way things are more encapsulated.)

Add the code highlighted below to return the index of a specified child, the child that corresponds to a given index, and the count of child nodes:

```
public class AdapterNode
{
    ...
    public String toString() {
        ...
    }

    public int index(AdapterNode child) {
        //System.err.println("Looking for index of " + child);
        int count = childCount();
        for (int i=0; i<count; i++) {
            AdapterNode n = this.child(i);
            if (child == n) return i;
        }
        return -1; // Should never get here.
    }
```

```
        public AdapterNode child(int searchIndex) {
            //Note: JTree index is zero-based.
            org.w3c.dom.Node node =
                domNode.getChildNodes().item(searchIndex);
            return new AdapterNode(node);
        }

        public int childCount() {
            return domNode.getChildNodes().getLength();
        }
    } // AdapterNode
    } // DomEcho
```

Note: During development, it was only after I started writing the TreeModel adapter that I realized these were needed, and went back to add them. In just a moment, you'll see why.

Define the TreeModel Adapter

Now, at last, you are ready to write the TreeModel adapter. One of the really nice things about the JTree model is the relative ease with which you convert an existing tree for display. One of the reasons for that is the clear separation between the displayable view, which JTree uses, and the modifiable view, which the application uses. For more on that separation, see Understanding the TreeModel at http://java.sun.com/products/jfc/tsc/articles/jtree/index.html. For now, the important point is that to satisfy the TreeModel interface we only need to (a) provide methods to access and report on children and (b) register the appropriate JTree listener, so it knows to update its view when the underlying model changes.

Add the code highlighted below to create the TreeModel adapter and specify the child-processing methods:

```
        ...

    } // AdapterNode

    // This adapter converts the current Document (a DOM) into
    // a JTree model.
    public class DomToTreeModelAdapter implements
    javax.swing.tree.TreeModel
    {
        // Basic TreeModel operations
        public Object  getRoot() {
```

```
        //System.err.println("Returning root: " +document);
        return new AdapterNode(document);
    }

    public boolean isLeaf(Object aNode) {
        // Determines whether the icon shows up to the left.
        // Return true for any node with no children
        AdapterNode node = (AdapterNode) aNode;
        if (node.childCount() > 0) return false;
        return true;
    }
    public int     getChildCount(Object parent)
        AdapterNode node = (AdapterNode) parent;
        return node.childCount();
    }
    public Object  getChild(Object parent, int index) {
    AdapterNode node = (AdapterNode) parent;
    return node.child(index);
    }
    public int     getIndexOfChild(Object parent, Object child) {
        AdapterNode node = (AdapterNode) parent;
        return node.index((AdapterNode) child);
    }
    public void   valueForPathChanged(TreePath path, Object newValue) {
        // Null. We won't be making changes in the GUI
        // If we did, we would ensure the new value was really new
        // and then fire a TreeNodesChanged event.
    }
    } // DomToTreeModelAdapter
    } // DomEcho
```

In this code, the `getRoot` method returns the root node of the DOM, wrapped as an `AdapterNode` object. From here on, all nodes returned by the adapter will be `AdapterNodes` that wrap DOM nodes. By the same token, whenever the `JTree` asks for the child of a given parent, the number of children that parent has and so on the `JTree` will be passing us an `AdapterNode`. We know that because we control every node the `JTree` sees, starting with the root node.

`JTree` uses the `isLeaf` method to determine whether or not to display a clickable expand/contract icon to the left of the node, so that method returns true only if the node has children. In this method, we see the cast from the generic object

JTree sends us to the AdapterNode object we know it has to be. *We* know it is sending us an adapter object but the interface, to be general, defines objects so we have to do the casts.

The next three methods return the number of children for a given node, the child that lives at a given index, and the index of a given child, respectively. That's all pretty straightforward.

The last method is invoked when the user changes a value stored in the JTree. In this app, we won't support that. But if we did, the app would have to make the change to the underlying model and then inform any listeners that a change had occurred. (The JTree might not be the only listener. In many an application it isn't, in fact.)

To inform listeners that a change occurred, you'll need the ability to register them. That brings us to the last two methods required to implement the TreeModel interface. Add the code highlighted below to define them:

```
public class DomToTreeModelAdapter ...
{
    ...
    public void    valueForPathChanged(TreePath path, Object
newValue) {
        ...
    }
    private Vector listenerList = new Vector();
    public void addTreeModelListener(
        TreeModelListener listener ) {
        if ( listener != null && ! listenerList.contains(
            listener ) ) {
        listenerList.addElement( listener );
        }
    }
    public void removeTreeModelListener( TreeModelListener
    listener ) {
    if ( listener != null ) {
        listenerList.removeElement( listener );
        }
    }
} // DomToTreeModelAdapter
```

Since this app won't be making changes to the tree, these methods will go unused, for now. However, they'll be there in the future, when you need them.

Note: This example uses `Vector` so it will work with 1.1 apps. If coding for 1.2 or later, though, I'd use the excellent collections framework instead:

```
private LinkedList listenerList = new LinkedList();
```

The operations on the `List` are then `add` and `remove`. To iterate over the list, as in the operations below, you would use:

```
Iterator it = listenerList.iterator();
while ( it.hasNext() ) {
    TreeModelListener listener = (TreeModelListener) it.next();
        ...
}
```

Here, too, are some optional methods you won't be using in this app. At this point, though, you have constructed a reasonable template for a TreeModel adapter. In the interests of completeness, you might want to add the code highlighted below. You can then invoke them whenever you need to notify `JTree` listeners of a change:

```
public void removeTreeModelListener( TreeModelListener listener ) {
    ...
}
public void fireTreeNodesChanged( TreeModelEvent e ) {
    Enumeration listeners = listenerList.elements();
    while ( listeners.hasMoreElements() ) {
        TreeModelListener listener = (TreeModelListener)
listeners.nextElement();
        listener.treeNodesChanged( e );
    }
}
public void fireTreeNodesInserted( TreeModelEvent e ) {
    Enumeration listeners = listenerList.elements();
    while ( listeners.hasMoreElements() ) {
        TreeModelListener listener = (TreeModelListener)
listeners.nextElement();
        listener.treeNodesInserted( e );
    }
}
```

```
public void fireTreeNodesRemoved( TreeModelEvent e ) {
    Enumeration listeners = listenerList.elements();
    while ( listeners.hasMoreElements() ) {
        TreeModelListener listener = (TreeModelListener)
listeners.nextElement();
        listener.treeNodesRemoved( e );
    }
}
public void fireTreeStructureChanged( TreeModelEvent e ) {
    Enumeration listeners = listenerList.elements();
    while ( listeners.hasMoreElements() ) {
        TreeModelListener listener = (TreeModelListener)
listeners.nextElement();
        listener.treeStructureChanged( e );
    }
}
} // DomToTreeModelAdapter
```

Note: These methods are taken from the `TreeModelSupport` class described in Understanding the TreeModel. That architecture was produced by Tom Santos and Steve Wilson, and is a lot more elegant than the quick hack going on here. It seemed worthwhile to put them here, though, so they would be immediately at hand when and if they're needed.

6.2.4 Finishing Up

At this point, you are basically done. All you need to do is jump back to the constructor and add the code to construct an adapter and deliver it to the `JTree` as the `TreeModel`:

```
// Set up the tree
JTree tree = new JTree(new DomToTreeModelAdapter());
```

You can now compile and run the code on an XML file. In the next section, you will do that, and explore the DOM structures that result.

6.3 Examining the Structure of a DOM

In this section, you'll use the GUI-fied `DomEcho` app you created in the last section to visually examine a DOM. You'll see what nodes make up the DOM, and how they are arranged. With the understanding you acquire, you'll be well prepared to construct and modify Document Object Model structures in the future.

6.3.1 Displaying A Simple Tree

We'll start out by displaying a simple file, so you get an idea of basic DOM structure. Then we'll look at the structure that results when you include some of the more advanced XML elements.

Note: The code used to create the figures in this section is in `DomEcho02.java`. The file displayed is `slideSample01.xml`. (The browsable version is `slideSample01-xml.html`.)

Figure 6.1 shows the tree you see when you run the DomEcho program on the first XML file you created in the DOM tutorial.

Recall that the first bit of text displayed for each node is the element `type`. After that comes the element `name`, if any, and then the element `value`. This view shows three element types: `Document`, `Comment`, and `Element`. There is only `Document` type for the whole tree—that is the root node. The `Comment` node displays the `value` attribute, while the `Element` node displays the element `name`, "slideshow".

Compare the Table 6.1 with the code in the AdapterNode's `toString` method to see whether the name or value is being displayed for a particular node. If you need to make it more clear, modify the program to indicate which property is being displayed (for example, with N: *name*, V: *value*).

Expanding the slideshow element brings up the display shown in Figure 6.2.

Here, you can see the `Text` nodes and `Comment` nodes that are interspersed between Slide elements. The empty `Text` nodes exist because there is no DTD to tell the parser that no text exists. (Generally, the vast majority of nodes in a DOM tree will be `Element` and `Text` nodes.)

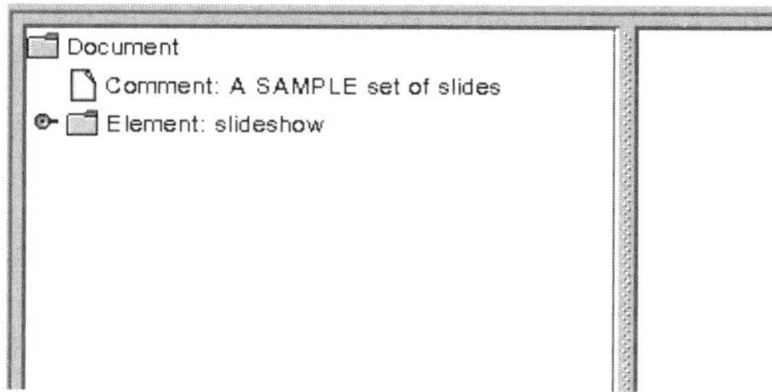

Figure 6.1 Document, Comment, and Element Nodes Displayed

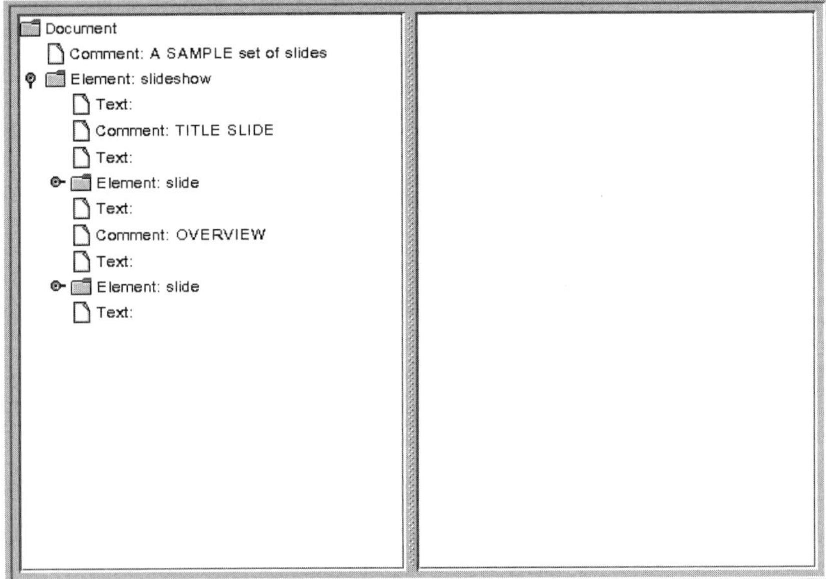

Figure 6.2 Element Node Expanded, No Attribute Nodes Showing

Important!

Text nodes exist *under* element nodes in a DOM, and data is *always* stored in text nodes. Perhaps the most common error in DOM processing is to navigate to an element node and expect it to contain the data that is stored in the XML file. Not so! Even the simplest element node has a text node under it. For example, given `<size>12</size>`, there is an element node (`size`), *and a text node under it* which contains the actual data (`12`).

Notably absent from this picture are the `Attribute` nodes. An inspection of the table in `org.w3c.dom.Node` shows that there is indeed an Attribute node type. But they are not included as children in the DOM hierarchy. They are instead obtained via the Node interface `getAttributes` method.

Note: The display of the text nodes is the reason for including the lines below in the AdapterNode's `toString` method. If your remove them, you'll see the funny characters (typically square blocks) that are generated by the newline characters that are in the text.

```
String t = domNode.getNodeValue().trim();
int x = t.indexOf(");
if (x >= 0) t = t.substring(0, x);
s += t;
```

6.3.2 Displaying a More Complex Tree

Here, you'll display the example XML file you created at the end of the SAX tutorial to see how entity references, processing instructions, and CDATA sections appear in the DOM.

Note: The file displayed in this section is `slideSample10.xml`. The `slideSample10.xml` file references `slideshow3.dtd` which, in turn, references `copyright.xml` and a (very simplistic) `xhtml.dtd`. (The browsable versions are `slideSample10-xml.html`, `slideshow3-dtd.html`, `copyright-xml.html`, and `xhtml-dtd.html`.)

Figure 6.3 shows the result of running the `DomEcho` app on `slideSample10.xml`, which includes a `DOCTYPE` entry that identifies the document's DTD.

The `DocType` interface is actually an extension of `w3c.org.dom.Node`. It defines a `getEntities` method that you would use to obtain `Entity` nodes—the nodes that define entities like the `product` entity, which has the value "WonderWidgets". Like `Attribute` nodes, `Entity` nodes do not appear as children of DOM nodes.

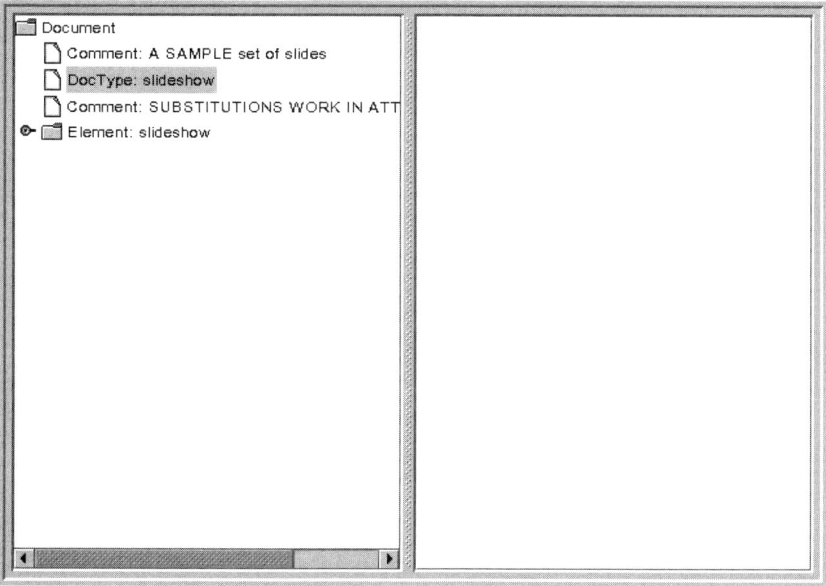

Figure 6.3 DocType Node Displayed

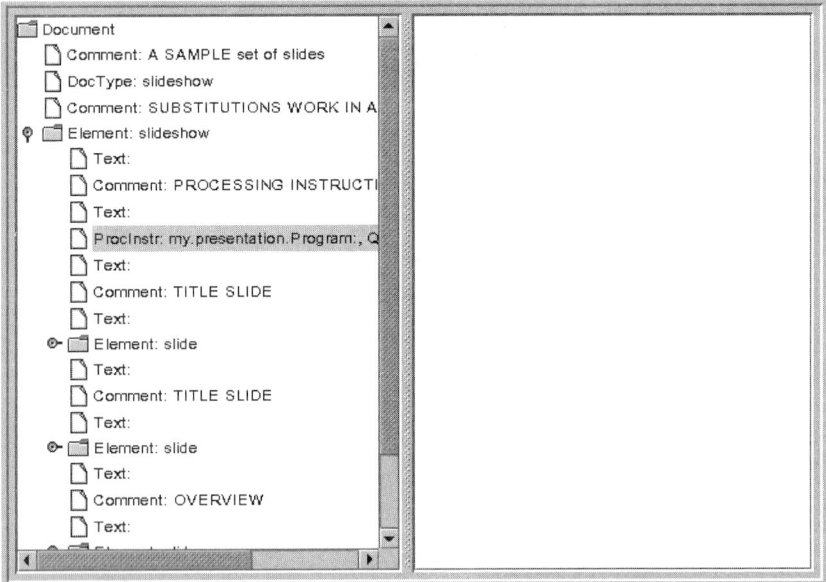

Figure 6.4 Processing Instruction Node Displayed

When you expand the `slideshow` node, you get the display shown in Figure 6.4.

Here, the processing instruction node is highlighted, showing that those nodes do appear in the tree. The `name` property contains the target-specification, which identifies the app that the instruction is directed to. The `value` property contains the text of the instruction.

Note that empty text nodes are also shown here, even though the DTD specifies that a `slideshow` can contain `slide` elements only, never text. Logically, then, you might think that these nodes would not appear. (When this file was run through the SAX parser, those elements generated `ignorableWhitespace` events, rather than `character` events.)

The empty text elements are included because by default, `DocumentBuilder` creates a DOM that includes *all the lexical information necessary to reconstruct the original document, in its original form*. That includes comment nodes as well as text nodes. There is as yet no standard mechanism for eliminating such lexical information in the DOM so you are left with the logical structure.

Moving down to the second `slide` element and opening the `item` element under it brings up the display shown in Figure 6.5.

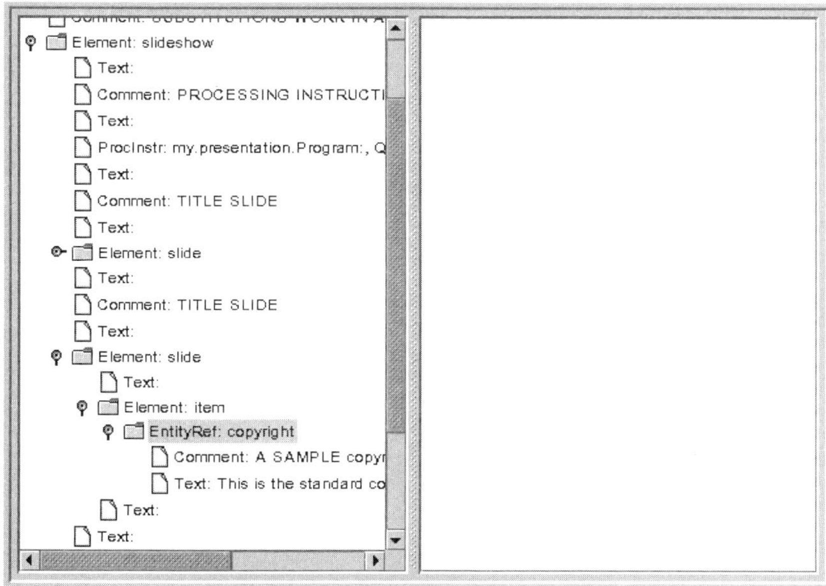

Figure 6.5 Entity Reference Node Displayed

Here, the Entity Reference node is highlighted. Note that the entity reference contains multiple nodes under it. This example shows only comment and a text nodes, but the entity could conceivable contain other element nodes, as well.

Moving down to the last `item` element under the last `slide` brings up the display shown in Figure 6.6.

Here, the `CDATA` node is highlighted. Note that there are no nodes under it. Since a `CDATA` section is entirely uninterpreted, all of its contents are contained in the node's `value` property.

6.3.3 Finishing Up

At this point, you have seen most of the nodes you will ever encounter in a DOM tree. There are one or two more that we'll mention in the next section, but you now know what you need to know to create or modify a DOM structure. In the next section, you'll see how to convert a DOM into a `JTree` that is suitable for an interactive GUI. Or, if you prefer, you can skip ahead to the DOM tutorial, Creating and Manipulating a DOM (page 193), where you'll learn how to create a DOM from scratch.

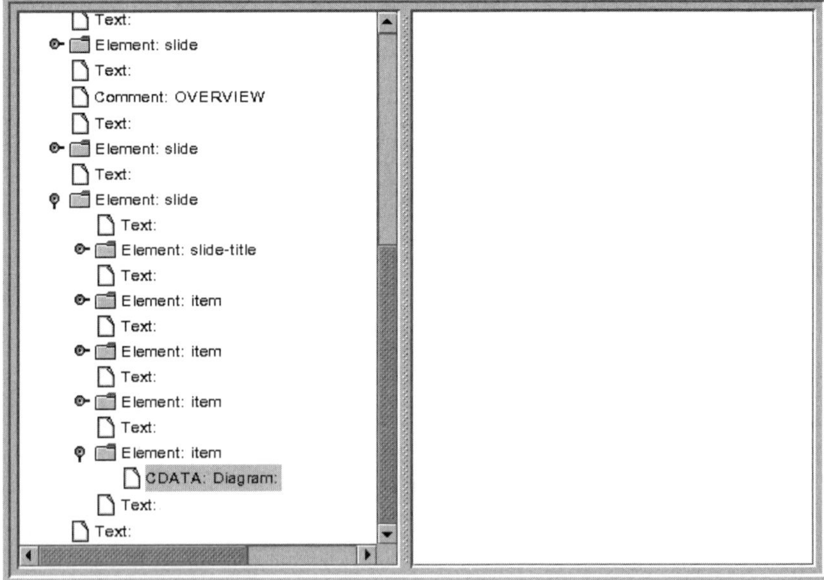

Figure 6.6 CDATA Node Displayed

6.4 Constructing a User-Friendly JTree from a DOM

Now that you know what a DOM looks like internally, you'll be better prepared to modify a DOM or construct one from scratch. Before going on to that, though, this section presents some modifications to the `JTreeModel` that let you produce a more user-friendly version of the `JTree` suitable for use in a GUI.

6.4.1 Compressing the Tree View

Displaying the DOM in tree form is all very well for experimenting and to learn how a DOM works. But it's not the kind of "friendly" display that most users want to see in a `JTree`. However, it turns out that very few modifications are needed to turn the `TreeModel` adapter into something that *will* present a user-friendly display. In this section, you'll make those modifications.

Note: The code discussed in this section is in `DomEcho03.java`. The file it operates on is `slideSample01.xml`. (The browsable version is `slideSample01-xml.html`.)

Make the Operation Selectable

When you modify the adapter, you're going to *compress* the view of the DOM, eliminating all but the nodes you really want to display. Start by defining a boolean variable that controls whether you want the compressed or uncompressed view of the DOM:

```
public class DomEcho extends JPanel
{
    static Document document;
     Boolean compress = true;
     static final int windowHeight = 460;
     ...
```

Identify "Tree" Nodes

The next step is to identify the nodes you want to show up in the tree. To do that, go to the area where you defined the names of all the element types (in the `typeName` array), and add the code highlighted below:

```
public class DomEcho extends JPanel
{
    ...

    public static void makeFrame() {
        ...
    }
    // An array of names for DOM node-type
    static String[] typeName = {
        ...
    };
    final int ELEMENT_TYPE =   1;
    // The list of elements to display in the tree
    static String[] treeElementNames = {
        "slideshow",
        "slide",
        "title",         // For slideshow #1
        "slide-title",   // For slideshow #10
        "item",
    };
```

```
Boolean treeElement(String elementName) {
    for (int i=0; i<treeElementNames.length; i++) {
        if ( elementName.equals(treeElementNames[i]) )
            return true;
    }
    return false;
}
```

With this code, you set up a constant you can use to identify the ELEMENT node type, declared the names of the elements you want in the tree, and created a method tells whether or not a given element name is a "tree element". Since slideSample01.xml has title elements and slideSample10.xml has slide-title elements, you set up the contents of this arrays so it would work with either data file.

Note: The mechanism you are creating here depends on the fact that *structure* nodes like slideshow and slide never contain text, while text usually does appear in *content* nodes like item. Although those "content" nodes may contain subelements in slideShow10.xml, the DTD constrains those subelements to be XHTML nodes. Because they are XHTML nodes (an XML version of HTML that is constrained to be well-formed), the entire sub-structure under an item node can be combined into a single string and displayed in the htmlPane that makes up the other half of the application window. In the second part of this section, you'll do that concatenation, displaying the text and XHTML as content in the htmlPane.

Control Node Visibility

The next step is to modify the AdapterNode's childCount function so that it only counts "tree element" nodes—nodes which are designated as displayable in the JTree. Make the modifications highlighted below to do that:

```
public class DomEcho extends JPanel
{
    ...
    public class AdapterNode
    {
        ...
        public AdapterNode child(int searchIndex) {
            ...
        }
        public int childCount() {
```

```
            if (!compress) {
                // Indent this
                return domNode.getChildNodes().getLength();
            }
            int count = 0;
            for (int i=0;
                i<domNode.getChildNodes().getLength(); i++) {
                org.w3c.dom.Node node =
                    domNode.getChildNodes().item(i);
                if (node.getNodeType() == ELEMENT_TYPE
                && treeElement( node.getNodeName() ))
                {
                    ++count;
                }
            }
            return count;
        }
    } // AdapterNode
```

The only tricky part about this code is checking to make sure the node is an element node before comparing the node. The DocType node makes that necessary, because it has the same name, "slideshow," as the `slideshow` element.

Control Child Access

Finally, you need to modify the `AdapterNode`'s child function to return the Nth item from the list of displayable nodes, rather than the Nth item from all nodes in the list. Add the code highlighted below to do that:

```
public class DomEcho extends JPanel
{
    ...
    public class AdapterNode
    {
        ...
        public int index(AdapterNode child) {
            ...
        }
        public AdapterNode child(int searchIndex) {
        //Note: JTree index is zero-based.
        org.w3c.dom.Node node =
            domNode.getChildNodes()Item(searchIndex);
```

```
            if (compress) {
                // Return Nth displayable node
                int elementNodeIndex = 0;
                for (int i=0;
                    i<domNode.getChildNodes().getLength(); i++) {
                    node = domNode.getChildNodes()Item(i);
                    if (node.getNodeType() == ELEMENT_TYPE
                    && treeElement( node.getNodeName() )
                    && elementNodeIndex++ == searchIndex) {
                        break;
                    }
                }
            }
            return new AdapterNode(node);
        } // child
    } // AdapterNode
```

There's nothing special going on here. It's a slightly modified version of the same logic you used when returning the child count.

Check the Results

When you compile and run this version of the app on `slideSample01.xml`, and then expand the nodes in the tree, you see the results shown in Figure 6.7. The only nodes remaining in the tree are the high-level "structure" nodes.

Extra Credit

The way the app stands now, the information that tells the app how to compress the tree for display is "hard-coded". Here are some ways you could consider extending the app:

Use a Command Line Argument

Whether you compress or don't compress the tree could be determined by a command line argument, rather than being a hard-coded Boolean variable. On the other hand, the list the list of elements that goes into the tree is still hard coded, so maybe that option doesn't make much sense, unless...

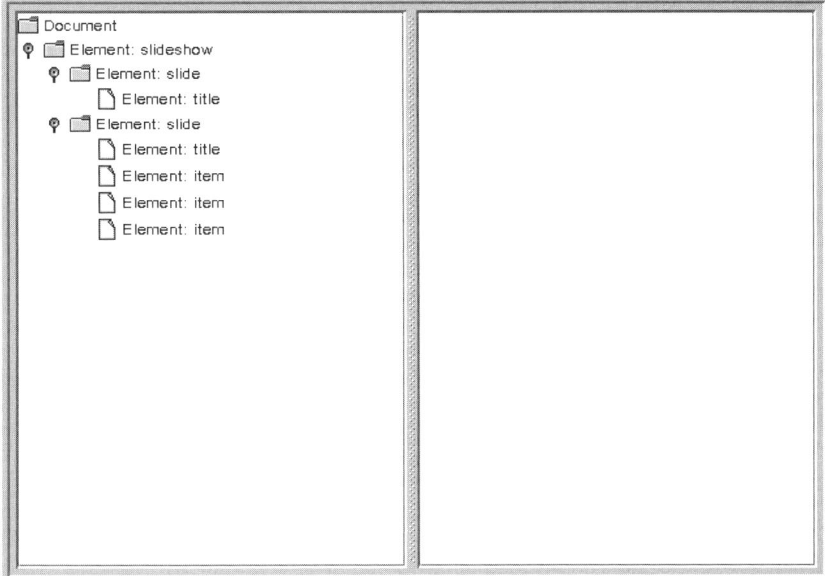

Figure 6.7 Tree View with a Collapsed Hierarchy

Read the TreeElement List from a File

If you read the list of elements to include in the tree from an external file, that would make the whole app command driven. That would be good. But wouldn't it be really nice to derive that information from the DTD or schema, instead? So you might want to consider...

Automatically Build the List

Watch out, though! As things stand right now, there are no standard DTD parsers! If you use a DTD, then, you'll need to write your parser to make sense out of its somewhat arcane syntax. You'll probably have better luck if you use a schema, instead of a DTD. The nice thing about schemas is that they use XML syntax, so you can use an XML parser to read the schema the same way you use any other file.

As you analyze the schema, note that the `JTree`-displayable *structure* nodes are those that have no text, while the *content* nodes may contain text and, optionally, XHTML subnodes. That distinction works for this example, and will likely work for a large body of real-world applications. It's pretty easy to construct cases that will create a problem, though, so you'll have to be on the lookout for schema/DTD specifications that embed non-XHTML elements in text-capable nodes, and take the appropriate action.

6.4.2 Acting on Tree Selections

Now that the tree is being displayed properly, the next step is to concatenate the subtrees under selected nodes to display them in the `htmlPane`. While you're at it, you'll use the concatenated text to put node-identifying information back in the `JTree`.

Note: The code discussed in this section is in `DomEcho04.java`.

Identify Node Types

When you concatenate the sub nodes under an element, the processing you do is going to depend on the type of node. So the first thing to is to define constants for the remaining node types. Add the code highlighted below to do that:

```
public class DomEcho extends JPanel
{
    ...
    // An array of names for DOM node-types
    static String[] typeName = {
        ...
    };
    static final int ELEMENT_TYPE =   1;
    static final int ATTR_TYPE =      2;
    static final int TEXT_TYPE =      3;
    static final int CDATA_TYPE =     4;
    static final int ENTITYREF_TYPE = 5;
    static final int ENTITY_TYPE =    6;
    static final int PROCINSTR_TYPE = 7;
    static final int COMMENT_TYPE =   8;
    static final int DOCUMENT_TYPE =  9;
    static final int DOCTYPE_TYPE =  10;
    static final int DOCFRAG_TYPE =  11;
    static final int NOTATION_TYPE = 12;
```

Concatenate Subnodes to Define Element Content

Next, you need to define the method that concatenates the text and subnodes for an element and returns it as the element's "content." To define the `content` method, you'll need to add the big chunk of code highlighted below, but this is the last big chunk of code in the DOM tutorial!

```
public class DomEcho extends JPanel
{
    ...
    public class AdapterNode
    {
        ...
        public String toString() {
        ...
        }
        public String content() {
            String s = "";
            org.w3c.dom.NodeList nodeList =
                domNode.getChildNodes();
            for (int i=0; i<nodeList.getLength(); i++) {
                org.w3c.dom.Node node = nodeList.item(i);
                int type = node.getNodeType();
                AdapterNode adpNode = new AdapterNode(node);
                if (type == ELEMENT_TYPE) {
                    if ( treeElement(node.getNodeName()) )
                        continue;
                    s += "<" + node.getNodeName() + ">";
                    s += adpNode.content();
                    s += "</" + node.getNodeName() + ">";
                } else if (type == TEXT_TYPE) {
                    s += node.getNodeValue();
                } else if (type == ENTITYREF_TYPE) {
                    // The content is in the TEXT node under it
                    s += adpNode.content();
                } else if (type == CDATA_TYPE) {
                    StringBuffer sb = new StringBuffer(
                        node.getNodeValue() );
                    for (int j=0; j<sb.length(); j++) {
                        if (sb.charAt(j) == '<') {
                            sb.setCharAt(j, '&');
```

```
                    sb.insert(j+1, "lt;");
                    j += 3;
                } else if (sb.charAt(j) == '&') {
                    sb.setCharAt(j, '&');
                    sb.insert(j+1, "amp;");
                    j += 4;
                }
            }
            s += "<pre>" + sb + "</pre>";
        }
    }
    return s;
}
...
} // AdapterNode
```

This is not the most efficient code anyone ever wrote, but it works and will do fine for our purposes. In this code, you are recognizing and dealing with the following data types:

Element

For elements with names like the XHTML "em" node, you return the node's content sandwiched between the appropriate `<em>` and `</em>` tags. However, when processing the content for the `slideshow` element, for example, you don't include tags for the `slide` elements it contains so, when returning a node's content, you skip any subelements that are themselves displayed in the tree.

Text

No surprise here. For a text node, you simply return the node's `value`.

Entity Reference

Unlike CDATA nodes, Entity References can contain multiple subelements. So the strategy here is to return the concatenation of those subelements.

CDATA

Like a text node, you return the node's `value`. However, since the text in this case may contain angle brackets and ampersands, you need to convert them to a form that displays properly in an HTML pane. Unlike the XML CDATA tag, the HTML <pre> tag does not prevent the parsing of character-format tags, break tags and the like. So you have to convert left-angle brackets (<) and ampersands (&) to get them to display properly.

On the other hand, there are quite a few node types you are *not* processing with the code above. It's worth a moment to examine them and understand why:

Attribute

These nodes do not appear in the DOM, but are obtained by invoking `getAttributes` on element nodes.

Entity

These nodes also do not appear in the DOM. They are obtained by invoking `getEntities` on `DocType` nodes.

Processing Instruction

These nodes don't contain displayable data.

Comment

Ditto. Nothing you want to display here.

Document

This is the root node for the DOM. There's no data to display for that.

DocType

The `DocType` node contains the DTD specification, with or without external pointers. It only appears under the root node, and has no data to display in the tree.

Document Fragment

This node is equivalent to a document node. It's a root node that the DOM specification intends for holding intermediate results during cut/paste operations, for example. Like a document node, there's no data to display.

Notation

We're just flat out ignoring this one. These nodes are used to include binary data in the DOM. As discussed earlier in Referencing Binary Entities (page 128) and , the MIME types (in conjunction with namespaces) make a better mechanism for that.

Display the Content in the JTree

With the content-concatenation out of the way, only a few small programming steps remain. The first is to modify `toString` so that it uses the node's content for identifying information. Add the code highlighted below to do that:

```
public class DomEcho extends JPanel
{
    ...
    public class AdapterNode
    {
        ...
        public String toString() {
            ...
            if (! nodeName.startsWith("#")) {
                s += ": " + nodeName;
            }
            if (compress) {
                String t = content().trim();
                int x = t.indexOf(");
                if (x >= 0) t = t.substring(0, x);
                s += " " + t;
                return s;
            }
            if (domNode.getNodeValue() != null) {
                ...
            }
            return s;
        }
```

Wire the JTree to the JEditorPane

Returning now to the app's constructor, create a tree selection listener and use to wire the `JTree` to the `JEditorPane`:

```
public class DomEcho extends JPanel
{
    ...
    public DomEcho()
    {
        ...
        // Build right-side view
        JEditorPane htmlPane = new JEditorPane("text/html","");
        htmlPane.setEditable(false);
        JScrollPane htmlView = new JScrollPane(htmlPane);
        htmlView.setPreferredSize(
            new Dimension( rightWidth, windowHeight ));
         tree.addTreeSelectionListener(
            new TreeSelectionListener() {
                public void valueChanged(TreeSelectionEvent e)
                {
                    TreePath p = e.getNewLeadSelectionPath();
                    if (p != null) {
                        AdapterNode adpNode =
                            (AdapterNode)
                                p.getLastPathComponent();
                        htmlPane.setText(adpNode.content());
                    }
                }
            }
        );
```

Now, when a `JTree` node is selected, its contents are delivered to the `htmlPane`.

Note: The `TreeSelectionListener` in this example is created using an anonymous inner-class adapter. If you are programming for the 1.1 version of the platform, you'll need to define an external class for this purpose.

If you compile this version of the app, you'll discover immediately that the `htmlPane` needs to be specified as `final` to be referenced in an inner class, so add the keyword highlighted below:

```
public DomEcho04()
{
    ...
```

```
// Build right-side view
final JEditorPane htmlPane = new
    JEditorPane("text/html","");
htmlPane.setEditable(false);
JScrollPane htmlView = new JScrollPane(htmlPane);
htmlView.setPreferredSize(
    new Dimension( rightWidth, windowHeight ));
```

Run the App

When you compile the app and run it on `slideSample10.xml` (the browsable version is `slideSample10-xml.html`), you get a display like that shown in Figure 6.8. Expanding the hierarchy shows that the `JTree` now includes identifying text for a node whenever possible.

Selecting an item that includes XHTML subelements produces a display like that shown in Figure 6.9.

Selecting a node that contains an entity reference causes the entity text to be included, as shown in Figure 6.10.

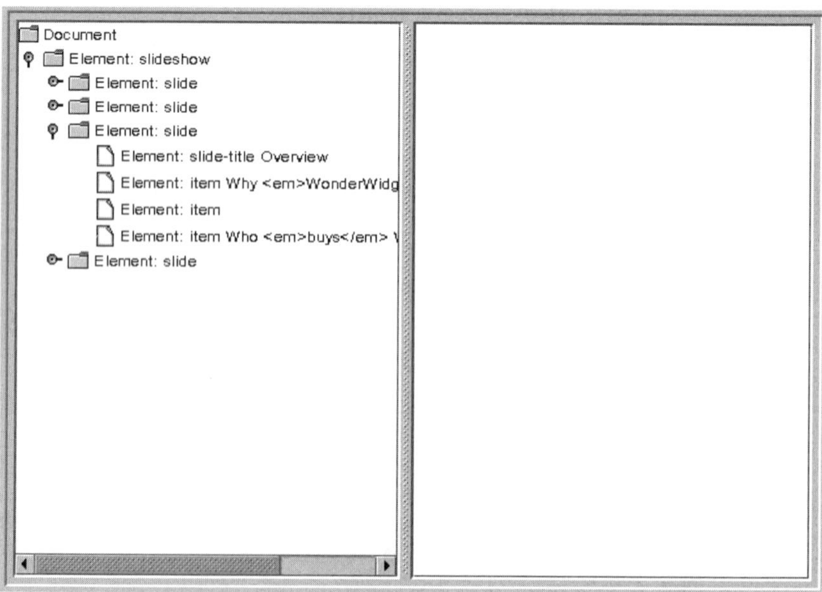

Figure 6.8 Collapsed Hierarchy Showing Text in Nodes

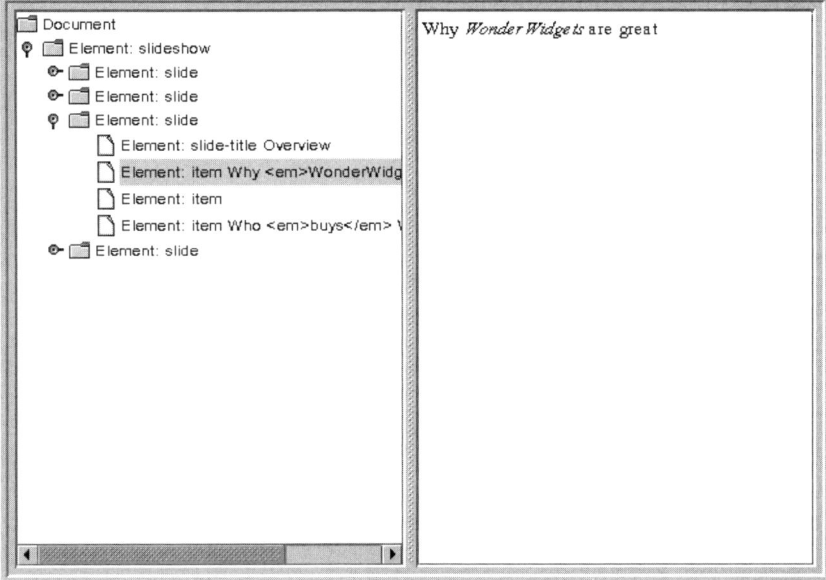

Figure 6.9 Node with <em> Tag Selected

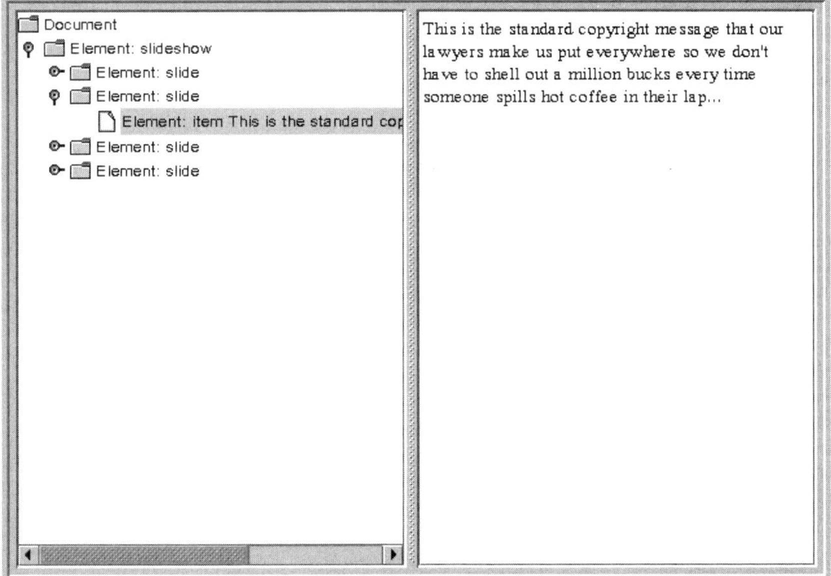

Figure 6.10 Node with Entity Reference Selected

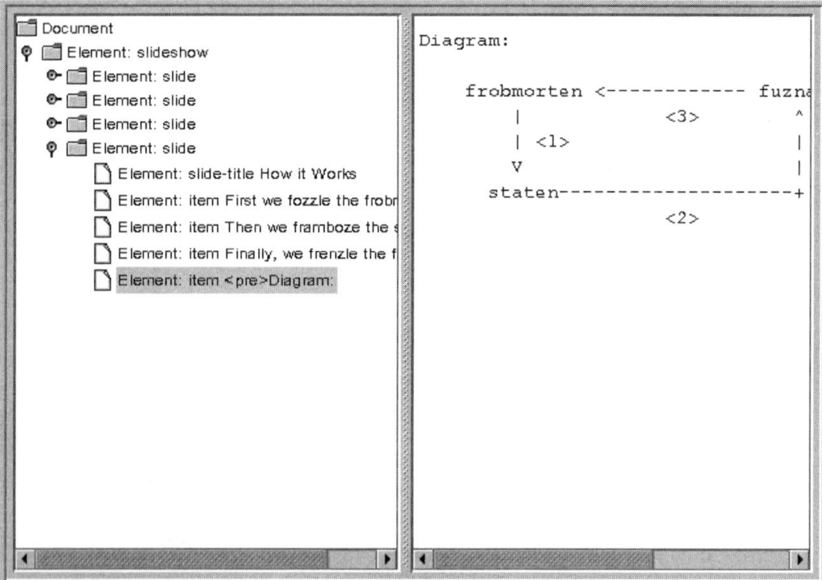

Figure 6.11 Node with CDATA Component Selected

Finally, selecting a node that includes a CDATA section produces results like those shown in Figure 6.11.

Extra Credit

Now that you have the app working, here are some ways you might think about extending it in the future:

Use Title Text to Identify Slides

Special case the `slide` element so that the contents of the `title` node is used as the identifying text. When selected, convert the title node's contents to a centered `H1` tag, and ignore the `title` element when constructing the tree.

Convert Item Elements to Lists

Remove `item` elements from the `JTree` and convert them to HTML lists using `<ul>`, `<li>`, `</ul>` tags, including them in the slide's content when the slide is selected.

6.4.3 Handling Modifications

A full discussion of the mechanisms for modifying the `JTree`'s underlying data model is beyond the scope of this tutorial. However, a few words on the subject are in order.

Most importantly, note that if you allow the user to modifying the structure by manipulating the `JTree`, you have take the compression into account when you figure out where to apply the change. For example, if you are displaying text in the tree and the user modifies that, the changes would have to be applied to text subelements, and perhaps require a rearrangement of the XHTML subtree.

When you make those changes, you'll need to understand more about the interactions between a `JTree`, it's `TreeModel`, and an underlying data model. That subject is covered in depth in the Swing Connection article, *Understanding the TreeModel*.

6.4.4 Finishing Up

You now understand pretty much what there is to know about the structure of a DOM, and you know how to adapt a DOM to create a user-friendly display in a `JTree`. It has taken quite a bit of coding, but in return you have obtained valuable tools for exposing a DOM's structure and a template for GUI apps. In the next section, you'll make a couple of minor modifications to the code that turn the app into a vehicle for experimentation, and then experiment with building and manipulating a DOM.

6.5 Creating and Manipulating a DOM

By now, you understand the structure of the nodes that make up a DOM. A DOM is actually very easy to create. This section of the DOM tutorial is going to take much less work than anything you've see up to now. All the foregoing work, however, generated the basic understanding that will make this section a piece of cake.

6.5.1 Obtaining a DOM from the Factory

In this version of the application, you're still going to create a document builder factory, but this time you're going to tell it create a new DOM instead of parsing an existing XML document. You'll keep all the existing functionality intact, however, and add the new functionality in such a way that you can "flick a switch" to get back the parsing behavior.

Note: The code discussed in this section is in `DomEcho05.java`.

Modify the Code

Start by turning off the compression feature. As you work with the DOM in this section, you're going to want to see all the nodes:

```
public class DomEcho05  extends JPanel
{
    ...
    boolean compress = true;
    boolean compress = false;
```

Next, you need to create a `buildDom` method that creates the `document` object. The easiest way to do that is to create the method and then copy the DOM-construction section from the `main` method to create the `buildDom`. The modifications shown below show you the changes you need to make to make that code suitable for the `buildDom` method.

```
public class DomEcho05  extends JPanel
{
    ...
    public static void makeFrame() {
        ...
    }
    public static void buildDom()
    {
        DocumentBuilderFactory factory =
DocumentBuilderFactory.newInstance();
        try {
            DocumentBuilder builder = factory.newDocumentBuilder();
            document = builder.parse( new File(argv[0]) );
           document = builder.newDocument();  // Create from whole
cloth
         } catch (SAXException sxe) {
            ...
         } catch (ParserConfigurationException pce) {
            // Parser with specified options can't be built
            pce.printStackTrace();
         } catch (IOException ioe) {
            ...
        }
    }
```

In this code, you replaced the line that does the parsing with one that creates a DOM. Then, since the code is no longer parsing an existing file, you removed exceptions which are no longer thrown: SAXException and IOException.

And since you are going to be working with Element objects, add the statement to import that class at the top of the program:

```
import org.w3c.dom.Document;
import org.w3c.dom.DOMException;
import org.w3c.dom.Element;
```

Create Element and Text Nodes

Now, for your first experiment, add the Document operations to create a root node and several children:

```
public class DomEcho05  extends JPanel
{
    ...
    public static void buildDom()
    {
        DocumentBuilderFactory factory =
            DocumentBuilderFactory.newInstance();
        try {
            DocumentBuilder builder =
                factory.newDocumentBuilder();
            document = builder.newDocument();
            // Create from whole cloth
             Element root =
                (Element)
                    document.createElement("rootElement");
            document.appendChild(root);
            root.appendChild(
                document.createTextNode("Some") );
            root.appendChild(
                document.createTextNode(" ")    );
            root.appendChild(
                document.createTextNode("text") );
        } catch (ParserConfigurationException pce) {
            // Parser with specified options can't be built
            pce.printStackTrace();
        }
    }
```

Finally, modify the argument-list checking code at the top of the `main` method so you invoke `buildDom` and `makeFrame` instead of generating an error, as shown below:

```
public class DomEcho05  extends JPanel
{
    ...
    public static void main(String argv[])
    {
        if (argv.length != 1) {
            System.err.println("Usage: java DomEcho filename");
            System.exit(1);
            buildDom();
            makeFrame();
            return;
        }
```

That's all there is to it! Now, if you supply an argument the specified file is parsed and, if you don't, the experimental code that builds a DOM is executed.

Run the App

Compiling and running the program with no arguments will produce the result shown in Figure 6.12.

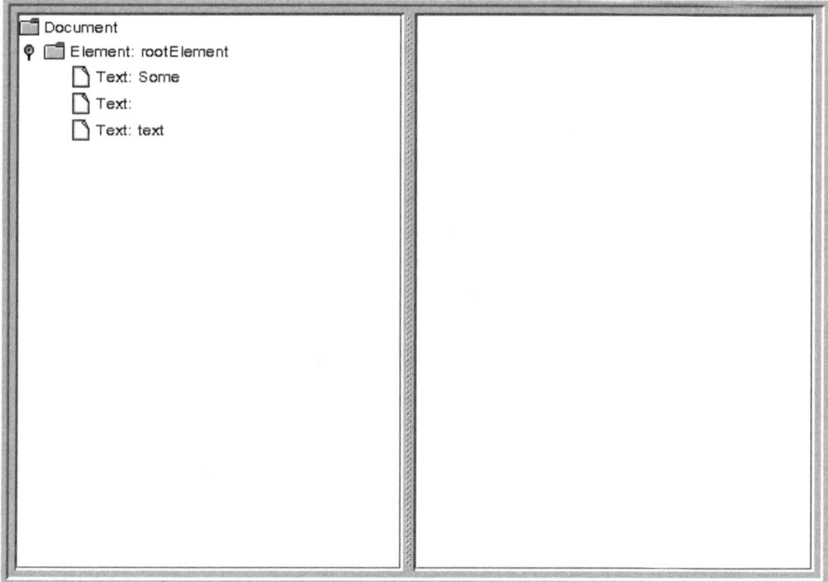

Figure 6.12 Element Node and Text Nodes Created

6.5.2 Normalizing the DOM

In this experiment, you'll manipulate the DOM you created by normalizing it after it has been constructed.

Note: The code discussed in this section is in `DomEcho06.java`.

Add the code highlighted below to normalize the DOM:

```
public static void buildDom()
{
    DocumentBuilderFactory factory =
DocumentBuilderFactory.newInstance();
    try {
        ...
        root.appendChild( document.createTextNode("Some") );
        root.appendChild( document.createTextNode(" ")    );
        root.appendChild( document.createTextNode("text") );
        document.getDocumentElement().normalize();
    } catch (ParserConfigurationException pce) {
          ...
```

In this code, `getDocumentElement` returns the document's root node, and the `normalize` operation manipulates the tree under it.

When you compile and run the app now, the result looks like Figure 6.13.

Here, you can see that the adjacent text nodes have been combined into a single node. The normalize operation is one that you will typically want to use after making modifications to a DOM, to ensure that the resulting DOM is as compact as possible.

Note: Now that you have this program to experiment with, see what happens to other combinations of `CDATA`, entity references, and text nodes when you normalize the tree.

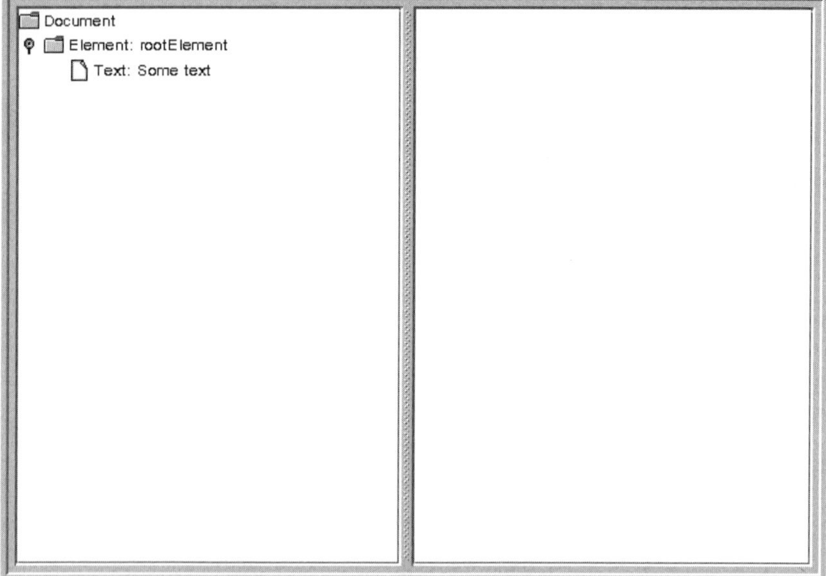

Figure 6.13 Text Nodes Merged After Normalization

6.5.3 Other Operations

To complete this section, we'll take a quick look at some of the other operations you might want to apply to a DOM, including:

- Traversing nodes
- Creating attributes
- Removing nodes

Traversing Nodes

The `org.w3c.dom.Node` interface defines a number of methods you can use to traverse nodes, including `getFirstChild`, `getLastChild`, `getNextSibling`, `getPreviousSibling`, and `getParentNode`. Those operations are sufficient to get from anywhere in the tree to any other location in the tree.

Creating Attributes

The `org.w3c.dom.Element` interface, which extends Node, defines a `setAttribute` operation, which adds an attribute to that node. (A better name from the Java platform standpoint would have been `addAttribute`, since the attribute is not a property of the class, and since a new object is created.)

You can also use the `Document`'s `createAttribute` operation to create an instance of `Attribute`, and use an overloaded version of `setAttribute` to add that.

Removing and Changing Nodes

To remove a node, you use its parent `Node`'s `removeChild` method. To change it, you can either use the parent node's `replaceChild` operation or the node's `setNodeValue` operation.

6.5.4 Finishing Up

Congratulations! You've learned how a DOM is structured and how to manipulate it. And you now have a DomEcho application that you can use to display a DOM's structure, condense it down to GUI-compatible dimensions, and experiment with to see how various operations affect the structure. Have fun with it!

6.6 Using Namespaces

As you saw previously, one way or another it is necessary to resolve the conflict between the `title` element defined in `slideshow.dtd` and the one defined in `xhtml.dtd`. In the previous exercise, you hyphenated the name in order to put it into a different "namespace". In this section, you'll see how to use the XML namespace standard to do the same thing without renaming the element.

Note: At this point in time, the Java XML parsers do not support namespaces. This section is for information only.

The primary goal of the namespace specification is to let the document author tell the parser which DTD to use when parsing a given element. The parser can then consult the appropriate DTD for an element definition. Of course, it is also important to keep the parser from aborting when a "duplicate" definition is found, and yet still generate an error if the document references an element like `title` without *qualifying* it (identifying the DTD to use for the definition).

Note: Namespaces apply to attributes as well as to elements. In this section, we consider only elements. For more information on attributes, consult the namespace specification at `http://www.w3.org/TR/REC-xml-names/`.

6.6.1 Defining a Namespace

To define a namespace that an element belongs to, it is necessary to add an attribute to the element's definition, where the attribute name is `xmlns` ("xml namespace"). For example, you could do that in `slideshow.dtd` by adding an entry like the following in the `title` element's attribute-list definition:

```
<!ELEMENT title (%inline;)*>
<!ATTLIST title
    xmlns CDATA #FIXED "http://www.example.com/slideshow"
>
```

Declaring the attribute as `FIXED` has several important features:

- It prevents the document from specifying any non-matching value for the `xmlns` attribute (as described in Defining Attributes in the DTD (page 122)).
- The element defined in this DTD is made unique (because the parser understands the `xmlns` attribute), so it does not conflict with an element that has the same name in another DTD. That allows multiple DTDs to use the same element name without generating a parser error.
- When a document specifies the `xmlns` attribute for a tag, the document selects the element definition with a matching attribute.

To be thorough, every element name in your DTD would get the exact same attribute, with the same value. (Here, though, we're only concerned about the `title` element.) Note, too, that you are using a `CDATA` string to supply the URI. In this case, we've specified an URL. But you could also specify a URN, possibly by specifying a prefix like `urn:` instead of `http:`. (URNs are currently being researched. They're not seeing a lot of action at the moment, but that could change in the future.)

6.6.2 Referencing a Namespace

When a document uses an element name that exists in only one of the `.dtd` files it references, the name does not need to be qualified. But when an element name that has multiple definitions is used, some sort of qualification is a necessity.

Note: In point of fact, an element name is always qualified by its *default namespace*, as defined by name of the DTD file it resides in. As long as there as is only one definition for the name, the qualification is implicit.

You qualify a reference to an element name by specifying the `xmlns` attribute, as shown here:

```
<title xmlns="http://www.example.com/slideshow">
    Overview
</title>
```

The specified namespace applies to that element, and to any elements contained within it.

6.6.3 Defining a Namespace Prefix

When you only need one namespace reference, it's not such a big deal. But when you need to make the same reference several times, adding `xmlns` attributes becomes unwieldy. It also makes it harder to change the name of the namespace at a later date.

The alternative is to define a *namespace prefix*, which is as simple as specifying xmlns, a colon (:) and the prefix name before the attribute value, as shown here:

```
<sl:slideshow xmlns:SL='http:/www.example.com/slideshow'
        ...>
    ...
</SL:slideshow>
```

This definition sets up `SL` as a prefix that can be used to qualify the current element name and any element within it. Since the prefix can be used on any of the contained elements, it makes the most sense to define it on the XML document's root element, as shown here.

Note: The namespace URI can contain characters that are not valid in an XML name, so it cannot be used as a prefix directly. The prefix definition associates an XML name with the URI, which allows the prefix name to be used instead. It also makes it easier to change references to the URI in the future.

When the prefix is used to qualify an element name, the end-tag also includes the prefix, as highlighted here:

```
<SL:slideshow xmlns:SL='http:/www.example.com/slideshow'
          ...>
   ...
   <slide>
      <SL:title>Overview<SL:title>
   </slide>
   ...
</SL:slideshow>
```

Finally, note that multiple prefixes can be defined in the same element, as shown here:

```
<SL:slideshow xmlns:SL='http:/www.example.com/slideshow'
          xmlns:xhtml='urn:...'>
   ...
</SL:slideshow>
```

With this kind of arrangement, all of the prefix definitions are together in one place, and you can use them anywhere they are needed in the document. This example also suggests the use of URN to define the xhtml prefix, instead of a URL. That definition would conceivably allow the app to reference a local copy of the XHTML DTD or some mirrored version, with a potentially beneficial impact on performance.

CHAPTER 7

XML Stylesheet Language for Transformations

Eric Armstrong

In This Chapter

THE XML Stylesheet Language for Transformations (XSLT) defines mechanisms for addressing XML data (XPath) and for specifying transformations on the data, in order to convert it into other forms. In this chapter, you'll learn how to use XSLT to write out a DOM as an XML file. You'll also see how to generate a DOM from an arbitrary data file in order to convert it to XML. Finally, you'll use XSLT to convert XML data into a different form, unlocking the mysteries of the XPath addressing mechanism along the way.

In this chapter, you'll parse an existing XML file to construct a DOM, display and inspect the DOM hierarchy, convert the DOM into a user-friendly JTree, and explore the syntax of namespaces. You'll also create a DOM from scratch, and see how to use some of the implementation-specific features in Sun's JAXP reference implementation to convert an existing data set to XML.

Note: The examples in this chapter can be found in `docs/tutorial/examples/jaxp/xslt/samples`.

7.1 Introducing XSLT and XPath

The XML Stylesheet Language (XSL) has three major subcomponents:

XSL-FO

The "flow object" standard. By far the largest subcomponent, this standard gives mechanisms for describing font sizes, page layouts, and how information "flows" from one page to another. This subcomponent is *not* covered by JAXP, nor is it included in this tutorial.

XSLT

This the transformation language, which lets you transform XML into some other format. For example, you might use XSLT to produce HTML, or a different XML structure. You could even use it to produce plain text or to put the information in some other document format. (And as you'll see in Generating XML from an Arbitrary Data Structure, a clever application can press it into service to manipulate non-XML data, as well.)

XPath

XSLT is a language that lets you specify what sorts of things to do when a particular element is encountered. But to write a program for different parts of an XML data structure, you need to be able to specify the part of the structure you are talking about at any given time. XPath is that specification language. It is an addressing mechanism that lets you specify a path to an element so, for example, `<article><title>` can be distinguished from `<person><title>`. That way, you can describe different kinds of translations for the different `<title>` elements.

The remainder of this section describes the XSLT package structure, and discusses the XPath addressing mechanism in a bit more depth.

7.1.1 The XSLT Packages

There XSLT packages break down as follows:

`javax.xml.transform`

This package defines the factory class you use to get a `Transformer` object. You then configure the transformer with input (Source) and output (Result) objects, and invoke its `transform()` method to make the transformation happen. The source and result objects are created using classes from one of the other three packages.

`javax.xml.transform.dom`

Defines the `DOMSource` and `DOMResult` classes that let you use a DOM as an input to or output from a transformation.

`javax.xml.transform.sax`

Defines the `SAXSource` and `SAXResult` classes that let you use a SAX event generator as input to a transformation, or deliver SAX events as output to a SAX event processor.

`javax.xml.transform.stream`

Defines the `StreamSource` and `StreamResult` classes that let you use an I/O stream as an input to or output from a transformation.

7.1.2 How XPath Works

The XPath specification is the foundation for a variety of specifications, including XSLT and linking/addressing specifications like XPointer. So an understanding of XPath is fundamental to a lot of advanced XML usage. This section provides a thorough introduction to XSLT, so you can refer to it as needed later on.

Note: In this tutorial, you won't actually use XPath until you get to the last page of this section, Transforming XML Data with XSLT (page 233). So, if you like, you can skip this section and go on ahead to the next page, Writing Out a DOM as an XML File (page 214). (When you get to the last page, there will be a note that refers you back here, so you don't forget!)

In general, an XPath expression specifies a *pattern* that selects a set of XML nodes. XSLT templates then use those patterns when applying transformations. (XPointer, on the other hand, adds mechanisms for defining a *point* or a *range*, so that XPath expressions can be used for addressing.)

The nodes in an XPath expression refer to more than just elements. They also refer to text and attributes, among other things. In fact, the XPath specification defines an abstract document model that defines seven different kinds of nodes:

- root
- element
- text
- attribute
- comment
- processing instruction
- namespace

Note: The root element of the XML data is modeled by an *element* node. The XPath root node contains the document's root element, as well as other information relating to the document.

The data model is described in the last section of the XPath Specification, Section 5. (Like many specifications, it is frequently helpful to start reading near the end! Frequently, many of the important terms and underlying assumptions are documented there. That sequence has often been the "magic key" that unlocks the contents of a W3C specification.)

In this abstract model, syntactic distinctions disappear, and you are left with a normalized view of the data. In a text node, for example, it makes no difference whether the text was defined in a CDATA section, or if it included entity references. The text node will consist of normalized data, as it exists after all parsing is complete. So the text will contain a < character, regardless of whether an entity reference like `<` or a CDATA section was used to include it (similarly for the & character).

In this section of the tutorial, we'll deal mostly with element nodes and text nodes. For the other addressing mechanisms, see the XPath Specification.

Basic XPath Addressing

An XML document is a tree-structured (hierarchical) collection of nodes. Like a hierarchical directory structure, it is useful to specify a *path* that points a particular node in the hierarchy. (Hence the name of the specification: XPath). In fact, much of the notation of directory paths is carried over intact:

- The forward slash / is used as a path separator.
- An absolute path from the root of the document starts with a /.
- A relative path from a given location starts with anything else.
- A double period `..` indicates the parent of the current node.
- A single period `.` indicates the current node.

In an xHTML document, for example, the path `/h1/h2/` would indicate an h2 element under an h1. (Recall that in XML, element names are case sensitive, so this kind of specification works much better in xHTML than it would in HTML.)

In a pattern-matching specification like XSLT, the specification `/h1/h2` selects *all* h2 elements that lie under an h1 element. To select a specific h2 element, square brackets `[]` are used for indexing (like those used for arrays). The path `/h1[4]/h2[5]` would therefore select the fifth h2 element under the fourth h1 element.

Note: In xHTML, all element names are in lowercase. But as a matter of style, uppercase names are easier to read and easier to write about. (Although they are admittedly harder to write.) For the remainder of XPATH tutorial, then, and for the section on using XSLT transforms, all XML element names will be in uppercase. (Attribute names, on the other hand, will remain in lowercase.)

As you've seen, a name in XPath specification refers to an element. To refer to attribute, you prefix its name with an `@` sign. For example, `@type` refers to the `type` attribute of an element. Assuming you have an XML document with `list` elements, for example, the expression `list/@type` selects the `type` attribute of the `list` element.

Note: (Since the expression does not begin with /, the reference specifies a list node relative to the current context—whatever position in the document that happens to be.)

Basic XPath Expressions

The full range of XPath expressions takes advantage of the wildcards, operators, and functions that XPath defines. You'll be learning more about those shortly. Here, we'll take a look at a couple of the most common XPath expressions, simply to introduce the concept.

The expression `@type="unordered"` specifies an attribute named type whose value is "unordered." So an expression like `LIST/@type` specifies the `type attribute` of a `LIST` element.

But now for something a little different! In XPath, the square-bracket notation (`[]`) normally associated with indexing is extended to specify selection-criteria. For example, the expression `LIST[@type="unordered"]` selects all `LIST` elements whose `type` value is "unordered."

Similar expressions exist for elements, where each element has an associated *string-value*. (You'll see how the string-value is determined for a complicated element in a little while. For now, we'll stick with super-simple elements that have a single text string.)

Suppose you model what's going on in your organization with an XML structure that consists of `PROJECT` elements and `ACTIVITY` elements that have a text string with the project name, multiple `PERSON` elements to list the people involved and, optionally, a `STATUS` element that records the projects status. Here are some more examples that use the extended square-bracket notation:

- `/PROJECT[.="MyProject"]`—selects a `PROJECT` named "MyProject."
- `/PROJECT[STATUS]`—selects all projects that have a `STATUS` child element.
- `/PROJECT[STATUS="Critical"]`—selects all projects that have a STATUS child element with the string-value "Critical."

Combining Index Addresses

The XPath specification defines quite a few addressing mechanisms, and they can be combined in many different ways. As a result, XPath delivers a lot of expressive power for a relatively simple specification. This section illustrates two more interesting combinations:

- `LIST[@type="ordered"][3]`—selects all LIST elements of type "ordered," and returns the third.
- `LIST[3][@type="ordered"]`—selects the third LIST element, but only if it is of "ordered" type.

Note: Many more combinations of address operators are listed in section 2.5 of the XPath Specification. This is arguably the most useful section of the spec for defining an XSLT transform.

Wildcards

By definition, an unqualified XPath expression selects a set of XML nodes that matches that specified pattern. For example, `/HEAD` matches all top-level `HEAD` entries, while `/HEAD[1]` matches only the first. Table 7.1 lists the wildcards that can be used in XPath expressions to broaden the scope of the pattern matching.

Table 7.1 XPath Wildcards

*	matches any element node (not attributes or text)
`node()`	matches all nodes of any kind: element nodes, text nodes, attribute nodes, processing instruction nodes, namespace nodes, and comment nodes
@*	matches all attribute nodes

In the project database example, for instance, `/*/PERSON[.="Fred"]` matches any `PROJECT` or `ACTIVITY` element that includes Fred.

Extended-Path Addressing

So far, all of the patterns we've seen have specified an exact number of levels in the hierarchy. For example, `/HEAD` specifies any `HEAD` element at the first level in the hierarchy, while /*/* specifies any element at the second level in the hierarchy. To specify an indeterminate level in the hierarchy, use a double forward slash (//). For example, the XPath expression `//PARA` selects all `paragraph` elements in a document, wherever they may be found.

The // pattern can also be used within a path. So the expression `/HEAD/LIST//PARA` indicates all paragraph elements in a subtree that begins from `/HEAD/LIST`.

XPath Data Types and Operators

XPath expressions yield either a set of nodes, a string, a boolean (true/false value), or a number. Table 7.2 lists the operations that can be applied in an Xpath expressions.

Table 7.2 XPath Operators

|	Alternative. So `PARA|LIST` selects all `PARA` and `LIST` elements.
or, and	Returns the or/and of two boolean values.
=, !=	Equal or not equal, for booleans, strings, and numbers.
<, >, <=, >=	Less than, greater than, less than or equal to, greater than or equal to—for numbers.
+, -, *, div, mod	Add, subtract, multiply, floating-point divide, and modulus (remainder) operations (e.g., 6 mod 4 = 2)

Finally, expressions can be grouped in parentheses, so you don't have to worry about operator precedence. (Which, for those of you who are good at such things, is roughly the same as that shown in the table.)

String-Value of an Element

Before going on, it's worthwhile to understand how the string-value of more complex element is determined. We'll do that now.

The string-value of an element is the concatenation of all descendant text nodes, no matter how deep. So, for a "mixed-model" XML data element like this:

```
<PARA>This_paragraph_contains_a_<B>bold</B>_word</PARA>
```

The string-value of `<PARA>` is "This paragraph contains a bold word." In particular, note that `<B>` is a child of `<PARA>` and that the text contained in all children is concatenated to form the string-value.

Also, it is worth understanding that the text in the abstract data model defined by XPath is fully normalized. So whether the XML structure contains the entity reference "`<`" or "<" in a CDATA section, the element's string-value will contain the "<" character. Therefore, when generating HTML or XML with an XSLT stylesheet, occurrences of "<" will have to be converted to `<` or enclosed in a CDATA section. Similarly, occurrences of "&" will need to be converted to `&`.

XPath Functions

This section ends with an overview of the XPath functions. You can use XPath functions to select a collection of nodes in the same way that you would use an element-specification. Other functions return a string, a number, or a boolean value. For example, the expression `/PROJECT/text()` gets the string-value of project nodes.

Many functions depend on the current context. In the example above, the *context* for each invocation of the `text()` function is the `PROJECT` node that is currently selected.

There are many XPath functions—too many to describe in detail here. This section provides a quick listing that shows the available XPath functions, along with a summary of what they do.

Note: Skim the list of functions to get an idea of what's there. For more information, see section 4 of the XPath Specification.

Node-Set Functions

Many XPath expressions select a set of nodes. In essence, they return a *node-set*. One function does that, too.

- `id(...)`—returns the node with the specified id.

(Elements only have an ID when the document has a DTD, which specifies which attribute has the `ID` type.)

Positional Functions

These functions return positionally-based numeric values.

- `last()`—returns the index of the last element. Ex: `/HEAD[last()]` selects the last `HEAD` element.
- `position()`—returns the index position. Ex: `/HEAD[position() <= 5]` selects the first five `HEAD` elements.
- `count(...)`—returns the count of elements. Ex: `/HEAD[count(HEAD)=0]` selects all `HEAD` elements that have no subheads.

String Functions

These functions operate on or return strings.

- `concat(string, string, ...)`—concatenates the string values
- `starts-with(string1, string2)`—returns true if string1 starts with string2
- `contains(string1, string2)`—returns true if string1 contains string2
- `substring-before(string1, string2)`—returns the start of string1 before string2 occurs in it
- `substring-after(string1, string2)`—returns the remainder of string1 after string2 occurs in it
- `substring(string, idx)`—returns the substring from the index position to the end, where the index of the first char = 1
- `substring(string, idx, len)`—returns the substring from the index position, of the specified length
- `string-length()`—returns the size of the context-node's string-value

- `string-length(string)`—returns the size of the specified string
- `normalize-space()`—returns the normalized string-value of the current node (no leading or trailing whitespace, and sequences of whitespace characters converted to a single space)
- `normalize-space(string)`—returns the normalized string-value of the specified string
- `translate(string1, string2, string3)`—converts string1, replacing occurrences of characters in string2 with the corresponding character from string3

Note: XPath defines three ways to get the text of an element: `text()`, `string(object)`, and the string-value implied by an element name in an expression like this: `/PROJECT[PERSON="Fred"]`.

Boolean Functions

These functions operate on or return boolean values:

- `not(...)`—negates the specified boolean value
- `true()`—returns true
- `false()`—returns false
- `lang(string)`—returns true if the language of the context node (specified by `xml:Lang` attributes) is the same as (or a sublanguage of) the specified language. Ex: `Lang("en")` is true for `<PARA_xml:Lang="en">...</PARA>`

Numeric Functions

These functions operate on or return numeric values.

- `sum(...)`—returns the sum of the numeric value of each node in the specified node-set
- `floor(N)`—returns the largest integer that is not greater than N
- `ceiling(N)`—returns the smallest integer that is greater than N
- `round(N)`—returns the integer that is closest to N

Conversion Functions

These functions convert one data type to another.

- `string(...)`—returns the string value of a number, boolean, or node-set
- `boolean(...)`—returns the boolean-equivalent for a number, string, or node-set

(a non-zero number, a non-empty node-set, and a non-empty string are all true)

- `number(...)`—returns the numeric value of a boolean, string, or node-set

(true is 1, false is 0, a string containing a number becomes that number, the string-value of a node-set is converted to a number)

Namespace Functions

These functions let you determine the namespace characteristics of a node.

- `local-name()`—returns the name of the current node, minus the namespace-extension
- `local-name(...)`—returns the name of the first node in the specified node set, minus the namespace-extension
- `namespace-uri()`—returns the namespace URI from the current node
- `namespace-uri(...)`—returns the namespace URI from the first node in the specified node set
- `name()`—returns the expanded name (URI + local name) of the current node
- `name(...)`—returns the expanded name (URI + local name) of the first node in the specified node set

7.1.3 Summary

XPath operators, functions, wildcards, and node-addressing mechanisms can be combined in wide variety of ways. The introduction you've had so far should give you a good head start at specifying the pattern you need for any particular purpose.

7.2 Writing Out a DOM as an XML File

Once you have constructed a DOM, either by parsing an XML file or building it programmatically, you frequently want to save it as XML. This section shows you how to do that using the XSLT transform package.

Using that package, you'll create a transformer object to wire a `DomSource` to a `StreamResult`. You'll then invoke the transformer's `transform()` method to do the job!

7.2.1 Reading the XML

The first step is to create a DOM in memory by parsing an XML file. By now, you should be getting pretty comfortable with the process!

Note: The code discussed in this section is in `TransformationApp01.java`.

The code below provides a basic template to start from. (It should be familiar. It's basically the same code you wrote at the start of the DOM tutorial. If you saved it then, that version should be pretty much the equivalent of what you see below.)

```
import javax.xml.parsers.DocumentBuilder;
import javax.xml.parsers.DocumentBuilderFactory;
import javax.xml.parsers.FactoryConfigurationError;
import javax.xml.parsers.ParserConfigurationException;

import org.xml.sax.SAXException;
import org.xml.sax.SAXParseException;
import org.w3c.dom.Document;
import org.w3c.dom.DOMException;
import java.io.*;
public class TransformationApp
{
    static Document document;
    public static void main(String argv[])
    {
        if (argv.length != 1) {
            System.err.println ("Usage: java TransformationApp
filename");
            System.exit (1);
```

```
        }
        DocumentBuilderFactory factory =
            DocumentBuilderFactory.newInstance();
        //factory.setNamespaceAware(true);
        //factory.setValidating(true);
         try {
            File f = new File(argv[0]);
            DocumentBuilder builder = factory.newDocumentBuilder();
            document = builder.parse(f);
         } catch (SAXException sxe) {
            // Error generated by this application
            // (or a parser-initialization error)
            Exception  x = sxe;
            if (sxe.getException() != null)
                x = sxe.getException();
            x.printStackTrace();
         } catch (ParserConfigurationException pce) {
            // Parser with specified options can't be built
            pce.printStackTrace();
         } catch (IOException ioe) {
            // I/O error
            ioe.printStackTrace();
        }
} // main
}
```

7.2.2 Creating a Transformer

The next step is to create a transformer you can use to transmit the XML to System.out.

Note: The code discussed in this section is in `TransformationApp02.java`. The file it runs on is `slideSample01.xml`. (The browsable version is `slideSample01-xml.html`.) The output is in `TransformationLog02`.

Start by adding the import statements highlighted below:

```
import javax.xml.transform.Transformer;
import javax.xml.transform.TransformerFactory;
import javax.xml.transform.TransformerException;
import javax.xml.transform.TransformerConfigurationException;
```

```
import javax.xml.transform.dom.DOMSource;

import javax.xml.transform.stream.StreamResult;

import java.io.*;
```

Here, you've added a series of classes that should be now be forming a standard pattern: an entity (`Transformer`), the factory to create it (`TransformerFactory`), and the exceptions that can be generated by each. Since a transformation always has a *source* and a *result*, you then imported the classes necessary to use a DOM as a source (`DomSource`), and an output stream for the result (`StreamResult`).

Next, add the code to carry out the transformation:

```
try {
    File f = new File(argv[0]);
    DocumentBuilder builder = factory.newDocumentBuilder();
    document = builder.parse(f);

    // Use a Transformer for output
    TransformerFactory tFactory =
        TransformerFactory.newInstance();
    Transformer transformer = tFactory.newTransformer();

    DOMSource source = new DOMSource(document);
    StreamResult result = new StreamResult(System.out);
    transformer.transform(source, result);
```

Here, you created a transformer object, used the DOM to construct a source object, and used `System.out` to construct a result object. You then told the transformer to operate on the source object and output to the result object.

Note: In this case, the "transformer" isn't actually changing anything. In XSLT terminology, you are using the *identity transform*, which means that the "transformation" generates a copy of the source, unchanged.

Finally, add the code highlighted below to catch the new errors that can be generated:

```
} catch (TransformerConfigurationException tce) {
    // Error generated by the parser
    System.out.println ("* Transformer Factory error");
    System.out.println("    " + tce.getMessage() );
```

```
        // Use the contained exception, if any
        Throwable x = tce;
        if (tce.getException() != null)
            x = tce.getException();
        x.printStackTrace();

    } catch (TransformerException te) {
        // Error generated by the parser
        System.out.println ("* Transformation error");
        System.out.println("   " + te.getMessage() );

        // Use the contained exception, if any
        Throwable x = te;
        if (te.getException() != null)
            x = te.getException();
        x.printStackTrace();

    } catch (SAXException sxe) {
        ...
```

Note: `TransformerExceptions` are thrown by the transformer object.

`TransformerConfigurationExceptions` are thrown by the factory.

Addendum:

Astute reader Malcolm Gorman points out that, as it is currently written, the transformation app won't preserve the XML document's `DOCTYPE` setting. He proposes the following code to remedy the omission:

```
String systemValue = (new
File(document.getDoctype().getSystemId())).getName();
transformer.setOutputProperty(OutputKeys.DOCTYPE_SYSTEM,
    systemValue);
```

7.2.3 Writing the XML

For instructions on how to compile and run the program, see Compiling and Running the Program (page 91) from the SAX tutorial. (Substitute "TransformationApp" for "Echo" as the name of the program.). When you run the program on `slideSample01.xml`, following is the output you see.

```
<?xml version="1.0" encoding="UTF-8"?>
<!--  A SAMPLE set of slides  -->
<slideshow title="Sample Slide Show" date="Date of publication"
author="Yours Truly">
      <!-- TITLE SLIDE -->
      <slide type="all">
         <title>Wake up to WonderWidgets!</title>
      </slide>
      <!-- OVERVIEW -->
      <slide type="all">
          <title>Overview</title>
          <item>Why
        <em>WonderWidgets</em> are great
     </item>
          <item />
          <item>Who
      <em>buys</em> WonderWidgets
    </item>
      </slide>
</slideshow>
```

Note: See Additional Information (page 154) to find out more about configuring the factory and handling validation errors.

7.2.4 Writing Out a Subtree of the DOM

It is also possible to operate on a subtree of a DOM. In this section of the tutorial, you'll experiment with that option.

Note: The code discussed in this section is in `TransformationApp03.java`. The output is in `TransformationLog03`.

The only difference in the process is that now you will create a `DOMSource` using a node in the DOM, rather than the entire DOM. The first step will be to import the classes you need to get the node you want. Add the code highlighted below to do that:

```
import org.w3c.dom.DOMException;
import org.w3c.dom.Node;
import org.w3c.dom.NodeList;
```

The next step is to find a good node for the experiment. Add the code highlighted below to select the first `<slide>` element:

```
try {
    File f = new File(argv[0]);
    DocumentBuilder builder = factory.newDocumentBuilder();
    document = builder.parse(f);

    // Get the first <slide> element in the DOM
    NodeList list = document.getElementsByTagName("slide");
    Node node = list.item(0);
```

Finally, make the changes shown below to construct a source object that consists of the subtree rooted at that node:

```
DOMSource source = new DOMSource(document);
DOMSource source = new DOMSource(node);
StreamResult result = new StreamResult(System.out);
transformer.transform(source, result);
```

Now run the app. Your output should look like this:

```
    <?xml version="1.0" encoding="UTF-8"?>
<slide type="all">
        <title>Wake up to WonderWidgets!</title>
    </slide>
```

Clean Up

Because it will be easiest to do now, make the changes shown below to back out the additions you made in this section. (`TransformationApp04.java` contains these changes.)

```
Import org.w3c.dom.DOMException;
import org.w3c.dom.Node;
import org.w3c.dom.NodeList;
...
    try {
        ...
        // Get the first <slide> element in the DOM
        NodeList list = document.getElementsByTagName("slide");
        Node node = list.item(0);
        ...
```

```
DOMSource source = new DOMSource(node);
StreamResult result = new StreamResult(System.out);
transformer.transform(source, result);
```

7.2.5 Summary

At this point, you've seen how to use a transformer to write out a DOM, and how to use a subtree of a DOM as the source object in a transformation. In the next section, you'll see how to use a transformer to create XML from any data structure you are capable of parsing.

7.3 Generating XML from an Arbitrary Data Structure

In this section, you'll use an XSLT transformer to converting an *arbitrary data structure* to XML.

In general outline, then, you're going to:

1. Modify an existing program that reads the data and modify it to generate SAX events. (Whether that is a real parser or simply a data filter of some kind is irrelevant for the moment.)
2. You'll then use the SAX "parser" to construct a `SAXSource` for the transformation.
3. You'll use the same `StreamResult` object you created in the last exercise, so you can see the results. (But note that you could just as easily create a DOM-Result object to create a DOM in memory.)
4. You'll wire the source to the result, using the XSLT transformer object to make the conversion.

For starters, you need a data set you want to convert and some program which is capable of reading the data. In the next two sections, you'll create a simple data file and a program that reads it.

7.3.1 Creating a Simple File

We'll start by creating a data set for an address book. You can duplicate the process, if you like, or simply make use of the data stored in PersonalAddressBook.ldif.

The file shown below was produced by creating a new address book in Netscape messenger, giving it some dummy data (one address card) and then exporting it in LDIF format. Figure 7.1 shows the address book entry that was created.

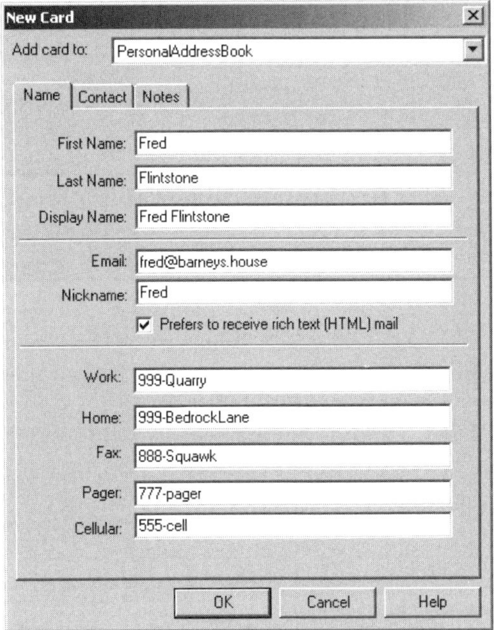

Figure 7.1 Address Book Entry

Exporting the address book produces a file like the one shown below. The parts of the file that we care about are shown in bold.

```
dn: cn=Fred Flinstone,mail=fred@barneys.house
modifytimestamp: 20010409210816Z
cn: Fred Flinstone
xmozillanickname: Fred
mail: Fred@barneys.house
xmozillausehtmlmail: TRUE
givenname: Fred
sn: Flinstone
telephonenumber: 999-Quarry
homephone: 999-BedrockLane
facsimiletelephonenumber: 888-Squawk
pagerphone: 777-pager
cellphone: 555-cell
xmozillaanyphone: 999-Quarry
objectclass: top
objectclass: person
```

Note that each line of the file contains a variable name, a colon, and a space followed by a value for the variable. The "sn" variable contains the person's surname (last name) and, for some reason, the variable "cn" contains the DisplayName field from the address book entry.

Note: LDIF stands for LDAP Data Interchange Format, according to the Netscape pages. And LDAP, turn, stands for Lightweight Directory Access Protocol. I prefer to think of LDIF as the "Line Delimited Interchange Format", since that is pretty much what it is.

7.3.2 Creating a Simple Parser

The next step is to create a program that parses the data. Again, you can follow the process to write your own if you like, or simply make a copy of the program so you can use it to do the XSLT-related exercises that follow.

Note: The code discussed in this section is in `AddressBookReader01.java`. The output is in `AddressBookReaderLog01`.

The text for the program is shown below. It's an absurdly simple program that doesn't even loop for multiple entries because, after all, it's just a demo!

```
import java.io.*;
public class AddressBookReader01
{

    public static void main(String argv[])
    {
        // Check the arguments
        if (argv.length != 1) {
            System.err.println (
                "Usage: java AddressBookReader filename");
            System.exit (1);
        }
        String filename = argv[0];
        File f = new File(filename);
        AddressBookReader01 reader = new AddressBookReader01();
        reader.parse(f);
    }
```

```
/** Parse the input */
public void parse(File f)
{
    try {
        // Get an efficient reader for the file
        FileReader r = new FileReader(f);
        BufferedReader br = new BufferedReader(r);

         // Read the file and display it's contents.
        String line = br.readLine();
        while (null != (line = br.readLine())) {
            if (line.startsWith("xmozillanickname: "))
                break;
        }
        output("nickname", "xmozillanickname", line);
        line = br.readLine();
        output("email",    "mail",             line);
        line = br.readLine();
        output("html",     "xmozillausehtmlmail", line);
        line = br.readLine();
        output("firstname","givenname",        line);
        line = br.readLine();
        output("lastname", "sn",               line);
        line = br.readLine();
        output("work",     "telephonenumber",  line);
        line = br.readLine();
        output("home",     "homephone",        line);
        line = br.readLine();
        output("fax",      "facsimiletelephonenumber",
            line);
        line = br.readLine();
        output("pager",    "pagerphone",       line);
        line = br.readLine();
        output("cell",     "cellphone",        line);

    }
    catch (Exception e) {
        e.printStackTrace();
    }
}
```

```
    void output(String name, String prefix, String line)
    {
        int startIndex = prefix.length() + 2;
        // 2=length of ": "
        String text = line.substring(startIndex);
        System.out.println(name + ": " + text);
    }
}
```

This program contains 3 methods:

main

The main method gets the name of the file from the command line, creates an instance of the parser, and sets it to work parsing the file. This method will be going away when we convert the program into a SAX parser. (That's one reason for putting the parsing code into a separate method.)

parse

This method operates on the File object sent to it by the main routine. As you can see, its about as simple as it can get! The only nod to efficiency is the use of a `BufferedReader`, which can become important when you start operating on large files.

output

The output method contains the smarts about the structure of a line. Starting from the right It takes three arguments. The first argument gives the method a name to display, so we can output "html" as a variable name, instead of "xmozillausehtmlmail". The second argument gives the variable name stored in the file (xmozillausehtmlmail). The third argument gives the line containing the data. The routine then strips off the variable name from the start of the line and outputs the desired name, plus the data.

Running this program on the address book file produces this output:

```
nickname: Fred
email: Fred@barneys.house
html: TRUE
firstname: Fred
lastname: Flintstone
work: 999-Quarry
```

```
home: 999-BedrockLane
fax: 888-Squawk
pager: 777-pager
cell: 555-cell
```

I think we can all agree that's a bit more readable!

7.3.3 Modifying the Parser to Generate SAX Events

The next step is to modify the parser to generate SAX events, so you can use it as the basis for a `SAXSource` object in an XSLT `transform`.

Note: The code discussed in this section is in `AddressBookReader02.java`.

Start by extending importing the additional classes you're going to need:

```
import java.io.*;


import org.xml.sax.*;
Import org.xml.sax.helpers.AttributesImpl;
```

Next, modify the application so that it extends `XmlReader`. That converts the app into a parser that generates the appropriate SAX events.

```
public class AddressBookReader02
    implements XMLReader
{
```

Now, remove the `main` method. You won't be needing that any more.

```
public static void main(String argv[])
{
    // Check the arguments
    if (argv.length != 1) {
        System.err.println ("Usage: Java AddressBookReader 
filename");
        System.exit (1);
    }
    String filename = argv[0];
    File f = new File(filename);
    AddressBookReader02 reader = new AddressBookReader02();
    reader.parse(f);
}
```

Add some global variables that will come in handy in a few minutes:

```
ContentHandler handler;

// We're not doing namespaces, and we have no
// attributes on our elements.
String nsu = "";  // NamespaceURI
Attributes atts = new AttributesImpl();
String rootElement = "addressbook";

String indent = "    "; // for readability!
```

The SAX `ContentHandler` is the thing that is going to get the SAX events the parser generates. To make the app into an `XmlReader`, you'll be defining a `setContentHandler` method. The `handler` variable will hold the result of that configuration step.

And, when the parser generates SAX *element* events, it will need to supply namespace and attribute information. Since this is a simple application, you're defining null values for both of those.

You're also defining a root element for the data structure (addressbook), and setting up an indent string to improve the readability of the output.

Next, modify the parse method so that it takes an `InputSource` as an argument, rather than a `File`, and account for the exceptions it can generate:

```
public void parse(File f)InputSource input)
throws IOException, SAXException
```

Now make the changes shown below to get the reader encapsulated by the `InputSource` object:

```
try {
    // Get an efficient reader for the file
    FileReader r = new FileReader(f);
    java.io.Reader r = input.getCharacterStream();
    BufferedReader Br = new BufferedReader(r);
```

Note: In the next section, you'll create the input source object and what you put in it will, in fact, be a buffered reader. But the `AddressBookReader` could be used by someone else, somewhere down the line. This step makes sure that the processing will be efficient, regardless of the reader you are given.

The next step is to modify the `parse` method to generate SAX events for the start of the document and the root element. Add the code highlighted below to do that:

```
/** Parse the input */
public void parse(InputSource input)
...
{
    try {
        ...
        // Read the file and display its contents.
        String line = br.readLine();
        while (null != (line = br.readLine())) {
            if (line.startsWith("xmozillanickname: ")) break;
        }
         if (handler==null) {
            throw new SAXException("No content handler");
        }
        handler.startDocument();
        handler.startElement(nsu, rootElement,
            rootElement, atts);
        output("nickname", "xmozillanickname", line);
        ...
        output("cell",     "cellphone",       line);
        handler.ignorableWhitespace(".toCharArray(),
                        0, // start index
                        1  // length
                        );
        handler.endElement(nsu, rootElement, rootElement);
        handler.endDocument();
    }
    catch (Exception e) {
    ...
```

Here, you first checked to make sure that the parser was properly configured with a `ContentHandler`. (For this app, we don't care about anything else.) You then generated the events for the start of the document and the root element, and finished by sending the end-event for the root element and the end-event for the document.

A couple of items are noteworthy, at this point:

- We haven't bothered to send the `setDocumentLocator` event, since that is optional. Were it important, that event would be sent immediately before the `startDocument` event.
- We've generated an `ignorableWhitespace` event before the end of the root element. This, too, is optional, but it drastically improves readability of the output, as you'll see in a few moments. (In this case, the whitespace consists of a single newline, which is sent the same way that `characters` method are sent: as a character array, a starting index, and a length.)

Now that SAX events are being generated for the document and the root element, the next step is to modify the `output` method to generate the appropriate element events for each data item. Make the changes shown below to do that:

```
void output(String name, String prefix, String line)
throws SAXException
{
    int startIndex = prefix.length() + 2; // 2=length of ": "
    String text = line.substring(startIndex);
    System.out.println(name + ": " + text);

    int textLength = line.length() - startIndex;
    handler.ignorableWhitespace(indent.toCharArray(),
                                0, // start index
                                indent.length()
                                );
    handler.startElement(nsu, name, name /*"qName"*/, atts);
    handler.characters(line.toCharArray(),
                       startIndex,
                       textLength);
    handler.endElement(nsu, name, name);
}
```

Since the `ContentHandler` methods can send `SAXExceptions` back to the parser, the parser has to be prepared to deal with them. In this case, we don't expect any, so we'll simply allow the app to fall on its sword and die if any occur.

You then calculate the length of the data, and once again generate some ignorable whitespace for readability. In this case, there is only one level of data, so we can use a fixed indent string. (If the data were more structured, we would have to calculate how much space to indent, depending on the nesting of the data.)

Note: The indent string makes no difference to the data, but will make the output a lot easier to read. Once everything is working, try generating the result without that string! All of the elements will wind up concatenated end to end, like this:

```
<addressbook><nickname>Fred</nickname><email>...
```

Next, add the method that configures the parser with the `ContentHandler` that is to receive the events it generates:

```
/** Allow an application to register a content event handler. */
public void setContentHandler(ContentHandler handler) {
    this.handler = handler;
}

/** Return the current content handler. */
public ContentHandler getContentHandler() {
    return this.handler;
}
```

There are several more methods that must be implemented in order to satisfy the XmlReader interface. For the purpose of this exercise, we'll generate null methods for all of them. For a production application, though, you may want to consider implementing the error handler methods to produce a more robust app. For now, though, add the code highlighted below to generate null methods for them:

```
/** Allow an application to register an error event handler. */
public void setErrorHandler(ErrorHandler handler)
{ }

/** Return the current error handler. */
public ErrorHandler getErrorHandler()
{ return null; }
```

Finally, add the code highlighted below to generate null methods for the remainder of the XmlReader interface. (Most of them are of value to a real SAX parser, but have little bearing on a data-conversion application like this one.)

```
/** Parse an XML document from a system identifier (URI). */
public void parse(String systemId)
throws IOException, SAXException
{ }
```

```
 /** Return the current DTD handler. */
public DTDHandler getDTDHandler()
{ return null; }

/** Return the current entity resolver. */
public EntityResolver getEntityResolver()
{ return null; }

/** Allow an application to register an entity resolver. */
public void setEntityResolver(EntityResolver resolver)
{ }

/** Allow an application to register a DTD event handler. */
public void setDTDHandler(DTDHandler handler)
{ }

/** Look up the value of a property. */
public Object getProperty(java.lang.String name)
{ return null; }

/** Set the value of a property. */
public void setProperty(java.lang.String name, java.lang.Object
value)
{ }

/** Set the state of a feature. */
public void setFeature(java.lang.String name, boolean value)
{ }

/** Look up the value of a feature. */
public boolean getFeature(java.lang.String name)
{ return false; }
```

Congratulations! You now have a parser you can use to generate SAX events. In the next section, you'll use it to construct a SAX source object that will let you transform the data into XML.

7.3.4 Using the Parser as a SAXSource

Given a SAX parser to use as an event source, you can (quite easily!) construct a transformer to produce a result. In this section, you'll modify the `TransformerApp` you've been working with to produce a stream output result, although you could just as easily produce a DOM result.

Note: The code discussed in this section is in `TransformationApp04.java`. The results of running it are in `TransformationLog04`.

Important!

Be sure to shift gears! Put the `AddressBookReader` aside and open up the `TransformationApp`. The work you do in this section affects the `TransformationApp`!

Start by making the changes shown below to import the classes you'll need to construct a `SAXSource` object. (You won't be needing the DOM classes at this point, so they are discarded here, although leaving them in doesn't do any harm.)

```
import org.xml.sax.SAXException;
import org.xml.sax.SAXParseException;
import org.xml.sax.ContentHandler;
import org.xml.sax.InputSource;
import org.w3c.dom.Document;
import org.w3c.dom.DOMException;
...
import javax.xml.transform.dom.DOMSource;
import javax.xml.transform.sax.SAXSource;
import javax.xml.transform.stream.StreamResult;
```

Next, remove a few other holdovers from our DOM-processing days, and add the code to create an instance of the AddressBookReader:

```
public class TransformationApp
{
    // Global value so it can be ref'd by the tree-adapter
    static Document document;

     public static void main(String argv[])
    {
        ...
        DocumentBuilderFactory factory =
            DocumentBuilderFactory.newInstance();
        //factory.setNamespaceAware(true);
        //factory.setValidating(true);
```

```
        // Create the sax "parser".
        AddressBookReader saxReader = new AddressBookReader();

         try {
            File f = new File(argv[0]);
            DocumentBuilder builder = factory.newDocumentBuilder();
            document = builder.parse(f);
```

Guess what! You're almost done. Just a couple of steps to go. Add the code highlighted below to construct a SAXSource object:

```
// Use a Transformer for output
...
Transformer transformer = tFactory.newTransformer();

// Use the parser as a SAX source for input
FileReader fr = new FileReader(f);
BufferedReader br = new BufferedReader(fr);
InputSource inputSource = new InputSource(br);
SAXSource source = new SAXSource(saxReader, inputSource);

StreamResult result = new StreamResult(System.out);
transformer.transform(source, result);
```

Here, you constructed a buffered reader (as mentioned earlier) and encapsulated it in an input source object. You then created a `SAXSource` object, passing it the reader and the `InputSource` object, and passed that to the transformer.

When the app runs, the transformer will configure itself as the `ContentHandler` for the SAX parser (the `AddressBookReader` and tell the parser to operate on the `inputSource` object. Events generated by the parser will then go to the transformer, which will do the appropriate thing and pass the data on to the result object.

Finally, remove the exceptions you no longer need to worry about, since the `TransformationApp` no longer generates them:

```
} catch (SAXException sxe) {
    // Error generated by this application
    // (or a parser initialization error)
    Exception  x = sxe;
    if (sxe.getException() != null)
        x = sxe.getException();
    x.printStackTrace();
```

```
} catch (ParserConfigurationException pce) {
    // Parser with specified options can't be built
    pce.printStackTrace();

} catch (IOException ioe) {
```

You're done! You have now created a transformer that will use a `SAXSource` as input, and produce a `StreamResult` as output.

7.3.5 Doing the Conversion

Now run the app on the address book file. Your output should look like this:

```
<?xml version="1.0" encoding="UTF-8"?>
<addressbook>
    <nickname>Fred</nickname>
    <email>fred@barneys.house</email>
    <html>TRUE</html>
    <firstname>Fred</firstname>
    <lastname>Flintstone</lastname>
    <work>999-Quarry</work>
    <home>999-BedrockLane</home>
    <fax>888-Squawk</fax>
    <pager>777-pager</pager>
    <cell>555-cell</cell>
</addressbook>
```

You have now successfully converted an existing data structure to XML. And it wasn't even that hard. Congratulations!

7.4 Transforming XML Data with XSLT

The XML Stylesheet Language for Transformations (XSLT) can be used for many purposes. For example, you could generate PDF or postscript from the XML data. But generally, XSLT is used to generated formatted HTML output, or to create an alternative XML representation of the data.

In this section of the tutorial, you'll use an XSLT transform to translate XML input data to HTML output.

Note: The XSLT specification is very large and quite complex. Rather thick books have been written on the subject. So this tutorial can only scratch the surface. It will give you enough a background to get started, so you can undertake simple XSLT processing tasks. It should also give you a head start when you investigate XSLT further.

7.4.1 Defining an Ultra-Simple Article Document Type

We'll start by defining a super simple document type that could be used for writing articles. Our `<article>` documents will contain these structure tags:

- `<TITLE>`—The title of the article.
- `<SECT>`—A section. (Consists of a *heading* and a *body*.)
- `<PARA>`—A paragraph.
- `<LIST>`—A list.
- `<ITEM>`—An entry in a list.
- `<NOTE>`—An aside, which will be offset from the main text.

The slightly unusual aspect of this structure is that we won't create a separate element tag for a section heading. Such elements are commonly created to distinguish the heading text (and any tags it contains) from the body of the section (that is, any structure elements underneath the heading).

Instead, we'll allow the heading to merge seamlessly into the body of a section. That arrangement adds some complexity to the stylesheet, but that will give us a chance to explore XSLT's template-selection mechanisms. It also matches our intuitive expectations about document structure, where the text of a heading is directly followed by structure elements, which can simplify outline-oriented editing.

Note: However, that structure is not easily validated, because XML's mixed-content model allows text anywhere in a section, whereas we want to confine text and inline elements so that they only appear before the first structure element in the body of the section. The assertion-based validator (Schematron) can do it, but most other schema mechanisms can't. So we'll dispense with defining a DTD for the document type.

In this structure, sections can be nested. The depth of the nesting will determine what kind of HTML formatting to use for the section heading (for example, h1 or h2.) That's also useful with outline-oriented editing, because it lets you can move sections around at will without having to worry about changing the heading tag—or any of the other section headings that are affected by the move.

For lists, we'll use a `type` attribute to specify whether the list entries are `unordered` (bulleted), `alpha` (enumerated with lowercase letters), `ALPHA` (enumerated with uppercase letters, or `numbered`.

We'll also allow for some inline tags that change the appearance of the text:

- `<B>`—bold
- `<I>`—italics
- `<U>`—underline
- `<DEF>`—definition
- `<LINK>`—link to a URL

Note: An *inline* tag does not generate a line break, so a style change caused by an inline tag does not affect the flow of text on the page (although it will affect the appearance of that text). A *structure* tag, on the other hand, demarcates a new segment of text, so at a minimum it always generates a line break, in addition to other format changes.

The `<DEF>` tag will help make things interesting. That tag will used for terms that are defined in the text. Such terms will be displayed in italics, the way they ordinarily are in a document. But using a special tag in the XML will allow an index program to one day find such definitions and add them to the index, along with keywords in headings. In the *Note* above, for example, the definitions of inline tags and structure tags could have been marked with `<DEF>` tags, for future indexing.

Finally, the `LINK` tag serves two purposes. First, it will let us create a link to a URL without having to put the URL in twice—so we can code `<link>http//...</link>` instead of `<a href="http//...">http//...</a>`. Of course, we'll also want to allow a form that looks like `<link target="...">...name...</link>`. That leads to the second reason for the `<link>` tag—it will give us an opportunity to play with conditional expressions in XSLT.

Note: As one college professor said, the trick to defining a research project is to find something that is "large enough to be feasible... but small enough to be feasible." Although the article structure is exceedingly simple (consisting of only 11 tags), it raises enough interesting problems to keep us busy exploring XSLT for a while! Along the way, we'll get a good view of its basic capabilities. But there will still be large areas of the spec that are left untouched. The last part of this tutorial will point out the major things we missed, to give you some sense of what sorts of features await you in the specification!

7.4.2 Creating a Test Document

Here, you'll create a simple test document using nested <SECT> elements, a few <PARA> elements, a <NOTE> element, a <LINK>, and a <LIST type="unordered">. The idea is to create a document with one of everything, so we can explore the more interesting translation mechanisms.

Note: The sample data described here is contained in `article1.xml`. (The browsable version is `article1-xml.html`.)

To make the test document, create a file called `article.xml` and enter the XML data shown below.

```
<?xml version="1.0"?>
<ARTICLE>
    <TITLE>A Sample Article</TITLE>
    <SECT>The First Major Section
        <PARA>This section will introduce a subsection.</PARA>
        <SECT>The Subsection Heading
            <PARA>This is the text of the subsection.
            </PARA>
        </SECT>
    </SECT>
</ARTICLE>
```

Note that in the XML file, the subsection is totally contained within the major section. (Unlike HTML, for example, where headings, do no *contain* the body of a section.) The result is an outline structure that is harder to edit in plain-text form, like this. But much easier to edit with an outline-oriented editor.

Someday, given an tree-oriented XML editor that understands inline tags like <B> and <I>, it should be possible to edit an article of this kind in outline form, without requiring a complicated stylesheet. (Thereby allowing the writer to focus on the structure of the article, leaving layout until much later in the process.) In such an editor, the article-fragment above would look something like this:

```
<ARTICLE>
    <TITLE>A Sample Article
    <SECT>The First Major  Section
        <PARA>This section  will introduce a subsection.
        <SECT>The Subheading
           <PARA>This  is the text of the subsection. Note that ...
```

At the moment, tree-structured editors exist, but they treat inline tags like <B> and <I> the same way that they treat other structure tags, which can make the "outline" a bit difficult to read. But hopefully, that situation will improve one day. Meanwhile, we'll press on...

7.4.3 Writing an XSLT Transform

In this part of the tutorial, you'll begin writing an XSLT transform that will convert the XML article and render it in HTML.

Note: The transform described in this section is contained in `article1a.xsl`. (The browsable version is `article1a-xsl.html`.)

Start by creating a normal XML document:

```
<?xml version="1.0" encoding="ISO-8859-1"?>
```

Then add the lines shown below to create an XSL stylesheet:

```
<?xml version="1.0" encoding="ISO-8859-1"?>
<xsl:stylesheet
    xmlns:xsl="http://www.w3.org/1999/XSL/Transform"
    version="1.0"
    >

</xsl:stylesheet>
```

Now, set it up to produce HTML-compatible output:

```
<xsl:stylesheet
    ...
    >
    <xsl:output method="html"/>

     ...

</xsl:stylesheet>
```

We'll get into the detailed reasons for that entry later on in this section. But for now, note that if you want to output anything besides well-formed XML, then you'll need an `<xsl:output>` tag like the one shown, specifying either `"text"` or `"html"`. (The default value is `"xml"`.)

Note: When you specify XML output, you can add the `indent` attribute to produce nicely indented XML output. The specification looks like this:

```
<xsl:output_method="xml"_indent="yes"/>.
```

7.4.4 Processing the Basic Structure Elements

You'll start filling in the stylesheet by processing the elements that go into creating a table of contents—the root element, the title element, and headings. You'll also process the PARA element defined in the test document.

Note: If on first reading you skipped the section of this tutorial that discusses the XPath addressing mechanisms, now is a good time to go back and review that section!

Begin by adding the main instruction that processes the root element:

```
<xsl:stylesheet ...
    <xsl:template match="/">
        <html><body>
            <xsl:apply-templates/>
        </body></html>
    </xsl:template>

</xsl:stylesheet>
```

The XSL commands are shown in bold. (Note that they are defined in the "`xsl`" namespace.) The instruction `<xsl:apply-templates>` processes the children of the current node. In the case, the current node is the root node.

Despite its simplicity, this example illustrates a number of important ideas, so it's worth understanding thoroughly. The first concept is that a stylesheet contains a number of *templates*, defined with the <xsl:template> tag. Each template contains a `match` attribute, which selects the elements that the template will be applied to, using the XPath addressing mechanisms.

Within the template, tags that do not start with the `xsl:` namespace prefix are simply copied. The newlines and whitespace that follow them are also copied, which helps to format make the resulting output readable.

Note: When a newline is not present, whitespace generally seems to be ignored. To include whitespace in the output in such cases, or to include other text, you can use the `<xsl:text>` tag. Basically, an XSLT stylesheet expects to process tags. So everything it sees needs to be either an `<xsl:...>` tag, some other tag, or whitespace.

In this case, the non-xsl tags are HTML tags (shown in red, for readability). So when the root tag is matched, XSLT outputs the HTML start-tags, processes any templates that apply to children of the root, and then outputs the HTML end-tags.

Process the <TITLE> Element

Next, add a template to process the article title:

```
    <xsl:template match="/ARTICLE/TITLE">
        <h1 align="center"> <xsl:apply-templates/> </h1>
    </xsl:template>

</xsl:stylesheet>
```

In this case, you specified a complete path to the TITLE element, and output some HTML to make the text of the title into a large, centered heading. In this case, the apply-templates tag ensures that if the title contains any inline tags like italics, links, or underlining, they will be processed as well.

More importantly, the apply-templates instruction causes the *text* of the title to be processed. Like the DOM data model, the XSLT data model is based on the concept of *text nodes* hanging off of *element nodes* (which, in turn, can hang off other element nodes, and so on). That hierarchical structure constitutes the source tree. There is also a result tree, which contains the output.

XSLT works by transforming the source tree into the result tree. To visualize the result of XSLT operations, it is helpful to understand the structure of those trees, and their contents. (For more on this subject, see the sidebar on The XSLT/XPath Data Model (page 257) later in this section.)

Process Headings

To continue processing the basic structure elements, add a template to process the top-level headings:

```
    <xsl:template match="/ARTICLE/SECT">
        <h1> <xsl:apply-templates select="text()|B|I|U|DEF|LINK"/>
</h1>
        <xsl:apply-templates select="SECT|PARA|LIST|NOTE"/>
    </xsl:template>

</xsl:stylesheet>
```

Here, you've specified the path to the topmost SECT elements. But this time, you've applied templates in two stages, using the `select` attribute. For the first stage, you selected text nodes using the XPath `text()` function, as well as inline tags like bold and italics. (The vertical pipe (|) is used to match multiple items—text, *or* a bold tag, *or* an italics tag, and so on) In the second stage, you selected the other structure elements contained in the file, for sections, paragraphs, lists, and notes.

Using the select tags let you put the text and inline elements between the `<h1>...</h1>` tags, while making sure that all of the structure tags in the section are processed afterwards. In other words, you made sure that the nesting of the headings in the XML document is *not* reflected in the HTML formatting, which is important for HTML output.

In general, the select clause lets you apply all templates to a selected subset of the information available at the current context. As another example, this template selects all attributes of the current node:

```
<xsl:apply-templates select="@*"/></attributes>
```

Next, add the virtually identical template to process the second-level headings:

```
    <xsl:template match="/ARTICLE/SECT/SECT">
        <h2> <xsl:apply-templates select="text()|B|I|U|DEF|LINK"/>
</h2>
        <xsl:apply-templates select="SECT|PARA|LIST|NOTE"/>
    </xsl:template>

</xsl:stylesheet>
```

Generate a Runtime Message

You could add templates for deeper headings, too, but at some point you have to stop, if only because HTML only goes down to five levels. But for this example, you'll stop at two levels of section headings. But if the XML input happens to contain a third level, you'll want to deliver an error message to the user. This section shows you how to do that.

Note: We *could* continue processing SECT elements that are further down, by selecting them with the expression `/SECT/SECT//SECT`. The `//` selects any SECT elements, at any "depth", as defined by XPath addressing mechanism. But we'll take the opportunity to play with messaging, instead.

Add the following template to generate an error when a section is encountered that is nested too deep:

```
    <xsl:template match="/ARTICLE/SECT/SECT/SECT">
        <xsl:message terminate="yes">Error: Sections can only be
nested 2 deep
        .</xsl:message>

</xsl:template>

</xsl:stylesheet>
```

The `terminate="yes"` clause causes the transformation process to stop after the message is generated. Without it, processing could still go on with everything in that section being ignored.

Extra-Credit Exercise:

Expand the stylesheet to handle sections nested up to five sections deep, generating <h1>...<h5> tags. Generate an error on any section nested six levels deep.

Finally, finish up the stylesheet by adding a template to process the PARA tag:

```
    <xsl:template match="PARA">
        <p><xsl:apply-templates/></p>
    </xsl:template>

</xsl:stylesheet>
```

Nothing unusual here. Just another template like the ones you're used to.

7.4.5 Writing the Basic Program

In this part of the tutorial, you'll modify the program that used XSLT to echo an XML file unchanged, and modify it so that it uses your stylesheet.

Note: The code shown in this section is contained in `Stylizer.java`. The result is the HTML code shown in `stylizer1a.txt`. (The displayable version is `stylizer1a.html`.)

Start by copying `TransformationApp02`, which parses an XML file and writes to System.out. Save it as `Stylizer.java`.

Next, modify occurrences of the class name and the usage-section of the program:

```
public class TransformationAppStylizer
{
    if (argv.length != 1 2) {
```

```
        System.err.println ("Usage: java TransformationAppStylizer
stylesheet
                                                    filename");
        System.exit (1);
    }
    ...
```

Then modify the program to use the stylesheet when creating the `Transformer` object.

```
...
import javax.xml.transform.dom.DOMSource;
import javax.xml.transform.stream.StreamSource;
import javax.xml.transform.stream.StreamResult;
...

public class Stylizer
{
    ...
    public static void main (String argv[])
    {
        ...
        try {
            File f = new File(arv[0]);
            File stylesheet = new File(argv[0]);
            File datafile   = new File(argv[1]);

            DocumentBuilder builder =
                factory.newDocumentBuilder();
            document = builder.parse(f datafile);
            ...
          StreamSource stylesource = new StreamSource(stylesheet);
            Transformer transformer =
                Factory.newTransformer(stylesource);
            ...
```

This code uses the file to create a `StreamSource` object, and then passes the source object to the factory class to get the transformer.

Note: You can simplify the code somewhat by eliminating the DOMSource class entirely. Instead of creating a DOMSource object for the XML file, create a StreamSource object for it, as well as for the stylesheet. (Take it on for extra credit!)

Now compile and run the program using `article1a.xsl` on `article1.xml`. The results should look like this:

```
<html>
<body>

<h1 align="center">A Sample Article</h1>

<h1>The First Major Section
            </h1>
<p>This section will introduce a subsection.</p>
<h2>The Subsection Heading

            </h2>

<p>This is the text of the subsection.

       </p>

</body>
</html>
```

At this point, there is quite a bit of excess whitespace in the output. You'll see how to eliminate most of it in the next section.

7.4.6 Trimming the Whitespace

If you recall, when you took a look at the structure of a DOM, there were many text nodes that contained nothing but ignorable whitespace. Most of the excess whitespace in the output came from them. Fortunately, XSL gives you a way to eliminate them. (For more about the node structure, see the sidebar: The XSLT/XPath Data Model (page 257)).

Note: The stylesheet described here is `article1b.xsl`. The result is the HTML code shown in `stylizer1b.txt`. (The displayable versions are `article1b-xsl.html` and `stylizer1b.html`.)

To do remove some of the excess whitespace, add the line highlighted below to the stylesheet.

```
<xsl:stylesheet ...
    >
    <xsl:output method="html"/>
    <xsl:strip-space elements="SECT"/>
    ...
```

This instruction tells XSL to remove any text nodes under SECT elements that contain nothing but whitespace. Nodes that contain text other than whitespace will not be affected, and other kinds of nodes are not affected.

Now, when you run the program, the result looks like this:

```
<html>
<body>

<h1 align="center">A Sample Article</h1>

<h1>The First Major Section
    </h1>
<p>This section will introduce a subsection.</p>
<h2>The Subsection Heading
    </h2>
<p>This is the text of the subsection.
    </p>

</body>
</html>
```

That's quite an improvement. There are still newline characters and white space after the headings, but those come from the way the XML is written:

```
<SECT>The First Major Section
____<PARA>This section will introduce a subsection.</PARA>
^^^^
```

Here, you can see that the section heading ends with a newline and indentation space, before the PARA entry starts. That's not a big worry, because the browsers that will process the HTML routinely compress and ignore the excess space. But there is still one more formatting at our disposal.

Note: The stylesheet described here is `article1c.xsl`. The result is the HTML code shown in `stylizer1c.txt`. (The displayable versions are `article1c-xsl.html` and `stylizer1c.html`.)

To get rid of that last little bit of whitespace, add this template to the stylesheet:

```
    <xsl:template match="text()">
        <xsl:value-of select="normalize-space()"/>
    </xsl:template>

</xsl:stylesheet>
```

The output now looks like this:

```
<html>
<body>
<h1 align="center">A Sample Article</h1>
<h1>The First Major Section</h1>
<p>This section will introduce a subsection.</p>
<h2>The Subsection Heading</h2>
<p>This is the text of the subsection.</p>
</body>
</html>
```

That is quite a bit better. Of course, it would be nicer if it were indented, but that turns out to be somewhat harder than expected! Here are some possible avenues of attack, along with the difficulties:

Indent option

Unfortunately, the `indent="yes"` option that can be applied to XML output is not available for HTML output. Even if that option were available, it wouldn't help, because HTML elements are rarely nested! Although HTML source is frequently indented to show the *implied* structure, the HTML tags themselves are not nested in a way that creates a *real* structure.

Indent variables

The `<xsl:text>` function lets you add any text you want, including whitespace. So, it could conceivably be used to output indentation space. The problem is to vary the *amount* of indentation space. XSLT variables seem like a good idea, but they don't work here. The reason is that when you assign a value to a variable in a template, the value is only known *within* that template (statically, at compile time value). Even if the variable is defined globally, the assigned value is not stored in a way that lets it be dynamically known by other templates at runtime. Once `<apply-templates/>` invokes other templates, they are unaware of any variable settings made in other templates.

Parameterized templates

Using a "parameterized template" is another way to modify a template's behavior. But determining the amount of indentation space to pass as the parameter remains the crux of the problem!

At the moment, then, there does not appear to be any good way to control the indentation of HTML-formatted output. Typically, that fact is of little consequence, since the data will usually be manipulated in its XML form, while the HTML version is only used for display a browser. It's only inconvenient in a tutorial like this, where it would be nice to see the structure you're creating! But when you click on the link to `stylizer1c.html`, you see the results you expect.

7.4.7 Processing the Remaining Structure Elements

In this section, you'll process the LIST and NOTE elements that add additional structure to an article.

Note: The sample document described in this section is `article2.xml`, the stylesheet used to manipulate it is `article2.xsl`. The result is the HTML code shown in `stylizer2.txt`. (The displayable versions are `article2-xml.html`, `article2-xsl.html`, and `stylizer2.html`.)

Start by adding some test data to the sample document:

```
<?xml version="1.0"?>
<ARTICLE>
    <TITLE>A Sample Article</TITLE>
    <SECT>The First Major Section
        ...
    </SECT>
    <SECT>The Second Major Section
        <PARA>This section adds a LIST and a NOTE.
        <PARA>Here is the LIST:
            <LIST type="ordered">
                <ITEM>Pears</ITEM>
                <ITEM>Grapes</ITEM>
            </LIST>
```

```
        </PARA>
        <PARA>And here is the NOTE:
            <NOTE>Don't forget to go to the hardware store on your
                                    way to the grocery!
            </NOTE>
        </PARA>
    </SECT>
</ARTICLE>
```

Note: Although the list and note in the XML file are contained in their respective paragraphs, it really makes no difference whether they are contained or not—the generated HTML will be the same, either way. But having them contained will make them easier to deal with in an outline-oriented editor.

Modify <PARA> handling

Next, modify the PARA template to account for the fact that we are now allowing some of the structure elements to be embedded with a paragraph:

```
<xsl:template match="PARA">
    <p><xsl:apply-templates/></p>
    <p> <xsl:apply-templates select="text()|B|I|U|DEF|LINK"/> </p>
    <xsl:apply-templates select="PARA|LIST|NOTE"/>
</xsl:template>
```

This modification uses the same technique you used for section headings. The only difference is that SECT elements are not expected within a paragraph.

Process <LIST> and <ITEM> elements

Now you're ready to add a template to process LIST elements:

```
    <xsl:template match="LIST">
        <xsl:if test="@type='ordered'">
            <ol>
                <xsl:apply-templates/>
            </ol>
        </xsl:if>
        <xsl:if test="@type='unordered'">
            <ul>
                <xsl:apply-templates/>
```

```
            </ul>
        </xsl:if>
    </xsl:template>

</xsl:stylesheet>
```

The <xsl:if> tag uses the `test=""` attribute to specify a boolean condition. In this case, the value of the `type` attribute is tested, and the list that is generated changes depending on whether the value is `ordered` or `unordered`.

The two important things to note for this example are:

- There is no `else` clause, nor is there a `return` or `exit` statement, so it takes two <xsl:if> tags to cover the two options. (Or the <xsl:choose> tag could have been used, which provides case-statement functionality.)
- Single quotes are required around the attribute values. Otherwise, the XSLT processor attempts to interpret the word `ordered` as an XPath function, instead of as a string.

Now finish up `LIST` processing by handling `ITEM` elements. Nothing spectacular here.

```
    <xsl:template match="ITEM">
        <li><xsl:apply-templates/>
        </li>
    </xsl:template>

</xsl:stylesheet>
```

Ordering Templates in a Stylesheet

By now, you should have the idea that templates are independent of one another, so it doesn't generally matter where they occur in a file. So from here on, we'll just show the template you need to add. (For the sake of comparison, they're always added at the end of the example stylesheet.)

Order *does* make a difference when two templates can apply to the same node, In that case, the one that is defined *last* is the one that is found and processed. For example, to change the ordering of an indented list to use lowercase alphabetics, you could specify a template pattern that looks like this: `//LIST//LIST`. In that template, you would use the HTML option to generate an alphabetic enumeration, instead of a numeric one.

But such an element could also be identified by the pattern `//LIST`. To make sure the proper processing is done, the template that specifies `//LIST` would have to appear *before* the template the specifies `//LIST//LIST`.

Process <NOTE> Elements

The last remaining structure element is the `NOTE` element. Add the template shown below to handle that.

```
<xsl:template match="NOTE">
    <blockquote><b>Note:</b><br/>
        <xsl:apply-templates/>
    </p></blockquote>
</xsl:template>
```

This code brings up an interesting issue that results from the inclusion of the `<br/>` tag. To be well-formed XML, the tag must be specified in the stylesheet as `<br/>`, but that tag is not recognized by many browsers. And while most browsers recognize the sequence `<br></br>`, they all treat it like a paragraph break, instead of a single line break.

In other words, the transformation *must* generate a `<br>` tag, but the stylesheet must specify `<br/>`. That brings us to the major reason for that special output tag we added early in the stylesheet:

```
<xsl:stylesheet ... >
    <xsl:output method="html"/>
    ...
</xsl:stylesheet>
```

That output specification converts empty tags like `<br/>` to their HTML form, `<br>`, on output. That conversion is important, because most browsers do not recognize the empty tags. Table 7.3 is a list of the affected tags.

Table 7.3 Empty Tags

- area	- frame	- link
- base	- hr	- meta
- basefont	- img	- param
- br	- input	
- col	- isindex	

Summarizing:

By default, XSLT produces well-formed XML on output. And since an XSL stylesheet is well-formed XML to start with, you cannot easily put a tag like `<br>` in the middle of it. The "`<xsl:output method="html"/>`" solves the problem, so you can code `<br/>` in the stylesheet, but get `<br>` in the output.

The other major reason for specifying `<xsl:output method="html"/>` is that, like the specification `<xsl:output method="text"/>`, generated text is *not* escaped. For example, if the stylesheet includes the `<` entity reference, it will appear as the "<" character in the generated text. When XML is generated, on the other hand, the `<` entity reference in the stylesheet would be unchanged, so it would appear as `<` in the generated text.

Note: If you actually want < to be generated as part of the HTML output, you'll need to encode it as `<`—that sequence becomes `<` on output, because only the `&` is converted to an & character.

Run the Program

Here is the HTML that is generated for the second section when you run the program now:

```
...
<h1>The Second Major Section</h1>
<p>This section adds a LIST and a NOTE.</p>
<p>Here is the LIST:</p>
<ol>
<li>Pears</li>
<li>Grapes</li>
</ol>
<p>And here is the NOTE:</p>
<blockquote>
<b>Note:</b>
<br>Don't forget to go to the hardware store on your way to the
grocery!
</blockquote>
```

7.4.8 Process Inline (Content) Elements

The only remaining tags in the `ARTICLE` type are the *inline* tags—the ones that don't create a line break in the output, but which instead are integrated into the stream of text they are part of.

Inline elements are different from structure elements, in that they are part of the content of a tag. If you think of an element as a node in a document tree, then each node has both *content* and *structure*. The content is composed of the text and inline tags it contains. The structure consists of the other elements (structure elements) under the tag.

Note: The sample document described in this section is `article3.xml`, the stylesheet used to manipulate it is `article3.xsl`. The result is the HTML code shown in `stylizer3.txt`. (The browser-displayable versions are `article3-xml.html`, `article3-xsl.html`, and `stylizer3.html`.)

Start by adding one more bit of test data to the sample document:

```
<?xml version="1.0"?>
<ARTICLE>
    <TITLE>A Sample Article</TITLE>
    <SECT>The First Major Section
        ...
    </SECT>
    <SECT>The Second Major Section
        ...
    </SECT>
    <SECT>The <I>Third</I> Major Section
        <PARA>In addition to the inline tag in the heading, this
section
           defines the term <DEF>inline</DEF>, which literally means
          "no line break." It also adds a simple link to the main page
           for the Java platform (<LINK>http://java.sun.com</LINK>),
             as well as a link to the
             <LINK target="http://java.sun.com/xml">XML</LINK> page.
        </PARA>
    </SECT>
</ARTICLE>
```

Now, process the inline <DEF> elements in paragraphs, renaming them to HTML italics tags:

```
<xsl:template match="DEF">
    <i> <xsl:apply-templates/> </i>
</xsl:template>
```

Next, comment out the text-node normalization. It has served its purpose, and new we're to the point that we need to preserve spaces important:

```
<!--
    <xsl:template match="text()">
        <xsl:value-of select="normalize-space()"/>
    </xsl:template>
-->
```

This modification keeps us from losing spaces before tags like <I> and <DEF>. (Try the program without this modification to see the result.)

Now, process basic inline HTML elements like <B>, <I>, <U> for bold, italics, and underlining.

```
<xsl:template match="B|I|U">
    <xsl:element name="{name()}">
        <xsl:apply-templates/>
    </xsl:element>
</xsl:template>
```

The `<xsl:element>` tag lets you compute the element you want to generate. Here, you generate the appropriate the inline tag using the name of the current element. In particular, note the use of curly braces (`{}`) in the `name=".."` expression. Those curly braces cause the text inside the quotes to be processed as an XPath expression, instead of being interpreted as a literal string. Here, they cause the XPath `name()` function to return the name of the current node.

Curly braces are recognized anywhere that an "attribute value template" can occur. (Attribute value templates are defined in section 7.6.2 of the specification, and they appear several places in the template definitions.). In such expressions, curly braces can also be used to refer to the value of an attribute, `{@foo}`, or to the content of an element `{foo}`.

Note: You can also generate attributes using `<xsl:attribute>`. For more information see section 7.1.3 of the XSLT Specification.

The last remaining element is the `LINK` tag. The easiest way to process that tag will be to set up a named-template that we can drive with a parameter:

```
<xsl:template name="htmLink">
    <xsl:param name="dest" select="UNDEFINED"/>
    <xsl:element name="a">
```

```
        <xsl:attribute name="href">
            <xsl:value-of select="$dest"/>
        </xsl:attribute>
        <xsl:apply-templates/>
    </xsl:element>
</xsl:template>
```

The major difference in this template is that, instead of specifying a `match` clause, you gave the template a name with the `name=""` clause. So this template only gets executed when you invoke it.

Within the template, you also specified a parameter named "dest", using the `<xsl:param>` tag. For a bit of error checking, you used the `select` clause to give that parameter a default value of "`UNDEFINED`". To reference the variable in the `<xsl:value-of>` tag, you specified `"$dest"`.

Note: Recall that an entry in quotes is interpreted as an expression, unless it is further enclosed in single quotes. That's why the single quotes were needed earlier, in `"@type='ordered'"`—to make sure that `ordered` was interpreted as a string.

The `<xsl:element>` tag generates an element. Previously, we have been able to simply specify the element we want by coding something like `<html>`. But here you are dynamically generating the content of the HTML anchor (<a>) in the body of the `<xsl:element>` tag. And you are dynamically generating the `href` attribute of the anchor using the `<xsl:attribute>` tag.

The last important part of the template is the `<apply-templates>` tag, which inserts the text from the text node under the `LINK` element. (Without it, there would be no text in the generated HTML link.)

Next, add the template for the `LINK` tag, and call the named template from within it:

```
<xsl:template match="LINK">
    <xsl:if test="@target">
        <!--Target attribute specified.-->
        <xsl:call-template name="htmLink">
            <xsl:with-param name="dest" select="@target"/>
        </xsl:call-template>
    </xsl:if>
</xsl:template>

<xsl:template name="htmLink">
    ...
```

The test="@target" clause returns true if the target attribute exists in the LINK tag. So this if-statement generates HTML links when the text of the link and the target defined for it are different.

The <xsl:call-template> tag invokes the named template, while <xsl:with-param> specifies a parameter using the name clause, and its value using the select clause.

As the very last step in the stylesheet construction process, add the if-clause shown below to process LINK tags that do not have a target attribute.

```
<xsl:template match="LINK">
    <xsl:if test="@target">
        ...
    </xsl:if>

    <xsl:if test="not(@target)">
        <xsl:call-template name="htmLink">
            <xsl:with-param name="dest">
                <xsl:apply-templates/>
            </xsl:with-param>
        </xsl:call-template>
    </xsl:if>
</xsl:template>
```

The not(...) clause inverts the previous test (there is no else clause, remember?). So this part of the template is interpreted when the target attribute is not specified. This time, the parameter value comes not from a select clause, but from the *contents* of the <xsl:with-param> element.

Note: Just to make it explicit: variables (which we'll mention a bit later) and parameters can have their value specified *either* by a select clause, which lets you use XPath expressions, *or* by the content of the element, which lets you use XSLT tags.

The content of the parameter, in this case, is generated by the <xsl:apply-templates/> tag, which inserts the contents of the text node under the LINK element.

Run the Program

When you run the program now, the results should look like this:

```
...
<h1>The <I>Third</I> Major Section
    </h1>
```

```
<p>In addition to the inline tag in the heading, this section
        defines the term <i>inline</i>, which literally means
       "no line break". It also adds a simple link to the main page
        for the Java platform (<a href="http://java.sun.com">http:/
/java.sun.com</a>),
        as well as a link to the
        <a href="http://java.sun.com/xml">XML</a> page.
    </p>
```

Awesome! You have now converted a rather complex XML file to HTML. (As seemingly simple as it was, it still provided a lot of opportunity for exploration.)

7.4.9 Printing the HTML

You have now converted an XML file to HTML. One day, someone will produce an HTML-aware printing engine that you'll be able to find and use through the Java Printing Service (JPS) API. At that point, you'll have ability to print an arbitrary XML file as formatted data—all you'll have to do is set up a stylesheet!

7.4.10 What Else Can XSLT Do?

As lengthy as this section of the tutorial has been, it has still only scratched the surface of XSLT's capabilities. Many additional possibilities await you in the XSLT Specification. Here are a few of the things to look for:

import (section 2.6.2) and include (section 2.6.1)

Use these statements to modularize and combine XSLT stylesheets. The `include` statement simply inserts any definitions from the included file. The `import` statement lets you override definitions in the imported file with definitions in your own stylesheet.

for-each loops (section 8)

Loop over a collection of items and process each one, in turn.

choose (case-statement) for conditional processing (section 9.2)

Branch to one of multiple processing paths depending on an input value.

generating numbers (section 7.7)

Dynamically generate numbered sections, numbered elements, and numeric literals. XSLT provides three numbering modes:

- **single**: Numbers items under a single heading, like an "ordered list" in HTML.
- **multiple:** Produces multi-level numbering like "A.1.3".
- **any:** Consecutively numbers items wherever they appear, like the footnotes in a chapter.

formatting numbers (section 12.3)

Control enumeration formatting, so you get numerics (`format="1"`), uppercase alphabetics (`format="A"`), lowercase alphabetics (`format="a"`), or compound numbers, like "A.1", as well as numbers and currency amounts suited for a specific international locale.

sorting output (section 10)

Produce output in some desired sorting order.

mode-based templates (section 5.7)

Lets you process an element multiple times, each time in a different "mode". You add a `mode` attribute to templates, and then specify `<apply-templates mode="...">` to apply only the templates with a matching mode. Combined with the `<apply-templates select="...">` to slice and dice the input processing, creating a matrix of elements to process and the templates to apply to them.

variables (section 11)

Variables, like parameters, let you control a template's behavior. But they are not as valuable as you might think. The value of a variable is only known within the scope of the current template or <xsl:if> clause (for example) in which it is defined. You can't pass a value from one template to another, or even from an enclosed part of a template to another part of the same template.

These statements are true even for a "global" variable. You can change its value in a template, but the change only applies to that template. And when the expression used to define the global variable is evaluated, that evaluation takes place in the context of the structure's root node. In other words, global variables are essentially runtime constants. Those constants can be useful to change the behavior of a template, especially when coupled with `include` and `import` statements. But variables are not a general-purpose data-management mechanism.

The XSLT/XPath Data Model

Like the DOM, the XSL/XPath data model consists of a tree containing a variety of nodes. Under any given element node, there are text nodes, attribute nodes, element nodes, comment nodes, and processing instruction nodes.

Once an XPath expression establishes a *context*, other expressions produce values that are relative to that context. For example, the expression `//LIST` establishes a context consisting of a LIST node. Within the XSLT template that processes such nodes, the expression `@type` refers to the element's type attribute. (Similarly, the expression `@*` refers to all of the element's attributes.)

The Trouble with Variables

It is awfully tempting to create a single template and set a variable for the destination of the link, rather than going to the trouble of setting up a parameterized template and calling it two different ways. The idea would be to set the variable to a default value (say, the text of the `LINK` tag) and then, if `target` attribute exists, set the destination variable to the value of the `target` attribute.

That would be a darn good idea—if it worked. But once again, the issue is that variables are only known in the scope within which they are defined. So when you code an `<xsl:if>` to change the value of the variable, the value is only known within the context of the `<xsl:if>` tag. Once `</xsl:if>` is encountered, any change to the variable's setting is lost.

A similarly tempting idea is the possibility of replacing the `text()|B|I|U|DEF|LINK` specification with a variable (`$inline`). But since the value of the variable is determined by where it is defined, the value of a global `inline` variable consists of text nodes, `<B>` nodes, etc. that happen to exist at the root level. In other words, the value of such a variable, in this case, is null.

Next...

The final page of the XSLT tutorial will show you how to concatenate multiple transformations together in a filter chain.

7.5 Concatenating XSLT Transformations with a Filter Chain

It is sometimes useful to create a "filter chain" of XSLT transformations, so that the output of one transformation becomes the input of the next. This section of the tutorial shows you how to do that.

7.5.1 Writing the Program

Start by writing a program to do the filtering. This example will show the full source code, but you can use one of the programs you've been working on as a basis, to make things easier.

Note: The code described here is contained in `FilterChain.java`.

The sample program includes the import statements that identify the package locations for each class:

```
import javax.xml.parsers.FactoryConfigurationError;
import javax.xml.parsers.ParserConfigurationException;
import javax.xml.parsers.SAXParser;
import javax.xml.parsers.SAXParserFactory;

import org.xml.sax.SAXException;
import org.xml.sax.SAXParseException;
import org.xml.sax.InputSource;
import org.xml.sax.XMLReader;
import org.xml.sax.XMLFilter;

import javax.xml.transform.Transformer;
import javax.xml.transform.TransformerException;
import javax.xml.transform.TransformerFactory;
import javax.xml.transform.TransformerConfigurationException;

import javax.xml.transform.sax.SAXTransformerFactory;
import javax.xml.transform.sax.SAXSource;
import javax.xml.transform.sax.SAXResult;

import javax.xml.transform.stream.StreamSource;
import javax.xml.transform.stream.StreamResult;

import java.io.*;
```

The program also includes the standard error handlers you're used to. They're listed here, just so they are all gathered together in one place:

```
}
catch (TransformerConfigurationException tce) {
    // Error generated by the parser
    System.out.println ("* Transformer Factory error");
    System.out.println("    " + tce.getMessage() );

    // Use the contained exception, if any
    Throwable x = tce;
    if (tce.getException() != null)
        x = tce.getException();
    x.printStackTrace();
}
catch (TransformerException te) {
    // Error generated by the parser
    System.out.println ("* Transformation error");
    System.out.println("    " + te.getMessage() );

    // Use the contained exception, if any
    Throwable x = te;
    if (te.getException() != null)
        x = te.getException();
    x.printStackTrace();
}
catch (SAXException sxe) {
    // Error generated by this application
    // (or a parser-initialization error)
    Exception  x = sxe;
    if (sxe.getException() != null)
        x = sxe.getException();
    x.printStackTrace();
}
catch (ParserConfigurationException pce) {
    // Parser with specified options can't be built
    pce.printStackTrace();
}
catch (IOException ioe) {
    // I/O error
    ioe.printStackTrace();
}
```

In between the import statements and the error handling, the core of the program consists of the code shown below.

```
public static void main (String argv[])
{
    if (argv.length != 3) {
        System.err.println ("Usage: java FilterChain stylesheet1
stylesheet2 xmlfile");
        System.exit (1);
    }

     try {
        // Read the arguments
        File stylesheet1 = new File(argv[0]);
        File stylesheet2 = new File(argv[1]);
        File datafile    = new File(argv[2]);

         // Set up the input stream
        BufferedInputStream bis = new

BufferedInputStream(newFileInputStream(datafile));
        InputSource input = new InputSource(bis);

         // Set up to read the input file
        SAXParserFactory spf = SAXParserFactory.newInstance();
        SAXParser parser = spf.newSAXParser();
        XMLReader reader = parser.getXMLReader();

         // Create the filters (see Note #1)
        SAXTransformerFactory stf =
            (SAXTransformerFactory)
                TransformerFactory.newInstance();
        XMLFilter filter1 = stf.newXMLFilter(
            new StreamSource(stylesheet1));
        XMLFilter filter2 = stf.newXMLFilter(
            new StreamSource(stylesheet2));

        // Wire the output of the reader to filter1 (see Note #2)
        // and the output of filter1 to filter2
        filter1.setParent(reader);
        filter2.setParent(filter1);
```

```
        // Set up the output stream
        StreamResult result = new StreamResult(System.out);

    // Set up the transformer to process the SAX events generated
    // by the last filter in the chain
        Transformer transformer = stf.newTransformer();
        SAXSource transformSource = new SAXSource(
            filter2, input);
        transformer.transform(transformSource, result);
    } catch (...) {
        ...
```

Note: This weird bit of code is explained by the fact that `SAXTransformerFactory` extends `TransformerFactory`, adding methods to obtain filter objects. The `newInstance()` method is a static method defined in `TransformerFactory`, which (naturally enough) returns a `TransformerFactory` object. In reality, though, it returns a `SAXTransformer-Factory`. So, to get at the extra methods defined by `SAXTransformerFactory`, the return value must be cast to the actual type.

An XMLFilter object is both a SAX reader and a SAX content handler. As a SAX reader, it generates SAX events to whatever object has registered to receive them. As a content handler, it consumes SAX events generated by its "parent" object—which is, of necessity, a SAX reader, as well. (Calling the event generator a "parent" must make sense when looking at the internal architecture. From the external perspective, the name doesn't appear to be particularly fitting.) The fact that filters both generate and consume SAX events allows them to be chained together.

7.5.2 Understanding How it Works

The code listed above shows you how to set up the transformation. Figure 7.2 should help you get a better feel for what's happening when it executes.

When you create the transformer, you pass it at a `SAXSource` object, which encapsulates a reader (in this case, `filter2`) and an input stream. You also pass it a pointer to the result stream, where it directs its output. The diagram shows what happens when you invoke `transform()` on the transformer. Here is an explanation of the steps:

1. The transformer sets up an internal object as the content handler for `filter2`, and tells it to parse the input source.
2. `filter2`, in turn, sets itself up as the content handler for `filter1`, and tells *it* to parse the input source.

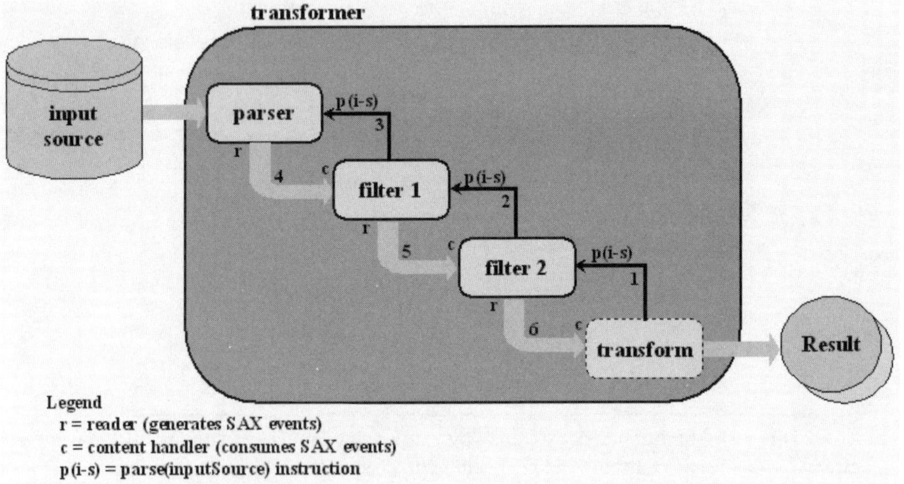

Figure 7.2 Operation of chained filters

3. Continuing to pass the buck, `filter1` asks the `parser` object to please parse the input source.
4. The `parser` does so, generating SAX events which it passes to `filter1`.
5. `filter1`, acting in its capacity as a content handler, processes the events and does its transformations. Then, acting in its capacity as a SAX reader (XMLReader), it sends SAX events to `filter2`.
6. `filter2` does the same, sending its events to the transformer's content handler, which generates the output stream.

7.5.3 Testing the Program

To try out the program, you'll create an XML file based on a tiny fraction of the XML DocBook format, and convert it to the `ARTICLE` format defined here. Then you'll apply the `ARTICLE` stylesheet to generate an HTML version.

Note: This example processes `small-docbook-article.xml` using `docbookToArticle.xsl`, and `article1c.xsl`. The result is the HTML code shown in `filterout.txt`. (The browser-displayable versions are `small-docbook-article-xml.html`, `docbookToArticle-xsl.html`, `article1c-xsl.html`, and `filterout.html`.) See the O'Reilly Web pages for a good description of the DocBook article format.

Start by creating a small article that uses a minute subset of the XML DocBook format:

```
<?xml version="1.0"?>
<Article>
    <ArtHeader>
        <Title>Title of my (Docbook) article</Title>
    </ArtHeader>
    <Sect1>
        <Title>Title of Section 1.</Title>
        <Para>This is a paragraph.</Para>
    </Sect1>
</Article>
```

Next, create a stylesheet to convert it into the `ARTICLE` format:

```
<xsl:stylesheet
    xmlns:xsl="http://www.w3.org/1999/XSL/Transform"
    version="1.0"
    >
    <xsl:output method="xml"/> (see Note #1)

     <xsl:template match="/">
        <ARTICLE>
            <xsl:apply-templates/>
        </ARTICLE>
    </xsl:template>

     <!-- Lower level titles strip out the element tag --> (see
Note #2)

    <!-- Top-level title -->
    <xsl:template match="/Article/ArtHeader/Title"> (see Note #3)
        <TITLE> <xsl:apply-templates/> </TITLE>
    </xsl:template>

     <xsl:template match="//Sect1"> (see Note #4)
        <SECT><xsl:apply-templates/></SECT>
    </xsl:template>
```

```
    <xsl:template match="Para">
       <PARA><xsl:apply-templates/></PARA> (see Note #5)
    </xsl:template>

</xsl:stylesheet>
```

Note:

1. This time, the stylesheet is generating XML output.
2. The element below matches the main title. For section titles, the tag gets stripped. (Since no template conversion governs those title elements, they are ignored. The text nodes they contain, however, are still echoed as a result of XSLT's built in template rules. More on that below.)
3. The title from the DocBook article header becomes the `ARTICLE` title.
4. Numbered section tags are converted to plain `SECT` tags.
5. Carries out a case conversion, so `Para` becomes `PARA`.

Although it hasn't been mentioned explicitly, XSLT defines a number of built-in (default) template rules. The complete set is listed in section 5.8 of the spec. Mainly, they provide for the automatic copying of text and attribute nodes, and for skipping comments and processing instructions. They also dictate that inner elements are processed, even when their containing tags that don't have templates. That is the reason that the text node in the section title is processed, even though the section title is not covered by any template.

Now, run the `FilterChain` program, passing it the stylesheet above, the `ARTICLE` stylesheet, and the small DocBook file, in that order. The result should like this:

```
<html>
<body>
<h1 align="center">Title of my (Docbook) article</h1>
<h1>Title of Section 1.</h1>
<p>This is a paragraph.</p>
</body>
</html>
```

7.5.4 Conclusion

Congratulations! You have completed the XSLT tutorial! There is a lot you do with XML and XSLT, and you are now prepared to explore the many exciting possibilities that await.

CHAPTER 8

Java API for XML Messaging

Maydene Fisher

IN THIS CHAPTER

THE Java API for XML Messaging (JAXM) makes it possible for developers to do XML messaging using the Java platform. This document will help you learn how to use JAXM.

For more information on JAXM, see the JAXM documentation included with the Java Web Services Developer Pack (Java WSDP) at

```
<JWSDP_HOME>/docs/jaxm/index.html
```

The Java WSDP includes the following material related to JAXM:

- The API specification (Javadoc documentation) for JAXM
- The JAXM 1.0.1 EA1 Reference Implementation (RI)
- Various documents about the RI
- Sample applications that can be run with the JAXM RI

This document gives instructions for running the RI as a way to help you get started. You may prefer to go through both the overview and tutorial before running the samples to make it easier to understand what the RI is doing, or you may prefer to explore the RI first. The overview gives some of the conceptual background behind the JAXM API to help you understand why certain things are done the way they are. The tutorial shows you how to use the basic JAXM API, giving examples and explanations of the more commonly used features. Finally, the code examples show how to build an application that you can run.

8.1 Overview of JAXM

This overview presents a high level view of how JAXM messaging works and explains concepts in general terms. Its goal is to give you some terminology and a framework for the explanations and code examples that are presented in the tutorial section.

The overview looks at JAXM from three perspectives:

- Messages
- Connections
- Messaging providers

8.1.1 Messages

JAXM messages follow SOAP standards. That is, they conform to the Simple Object Access Protocol (SOAP) 1.1 and SOAP with Attachments specifications, which prescribe the format for messages and also specify some things that are required, optional, or not allowed. With the JAXM API, you can create XML messages that conform to these SOAP specifications simply by making Java API calls.

The Structure of an XML Document

Note: For more complete information on XML documents, see Understanding XML (page 29) and Java API for XML Processing (page 67).

An XML document has a hierarchical structure with elements, subelements, subsubelements, and so on. You will notice that many of the JAXM classes and interfaces represent XML elements in a SOAP message and have the word *element* or *SOAP* or both in their names.

An element is also referred to as a *node*. Accordingly, the JAXM API has the interface `Node`, which is the base class for all the classes and interfaces that represent XML elements in a SOAP message. There are also methods such as `SOAPElement.addTextNode`, `Node.detachNode`, and `Node.getValue`, which you will see how to use in the tutorial section.

What Is in a Message?

The two main types of SOAP messages are those that have attachments and those that do not.

Messages with No Attachments. The following outline shows the very high level structure of a JAXM message with no attachments. Except for the SOAP header, all the parts listed are required.

I. SOAP message

  A. SOAP part

    1. SOAP envelope

      a. SOAP header (optional)

      b. SOAP body

The JAXM API provides the `SOAPMessage` class to represent a SOAP message, `SOAPPart` to represent the SOAP part, `SOAPEnvelope` to represent the SOAP envelope, and so on.

When you create a new `SOAPMessage` object, it will automatically have the parts that are required to be in a SOAP message. In other words, a new `SOAPMessage` object has a `SOAPPart` object that contains a `SOAPEnvelope` object. The `SOAPEnvelope` object in turn automatically contains an empty `SOAPHeader` object followed by an empty `SOAPBody` object. If you do not need the `SOAPHeader` object, which is optional, you can delete it. The rationale for having it automatically included is that more often than not you will need it, so it is more convenient to have it provided.

Messages with Attachments. A SOAP message may include one or more attachment parts in addition to the SOAP part. The SOAP part may contain only XML content; as a result, if any of the content of a message is not in XML format, it must occur in an attachment part. So, if for example, you want your message to contain an image file or plain text, your message must have an attachment part for it. Note than an attachment part can contain any kind of content, so it can contain data in XML format as well.

The following outline shows the high-level structure of a SOAP message that has two attachments, one containing plain text and one containing an image.

I. SOAP message
  A. SOAP part
    1. SOAP envelope
      a. SOAP header (optional)
      b. SOAP body
  B. Attachment part (content is plain text)
  C. Attachment part (content is an image file)

JAXM provides the `AttachmentPart` class to represent the attachment part of a SOAP message.

A `SOAPMessage` object automatically has a `SOAPPart` object and its required subelements, but because `AttachmentPart` objects are optional, you have to create and add them yourself.

The tutorial section will walk you through creating and populating messages with and without attachment parts.

Another way to look at JAXM messaging is from the perspective of whether or not a messaging provider is used, which is discussed at the end of the section Messaging Providers (page 270).

8.1.2 Connections

All JAXM messages are sent and received over a connection. The connection can go directly to a particular destination or to a messaging provider. (A messaging provider is a service that handles the transmission and routing of messages and provides features not available when you use a connection that goes directly to its ultimate destination. Messaging providers are explained in more detail later.)

The JAXM API supplies the following class and interface to represent these two kinds of connections:

1. `SOAPConnection`—a connection from the sender directly to the receiver (a point-to-point connection)
2. `ProviderConnection`—a connection to a messaging provider

SOAPConnection

A SOAPConnection object, which represents a point-to-point connection, is simple to create and use. One reason is that you do not have to do any configuration to use a SOAPConnection object because it does not need to run in a servlet container (like Tomcat) or a J2EE container. It is the only kind of connection available to a client that does not use a messaging provider.

The following code fragment creates a SOAPConnection object and then, after creating and populating the message, uses the connection to send the message. The parameter *request* is the message being sent; *endpoint* represents where it is being sent.

```
SOAPConnectionFactory factory =
                SOAPConnectionFactory.newInstance();
SOAPConnection con = factory.createConnection();

. . .// create a request message and give it content

SOAPMessage response = con.call(request, endpoint);
```

When a SOAPConnection object is used, the only way to send a message is with the method call, which transmits its message and then blocks until it receives a reply. Because the method call requires that a response be returned to it, this type of messaging is referred to as *request-response* messaging.

A Web service implemented for request-response messaging must return a response to any message it receives. As stated in the previous section, a request-response message will always be sent using the SOAPConnection.call method, which requires that a message be returned to unblock it. Most often, the message being sent is a request, and the message that is returned is the response.

When the message is an update, the response is an acknowledgement that the update was received. Such an acknowledgement implies that the update was successful. Some messages may not require any response at all. The service that gets such a message is still required to send back a response because one is needed to unblock the call method. In this case, the response is not related to the content of the message; it is simply a message to unblock the call method.

Unlike a client with no messaging provider, which is limited to using only a SOAPConnection object, a client that uses a messaging provider is free to use a SOAPConnection object or a ProviderConnection object. It is expected that ProviderConnection objects will be used most of the time.

ProviderConnection

A `ProviderConnection` object represents a connection to a messaging provider. (The next section explains more about messaging providers.) When you send a message via a `ProviderConnection` object, the message goes to the messaging provider. The messaging provider forwards the message, following the message's routing instructions, until the message gets to the ultimate recipient's messaging provider, which in turn forwards the message to the ultimate recipient.

When an application is using a `ProviderConnection` object, it must use the method `ProviderConnection.send` to send a message. This method transmits the message one way and returns immediately, without having to block until it gets a response. The messaging provider that receives the message will forward it to the intended destination and return the response, if any, at a later time. The interval between sending a request and getting the response may be very short, or it may be measured in days. In this style of messaging, the original message is sent as a one-way message, and any response is sent subsequently as a one-way message. Not surprisingly, this style of messaging is referred to as *one-way* messaging.

8.1.3 Messaging Providers

A messaging provider is a service that handles the transmission and routing of messages. It works behind the scenes to keep track of messages and see that they are sent to the proper destination or destinations.

Transparency

One of the great features of a messaging provider is that you are not even aware of it. You just write your JAXM application, and the right things happen. For example, when you are using a messaging provider and send a message by calling the `ProviderConnection.send` method, the messaging provider receives the message and works with other parts of the communications infrastructure to perform various tasks, depending on what the message's header contains and how the messaging provider itself has been implemented. The result is that the message arrives at its final destination without your being aware of any of the details involved in accomplishing the delivery.

Profiles

JAXM offers the ability to plug in additional protocols that are built on top of SOAP. A JAXM provider implementation is not required to implement features beyond what the SOAP 1.1 and SOAP with Attachments specifications require, but it is free to incorporate other standard protocols, called *profiles*, that are implemented on top of SOAP. For example, the "ebXML Routing, Transport, and Packaging V1.0—Message Service Specification" defines levels of service that are not included in the two SOAP specifications. A messaging provider that is implemented to include ebXML capabilities on top of SOAP capabilities is said to support an ebXML profile. A messaging provider may support multiple profiles, but an application can use only one at a time and must have a prior agreement with each of the parties to whom it sends messages about what profile is being used.

Profiles affect a message's headers. For example, depending on the profile, a new `SOAPMessage` object will come with certain headers already set. Also a profile implementation may provide API that makes it easier to create a header and set its content. The JAXM RI includes APIs for both the ebXML and SOAP-RP profiles. The Javadoc documentation for these profiles is at `<JWSDP_HOME>/docs/jaxm/profiles/index.html`. (You will find links to the Javadoc documentation for the JAXM API at `<JWSDP_HOME>/api/index.html`.)

Continuously Active

A messaging provider works continuously. A JAXM client may make a connection with its provider, send one or more messages, and then close the connection. The provider will store the message and then send it. Depending on how the provider has been configured, it will resend a message that was not successfully delivered until it is successfully delivered or until the limit for the number of resends is reached. Also, the provider will stay in a waiting state, ready to receive any messages that are intended for the client. The provider will store incoming messages so that when the client connects with the provider again, the provider will be able to forward the messages. In addition, the provider generates error messages as needed and maintains a log where messages and their related error messages are stored.

Intermediate Destinations

When a messaging provider is used, a message can be sent to one or more intermediate destinations before going to the final recipient. These intermediate destinations, called *actors*, are specified in the message's `SOAPHeader` object. For example, assume that a message is an incoming Purchase Order. The header might route the message to the order input desk, the order confirmation desk, the shipping desk, and the billing department. Each of these destinations is an actor that will take the appropriate action, remove the header information relevant to it, and send the message to the next actor. The default actor is the final destination, so if no actors are specified, the message is routed to the final recipient.

The attribute *`actor`* is used to specify an intermediate recipient. A related attribute is *`mustUnderstand`*, which, when its value is `true`, means that an actor must understand what it is supposed to do and carry it out successfully. A `SOAP-Header` object uses the method `addAttribute` to add these attributes, and the `SOAPHeaderElement` interface provides methods for setting and getting the values of these attributes.

When to Use a Messaging Provider

A JAXM client may or may not use a messaging provider. Generally speaking, if you just want to be a consumer of Web services, you do not need a messaging provider. The following list shows some of the advantages of not using a messaging provider:

- The application can be written using the J2SE platform.
- The application is not required to be deployed in a container such as Tomcat or a J2EE container.
- No configuration is required.

The limitations of not using a messaging provider are the following:

- The client can send only request-response messages.
- The client can act in the client role only.

It follows that if you want to provide a Web service, meaning that you must be able to get and save requests that are sent to you at any time, you must use a messaging provider. You will also need to run in a container, which provides the messaging infrastructure used by the provider. A messaging provider gives you the flexibility to assume both the client and service roles, and it also lets you send one-way messages. In addition, if your messaging provider supports a protocol such as ebXML or SOAP-RP on top of SOAP, you can take advantage of the additional quality of service features that it provides.

Messaging with and without a Provider

JAXM clients can be categorized according to whether or not they use a messaging provider. Those that do not use a messaging provider can be further divided into those that run in a container and those that do not. A JAXM client that does not use a messaging provider and also does not run in a container is called a *standalone* client.

8.2 Running the Samples

The JAXM Reference Implementation (RI) is an implementation of the JAXM API plus an implementation of a messaging provider. The RI also includes basic implementations of ebXML and SOAP-RP profiles, which run on top of SOAP. When an enterprise shops for a messaging provider, one of the main considerations is which profiles the messaging provider supports.

The RI also provides some simple examples of JAXM applications that you can run and also a Provider Administration tool that makes it easy to configure the messaging provider.

Before you can run the samples that run in a container or use the Provider Administration tool, you need to start up Tomcat. These are the steps to follow:

1. Type the following at the command line:

   UNIX:

   ```
   cd $JWSDP_HOME/bin
   startup.sh
   ```

   Windows:

   ```
   cd %JWSDP_HOME%\bin
   startup.bat
   ```

2. Open a browser window and set it to

   ```
   http://localhost:8080/index.html
   ```

3. On the page that comes up, click on one of the sample programs listed. Then follow the instructions in the new window that comes up.

8.2.1 The Sample Programs

The sample programs illustrate various kinds of applications you can write with the JAXM API. Once Tomcat is running, you can run the following sample programs provided with the RI simply by setting your browser to the appropriate URL and following the instructions on the Web page that comes up.

- Simple—A simple example of sending and receiving a message using the local messaging provider
- Translator—A simple translation service that translates text into different languages

- JAXM Tags—An example that uses JSP tags to generate and consume a SOAP message
- Remote—An example of a round-trip message that uses a JAXM messaging provider that supports the basic ebXML profile to send and receive a message
- SOAP-RP—An example of a round-trip message that uses a JAXM messaging provider that supports the basic SOAP-RP profile to send and receive a message

There are two other sample programs, `jaxm-uddiping` and `jaxm-standalone`, that do not run in Tomcat. To run them, go to the `<JWSDP_HOME>/samples/jaxm` directory, where you will find the directories `uddiping` and `standalone`. Each directory contains a `README` file that explains what to do.

The last part of the JAXM tutorial modifies the code in `UddiPing.java` and also explains in detail how to run it. You might find it more convenient to wait until you have reached that section before trying to run the `jaxm-uddiping` and `jaxm-standalone` samples.

The preceding list presented the sample applications according to what they do. You can also look at the sample applications as examples of the three possible types of JAXM clients:

- **Those that do not use a messaging provider and also do not run in a container**

  These are called *standalone* applications. The samples `jaxm-standalone` and `jaxm-uddiping` are examples of standalone clients.

- **Those that do not use a messaging provider and run in a container**

  The samples Simple, Translator, and JAXM Tags are examples of this type. Simple differs from the other two in that it uses a *local provider*, which should not be confused with a messaging provider. The local provider is simply a mechanism for returning the reply to a message that was sent using the method `SOAPConnection.call`.

- **Those that use a messaging provider and run in a container**

  The samples Remote and SOAP-RP are examples of this type. The JAXM RI includes an implementation of a messaging provider and also implementations of two profiles that operate on top of SOAP. Remote uses the implementation of an ebXML profile, and SOAP-RP uses the implementation of a SOAP-RP profile.

8.2.2 The Provider Administration Tool

The same `index.html` page with links to the samples has a link to the Provider Administration tool. This tool requires a user name and password for authentication, which you will have to set up before you can use the tool. All that is involved in the setup is simply opening the file `tomcat-users.xml` and uncommenting the element for `provideradmin`. Here are the steps to follow:

1. Open the file `<JWSDP_HOME>/conf/tomcat-users.xml` in your favorite editor.
2. Delete the comment tags (`<!--`) and (`-->`) that are before and after the following element:

```
<users name="jaxm-provideradmin" password="changeme"
            role="provider"/>
```

3. If Tomcat is running, you will need to shut it down and start it up again. This is so that Tomcat will see the revised version of `tomcat-users.xml`. Here are the instructions for shutting Tomcat down and then starting it up again:

   UNIX:

```
cd $JWSDP_HOME/bin
shutdown.sh
startup.sh
```

   Windows:

```
cd %JWSDP_HOME%\bin
shutdown.bat
startup.bat
```

4. Set your browser window to

```
http://localhost:8080/index.html
```

5. Click on the link "JAXM Provider Administration Tool." A window will come up with text boxes for your login name and password. Use the name and password in the file `tomcat-users.xml`, which are

```
user name: jaxm-provideradmin
password: changeme
```

When the Provider Administration tool comes up, follow the instructions it gives. This tool is normally used by System Administrators, but others may use it as well. Exploring this tool gives you more of an idea of what a messaging provider needs to know. For example, some typical ways to change the provider properties are:

- To add, modify, or delete an endpoint
- To change the retry interval (the amount of time the provider will wait before trying to send a message again)
- To change the number of retries (the number of times the provider will try to send a message)
- To change the directory where the provider logs messages

8.3 Tutorial

This section will walk you through the basics of sending a SOAP message using the JAXM API. At the end of this chapter, you will know how to do the following:

- Get a connection
- Create a message
- Add content to a message
- Send the message
- Retrieve the content in a message and in an attachment

First, we'll walk through the steps in sending a request-response message for a client that does not use a messaging provider. Then we'll do a walkthrough of a client that uses a messaging provider sending a one-way message. Both types of client may add attachments to a message, so adding attachments is covered last as a separate topic.

8.3.1 Client without a Messaging Provider

An application that does not use a messaging provider is limited to operating in a client role and can send only request-response messages. Though limited, it can make use of Web services that are implemented to do request-response messaging.

Getting a SOAPConnection Object

The first thing any JAXM client needs to do is get a connection, either a SOAPConnection object or a ProviderConnection object. The overview section discusses these two types of connections and how they are used.

A client that does not use a messaging provider has only one choice for creating a connection, which is to create a SOAPConnection object. This kind of connection is a point-to-point connection, meaning that it goes directly from the sender to the URL that the sender specifies.

The first step is to obtain a SOAPConnectionFactory object that you can use to create your connection. The JAXM API makes this easy by providing the SOAPConnectionFactory class with a default implementation. You can get an instance of this implementation with the following line of code.

```
SOAPConnectionFactory scFactory =
                        SOAPConnectionFactory.newInstance();
```

Notice that because newInstance is a static method, you will always use the class name SOAPConnectionFactory when you invoke its newInstance method.

Now you can use *scFactory* to create a SOAPConnection object.

```
SOAPConnection con = scFactory.createConnection();
```

You will use *con* later to send the message that is created in the next part.

Creating a Message

The next step is to create a message, which you do using a MessageFactory object. If you are a standalone client, you can use the default implementation of the MessageFactory class that the JAXM API provides. The following code fragment illustrates getting an instance of this default message factory and then using it to create a message.

```
MessageFactory factory = MessageFactory.newInstance();
SOAPMessage message = factory.createMessage();
```

As is true of the newInstance method for SOAPConnectionFactory, the newInstance method for MessageFactory is static, so you invoke it by calling MessageFactory.newInstance. Note that it is possible to write your own implementation of a message factory and plug it in via system properties, but the default message factory is the one that will generally be used.

The other way to get a `MessageFactory` object is to retrieve it from a naming service where it has been registered. This way is available only to applications that use a messaging provider, and it will be covered later.

Parts of a Message. A `SOAPMessage` object is required to have certain elements, and the JAXM API simplifies things for you by returning a new `SOAPMessage` object that already contains these elements. So *`message`*, which was created in the preceding line of code, has the following:

I. A `SOAPPart` object that contains

   A. A `SOAPEnvelope` object that contains

      1. An empty `SOAPHeader` object

      2. An empty `SOAPBody` object

The `SOAPHeader` object, though optional, is included for convenience because most messages will use it. The `SOAPBody` object can hold the content of the message and can also contain fault messages that contain status information or details about a problem with the message.

Accessing Elements of a Message. The next step in creating a message is to access its parts so that content can be added. The `SOAPMessage` object *`message`*, created in the previous code fragment, is where to start. It contains a `SOAPPart` object, so you use *`message`* to retrieve it.

```
SOAPPart soapPart = message.getSOAPPart();
```

Next you can use *`soapPart`* to retrieve the `SOAPEnvelope` object that it contains.

```
SOAPEnvelope envelope = soapPart.getEnvelope();
```

You can now use *`envelope`* to retrieve its empty `SOAPHeader` and `SOAPBody` objects.

```
SOAPHeader header = envelope.getHeader();
SOAPBody body = envelope.getBody();
```

Our example of a standalone client does not use a SOAP header, so you will need to delete it. Because all `SOAPElement` objects, including `SOAPHeader` objects, are derived from the `Node` interface, you use the method `Node.detachNode` to delete *`header`*.

```
header.detachNode();
```

Adding Content to the Body. To add content to the body, you need to create a SOAPBodyElement object to hold the content. When you create any new element, you also need to create an associated Name object to identify it. Name objects are created using SOAPEnvelope methods, so you can use *envelope* from the previous code fragment to create the Name object for your new element.

Name objects associated with SOAPBody and SOAPHeader objects must be fully qualified; that is, they must be created with a local name, a prefix for the namespace being used, and a URI for the namespace. Specifying a namespace for an element makes clear which one is meant if there is more than one element with the same local name.

The code fragment that follows retrieves the SOAPBody object *body* from *envelope*, creates a Name object for the element to be added, and adds a new SOAPBodyElement object to *body*.

```
SOAPBody body = envelope.getBody();
Name bodyName = envelope.createName("GetLastTradePrice",
                    "m", "http://wombat.ztrade.com");
SOAPBodyElement gltp = body.addBodyElement(bodyName);
```

At this point, *body* contains a SOAPBodyElement object identified by the Name object *bodyName*, but there is still no content in *gltp*. Assuming that you want to get a quote for the stock of Sun Microsystems, Inc., you need to create a child element for the symbol using the method addChildElement. Then you need to give it the stock symbol using the method addTextNode. The Name object for the new SOAPElement object *symbol* is initialized with only a local name, which is allowed for child elements.

```
Name name = envelope.createName("symbol");
SOAPElement symbol = gltp.addChildElement(name);
symbol.addTextNode("SUNW");
```

You might recall that the headers and content in a SOAPPart object must be in XML format. The JAXM API takes care of this for you, building the appropriate XML constructs automatically when you call methods such as addBodyElement, addChildElement, and addTextNode. Note that you can call the method addTextNode only on an element such as *bodyElement* or any child elements that are added to it. You cannot call addTextNode on a SOAPHeader or SOAPBody object.

The content that you have just added to your SOAPBody object will look like the following when it is sent over the wire:

```
<SOAP-ENV:Envelope
 xmlns:SOAP-ENV="http://schemas.xmlsoap.org/soap/envelope/"
    <SOAP-ENV:Body>
        <m:GetLastTradePrice xmlns:m=
                                    "http://wombat.ztrade.com">
            <symbol>SUNW</symbol>
        </m:GetLastTradePrice>
    </SOAP-ENV:Body>
</SOAP-ENV:Envelope>
```

Let's examine this XML excerpt line by line to see how it relates to your JAXM code. Note that an XML parser does not care about indentations, but they are generally used to indicate element levels and thereby make it easier for a human reader to understand.

JAXM code:

```
SOAPPart soapPart = message.getSOAPPart();
SOAPEnvelope envelope = soapPart.getEnvelope();
```

XML it produces:

```
<SOAP-ENV:Envelope
 xmlns:SOAP-ENV="http://schemas.xmlsoap.org/soap/envelope/"
    . . . . . . (intervening elements omitted)
</SOAP-ENV:Envelope>
```

The outermost element in this XML example is the SOAP envelope element, indicated by SOAP-ENV:Envelope. Envelope is the name of the element, and SOAP-ENV is the namespace prefix. The interface SOAPEnvelope represents a SOAP envelope.

The first line signals the beginning of the SOAP envelope element, and the last line signals the end of it; everything in between is part of the SOAP envelope. The second line has an attribute for the SOAP envelope element. xmlns stands for "XML namespace," and its value is the URI of the namespace associated with Envelope. This attribute is automatically included for you.

JAXM code:

```
SOAPBody body = envelope.getBody();
```

XML it produces:

```
<SOAP-ENV:Body>
        . . . . . .
</SOAP-ENV:Body>
```

These two lines mark the beginning and end of the SOAP body, represented in JAXM by a `SOAPBody` object.

JAXM code:

```
Name bodyName = envelope.createName("GetLastTradePrice",
                    "m", "http://wombat.ztrade.com");
SOAPBodyElement gltp = body.addBodyElement(bodyName);
```

XML it produces:

```
<m:GetLastTradePrice xmlns:m=
                    "http://wombat.ztrade.com">
    . . . .
</m:GetLastTradePrice>
```

These lines are what the `SOAPBodyElement` *`gltp`* in your code represents. “GetLastTradePrice” is its local name, “m” is its namespace prefix, and “http://wombat.ztrade.com” is its namespace URI.

JAXM code:

```
Name name = envelope.createName("symbol");
SOAPElement symbol = gltp.addChildElement(name);
symbol.addTextNode("SUNW");
```

XML it produces:

```
<symbol>SUNW</symbol>
```

The `String` `"SUNW"` is the message content that your recipient, the stock quote service, receives.

Sending a Message

A standalone client uses a `SOAPConnection` object and must therefore use the `SOAPConnection` method `call` to send a message. This method takes two arguments, the message being sent and the destination to which the message should go. This message is going to the stock quote service indicated by the `URLEndpoint` object *`endpoint`*.

```
URLEndpoint endpoint = new URLEndpoint(
                    "http://wombat.ztrade.com/quotes");

SOAPMessage response = con.call(message, endpoint);
```

Your message sent the stock symbol SUNW; the `SOAPMessage` object *response* should contain the last stock price for Sun Microsystems, which you will retrieve in the next section.

A connection uses a fair amount of resources, so it is a good idea to close a connection as soon as you are through using it.

```
con.close();
```

Getting the Content of a Message

The initial steps for retrieving a message's content are the same as those for giving content to a message: You first access the `SOAPBody` object, using the message to get the envelope and the envelope to get the body. Then you access its `SOAPBodyElement` object because that is the element to which content was added in the example. (In a later section you will see how to add content directly to the `SOAPBody` object, in which case you would not need to access the `SOAPBodyElement` object for adding content or for retrieving it.) To get the content, which was added with the method `Node.addTextNode`, you call the method `Node.getValue`. Note that `getValue` returns the value of the immediate child of the element that calls the method. Therefore, in the following code fragment, `getValue` is called on *bodyElement*, the element on which the method `addTextNode` was called.

In order to access *bodyElement*, you need to call the method `getChildElement` on *body*. Passing *bodyName* to `getChildElement` returns a `java.util.Iterator` object that contains all of the child elements identified by the `Name` object *bodyName*. You already know that there is only one, so just calling the method `next` on it will return the `SOAPBodyElement` you want. Note that the method `Iterator.next` returns a Java `Object`, so it is necessary to cast the `Object` it returns to a `SOAPBodyElement` object before assigning it to the variable *bodyElement*.

```
SOAPPart sp = response.getSOAPPart();
SOAPEnvelop env = sp.getEnvelope();
SOAPBody sb = sp.getBody();
java.util.Iterator it = sb.getChildElements(bodyName);
SOAPBodyElement bodyElement = (SOAPBodyElement)it.next();
String lastPrice = bodyElement.getValue();
System.out.print("The last price for SUNW is ");
System.out.println(lastPrice);
```

If there were more than one element with the name *bodyName*, you would have had to use a `while` loop using the method `Iterator.hasNext` to make sure that you got all of them.

```
while (it.hasNext()) {
    SOAPBodyElement bodyElement = (SOAPBodyElement)it.next();
    String lastPrice = bodyElement.getValue();
    System.out.print("The last price for SUNW is ");
    System.out.println(lastPrice);
}
```

At this point, you have seen how to send a request-response message as a standalone client. You have also seen how to get the content from the response. The next part shows you how to send a message using a messaging provider.

8.3.2 Client with a Messaging Provider

Using a messaging provider gives you more flexibility than a standalone client has because it can take advantage of the additional functionality that a messaging provider can offer.

Getting a ProviderConnection Object

Whereas a `SOAPConnection` object is a point-to-point connection directly to a particular URL, a `ProviderConnection` object is a connection to a messaging provider. With this kind of connection, all messages that you send or receive go through the messaging provider.

As with getting a `SOAPConnection` object, the first step is to get a connection factory, but in this case, it is a `ProviderConnectionFactory` object. You can obtain a `ProviderConnectionFactory` object by retrieving it from a naming service. This is possible when your application is using a messaging provider and is deployed in a servlet or J2EE container. With a `ProviderConnectionFactory` object, you can create a connection to a particular messaging provider and thus be able to use the capabilities of a profile that the messaging provider supports.

To get a `ProviderConnectionFactory` object, you first supply the logical name of your messaging provider to the container at deployment time. This is the name associated with your messaging provider that has been registered with a naming service based on the Java Naming and Directory Interface (JNDI). You can then do a lookup using this name to obtain a `ProviderConnectionFactory` object that will create connections to your messaging provider. For example, if the name registered for your messaging provider is "ProviderABC," you can do a lookup on "ProviderABC" to get a `ProviderConnectionFactory` object and use it to create a connection to your messaging provider. This is what is done in the following code fragment. The first two lines use methods from the JNDI API to retrieve the `ProviderConnectionFactory` object, and the last line uses a method from the JAXM API to create the connection to the messaging provider. Note that because the JNDI method `lookup` returns a Java `Object`, you must convert it to a `ProviderConnectionFactory` object before assigning it to the variable *pcFactory*.

```
Context ctx = new InitialContext();
ProviderConnectionFactory pcFactory =
        (ProviderConnectionFactory)ctx.lookup("ProviderABC");

ProviderConnection pcCon = pcFactory.createConnection();
```

You will use *pcCon*, which represents a connection to your messaging provider, to get information about your messaging provider and to send the message you will create in the next section.

Creating a Message

You create all JAXM messages by getting a `MessageFactory` object and using it to create the `SOAPMessage` object. For the standalone client example, you simply used the default `MessageFactory` object obtained via the method `MessageFactory.newInstance`. However, when you are using a messaging provider, you obtain the `MessageFactory` object in a different way.

Getting a MessageFactory. If you are using a messaging provider, you create a `MessageFactory` object by using the method `ProviderConnection.createMessageFactory`. In addition, you pass it a `String` indicating the profile you want to use. To find out which profiles your messaging provider supports, you need to get a `ProviderMetaData` object with information about your provider. This is done by calling the method `getMetaData` on the connection to your provider. Then you need to call the method `getSupportedProfiles` to get an array of the profiles your messaging provider supports. Supposing that you want to use the ebXML profile, you need to see if any of the profiles in the array matches "ebxml". If there is a match, that profile is assigned to the variable *profile*, which can then be passed to the method `createMessageFactory`.

```
ProviderMetaData metaData = pcCon.getMetaData();
String[] supportedProfiles = metaData.getSupportedProfiles();
String profile = null;
```

```
for (int i=0; i < supportedProfiles.length; i++) {
    if (supportedProfiles[i].equals("ebxml")) {
        profile = supportedProfiles[i];
        break;
    }
}

MessageFactory factory = pcCon.createMessageFactory(profile);
```

You can now use *factory* to create a `SOAPMessage` object that conforms to the ebXML profile. This example uses the minimal ebXML profile used in the JAXM RI. Note that the following line of code uses the class `EbXMLMEssageImpl`, which is defined in the JAXM RI and is not part of the JAXM API.

```
EbXMLMessageImpl message = (EbXMLMessageImpl)factory.
                                        createMessage();
```

For this profile, instead of using `Endpoint` objects, you indicate `Party` objects for the sender and the receiver. This information will appear in the message's header, and the messaging provider will use it to determine where to send the message. The following lines of code use the methods `setSender` and `setReceiver`, which are provided by the ebXML profile implemented in the JAXM RI. These methods not only create a `SOAPHeader` object but also give it content. You can use these methods because your `SOAPMessage` object is an `EbXMLMessageImpl` object, giving you access to the methods defined in `EbXMLMessageImpl`.

```
message.setSender(new Party("http://grand.products.com"));
message.setReceiver(new Party("http://whiz.gizmos.com"));
```

If you are not using a profile or you want to set content for a header not covered by your profile's implementation, you need to follow the steps shown in the next section.

Adding Content to the Header. To add content to the header, you need to create a `SOAPHeaderElement` object. As with all new elements, it must have an associated `Name` object, which you create using the message's `SOAPEnvelope` object.

The following code fragment retrieves the `SOAPHeader` object from *envelope* and adds a new `SOAPHeaderElement` object to it.

```
SOAPHeader header = envelope.getHeader();
Name headerName = envelope.createName("Purchase Order",
                        "PO", "http://www.sonata.com/order");
SOAPHeaderElement headerElement =
                        header.addHeaderElement(headerName);
```

At this point, *header* contains the SOAPHeaderElement object *headerElement* identified by the Name object *headerName*. Note that the addHeaderElement method both creates *headerElement* and adds it to *header*.

Now that you have identified *headerElement* with *headerName* and added it to *header*, the next step is to add content to *headerElement*, which the next line of code does with the method addTextNode.

```
headerElement.addTextNode("order");
```

Now you have the SOAPHeader object *header* that contains a SOAPHeaderElement object whose content is "order."

Adding Content to the SOAP Body. The process for adding content to the SOAPBody object is the same for clients using a messaging provider as it is for standalone clients. This is also the same as the process for adding content to the SOAPHeader object. You access the SOAPBody object, add a SOAPBodyElement object to it, and add text to the SOAPBodyElement object. It is possible to add additional SOAPBodyElement objects, and it is possible to add subelements to the SOAPBodyElement objects with the method addChildElement. For each element or child element, you add content with the method addTextNode.

The section on the standalone client demonstrated adding one SOAPBodyElement object, adding a child element, and giving it some text. The following example shows adding more than one SOAPBodyElement and adding text to each of them.

The code first creates the SOAPBodyElement object *purchaseLineItems*, which has a fully-qualified namespace associated with it. That is, the Name object for it has a local name, a namespace prefix, and a namespace URI. As you saw earlier, a SOAPBodyElement object is required to have a fully-qualified namespace, but child elements added to it may have Name objects with only the local name.

```
SOAPBody body = envelope.getBody();
Name bodyName = envelope.createName("PurchaseLineItems", "PO",
                       "http://sonata.fruitsgalore.com");
SOAPBodyElement purchaseLineItems =
                           body.addBodyElement(bodyName);

Name childName = envelope.createName("Order");
SOAPElement order =
            purchaseLineItems.addChildElement(childName);
```

```
childName = envelope.createName("Product");
SOAPElement product = order.addChildElement(childName);
product.addTextNode("Apple");

childName = envelope.createName("Price");
SOAPElement price = order.addChildElement(childName);
price.addTextNode("1.56");

childName = envelope.createName("Order");
SOAPElement order2 =
            purchaseLineItems.addChildElement(childName);

childName = envelope.createName("Product");
SOAPElement product2 = order2.addChildElement(childName);
product2.addTextNode("Peach");

childName = envelope.createName("Price");
SOAPElement price2 = order2.addChildElement(childName);
price2.addTextNode("1.48");
```

The JAXM code in the preceding example produces the following XML in the SOAP body:

```
<PO:PurchaseLineItems
 xmlns:PO="http://www.sonata.fruitsgalore/order">
    <Order>
        <Product>Apple</Product>
        <Price>1.56</Price>
    </Order>

    <Order>
        <Product>Peach</Product>
        <Price>1.48</Price>
    </Order>
</PO:PurchaseLineItems>
```

Adding Content to the SOAPPart Object. If the content you want to send is in a file, JAXM provides an easy way to add it directly to the `SOAPPart` object. This means that you do not access the `SOAPBody` object and build the XML content yourself, as you did in the previous section.

To add a file directly to the `SOAPPart` object, you use a `javax.xml.transform.Source` object from JAXP (the Java API for XML Processing). There are three types of Source objects: SAXSource, DOMSource, and StreamSource. A StreamSource object holds content as an XML document. SAXSource and DOMSource objects hold content along with the instructions for transforming the content into an XML document.

The following code fragment uses JAXP API to build a DOMSource object that is passed to the SOAPPart.setContent method. The first two lines of code get a DocumentBuilderFactory object and use it to create the DocumentBuilder object *builder*. Then *builder* parses the content file to produce a Document object, which is used to initialize a new DOMSource object.

```
DocumentBuilderFactory dbFactory = DocumentBuilderFactory.
                                        newInstance();
DocumentBuilder builder = dbFactory.newDocumentBuilder();
Document doc = builder.parse("file:///music/order/soap.xml");
DOMSource domSource = new DOMSource(doc);
```

The following two lines of code access the SOAPPart object (using the SOAP-Message object *message*) and set the new DOMSource object as its content. The method SOAPPart.setContent not only sets content for the SOAPBody object but also sets the appropriate header for the SOAPHeader object.

```
SOAPPart soapPart = message.getSOAPPart();
soapPart.setContent(domSource);
```

You will see other ways to add content to a message in the section on AttachmentPart objects. One big difference to keep in mind is that a SOAPPart object must contain only XML data, whereas an AttachmentPart object may contain any type of content.

Sending the Message

When the connection is a ProviderConnection object, messages have to be sent using the method ProviderConnection.send. This method sends the message passed to it and returns immediately. Unlike the SOAPConnection method call, it does not have to block until it receives a response, which leaves the application free to do other things.

The send method takes only one argument, the message to be sent. It does not need to be given the destination because the messaging provider can use information in the header to figure out where the message needs to go.

```
pcCon.send(message);
pcCon.close();
```

8.3.3 Adding Attachments

Adding AttachmentPart objects to a message is the same for all clients, whether they use a messaging provider or not. As noted in earlier sections, you can put any type of content, including XML, in an AttachmentPart object. And because the SOAP part can contain only XML content, you must use an AttachmentPart object for any content that is not in XML format.

Creating an AttachmentPart Object and Adding Content

The SOAPMessage object creates an AttachmentPart object, and the message also has to add the attachment to itself after content has been added. The SOAPMessage class has three methods for creating an AttachmentPart object.

The first method creates an attachment with no content. In this case, an AttachmentPart method is used later to add content to the attachment.

```
AttachmentPart attachment = message.createAttachmentPart();
```

You add content to *attachment* with the AttachmentPart method setContent. This method takes two parameters, a Java Object for the content, and a String object that gives the content type. Content in the SOAPBody part of a message automatically has a Content-Type header with the value "text/xml" because the content has to be in XML. In contrast, the type of content in an AttachmentPart object has to be specified because it can be any type.

Each AttachmentPart object has one or more headers associated with it. When you specify a type to the method setContent, that type is used for the header Content-Type. Content-Type is the only header that is required. You may set other optional headers, such as Content-Id and Content-Location. For convenience, JAXM provides get and set methods for the headers Content-Type, Content-Id, and Content-Location. These headers can be helpful in accessing a particular attachment when a message has multiple attachments. For example, to access the attachments that have particular headers, you call the SOAPMessage method getAttachments and pass it the header or headers you are interested in.

The following code fragment shows one of the ways to use the method setContent. The Java Object being added is a String, which is plain text, so the second argument has to be "text/plain." The code also sets a content identifier, which can be used to identify this AttachmentPart object. After you have added content to *attachment*, you need to add *attachment* to the SOAPMessage object, which is done in the last line.

```
String stringContent = "Update address for Sunny Skies " +
    "Inc., to 10 Upbeat Street, Pleasant Grove, CA 95439";

attachment.setContent(stringContent, "text/plain");
attachment.setContentId("update_address");

message.addAttachmentPart(attachment);
```

The variable *attachment* now represents an AttachmentPart object that contains the String *stringContent* and has a header that contains the String "text/plain". It also has a Content-Id header with "update_address" as its value. And now *attachment* is part of *message*.

Let's say you also want to attach a jpeg image showing how beautiful the new location is. In this case, the second argument passed to setContent must be "image/jpeg" to match the content being added. The code for adding an image might look like the following. For the first attachment, the Object passed to the method setContent was a String. In this case, it is a stream.

```
AttachmentPart attachment2 = message.createAttachmentPart();

byte[] jpegData = . . .;
ByteArrayInputStream stream = new ByteArrayInputStream(
                                    jpegData);

attachment2.setContent(stream, "image/jpeg");

message.addAttachmentPart(attachment);
```

The other two SOAPMessage.createAttachment methods create an AttachmentPart object complete with content. One is very similar to the AttachmentPart.setContent method in that it takes the same parameters and does essentially the same thing. It takes a Java Object containing the content and a String giving the content type. As with AttachmentPart.setContent, the Object may be a String, a stream, a javax.xml.transform.Source, or a javax.activation.DataHandler object. You have already seen an example of using a Source object as content. The next example will show how to use a DataHandler object for content.

The other method for creating an AttachmentPart object with content takes a DataHandler object, which is part of the JavaBeans Activation Framework (JAF). Using a DataHandler object is fairly straightforward. First you create a java.net.URL object for the file you want to add as content. Then you create a DataHandler object initialized with the URL object and pass it to the method createAttachmentPart.

```
URL url = new URL("http://greatproducts.com/gizmos/img.jpg");
DataHandler dh = new DataHandler(url);
AttachmentPart attachment = message.createAttachmentPart(dh);
attachment.setContentId("gyro_image");

message.addAttachmentPart(attachment);
```

You might note two things about the previous code fragment. First, it sets a header for Content-ID with the method setContentId. This method takes a String that can be whatever you like to identify the attachment. Second, unlike the other methods for setting content, this one does not take a String for Content-Type. This method takes care of setting the Content-Type header for you, which is possible because one of the things a DataHandler object does is determine the data type of the file it contains.

Accessing an AttachmentPart Object

If you receive a message with attachments or want to change an attachment to a message you are building, you will need to access the attachment. When it is given no argument, the method SOAPMessage.getAttachments returns a java.util.Iterator object over all the AttachmentPart objects in a message. The following code prints out the content of each AttachmentPart object in the SOAPMessage object *message*.

```
java.util.Iterator it = message.getAttachments();
while (it.hasNext()) {
    AttachmentPart attachment = it.next();
    Object content = attachment.getContent();
    String id = attachment.getContentId();
    System.out.print("Attachment " + id + " contains: " +
                                                content);
    System.out.println("");
}
```

Summary

You have now used the basic JAXM API and seen how to create and send SOAP messages as a standalone client and as a client using a messaging provider. You have added content to a SOAP header and a SOAP body and also created attachments and given them content. In addition, you have seen how to retrieve the content from the SOAP part and from attachments.

Congratulations on learning how to use the basic JAXM API.

8.4 Code Examples

The first part of this tutorial used code fragments to walk you through the basics of using the JAXM API. In this section, you will use some of those code fragments to create the program `Request.java` and also create the application `MyUddiPing.java`, which you can run.

Note: `<JWSDP_HOME>` is the directory where you unpacked the Java Web Services Developer Pack. The code examples use the UNIX form `$JWSDP_HOME`; for Windows, substitute the equivalent form `%JWSDP_HOME%`.

8.4.1 Request.java

The class `Request.java` is shown here and is also included in the `<JWSDP_HOME>/docs/tutorial/examples/jaxm` directory. It is based on the message you built as an example of a standalone client sending a request-response message. In addition to putting all the code together, it adds `import` statements, a `main` method, and a `try/catch` block with exception handling.

```
import javax.xml.soap.*;
import javax.xml.messaging.*;
import java.io.*;
import java.util.*;

public class Request {
    public static void main(String[] args)    {
        try {
            SOAPConnectionFactory scFactory =
                    SOAPConnectionFactory.newInstance();
            SOAPConnection con = scFactory.createConnection();

            MessageFactory factory =
                    MessageFactory.newInstance();
            SOAPMessage message = factory.createMessage();
```

```
            SOAPPart soapPart = message.getSOAPPart();
            SOAPEnvelope envelope = soapPart.getEnvelope();
            SOAPHeader header = envelope.getHeader();
            SOAPBody body = envelope.getBody();
            header.detachNode();

            Name bodyName = envelope.createName(
                            "GetLastTradePrice", "m",
                            "http://wombats.ztrade.com");
            SOAPBodyElement gltp =
                    body.addBodyElement(bodyName);

            Name name = envelope.createName("symbol");
            SOAPElement symbol = gltp.addChildElement(name);
            symbol.addTextNode("SUNW");

            URLEndpoint endpoint = new URLEndpoint(
                    "http://wombat.ztrade.com/quotes");
            SOAPMessage response = con.call(message,
                                          endpoint);

            con.close();

            SOAPPart sp = response.getSOAPPart();
            SOAPEnvelope se = sp.getEnvelope();
            SOAPBody sb = se.getBody();

            Iterator it = sb.getChildElements(bodyName);
            SOAPBodyElement bodyElement =
                            (SOAPBodyElement)it.next();
            String lastPrice = bodyElement.getValue();

            System.out.print("The last price for SUNW is ");
            System.out.println(lastPrice);

        } catch (Exception ex) {
            ex.printStackTrace();
        }
    }
}
```

In order for `Request.java` to be runnable, the `URLEndpoint` object in it has to be a valid existing site, which is not true in this case. However, the application in the next section is one that you can run.

8.4.2 MyUddiPing.java

The sample program `UddiPing.java` is another example of a standalone application. A Universal Description, Discovery and Integration (UDDI) service is a business registry and repository from which you can get information about businesses that have registered themselves with the registry. In this case, the `UddiPing` application is not actually accessing a UDDI service registry but rather a test (demo) version. Because of this, the number of businesses you can get information about is limited. Nevertheless, `UddiPing` demonstrates a request being sent and a response being received. The application prints out the complete message that is returned, that is, the complete XML document as it looks when it comes over the wire. Later in this section you will see how to rewrite `UddiPing.java` so that in addition to printing out the entire XML document, it also prints out just the text content of the response. This makes it much easier to see the information you want.

In order to get a better idea of how to run the `UddiPing` example, take a look at the directory `<JWSDP_HOME>/samples/jaxm/uddiping`. This directory contains the subdirectory `src` and the files `run.sh` (or `run.bat`), `uddi.properties`, `UddiPing.class`, and `README`. The `README` file tells you what you need to do to run the application, which is explained more fully here.

The `README` file directs you to modify the file `uddi.properties`, which contains the URL of the destination (the UDDI test registry) and the proxy host and proxy port of the sender. You will need to modify this file so that it has your proxy host and your proxy port. If you are in the `uddiping` directory when you call the `run.sh` (or `run.bat`) script, the information in the `run` script should be correct already.

The `run.sh` script calls the `java` command on `UddiPing`. First it sets the location of the `java` command and then prints a usage message if two arguments are not supplied. Perhaps the main thing it does is to set your classpath so that the necessary `.jar` files can be found.

Here is what you type at the command line if you want to get information about, for example, Oracle:

```
run.sh uddi.properties Oracle
```

Executing the `run` script as shown in the preceding command line should produce an XML document with the name and description of Oracle as the content.

However, these are embedded in the XML document, which makes them difficult to see. The next section adds code to `UddiPing.java` that extracts the content so that it is readily visible.

Creating MyUddiPing.java. To make the response to `UddiPing.java` easier to read, you will create a new file called `MyUddiPing.java`, which extracts the content and prints it out. You will see how to write the new file later in this section after setting up a new directory with the necessary files. Because the name of the new file is `MyUddiPing.java`, create the directory `myuddiping` under the `<JWSDP_HOME>/samples/jaxm` directory. Then copy the `uddi.properties` file from the `uddiping` directory into the `myuddiping` directory.

```
cd $JWSDP_HOME/samples/jaxm
mkdir myuddiping
cp uddiping/uddi.properties myuddiping
```

The `run.sh` and `run.bat` scripts for `MyUddiPing` are located in the `examples` directory of the tutorial, so you will need to copy the appropriate one from there.

UNIX:

```
cd myuddiping
cp $JWSDP_HOME/docs/tutorial/jaxm/examples/run.sh .
```

Windows:

```
cd myuddiping
copy %JWSDP_HOME%\docs\tutorial\jaxm\examples\run.bat .
```

The `MyUddiPing.class` file will be added to the directory `myuddiping` later as part of the execution of the `run` script.

Next, you need to create a `src` directory as a subdirectory of `myuddiping`., which is where you will create the file `MyUddiPing.java`.

```
cd myuddiping
mkdir src
```

For convenience, you can copy `MyUddiPing.java` from the `examples` directory to your new `src` directory as follows:

UNIX:

```
cd src
cp $JWSDP_HOME/docs/tutorial/examples/jaxm/MyUddiPing.java .
```

Windows:

```
cd src
copy %JWSDP_HOME%\docs\tutorial\examples\jaxm\
                                        MyUddiPing.java .
```

Now let's go through the file a few lines at a time. Note that most of the class `MyUddiPing.java` is based on `UddiPing.java`. You will be adding a section at the end that accesses only the content you want from the response that is returned by the method `call`.

The first four lines of code import the packages used in the application.

```
import javax.xml.soap.*;
import javax.xml.messaging.*;
import java.util.*;
import java.io.*;
```

The next few lines begin the definition of the class `MyUddiPing`, which starts with the definition of its `main` method. The first thing it does is check to see if two arguments were supplied. If not, it prints a usage message and exits. (Note that if one of the `run` scripts is used, the check will already have been done, so there will always be two arguments to get to this point.)

```
public class MyUddiPing {
    public static void main(String[] args) {
        try {
            if (args.length != 2) {
                System.err.println("Usage: UddiPing " +
                    "properties-file business-name");
                System.exit(1);
            }
```

The following lines create a `java.util.Properties` file that contains the system properties and the properties from the file `uddi.properties` that is in the `myuddiping` directory.

```
            Properties myprops = new Properties();
            myprops.load(new FileInputStream(args[0]));
            Properties props = System.getProperties();
            Enumeration it = myprops.propertyNames();
            while (it.hasMoreElements()) {
                String s = (String) it.nextElement();
                props.put(s, myprops.getProperty(s));
            }
```

The next four lines create a `SOAPMessage` object. First, the code gets an instance of `SOAPConnectionFactory` and uses it to create a connection. Then it gets an instance of `MessageFactory` and uses it to create a message.

```
SOAPConnectionFactory scf =
        SOAPConnectionFactory.newInstance();
SOAPConnection connection =
        scf.createConnection();
MessageFactory msgFactory =
        MessageFactory.newInstance();
SOAPMessage msg = msgFactory.createMessage();
```

The new `SOAPMessage` object *msg* automatically contains a `SOAPPart` object that contains a `SOAPEnvelope` object. The `SOAPEnvelope` object contains a `SOAPBody` object, which is the element you want to access in order to add content to it. The next lines of code get the `SOAPPart` object, the `SOAPEnvelope` object, and the `SOAPBody` object.

```
SOAPEnvelope envelope =
            msg.getSOAPPart().getEnvelope();
SOAPBody body = envelope.getBody();
```

The following lines of code add an element with a fully-qualified name and then add two attributes to the new element. The first attribute has the name `"generic"` and the value `"1.0"`. The second attribute has the name `"maxRows"` and the value `"100"`. Then the code adds a child element with the name *name* and adds some text to it with the method `addTextNode`. The text added is the `String` object that was passed in as the second argument, which is the name of the business that is being searched for in the test registry.

```
SOAPBodyElement findBusiness =
        body.addBodyElement(
        envelope.createName("find_business",
        "", "urn:uddi-org:api"));
findBusiness.addAttribute(
        envelope.createName("generic", "1.0");
findBusiness.addAttribute(
        envelope.createName("maxRows", "100");
SOAPElement businessName =
        findBusiness.addChildElement(
        envelope.createName("name"));
businessName.addTextNode(args[1]);
```

The next line of code creates the URLEndpoint object that is the destination for this message. It gets the value of the property named "URL" from the system property file.

```
URLEndpoint endpoint = new URLEndpoint(
    System.getProperties().getProperty("URL"));
```

The following line of code saves the changes that have been made to the message. This method will be called automatically when the message is sent, but it does not hurt to call it explicitly.

```
msg.saveChanges();
```

Next the message *msg* is sent to the destination that *endpoint* represents, which is the test UDDI registry. The method call will block until it gets a SOAPMessage object back, at which point it returns the reply.

```
SOAPMessage reply = connection.call(msg,
                                endpoint);
```

In the next two lines, the first prints out a line giving the URL of the sender (the test registry), and the second prints out the returned message as an XML document.

```
System.out.println("Received reply from: " +
                                endpoint);
reply.writeTo(System.out);
```

The code thus far has been based on UddiPing.java. If you go to the uddiping directory and call the appropriate run script, you can see what the output looks like.

UNIX:

```
cd $JWSDP_HOME/samples/jaxm/uddiping
run.sh uddi.properties Microsoft
```

Windows:

```
cd %JWSDP_HOME%\samples\jaxm\uddiping
run.bat uddi.properties Microsoft
```

What appears on your screen will look something like this:

```
Received replyfrom:
http://www3.ibm.com/services/uddi/testregistry/inquiryapi<?xm
l version="1.0" encoding="UTF-8" ?><Envelope
xmlns="http://schemas.xmlsoap.org/soap/envelope/"><Body><busi
nessList generic="1.0" xmlns="urn:uddi-org:api"
operator="www.ibm.com/services/uddi"
truncated="false"><businessInfos><businessInfo
businessKey="D7475060-BF58-11D5-A432-
0004AC49CC1E"><name>Microsoft Corporation</name><description
xml:lang="en">Computer Software and Hardware
Manufacturer</description><serviceInfos></serviceInfos></busi
nessInfo></businessInfos></businessList></Body></Envelope>
```

Adding New Code

Now you are going to add code to make the reply more user-friendly. Your new code will get the content from certain elements rather than printing out the whole XML document as it was sent over the wire. Because the content is in the SOAP-Body object, the first thing you need to do is access it, as shown in the following line of code. You can access each element in separate method calls, as was done in earlier examples, or you can access the SOAPBody object using this shorthand version.

```
SOAPBody replyBody =
        reply.getSOAPPart().getEnvelope().getBody();
```

Next you might print out two blank lines to separate your results from the raw XML message and a third line that describes the text that follows.

```
System.out.println("");
System.out.println("");
System.out.print(
 "Content extracted from the reply message: ");
```

Now you can begin the process of getting all of the child elements from an element, getting the child elements from each of those, and so on, until you arrive at a text element that you can print out. Unfortunately, the registry used for this example code, being just a test registry, is not always consistent. The number of subelements sometimes varies, making it difficult to know how many levels down the code needs to go. And in some cases, there are multiple entries for the same company name. Note that by contrast, you can count on the structure and elements for a standard valid registry being consistent.

The code you will be adding drills down through the subelements within the SOAP body and retrieves the name and description of the company in most cases. The method you use to retrieve child elements is the `SOAPElement` method `getChildElements`. When you give this method no arguments, it retrieves all of the child elements of the element on which it is called. If you know the `Name` object used to name an element, you can supply that to `getChildElements` and retrieve only the children with that name. In this case, however, you need to retrieve all elements and keep drilling down until you get to the elements that contain text content.

Here is the basic pattern that is repeated for drilling down:

```
Iterator iter1 = replyBody.getChildElements();
while (iter1.hasNext()) {
    SOAPBodyElement bodyElement =
            (SOAPBodyElement)iter1.next();
    Iterator iter2 =
            bodyElement.getChildElements();
    while (iter2.hasNext()) {
```

The method `getChildElements` returns the elements in the form of a `java.util.Iterator` object. You access the child elements by calling the method `next` on the `Iterator` object. The method `Iterator.hasNext` can be used in a `while` loop because it returns `true` as long as the next call to the method `next` will return a child element. The loop ends when there are no more child elements to retrieve.

An immediate child of a `SOAPBody` object is a `SOAPBodyElement` object, which is why calling `iter1.next` returns a `SOAPBodyElement` object. Children of `SOAPBodyElement` objects and all child elements from there down are `SOAPElement` objects. For example, the call `iter2.next` returns the `SOAPElement` object *child2*. Note that the method `Iterator.next` returns an `Object`, which has to be narrowed (cast) to the specific kind of object you are retrieving. Thus, the result of calling `iter1.next` is cast to a `SOAPBodyElement` object, whereas the results of calling `iter2.next`, `iter3.next`, and so on, are all cast to a `SOAPElement` object.

Here is the code you add to access and print out the business name and description:

```
Iterator iter1 = replyBody.getChildElements();
while (iter1.hasNext()) {
    SOAPBodyElement bodyElement =
            (SOAPBodyElement)iter1.next();
```

```
                Iterator iter2 =
                        bodyElement.getChildElements();
                while (iter2.hasNext()) {
                    SOAPElement child2 =
                        (SOAPElement)iter2.next();
                    Iterator iter3 =
                        child2.getChildElements();
                    String content = child2.getValue();
                    System.out.println(content);
                    while (iter3.hasNext()) {
                        SOAPElement child3 =
                            (SOAPElement)iter3.next();
                        Iterator iter4 =
                                child3.getChildElements();
                        content = child3.getValue();
                        System.out.println(content);
                        while (iter4.hasNext()) {
                            SOAPElement child4 =
                                (SOAPElement)iter4.next();
                            content = child4.getValue();
                            System.out.println(content);
                        }
                    }
                }
            }
            connection.close();
        } catch (Exception ex) {
            ex.printStackTrace();
        }
    }
}
```

You are now ready to compile the code and move the new `.class` file to the directory `myuddiping`. If you have not already done so, you can copy the file `MyUddiPing.java` from *<JWSDP_HOME>*`/docs/tutorial/examples/jaxm` to *<JWSDP_HOME>*`/samples/jaxm/myuddiping/src`. You should already have copied the appropriate run script from *<JWSDP_HOME>*`/docs/tutorial/examples/jaxm` to the `myuddiping` directory. When you execute the appropriate `run` script, which you will do next, it will compile `MyUddiPing.java` and move the resulting `MyUddiPing.class` file to the `myuddiping` directory for you.

To execute the script for your platform, first be sure you are in the directory `myuddiping`. The `run` script takes two arguments, the file `uddi.properties`, and the name of the business you want to look up. To get a description of, for instance, Oracle, execute the appropriate `run` script as follows.

Note: If the `run` script is not executable, you will need to make it executable.

UNIX:

```
cd $JWSDP_HOME/samples/jaxm/myuddiping
run.sh uddi.properties Oracle
```

Windows:

```
cd %JWSDP_HOME%\samples\jaxm\myuddiping
run.bat uddi.properties Oracle
```

Here is the output that will appear after the full XML message. It is produced by the code added in `MyUddiPing.java`.

```
Content extracted from the reply message:

Oracle
oracle powers the internet

Oracle Corporation
Oracle Corporation provides the software and services for
e-business.
```

Running the script with Microsoft instead of Oracle produces the following output:

```
Received reply from: http://www-
3.ibm.com/services/uddi/testregistry/inquiryapi
<?xml version="1.0" encoding="UTF-8" ?><Envelope
xmlns="http://schemas.xmlsoap.org/soap/envelope/"><Body><busi
nessList generic="1.0" xmlns="urn:uddi-org:api"
operator="www.ibm.com/services/uddi"
truncated="false"><businessInfos><businessInfo
businessKey="D7475060-BF58-11D5-A432-
0004AC49CC1E"><name>Microsoft Corporation</name><description
xml:lang="en">Computer Software and Hardware
```

```
Manufacturer</description><serviceInfos></serviceInfos></busi
nessInfo></businessInfos></businessList></Body></Envelope>

Content extracted from the reply message:

Microsoft Corporation
Computer Software and Hardware Manufacturer
```

Conclusion

JAXM provides a Java API that simplifies writing and sending XML messages. You have learned how to use this API to write client code for JAXM request-response messages and one-way messages. You have also learned how to get the content from a reply message. Finally, you have seen how to write and run your own modification of the `uddiping` sample application. You now have first-hand experience of how JAXM makes it easier to do XML messaging.

CHAPTER 9

Java API for XML-based RPC

Dale Green

IN THIS CHAPTER

If you're new to the Java API for XML-based RPC ("JAX-RPC"), this chapter is the place to start. After briefly describing JAX-RPC, the chapter shows you how to build a simple Web service and client.

Although it starts with the basics, this chapter does have a few prerequisites. First, you should already be familiar with the Java programming language. You should also know how to install software, set environment variables, edit XML files, and run commands from a terminal window. A basic knowledge of Web servers is helpful, but not required.

Since this material is based on an early access (EA) release, it does not cover the full capabilities of JAX-RPC. If you're interested in learning more about JAX-RPC and its underlying technologies, please see the list of links on the <*JAXRPC_HOME*>/index.html page of your installation.

9.1 What is JAX-RPC?

JAX-RPC stands for Java API for XML-based RPC. It's an API for building Web services and clients using remote procedure calls (RPC) and XML. Often used in a distributed client/server model, an RPC mechanism enables clients to execute procedures on other systems.

In JAX-RPC, a remote procedure call is represented by an XML-based protocol such as SOAP. The SOAP specification defines envelope structure, encoding rules, and a convention for representing remote procedure calls and responses. These calls and responses are transmitted as SOAP messages over HTTP. The JAX-RPC reference implementation relies on SOAP 1.1 and HTTP 1.1.

Although JAX-RPC relies on complex protocols, the API hides this complexity from the application developer. On the server side, the developer specifies the remote procedures by defining methods in an interface written in the Java programming language. The developer also codes one or more classes that implement those methods. Client programs are also easy to code. After locating the service endpoint by specifying a URL, the client simply invokes the methods on a local object (a stub) that represents the remote service.

With JAX-RPC, clients and Web services have a big advantage—the platform independence of the Java programming language. In addition, JAX-RPC is not restrictive: a JAX-RPC client can access a Web service that is not running on the Java platform and vice versa. This flexibility is possible because JAX-RPC uses technologies defined by the World Wide Web Consortium (W3C): HTTP, SOAP, and the Web Service Description Language (WSDL). WSDL specifies an XML format for describing a service as a set of endpoints operating on messages. The JAX-RPC reference implementation includes a tool (`xrpcc`) that can read or write WSDL files. See the appendix, The xrpcc Tool (page 485).

9.2 A Simple Example: HelloWorld

This example shows you how to create a service named `HelloWorld`. A remote client of the `HelloWorld` service can invoke the `sayHello` method, which accepts a string parameter and then returns a string.

9.2.1 HelloWorld at Runtime

Figure 9.1 shows the structure of the `HelloWorld` service after it's been deployed. Here's what happens at runtime:

1. To call a remote procedure, the `HelloClient` program invokes a method on a stub, a local object that represents the remote service.

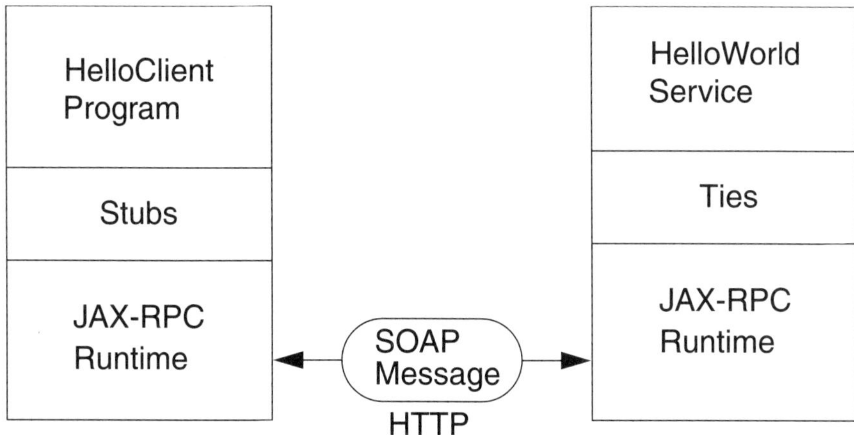

Figure 9.1 The `HelloWorld` Example at Runtime

2. The stub invokes routines in the JAX-RPC runtime system of the reference implementation.
3. The runtime system converts the remote method call into a SOAP message and then transmits the message as an HTTP request.
4. When the server receives the HTTP request, the JAX-RPC runtime system extracts the SOAP message from the request and translates it into a method call.
5. The JAX-RPC runtime system invokes the method on the tie object.
6. The tie object invokes the method on the implementation of the `HelloWorld` service.

The application developer only provides the top layers in the stacks depicted by Figure 9.1. Table 9.1 shows where the layers originate.

Table 9.1 Who (or What) Provides the Layers

Layer	Source
`HelloClient` Program `HelloWorld` Service (definition interface and implementation class)	Provided by the application developer
Stubs Ties	Generated by the `xrpcc` tool, which is run by the application developer
JAX-RPC Runtime System	Included with the reference implementation

9.2.2 HelloWorld Files

To create a service, an application developer needs to provide just a few files. For the `HelloWorld` example, these files are in the `docs/tutorial/examples/jaxrpc/hello` subdirectory:

- `HelloIF.java`—the service definition interface
- `HelloImpl.java`—the implementation class for the `HelloIF` interface
- `config.xml`—a configuration file read by the `xrpcc` tool, which creates the stub and tie classes
- `web.xml`—a deployment descriptor for the Web component (a servlet) that dispatches to the service
- `HelloClient.java`—the remote client that contacts the service and then invokes the `sayHello` method

9.2.3 Overview of Steps

The basic steps for developing a service definition are as follows:

1. Code the service definition interface and implementation class.
2. Compile the service definition code of step 1.
3. Create the configuration file.
4. Generate the stubs and ties.
5. Create the deployment descriptor.
6. Package the service definition.
7. Deploy the service definition.

On the client side, these are the steps:

1. Code the client.
2. Compile the client code.
3. Run the client.

9.2.4 Setting Up

Before you try out the `HelloWorld` example, verify that you've installed the required software and that you've set the necessary environment variables.

Required Software

For a list of the required software and supported operating systems, see the Release Notes of the Java Web Services Developer Pack.

The Java Web Services Developer Pack includes Tomcat and the `ant` build utility. You must use the included version of Tomcat to run the examples in this tutorial. Although you may use a separate installation of `ant`, we recommend that you run the included version in order to avoid confusion over incompatible versions.

Environment Variables

Before you try out the `HelloWorld` example, you must set some environment variables. For more information, see the Release Notes of the Java Web Services Developer Pack.

Setting build.xml Properties

If you are on a Windows system, you may skip this section.

1. In a text editor, open the `docs/tutorial/examples/jaxrpc/common/config-build.properties` file.
2. If you are on a UNIX system, change the value of the `script-suffix` property to `sh`. For Windows, the value should be `bat`, which is the default.
3. Save the `config-build.properties` file and exit the editor.

9.2.5 Coding the Service Definition Interface and Implementation Class

A service definition interface declares the methods that a remote client may invoke on the service. The interface must conform to a few rules:

- It extends the `java.rmi.Remote` interface.
- It must not have constant declarations, such as `public final static`.
- The methods must throw the `java.rmi.RemoteException` or one of its subclasses. (The methods may also throw service-specific exceptions.)

- Method parameters and return types must be supported JAX-RPC types. (See the JAX-RPC Specifications.)

In this example, the service definition interface is `HelloIF.java`:

```
package hello;

import java.rmi.Remote;
import java.rmi.RemoteException;

public interface HelloIF extends Remote {
    public String sayHello(String s) throws RemoteException;
}
```

In addition to the interface, you'll need to code the class that implements the interface. In this example, the implementation class is called `HelloImpl`:

```
package hello;

public class HelloImpl implements HelloIF {

    public String message = new String("Hello ");

    public String sayHello(String s) {
        return new String(message + s);
    }
}
```

9.2.6 Compiling the Service Definition Code

To compile `HelloIF.java` and `HelloImpl.java`, go to the `docs/tutorial/examples/jaxrpc/hello` directory and type the following:

```
ant compile-server
```

This command places the resulting class files in the `build` subdirectory.

9.2.7 Creating the Configuration File

The `config.xml` file contains information needed by the `xrpcc` tool, which you'll run in the next section.

In the file listing that follows, note the values defined in the `<service>` element. The name of the service, `HelloWorld`, will be used as the prefix of the `HelloWorldImpl` class name. Generated by the `xrpcc` tool, the `HelloWorldImpl` is instantiated by the client class. (See Coding the Client (page 315).) The `packageName` attribute, `hello`, is the name of the package of the classes generated by `xrpcc`. In the `<interface>` subelement, the `name` attribute corresponds to the fully qualified name of the service definition interface, `hello.HelloIF`. The `servantName` attribute is the name of the interface's implementation class, `hello.HelloImpl`.

Here is the `config.xml` file:

```
<?xml version="1.0" encoding="UTF-8"?>
<configuration
   xmlns="http://java.sun.com/jax-rpc-ri/xrpcc-config">
   <rmi name="HelloWorldService"
      targetNamespace="http://hello.org/wsdl"
      typeNamespace="http://hello.org/types">
      <service name="HelloWorld" packageName="hello">
         <interface name="hello.HelloIF"
         servantName="hello.HelloImpl"/>
      </service>
   </rmi>
</configuration>
```

For more information about the syntax of the tool's configuration file, see the section Configuration File (page 486).

Note: Although required for the reference implementation of JAX-RPC, the configuration file and `xrpcc` tool are not defined in the specifications. Their syntax and usage may change in future releases.

9.2.8 Generating the Stubs and Ties

The `xrpcc` tool generates the stubs and ties, which are lower-level classes that enable the client and server to communicate. The tool also creates a properties file and a WSDL file. Used internally by the reference implementation, the properties file is not defined in the specifications. For information about the relationship between JAX-RPC technology and WSDL files, please refer to the JAX-RPC Specifications.

In this example, the tool reads the service definition interface and the configuration file. (Alternatively, the tool may read a WSDL file instead of the interface. See Starting with a WSDL Document (page 488) for more information.)

The xrpcc tool is a script—xrpcc.sh for UNIX or xprcc.bat for Windows. To create the stubs and ties, run the tool as follows:

UNIX:

```
xrpcc.sh -classpath build -both -d build config.xml
```

Windows:

```
xrpcc.bat -classpath build -both -d build config.xml
```

The -both option instructs xrpcc to generate both stubs and ties. The -d option denotes the destination directory for the generated files. See the section Syntax (page 485) for the full syntax of the xrpcc tool.

9.2.9 Creating the Deployment Descriptor

A deployment descriptor is an XML file that provides configuration information for the Web server about the Web components (JSP pages or servlets) that are in a Web application. Because the HelloWorld service is deployed as a servlet, the deployment descriptor has some elements that are related to the service. This section describes only those elements; for more information about deployment descriptors, see the Java Servlet Specifications.

Let's take a quick look at a couple of the elements in the deployment descriptor (web.xml). First, note the HelloWorld_Config.properties value of the <init-param> element. This properties file was generated by the xrpcc tool. The name of the file is the HelloWorld service name (which was defined in the configuration file) appended by the _Config.properties string. The value of the <url-pattern> element, /jaxrpc/*, is part of the URL that designates the service's endpoint. This URL is passed to the HelloClient program as a command-line parameter. See Running the Client (page 316).

The web.xml deployment descriptor follows:

```
<?xml version="1.0" encoding="UTF-8"?>

 <!DOCTYPE web-app PUBLIC
     "-//Sun Microsystems, Inc.//DTD Web Application 2.3//EN"
     "http://java.sun.com/j2ee/dtds/web-app_2_3.dtd">
```

```
<web-app>
   <display-name>HelloWorldApplication</display-name>
   <description>Hello World Application</description>
   <servlet>
      <servlet-name>JAXRPCEndpoint</servlet-name>
      <display-name>JAXRPCEndpoint</display-name>
      <description>
         Endpoint for Hello World Application
      </description>
      <servlet-class>
        com.sun.xml.rpc.server.http.JAXRPCServlet
      </servlet-class>
      <init-param>
         <param-name>configuration.file</param-name>
         <param-value>
          /WEB_INF/HelloWorld_Config.properties
        </param-value>
      </init-param>
      <load-on-startup>0</load-on-startup>
   </servlet>
   <servlet-mapping>
      <servlet-name>JAXRPCEndpoint</servlet-name>
      <url-pattern>/jaxrpc/*</url-pattern>
   </servlet-mapping>
   <session-config>
      <session-timeout>60</session-timeout>
   </session-config>
</web-app>
```

9.2.10 Packaging the Service Definition

A service definition is packaged in a Web application archive (WAR), a JAR file whose contents is defined by the Java Servlet specifications. WAR files make it easy to distribute and install (deploy) the service on various sites. In a later step, you will deploy the `jaxrpc-hello.war` file on Tomcat. For JAX-RPC, a WAR file contains the following files:

- One or more service definition interfaces

  Each service definition has a single interface, but a WAR file may contain the files for more than one service. In this example, the service definition interface is `HelloIF.class`.

- One or more service definition classes that implement the interfaces

  For each service definition interface, you must provide a corresponding service implementation class (`HelloImpl.class`).

- Classes for pluggable serializers and deserializers

  This example does not require these files. (See the JAX-RPC Specifications for more information.)

- Other files required by the service implementation classes

  Examples of these files are: helper classes, JPEG images, and XML documents. Since it's so simple, the `HelloImpl` class does not need any of these other files.

- A deployment descriptor

  All WAR files require a deployment descriptor (`web.xml`).

- An optional WSDL file that describes the service

  In a previous section, you created the `HelloWorldService.wsdl` file by running the `xrpcc` tool.

In addition to the preceding list of files, in the JAX-RPC reference implementation a WAR file also contains several files generated by the `xrpcc` tool: tie, servlet, and helper classes; and a server configuration file (`HelloWorld_Config.properties`).

To package the `HelloWorld` service definition, type the following:

```
ant package
```

This command creates the `jaxrpc-hello.war` file.

9.2.11 Deploying the Service Definition

To deploy the service definition, you simply copy the WAR file to Tomcat's `webapps` directory:

```
ant deploy
```

The first time you deploy a WAR file, Tomcat must be started. For subsequent deployments of the same WAR file, you do not need to start or restart Tomcat. Because you are about to deploy the `jaxrpc-hello.war` file for the first time, if Tomcat is running now, you must shut it down and then restart it.

To shut down (stop) Tomcat, type the following command in a terminal window:

UNIX:

```
shutdown.sh
```

Windows:

```
shutdown
```

To start Tomcat, type this command:

UNIX:

```
startup.sh
```

Windows:

```
startup
```

To verify that the HelloWorld service has been deployed, open a browser window and specify this URL:

```
http://localhost:8080/jaxrpc-hello/jaxrpc
```

The browser should display these lines:

```
A Web Service is installed at this URL.

It supports the following ports: "HelloIF"
(http://localhost:8080/jaxrpc-hello/jaxrpc/HelloIF)
```

9.2.12 Coding the Client

The HelloClient is a standalone program that calls the sayHello method of the HelloWorld service. It makes this call through a stub, a local object which acts as a proxy for the remote service.

In the code listing that follows, note the names of the HelloIF_Stub and HelloWorldImpl classes, which were generated by the xrpcc tool. The HelloIF prefix matches the name of the service definition interface and the HelloWorld prefix corresponds to the service name specified in the configuration file. The HelloWorldImpl class is the implementation of a service as described in the JAX-RPC Specifications. The client gets a reference to the stub by calling the getHelloIF method of HelloWorldImpl.

The parameter of the _setTargetEndpoint method is a URI that denotes the address of the target service port. For details on this URI, see Running the Client (page 316).

The source code for the HelloClient follows:

```
package hello;

public class HelloClient {
    public static void main(String[] args) {
        try {
            HelloIF_Stub stub =
                (HelloIF_Stub)(new HelloWorldImpl().getHelloIF());
            stub._setTargetEndpoint(args[0]);
            System.out.println(stub.sayHello("Duke!"));
        } catch (Exception ex) {
            ex.printStackTrace();
        }
    }
}
```

9.2.13 Compiling the Client Code

Because the client code refers to classes generated by the xrpcc tool, be sure to run the tool before compiling the client. To compile the client, type the following:

```
ant compile-client
```

9.2.14 Running the Client

To run the HelloClient program, type the following:

```
ant run
```

The program should display this line:

```
Hello Duke!
```

The run target executes this command:

```
java -classpath <cpath> hello.HelloClient <endpoint>
```

We created the `run-hello` target because the classpath includes many JAR files. (The classpath will be simplified in a later release.) The command-line parameter for the `HelloClient` program is the service endpoint:

```
http://localhost:8080/jaxrpc-hello/jaxrpc/HelloIF
```

The `jaxrpc-hello` portion of the URL is the context of the servlet that implements the `HelloWorld` service. This portion corresponds to the prefix of the `jaxrpc-hello.war` file. The `jaxrpc` string matches the value of the `<url-pattern>` element of the `web.xml` deployment descriptor. And finally, `HelloIF` is the name of the interface that defines the service.

9.3 The Dynamic Invocation Interface

With the dynamic invocation interface (DII), a client can call a remote procedure even if the signature of the remote procedure or the name of the service are unknown until runtime.

9.3.1 When to Use DII

Although DII clients are flexible, they are more complex than clients that use static stubs. (For an example of a client with static stubs, see Coding the Client (page 315).) Compared to clients with static stubs, clients with DII are more difficult to code, debug, and test. Therefore, a client should use DII only if it cannot use static stubs.

However, there are two cases that require the flexibility of a DII client. The first case is a service broker that dynamically discovers services, configures the remote calls, and executes the calls. For example, an application for an online clothing store might access a service broker that specializes in shipping. This broker would use the Java API for XML Registries (JAXR) to locate the services of the shipping companies that meet certain criteria, such as low cost or fast delivery time. At runtime, the broker uses DII to call remote procedures on the web services of the shipping companies. As an intermediary between the clothing store and the shipping companies, the broker offers benefits to all parties. For the clothing store, it simplifies the shipping process, and for the shipping companies, it finds customers.

The second case requiring DII is less common: a development environment that does not support the generation of static stubs.

9.3.2 A DII Client Example

The source code for this example is in the `HelloClient.java` file of the `docs/tutorial/examples/jaxrpc/dynamic` directory.

The `HelloClient` program makes two remote procedure calls: `sayHello` and `sayHelloOneWay`. The `sayHello` call is synchronous and follows the familiar request-response model. During a synchronous call, the client makes the call (request) and waits for the call's return (response) before continuing. The `sayHelloOneWay` call has a one-way invocation mode. In the one-way mode, the client thread does not block and wait for the server to process the remote call. For more information about invocation modes, see the JAX-RPC Specifications.

DII Classes and Interfaces

The `HelloClient` program uses the following interfaces and classes for dynamic invocation.

- `Call`—supports the dynamic invocation of a remote operation on a service port
- `Service`—a factory for `Call` objects, dynamic proxies, and stubs; only generated services are factories for stubs
- `TypeMapping`—a set of tuples that describe the mapping between Java programming language types and XML data types; each `TypeMapping` is for a specific encoding; each tuple in a `TypeMapping` contains the following information:
    - Java programming language type
    - `SerializerFactory`
    - `DeserializerFactory`
    - XML data type
- `TypeMappingRegistry`—a storage area (registry) for `TypeMapping` instances; this registry enables you to store and retrieve `TypeMapping` instances for specific encodings
- `Qname`—a qualified name based on the Namespaces in XML Specifications

To see how to set up and invoke a dynamic invocation, refer to the `HelloClient` source code that is shown in the next section. As you examine the source code, note the classes and interfaces that belong to the packages whose names begin with `com.sun`. These packages are specific to the reference implementation and are not defined in the JAX-RPC Specifications.

DII HelloClient Listing

Here is the full listing for the `HelloClient.java` file of the `docs/tutorial/examples/jaxrpc/dynamic` directory. Note how much longer the DII client is than the static stub client shown in Coding the Client (page 315).

```
package dynamic;
import java.rmi.RemoteException;

import javax.xml.rpc.Call;
import javax.xml.rpc.Service;
import javax.xml.rpc.JAXRPCException;
import javax.xml.rpc.namespace.QName;
import javax.xml.rpc.encoding.TypeMapping;
import javax.xml.rpc.encoding.TypeMappingRegistry;

import com.sun.xml.rpc.client.ServiceImpl;
import com.sun.xml.rpc.client.dii.CallImpl;
import com.sun.xml.rpc.client.dii.CallPropertyConstants;

import com.sun.xml.rpc.encoding.Initializable;
import com.sun.xml.rpc.encoding.TypeMappingImpl;
import com.sun.xml.rpc.encoding.SerializerConstants;
import com.sun.xml.rpc.encoding.TypeMappingRegistryImpl;

import com.sun.xml.rpc.encoding.soap.SOAPConstants;
import com.sun.xml.rpc.encoding.soap.StandardSOAPTypeMappings;

import com.sun.xml.rpc.soap.streaming.SOAPNamespaceConstants;

public class HelloClient implements CallPropertyConstants,
    SerializerConstants {

    public static void main(String[] args) {

        try {

            String bodyNamespaceValue =
                new String("http://dynamic-hello.org/wsdl");

            QName stringQname =
                new QName(SOAPNamespaceConstants.XSD, "string");
```

```
            TypeMapping typeMapping =
                new StandardSOAPTypeMappings();
            TypeMappingRegistry registry =
                 new TypeMappingRegistryImpl();
            registry.register(typeMapping,
                SOAPConstants.URI_ENCODING);

            QName port = new QName("HelloIF");
            Service service =
                new ServiceImpl(new QName("Hello"));
            service.setTypeMappingRegistry(registry);

            Call call = service.createCall();
            call.setPortTypeName(port);
            call.setTargetEndpointAddress(args[0]);

            call.setProperty(BODY_NAMESPACE_PROPERTY,
                bodyNamespaceValue);
            call.setProperty(IS_SOAPACTION_USED_PROPERTY,
                new Boolean(true));
            call.setProperty(SOAPACTION_VALUE_PROPERTY, "");
            call.setProperty(ENCODING_STYLE_PROPERTY,
                SOAPConstants.URI_ENCODING);

            ((CallImpl)call).setReturnType(stringQname,
                 String.class);
            call.setOperationName("sayHello");
            call.addParameter("String_1", stringQname,
                Call.PARAM_MODE_IN);
            String[] params = { new String("Duke!") };
            String result = (String)call.invoke(params);
            System.out.println(result);

            call.setOperationName("sayHelloOneWay");
            call.removeAllParameters();
            call.invokeOneWay(null);
            System.out.println("One-way invoked");

        } catch (Exception ex) {
            ex.printStackTrace();
        }
    }
}
```

Building and Running the DII Example

To build this example, follow these steps:

1. Make sure that you've performed the set up instructions in Setting Up (page 309) and Coding the Service Definition Interface and Implementation Class (page 309).
2. Go to the `docs/tutorial/examples/jaxrpc/dynamic` directory.
3. Type the following:

   ```
   ant build
   ```

   This command compiles the code, runs the `xrpcc` tool, packages the WAR file, and deploys the WAR file onto the Tomcat server. The section, A Simple Example: HelloWorld (page 306), instructed you to perform each of these tasks by executing separate `ant` targets. The `build` target executes the same set of targets, but is more convenient because it requires less typing.
4. To run the client, type the following command:

   ```
   ant run
   ```

   The client should display the following lines:

   ```
   A dynamic hello to Duke! <time-stamp>
   One-way invoked
   ```

(Useful for debugging, the *`time-stamp`* indicates when the server code for the example was compiled. You can check the *`time-stamp`* to make sure that the client is accessing the WAR file most recently built.)

CHAPTER 10

Java API for XML Registries

by Kim Haase

IN THIS CHAPTER

THE Java API for XML Registries (JAXR) provides a uniform and standard Java API for accessing different kinds of XML Registries.

The release of JAXR 1.0 that you have downloaded as part of the Java Web Services Developer Pack (Java WSDP) includes the following:

- The JAXR 1.0 Early Access Reference Implementation (RI)
- API documentation
- Sample programs, including a Registry Browser

To learn how to configure JAXR in preparation for running JAXR client programs, see the JAXR home page (`<JWSDP_HOME>/docs/jaxr/index.html` on UNIX systems; `<JWSDP_HOME>\docs\jaxr\index.html` on Microsoft Windows systems).

10.1 Overview of JAXR

This section provides a brief overview of JAXR.

10.1.1 What is a Registry?

An XML registry is an infrastructure that enables the building, deployment, and discovery of Web services. It is a neutral third party that facilitates dynamic and loosely coupled business-to-business (B2B) interactions. A registry is available to organizations as a shared resource, often in the form of a Web-based service.

Currently there are a variety of specifications for XML registries. These include:

- The ebXML Registry and Repository standard, which is being developed by the Organization for the Advancement of Structured Information Standards (OASIS) and the United Nations Centre for the Facilitation of Procedures and Practices in Administration, Commerce and Transport (U.N./CEFACT).
- The Universal Description, Discovery, and Integration (UDDI) project, which is being developed by a vendor consortium.

10.1.2 What Is JAXR?

JAXR enables Java software programmers to use a single, easy-to-use abstraction API to access a variety of XML registries. A unified JAXR information model describes content and metadata within XML registries.

JAXR gives developers the ability to write registry client programs that are portable across different target registries. JAXR also enables value-added capabilities beyond those of the underlying registries.

The current version of the JAXR specification includes detailed bindings between the JAXR information model and both the ebXML Registry and the UDDI v1.0 Specifications. You can find the latest version of the specification at

```
http://java.sun.com/xml/downloads/jaxr.html
```

At this release, the JAXR RI implements the level 0 capability profile defined by the JAXR Specification. This level allows access to both UDDI and ebXML registries at a basic level. The RI, however, currently supports access only to UDDI registries.

Currently several UDDI registries exist. The Java WSDP Registry Server provides a UDDI-compliant registry that you can use to test your JAXR applications.

Some ebXML registries are under development, but they are not yet generally available.

10.1.3 JAXR Architecture

The high-level architecture of JAXR consists of the following parts:

- A JAXR client, which uses the JAXR API to access a registry via a JAXR provider.
- A JAXR provider, which implements the RegistryService interface and various interfaces in order to allow a client to access registries.

  A JAXR provider implements two main packages:

- `javax.xml.registry`, which consists of the API interfaces and classes that define the registry access interface.
- `javax.xml.registry.infomodel`, which consists of interfaces that define the information model for JAXR. These interfaces define the types of objects that reside in a registry and how they relate to each other. The basic interface in this package is the `RegistryObject` interface. Its subinterfaces include `Organization`, `Service`, and `ServiceBinding`.

  The most basic interfaces in the `javax.xml.registry` package are:

- `Connection`. The `Connection` interface represents a client session with a registry provider. The client must create a connection with the JAXR provider in order to use a registry.
- `RegistryService`. The client obtains a `RegistryService` object from its connection. The `RegistryService` object in turn enables the client to obtain the interfaces it uses to access the registry.

  The primary interfaces, also part of the `javax.xml.registry` package, are:

- `BusinessQueryManager`, which allows the client to search a registry for information in accordance with the `javax.xml.registry.infomodel` interfaces. An optional interface, `DeclarativeQueryManager`, allows the client to use SQL syntax for queries. (This release of the JAXR RI does not implement `DeclarativeQueryManager`.)
- `BusinessLifeCycleManager`, which allows the client to modify the information in a registry by either saving it (updating it) or deleting it.

When an error occurs, JAXR API methods throw a `JAXRException` or one of its subclasses.

Many methods in the JAXR API use a `Collection` object as an argument or a returned value. Using a `Collection` object allows operations on several registry objects at a time.

10.2 Implementing a JAXR Client

This section describes the basic steps to follow in order to implement a JAXR client that can perform queries and updates to a UDDI registry. A JAXR client is a client program that can access registries using the JAXR API.

This tutorial does not describe how to implement a JAXR provider. A JAXR provider provides an implementation of the JAXR Specification, usually as a façade around an existing registry provider, such as a UDDI or ebXML registry. The JAXR RI itself is an example of a JAXR provider.

This tutorial includes several client examples:

- `JAXRQuery.java` shows how to search a registry.
- `JAXRPublish.java` shows how to publish an organization to a registry.
- `JAXRDelete.java` shows how to remove an organization from a registry.

The JAXR release also includes several sample JAXR clients, the most complete of which is a Registry Browser that includes a graphical user interface (GUI). The Registry Browser allows access to any registry, but includes some of the most commonly used registries as preset URLs:

- `http://uddi.microsoft.com:80/inquire` (the Microsoft query registry)
- `http://www-3.ibm.com/services/uddi/testregistry/inquiryapi` (the IBM query registry)
- `http://test.uddi.microsoft.com:80/inquire` (the Microsoft test query registry)
- `https://test.uddi.microsoft.com:443/publish` (the Microsoft test update registry)

The Registry Browser source code is in the directory `<JWSDP_HOME>/samples/jaxr/jaxr-browser` (on UNIX systems) or `<JWSDP_HOME>\samples\jaxr\jaxr-browser` (on Microsoft Windows systems). Much of the source code implements the GUI. The JAXR code is in the file `JAXRClient.java`.

10.2.1 Establishing a Connection

The first task a JAXR client must complete is to establish a connection to a registry.

Preliminaries: Getting Access to a Registry

Any user of a JAXR client may perform queries on a public registry. In order to add data to the registry or to update registry data, however, a user must obtain permission from the registry to access it through a user name and password. To register with one of the test registries, go to one of the following Web sites and follow the instructions:

- `http://uddi.microsoft.com/`
- `http://www-3.ibm.com/services/uddi/`

You do not need access permission to use the Java WSDP Registry Server.

Creating or Looking Up a Connection Factory

A client creates a connection from a connection factory. A JAXR provider may supply one or more preconfigured connection factories that clients can obtain by looking them up using the Java Naming and Directory Interface (JNDI) API.

The JAXR RI does not currently supply preconfigured connection factories. Instead, a client creates an instance of the abstract class `ConnectionFactory`:

```
import javax.xml.registry.*;
...
ConnectionFactory connFactory =
    ConnectionFactory.newInstance();
```

Creating a Connection

To create a connection, a client first creates a set of properties that specify the URL of the registry or registries being accessed and the type of registry (UDDI or ebXML). For example, the following code provides the URL of the IBM test query registry and specifies the JAXR RI implementation of the connection factory for the UDDI registry. (There should be no line break in the string.)

```
Properties props = new Properties();
props.setProperty("javax.xml.registry.queryManagerURL",
    "http://www-3.ibm.com/services/uddi/testregistry/inquiryapi");
props.setProperty("javax.xml.registry.factoryClass",
    "com.sun.xml.registry.uddi.ConnectionFactoryImpl");
```

The client then sets the properties for the connection factory and creates the connection:

```
connFactory.setProperties(props);
Connection connection = connFactory.createConnection();
```

The `makeConnection` method in `JAXRPublish.java` and `JAXRDelete.java` shows the steps used to create a JAXR connection.

Obtaining and Using a RegistryService Object

After creating the connection, the client uses the connection to obtain a `RegistryService` object and then the interface or interfaces it will use:

```
RegistryService rs = connection.getRegistryService();
BusinessQueryManager bqm = rs.getBusinessQueryManager();
BusinessLifeCycleManager blcm =
    rs.getBusinessLifeCycleManager();
```

Typically, a client obtains both a `BusinessQueryManager` object and a `BusinessLifeCycleManager` object from the `RegistryService` object. If it is using the registry for queries only, it may need to obtain only a `BusinessQueryManager` object.

10.2.2 Querying a Registry

The simplest way for a client to use a registry is to query it for information about the organizations that have submitted data to it. The `BusinessQueryManager` interface supports a number of find methods that allow clients to search for data using the JAXR information model. Many of these methods return a `BulkResponse` (a collection of objects) that meets a set of criteria specified in the method arguments. At this release the most useful of these methods are likely to be the following:

- `findOrganizations`, which returns a list of organizations that meet the specified criteria—often a name pattern or a classification within a classification scheme
- `findServices`, which returns a set of services offered by a specified organization
- `findServiceBindings`, which returns the service bindings supported by a specified service

The `JAXRQuery` program illustrates how to query a registry and display the data returned.

The following sections describe how to perform some common queries.

Finding Organizations by Name

The following fragment of the `executeQuery` method in `JAXRQuery.java` shows how to find all the organizations in the registry whose names begin with a specified string, `qString`, and to sort them in alphabetical order.

```
// Define find qualifiers and name patterns
Collection findQualifiers = new ArrayList();
findQualifiers.add(FindQualifier.SORT_BY_NAME_DESC);
Collection namePatterns = new ArrayList();
namePatterns.add(qString);

// Find using the name
BulkResponse response =
    bqm.findOrganizations(findQualifiers,
        namePatterns, null, null, null, null);
Collection orgs = response.getCollection();
```

A client can specify a case-sensitive search by using the first argument of the `findOrganizations` method to specify a collection of `findQualifiers`. For example, the following code fragment finds organizations whose names contain the string "Coffee":

```
Collection findQualifiers = new ArrayList();
findQualifiers.add(FindQualifier.CASE_SENSITIVE_MATCH);
Collection namePatterns = new ArrayList();
namePatterns.add("%Coffee%");

// Find orgs with name containing 'Coffee'
BulkResponse response =
    bqm.findOrganizations(findQualifiers, namePatterns, null,
        null, null, null);
Collection orgs = response.getCollection();
```

Finding Organizations by Classification

To find organizations by classification, you need to establish the classification within a particular classification scheme and then specify the classification as an argument to the `findOrganizations` method. The following code fragment finds all organizations that correspond to a particular classification within the North

American Industry Classification System (NAICS) taxonomy. (You can find the NAICS codes at `http://www.census.gov/epcd/naics/naicscod.txt`.)

```
BusinessLifeCycleManager lcm =
    rs.getBusinessLifeCycleManager();
ClassificationScheme cScheme =
    lcm.findClassificationSchemeByName("ntis-gov:naics");
Classification classification = (Classification)
    lcm.createClassification(cScheme, "Snack and Nonalcoholic
         Beverage Bars", "722213");
Collection classifications = new ArrayList();
classifications.add(classification);

// make JAXR request
BulkResponse response = bqManager.findOrganizations(null,
    null, classifications, null, null, null);
Collection orgs = response.getCollection();
```

Finding Services and ServiceBindings

After a client has located an organization, it can find that organization's services and the service bindings associated with those services.

```
Iterator orgIter = orgs.iterator();
while (orgIter.hasNext()) {
    Organization org = (Organization) orgIter.next();
    Collection services = org.getServices();
    Iterator svcIter = services.iterator();
    while (svcIter.hasNext()) {
        Service svc = (Service) svcIter.next();
        Collection serviceBindings =
            svc.getServiceBindings();
        Iterator sbIter = serviceBindings.iterator();
        while (sbIter.hasNext()) {
            ServiceBinding sb =
                (ServiceBinding) sbIter.next();
        }
    }
}
```

10.2.3 Managing Registry Data

If a client has authorization to do so, it can submit data to a registry, modify it, and remove it. It uses the BusinessLifeCycleManager interface to perform these tasks.

Registries usually allow a client to modify data only if the data is being modified by the same user who first submitted the data.

Getting Authorization from the Registry

Before it can submit data, the client must send its username and password to the registry in a set of credentials. The following code fragment shows how to do this.

```
// Edit to provide your own username and password
String username = "";
String password = "";

// Get authorization from the registry
PasswordAuthentication passwdAuth =
    new PasswordAuthentication(username,
        password.toCharArray());

Set creds = new HashSet();
creds.add(passwdAuth);
connection.setCredentials(creds);
```

Creating an Organization

The client creates the organization and populates it with data before saving it.

An Organization object is one of the more complex data items in the JAXR API. It normally includes the following:

- A Name object.
- A Description object.
- A Key object, representing the ID by which the organization is known to the registry.
- A PrimaryContact object, which is a User object that refers to an authorized user of the registry. A User object normally includes a PersonName object and collections of TelephoneNumber and EmailAddress objects.
- A collection of Classification objects.
- Service objects and their associated ServiceBinding objects.

For example, the following code fragment creates an organization and specifies its name, description, and primary contact. When a client creates an organization, it does not include a key; the registry normally returns the new key when it accepts the newly created organization. The `blcm` object in this code fragment is the `BusinessLifeCycleManager` object returned in Obtaining and Using a RegistryService Object (page 328). An `InternationalString` object is used for string values that may need to be localized.

```
// Create organization name and description
Organization org = blcm.createOrganization("The Coffee Break");
InternationalString s =
    blcm.createInternationalString("Purveyor of only the " +
        "finest coffees. Established 1895");
org.setDescription(s);

// Create primary contact, set name
User primaryContact = blcm.createUser();
PersonName pName = blcm.createPersonName("Jane Doe");
primaryContact.setPersonName(pName);

// Set primary contact phone number
TelephoneNumber tNum = blcm.createTelephoneNumber();
tNum.setNumber("(800) 555-1212");
Collection phoneNums = new ArrayList();
phoneNums.add(tNum);
primaryContact.setTelephoneNumbers(phoneNums);

// Set primary contact email address
EmailAddress emailAddress =
    blcm.createEmailAddress("jane.doe@TheCoffeeBreak.com");
Collection emailAddresses = new ArrayList();
emailAddresses.add(emailAddress);
primaryContact.setEmailAddresses(emailAddresses);

// Set primary contact for organization
org.setPrimaryContact(primaryContact);
```

Adding Classifications

Organizations commonly belong to one or more classifications within one or more classification schemes (taxonomies). To establish a classification for an organization within a taxonomy, the client locates the taxonomy it wants to use, then creates a classification. It uses the BusinessQueryManager to find the taxonomy. For example, the following code sets up a classification for the organization within the NAICS taxonomy.

```
// Set classification scheme to NAICS
ClassificationScheme cScheme =
    bqm.findClassificationSchemeByName("ntis-gov:naics");

// Create and add classification
Classification classification = (Classification)
    blcm.createClassification(cScheme,
        "Snack and Nonalcoholic Beverage Bars", "722213");
Collection classifications = new ArrayList();
classifications.add(classification);
org.addClassifications(classifications);
```

Services also use classifications, so you can use similar code to add a classification to a Service object.

Adding Services and Service Bindings to an Organization

Most organizations add themselves to a registry in order to offer services, so the JAXR API has facilities to add services and service bindings to an organization.

Like an Organization object, a Service object has a name and a description. Also like an Organization object, it has a unique key that is generated by the registry when the service is registered. It may also have classifications associated with it.

A service also commonly has service bindings, which provide information about how to access the service. A ServiceBinding object normally has a description, an access URI, and a specification link, which provides the linkage between a service binding and a technical specification that describes how to use the service using the service binding.

The following code fragment shows how to create a collection of services, add service bindings to a service, then add the services to the organization. It specifies an access URI but not a specification link.

```
// Create services and service
Collection services = new ArrayList();
Service service = blcm.createService("My Service Name");
InternationalString is =
  blcm.createInternationalString("My Service Description");
service.setDescription(is);
```

```
// Create service bindings
Collection serviceBindings = new ArrayList();
ServiceBinding binding = blcm.createServiceBinding();
is = blcm.createInternationalString("My Service Binding " +
    "Description");
binding.setDescription(is);
binding.setAccessURI("http://TheCoffeeBreak.com:8080/sb/");
serviceBindings.add(binding);

// Add service bindings to service
service.addServiceBindings(serviceBindings);

// Add service to services, then add services to organization
services.add(service);
org.addServices(services);
```

Saving an Organization

The primary method a client uses to add or modify organization data is the `saveOrganizations` method, which creates one or more new organizations in a registry if they did not exist previously. If one of the organizations exists but some of the data have changed, the `saveOrganizations` method updates the data.

After a client populates an organization with the information it wants to make public, it saves the organization. The registry returns the key in its response, and the client retrieves it.

```
// Add organization and submit to registry
// Retrieve key if successful
Collection orgs = new ArrayList();
orgs.add(org);
BulkResponse response = blcm.saveOrganizations(orgs);
Collection exceptions = response.getException();
if (exceptions == null) {
    System.out.println("Organization saved");

    Collection keys = response.getCollection();
    Iterator keyIter = keys.iterator();
    if (keyIter.hasNext()) {
        javax.xml.registry.infomodel.Key orgKey =
            (javax.xml.registry.infomodel.Key) keyIter.next();
        String id = orgKey.getId();
```

```
            System.out.println("Organization key is " + id);
            org.setKey(orgKey);
        }
    }
```

Removing Data from the Registry

A registry allows you to remove from the registry any data that you have submitted to it. You use the key returned by the registry as an argument to one of the BusinessLifeCycleManager delete methods: deleteOrganizations, deleteServices, deleteServiceBindings, and others.

The JAXRDelete sample program deletes the organization created by the JAXRPublish program. It searches the registry by name for the organization and uses the key string displayed by the JAXRPublish program to verify that it is removing the correct organization. Once it has the key, it deletes the organization and then displays the key again so that the user can confirm that it has deleted the correct one.

```
String id = key.getId();
System.out.println("Deleting organization with id " + id);
Collection keys = new ArrayList();
keys.add(key);
BulkResponse response = blcm.deleteOrganizations(keys);
Collection exceptions = response.getException();
if (exceptions == null) {
    System.out.println("Organization deleted");
    Collection retKeys = response.getCollection();
    Iterator keyIter = retKeys.iterator();
    javax.xml.registry.infomodel.Key orgKey = null;
    if (keyIter.hasNext()) {
        orgKey =
            (javax.xml.registry.infomodel.Key) keyIter.next();
        id = orgKey.getId();
        System.out.println("Organization key was " + id);
    }
}
```

A client can use a similar mechanism to delete services and service bindings.

10.2.4 Running the Client Examples

The simple client programs provided with this tutorial can be run from the command line. You can modify them to suit your needs. Currently they specify the IBM test registry for queries and updates; you can specify another registry.

Before you compile the `JAXRPublish` and `JAXRDelete` examples, edit the lines containing the empty strings for the username and password to specify your username and password. Feel free to change any of the organization data in the `JAXRPublish` program.

Set the `JAVA_HOME`, `JAXR_HOME`, and `CATALINA_HOME` environment variables as specified in the JAXR home page (`<JWSDP_HOME>/docs/jaxr/index.html` on UNIX systems; `<JWSDP_HOME>\docs\jaxr\index.html` on Microsoft Windows systems).

To compile the programs, go to the `docs/tutorial/examples/jaxr` directory (on UNIX systems) or the `docs\tutorial\examples\jaxr` directory (on Microsoft Windows systems). A `build.xml` file allows you to use the command

```
ant build
```

to compile all the examples. The `ant` tool creates a subdirectory called `build` and places the class files there.

Before you run the examples, start Tomcat. See the JAXR home page (`<JWSDP_HOME>/docs/jaxr/index.html` on UNIX systems; `<JWSDP_HOME>\docs\jaxr\index.html` on Microsoft Windows systems) for details.

To run the `JAXRQuery` example, use the `ant` target `run-query`. Specify a `query-string` argument on the command line to search the registry for organizations whose names contain that string. For example, the following command line searches for organizations whose names contain the string "sun":

```
ant -Dquery-string=sun run-query
```

To run the `JAXRPublish` program, use the `run-publish` target with no command line arguments:

```
ant run-publish
```

The program output displays the string value of the key of the new organization.

If you forgot to fill in the username and password strings, you will get a "No Credentials present" error message.

After you run the `JAXRPublish` program but before you run `JAXRDelete`, you can run `JAXRQuery` to look up the organization you published. You can also use the Registry Browser to search for it.

To run the JAXRDelete program, specify the string returned by the JAXR-Publish program as input to the run-delete target:

```
ant -Dkey-string=string-value run-delete
```

To remove the build directory and class files, use the command

```
ant clean
```

To obtain a syntax reminder for the run-query, run-publish, and run-delete targets, use the command

```
ant help
```

10.3 Using the Registry Browser

The Registry Browser is both a working example of a JAXR client and a GUI tool that enables you to search registries. You can examine the source code, as described in Implementing a JAXR Client (page 326).

Before you run the Registry Browser, start Tomcat. See Starting Tomcat (page 62) for details.

To start the browser, go to the bin directory of your Java WSDP installation or place this directory in your path.

To start the browser on a UNIX system, enter the following command:

```
jaxr-browser.sh
```

On a Microsoft Windows system, enter the following command:

```
jaxr-browser
```

After the browser starts, enter the URL of the registry you want to use in the Registry Location combo box, or select a URL from the drop-down menu in the combo box. There may be a delay of a few seconds while a busy cursor is visible.

When the busy cursor disappears, you have a connection to the URL. However, you do not establish a connection to the registry itself until you perform a query or update, so the browser will not report an invalid URL until then.

The browser contains two main panes, Browse and Submissions.

10.3.1 Querying a Registry

You use the Browse pane to query a registry.

Querying by Name

To search for organizations by name, perform the following steps.

1. Click the Browse tab if it is not already selected.
2. In the Find By panel on the left side of the Registry Browser window, do the following:
   a. Select Name in the Find By combo box if it is not already selected.
   b. Enter a string in the text field.
   c. Press Enter or click the Search button in the toolbar.

After a few seconds, the organizations whose names begin with the text string appear in the right side of the Registry Browser window. An informational dialog box appears if no matching organizations are found.

Double-click on an organization to show its details. An Organization dialog box appears. In this dialog box, you can click Show Services to display the Services dialog box for the organization. In the Services dialog box, you can click Show ServiceBindings to display the ServiceBindings dialog box for that service.

Querying by Classification

To query a registry by classification, perform the following steps.

1. Select Classification in the Find By combo box.
2. In the Classifications pane that appears below the combo box, double-click a classification scheme.
3. Continue to double-click until you reach the node you want to search on.
4. Click the Search button in the toolbar.

After a few seconds, one or more organizations in the chosen classification may appear in the right side of the Registry Browser window. An informational dialog box appears if no matching organizations are found.

10.3.2 Managing Registry Data

You use the Submissions pane to add, modify, or delete registry data.

To get to the Submissions pane, do either of the following:

- Click the Submissions tab.

- If you used the Browse pane to locate an organization for which you want to modify data, right-click on the organization and choose either Edit RegistryObject or Delete RegistryObject from the pop-up menu. In order to modify data, you need to be connected to a registry that allows you to publish data. If you were previously using a URL that only allows queries, change the URL to the publish URL.

If you click Delete RegistryObject, an authorization dialog box appears. To delete the organization, enter your username and password and click OK. To close the window without deleting the organization, click Cancel.

Adding an Organization

To enter or modify information about an organization, use the Organization panel on the left side of the Submissions pane.

Use the Organization Information fields as follows:

- Name: Enter the name of the organization.
- Id: You cannot enter or modify data in this field; the ID value is returned by the registry after you submit the data.
- Description: Enter a description of the organization.

Use the Primary Contact Information fields as follows:

- Name: Enter the name of the primary contact person for the organization.
- Phone: Enter the primary contact's phone number.
- Email: Enter the primary contact's e-mail address.

For information on adding or removing classifications, see Adding and Removing Classifications (page 341).

Adding Services to an Organization

To add or modify information about an organization's services, Use the Services panel on the right side of the Submissions pane.

To add a service, click the Add Services button in the toolbar. A subpanel for the service appears in the Services panel. Click the Add Services button more than once to add more services in the Services panel.

Each service subpanel has the following components:

- Name, Id, and Description fields
- Edit Bindings and Remove Service buttons
- A Classifications panel

Use these components as follows:

- Name field: Enter a name for the service.
- Id field: You cannot enter or modify data in this field; the ID value is returned by the registry after you submit the data.
- Description field: Enter a description of the service.
- Click the Edit Bindings button to add or edit service bindings for the service. An Edit ServiceBindings dialog box appears.
- Click the Remove Service button to remove this service from the organization. The service subpanel disappears from the Services panel.
- To add or remove classifications, use the Classifications panel.

Adding Service Bindings to a Service

To add service bindings for a service, click the Edit Bindings button in a service subpanel in the Submissions pane. The Edit ServiceBindings dialog box appears.

If there are no existing service bindings when the dialog box first appears, it contains an empty Service Bindings panel and two buttons, Add Binding and Done. If the service already has service bindings, the Service Bindings panel contains a subpanel for each service binding.

Click Add Binding to add a service binding. Click Add Binding more than once to add multiple service bindings.

After you click Add Binding, a new service binding subpanel appears. It contains three text fields and a Remove Binding button.

Use the text fields as follows:

- Description: Enter a description of the service binding.
- Access URI: Enter the URI used to access the service.

Use the Remove Binding button to remove the service binding from the service.

Click Done to close the dialog box when you have finished adding or removing service bindings.

Adding and Removing Classifications

To add classifications to, or remove classifications from, an organization or service, use a Classifications panel. A Classifications panel appears in an Organization panel or service subpanel.

To add a classification:

1. Click Add.
2. In the Select Classifications dialog, double-click one of the classification schemes.
   - If you clicked ntis-gov:naics, you can add the classification at any level of the taxonomy hierarchy. When you reach the level you want, click Add.
   - If you clicked Geography, locate the appropriate leaf node (the country) and click Add.

The classification appears in a table in the Classifications panel below the buttons.

Follow these steps more than once to add multiple classifications to the organization or service.

Click Close to dismiss the window when you have finished.

To remove a classification, select the appropriate table row in the Classifications panel and click Remove. The classification disappears from the table.

Submitting the Data

When you have finished entering the data you want to add or modify, click the Submit button in the toolbar.

An authorization dialog box appears. To continue with the submission, enter your username and password and click OK. To close the window without submitting the data, click Cancel.

CHAPTER 11

The Java WSDP Registry Server

by Kim Haase

In This Chapter

A registry offers a mechanism for humans or software applications to advertise and discover Web services. The Java Web Services Developer Pack (Java WSDP) Registry Server implements Version 1 of the Universal Description, Discovery and Integration (UDDI) project, providing a UDDI-compliant registry for Web services in a private environment. You can use it with the Java WSDP APIs as a test registry for Web services application development.

You can use the Registry Server to test applications that you develop that use the Java API for XML Registries (JAXR), described in the chapter Java API for XML Registries (page 323). You can also use the JAXR Registry Browser provided with the Java WSDP to perform queries and updates on registry data.

The release of the Registry Server that you have downloaded as part of the Java WSDP includes the following:

- The Java WSDP Registry Server 1.0 Early Access release
- A database based on the native XML database Xindice, which is part of the Apache XML project. This database provides the repository for registry data.
- A tool named Indri that allows you to create and inspect database data using a graphical user interface

Before you can access the Registry Server, you must start Tomcat and the database. For details, see the Registry Server home page.

At this release, the Registry Server has limited capabilities. It supports only the following messages defined in the UDDI Programmer's API 1.0 Specification:

- `<save_business>`
- `<find_business>`
- `<get_businessDetail>`
- `<delete_business>`

11.1 Setting Up the Registry Server

Before you can use the Java WSDP Registry Server, you must start both Tomcat and the Xindice database.

Instructions for starting and stopping Tomcat are in Starting Tomcat (page 62).

Go to the `bin` directory of your Java WSDP installation (or place this directory in your PATH). To start the Xindice database, use the command

```
xindice-start       (on a Microsoft Windows system)
xindice-start.sh    (on a UNIX system)
```

This command runs in the background. The database may take several seconds to start up.

To stop the database, use the command

```
xindice-stop       (on a Microsoft Windows system)
xindice-stop.sh    (on a UNIX system)
```

11.2 Using the JAXR Registry Browser with the Registry Server

You can use the JAXR Registry Browser to access the Registry Server.

For basic information on the Registry Browser, see Using the Registry Browser in Java API for XML Registries (page 323).

After you start the Registry Browser using the `jaxr-browser.sh` or `jaxr-browser.bat` script, enter the following URL in the Registry Location combo box (all on one line):

```
http://hostname:8080/registry-server/RegistryServerServlet
```

The hostname must be fully qualified; do not specify `localhost`. If you enter the name incorrectly, no error message appears until you try to perform a query or update.

You specify `http:` for both queries and updates. The registry server does not support authentication at this release.

11.2.1 Adding Organizations

When you submit an organization and the authorization dialog box appears, enter any string in the username and password fields. The Registry Server does not check the values you enter, but you may not enter an empty string.

The Registry Server supports adding and deleting organizations, but does not support modifying organizations. If you submit an organization and then choose the Edit Registry Object menu item to modify it, a new organization is created when you submit the modified data.

11.2.2 Querying the Registry

To perform queries by name against the Registry Server, enter the string in the Name text field. Searches against the Registry Server are case-sensitive. A search will find all organizations whose names contain the exact string entered.

11.3 Using the Command Line Client Scripts with the Registry Server

You will find a shell script called `<JWSDP_HOME>/samples/registry-server/registry-server-test.sh` (on UNIX systems) or `<JWSDP_HOME>\samples\registry-server/registry-server-test.bat` (on Microsoft Windows systems).

The script uses XML files in the xml subdirectory to send messages to the Registry Server.

Before you use the script, make sure it is executable (make it so if it is not).

1. Save a business.

   To save a business, the script uses the file SaveBusiness.xml in the xml subdirectory. Edit this file if you wish.

   To save the business, use the following command (on a UNIX system, add the .sh suffix):

   ```
   registry-server-test run-cli-save
   ```

   Output appears in the terminal window in which you run the command. Notice the businessKey value returned in the <businessEntity> tag. You will use it in step 2.

2. Obtain business details.

   To obtain details about a business, the script uses the file GetBusinessDetail.xml in the xml subdirectory.

   Before you run the script this time, edit this file by copying the businessKey value from the output of the command in step 1 into the <businessKey> tag.

   To obtain details about the business you saved, use the following command:

   ```
   registry-server-test run-cli-get
   ```

   Output appears in the terminal window.

3. Find a business.

   To find a business by name, the script uses the file FindBusiness.xml in the xml subdirectory.

   Before you run the script this time, edit the file by changing the value in the <name> tag to the name you specified in the SaveBusiness.xml file.

   To find the business, use the following command:

   ```
   registry-server-test run-cli-find
   ```

   Output appears in the terminal window.

   You can create your own XML files to run with the script. To use the <save_business> message, specify the following in the <authInfo> tag:

   ```
   <authInfo>magicCookie</authInfo>
   ```

11.4 Using the JAXR API to Access the Registry Server

You can access the Registry Server by using the sample programs in the `docs/tutorial/examples/jaxr` directory (on UNIX systems) or the `docs\tutorial\examples\jaxr` directory (on Microsoft Windows systems). You need to edit them as follows.

In `JAXRPublish.java` and `JAXRDelete.java`, for both the `queryURL` and the `publishURL`, specify the Registry Server by using the following string (on one line):

```
"http://hostname:8080/registry-server/RegistryServerServlet";
```

where *`hostname`* is the fully qualified host name. Do not use `https:` for the `publishURL`.

Edit the lines that specify a username and password by providing any non-empty string. For example:

```
// Edit to provide your own username and password
String username = "x";
String password = "y";
```

In `JAXRQuery.java`, specify the Registry Server as follows:

```
props.setProperty("javax.xml.registry.queryManagerURL",
"http://hostname:8080/registry-server/RegistryServerServlet");
```

Also in `JAXRQuery.java`, remove the percent (%) signs from the following line:

```
namePatterns.add("%" + qString + "%");
```

Instead, specify the `namePatterns` for the query string as follows:

```
namePatterns.add(qString);
```

11.5 Using the Indri Tool to Access the Registry Server Database

The Indri tool provides a graphic user interface (GUI) that allows you to access the Registry Server database directly. You can use this tool to save and find businesses and to obtain business details.

Note: The Indri is a large lemur. It is reported that when Europeans first arrived in Madagascar, they heard its cry from the trees and asked what was making that sound. The reply was "Indri! Indri!" which is Malagasy for "Look up! Look up!" This seems an appropriate name for a database lookup tool.

You invoke the Indri tool through the `registry-server-test` script. Use the following command:

```
registry-server-test.sh run-indri (UNIX systems)
registry-server-test.bat run-indri (Microsoft Windows systems)
```

To save a business, perform the following steps.

1. Open the file `SaveBusiness.xml` in the `xml` subdirectory. Edit it if you wish.
2. Copy the contents of the file and paste them into the large text area labeled Node.
3. Choose Check Content from the Process menu and verify that the message

   ```
   document is well-formed
   ```

   appears in the status area at the bottom of the Indri window.
4. In the Collection panel on the top left side of the Indri window, make sure `uddi` is selected.
5. Choose Create Node from the Database menu. The message

   ```
   node 'nid' in collection 'uddi' created
   ```

   appears in the status area.

To obtain business details, perform the following steps:

1. Select Clear Text Area from the Database menu to clear the Node text area.
2. Select Get Node from the Database menu. The XML code you submitted when you saved the business appears in the text area.

To find a business by name, perform the following steps:

1. Select Clear Text Area from the Database menu to clear the Node text area.

2. Copy the following string into the XPath Query text field. If necessary, replace "Alter" with a string that appears in the name of the business you saved.

```
//uddi:businessEntity/uddi:name[contains(text(),"Alter")]
```

3. Click Find.
4. Check the status area for a message like the following:

```
query complete: 1 matches.
```

5. If there are any matches, select a node from the XNodes panel on the bottom left side of the Indri window. The content of the node appears in the Node area. To exit the Indri tool, choose Exit from the File menu.

CHAPTER 12

Web Applications

Stephanie Bodoff

IN THIS CHAPTER

A Web application is a dynamic extension of a Web server. A Web application can consist of dynamic Web pages containing various types of markup language (HTML, XML, and so on) as well as static resources such as images. A Web application can also be the endpoint of a fine-grained Web service that is used by the dynamic Web pages. In the Java 2 Platform, *Web components* provide the dynamic extension capabilities for a Web server. Web components are supported by the services of a runtime platform called a *Web container*. In the Java Web Services Developer Pack (Java WSDP), Web components are either Java Servlets and JSP pages and they run in the Tomcat Web container.

This chapter describes the organization of and configuration, and deployment procedures for Web applications. Subsequent chapters, Java Servlet Technology (page 367) and JavaServer Pages Technology (page 401), cover how to develop the Web components. Many features of JSP technology are determined by Java Servlet technology so you should familiarize yourself with that material.

Most Web applications use the HTTP protocol and support for HTTP is a major aspect of Web components. For a brief summary of HTTP protocol features see HTTP Overview (page 491).

12.1 Web Application Life Cycle

The server-side portion of a Web application consists of Web components, static resource files such as images, and helper classes and libraries. The JWSDP provides many supporting services that enhance the capabilities of Web components and make them easier to develop. However, because it must take these services into account, the process for creating and running a Web application is different than that of traditional standalone Java classes.

Web components run within an environment called a *Web container.* The Web container provides services such as request dispatching, security, concurrency, and life cycle management. It also gives Web components access to APIs such as naming, transactions, and e-mail.

Certain aspects of Web application behavior can be configured when it is deployed. The configuration information is maintained in a text file in XML format called a *Web application deployment descriptor.* A deployment descriptor must conform to the schema described in the Java Servlet Specification.

The process for creating, deploying, and executing a Web application can be summarized as follows:

1. Develop the Web component code (including possibly a deployment descriptor).
2. Build the Web application components along with any static resources (for example, images) and helper classes referenced by the component.
3. Deploy the application.
4. Access a URL that references the Web application.

Developing Web component code is covered in the chapters on servlet and JSP technology. Steps 2. through 4. are expanded on in the following sections illustrated with a HelloWorld–style application. This application allows a user to enter a name into an HTML form as in Figure 12.1.

It then displays a greeting after the name is submitted as in Figure 12.2.

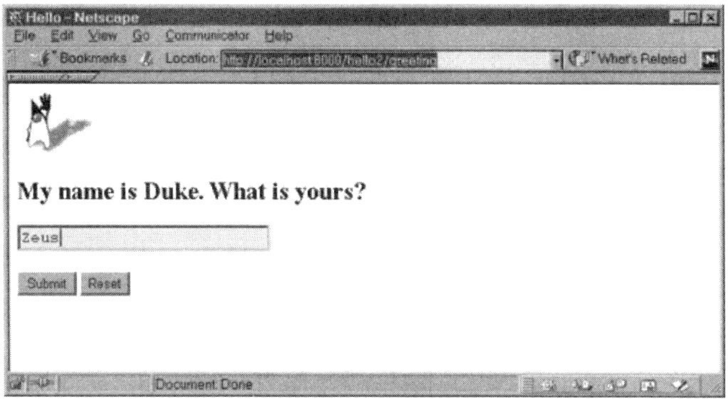

Figure 12.1 Greeting Form

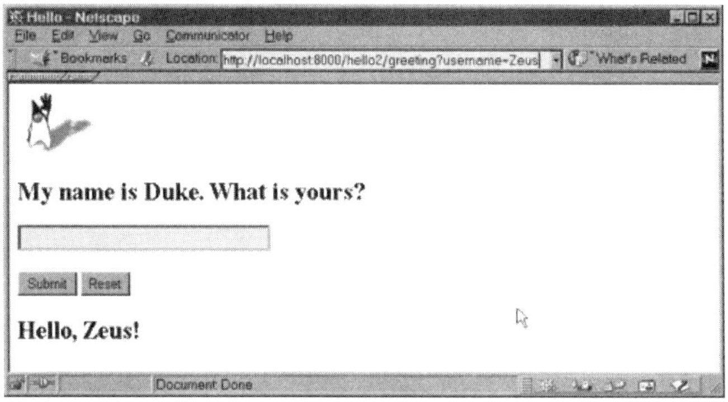

Figure 12.2 Response

The Hello application contains two Web components that generate the greeting and the response. This tutorial has two versions of this application: a servlet version called `Hello1`, in which the components are implemented by two servlet classes, `GreetingServlet.java` and `ResponseServlet.java` and a JSP version called `Hello2`, in which the components are implemented by two JSP pages `greeting.jsp` and `response.jsp`. The two versions are used to illustrate the tasks involved in packaging, deploying, and running an application that contains Web components. If you are viewing this tutorial online, you must download the tutorial bundle to get the source code for this example. See Running the Examples (page xx).

12.2 Web Application Archives

If you want to distribute a Web application and run it on another server you package it in a Web application archive (WAR), which is a JAR similar to the package used for Java class libraries, and installed (or *deployed*) into a Web container. In addition to Web components, a Web application archive usually contains other files including:

- Server-side utility classes (database beans, shopping carts, and so on). Often these classes conform to the JavaBeans component architecture.
- Static Web content (HTML, image, and sound files, and so on).
- Client-side classes (applets and utility classes).

Web components and static Web content files are called *Web resources*.

A WAR has a specific directory structure. The top-level directory of a WAR is the *document root* of the application. The document root is where JSP pages, client-side classes and archives, and static Web resources are stored.

The document root contains a subdirectory called `WEB-INF`, which contains the following files and directories:

- `web.xml`—the Web application deployment descriptor
- Tag library descriptor files (see Tag Library Descriptors (page 440)).
- `classes`—a directory that contains server-side classes: servlets, utility classes, and JavaBeans components.
- `lib`—a directory that contains JAR archives of libraries (tag libraries and any utility libraries called by server-side classes).

You can also create application-specific subdirectories (that is, package directories) in either the document root or the `WEB-INF/classes` directory.

The ant build files distributed with the tutorial examples construct this directory structure in the `build` subdirectory.

12.2.1 Creating a WAR File

You can manually create a WAR in two ways:

- With the JAR tool distributed with the J2SE SDK. You simply execute the following command in the build directory of a tutorial example:

  ```
  jar cvf archiveName.war
  ```

- With the `war` task of the `ant` portable build tool

12.3 Web Application Deployment Descriptors

The following sections give a brief introduction to the Web application deployment descriptor elements you will usually want to specify. A number of security parameters can be specified but this release of the tutorial does not cover them. For a complete listing and description of the elements, see the Java Servlet Specification. The simpler applications discussed in Creating the Getting Started Application (page 57), Updating Web Applications (page 360), and What is a JSP Page? (page 402) do not need a Web application deployment descriptor, but all the others are distributed with a descriptor.

Note: Descriptor elements must appear in the deployment descriptor in the following order: `icon`, `display-name`, `description`, `distributable`, `context-param`, `filter`, `filter-mapping`, `listener`, `servlet`, `servlet-mapping`, `session-config`, `mime-mapping`, `welcome-file-list`, `error-page`, `taglib`, `resource-env-ref`, `resource-ref`, `security-constraint`, `login-config`, `security-role`, `env-entry`.

12.3.1 Prolog

The prolog of the Web application deployment descriptor is as follows:

```
<?xml version="1.0" encoding="ISO-8859-1"?>
<!DOCTYPE web-app PUBLIC "-//Sun Microsystems, Inc.//DTD Web
Application 2.3//EN" "http://java.sun.com/j2ee/dtds/
web-app_2_3.dtd">
```

12.3.2 Context Parameters

The Web components in a WAR share an object that represents their Web context (see Accessing the Web Context (page 392)). To pass initialization parameters to the context, you must add a `context-param` element to the Web application deployment descriptor. Here is the element used to declare a context parameter that sets the resource bundle used in the example discussed in JavaServer Pages Standard Tag Library (page 465):

```
<context-param>
    <param-name>
        javax.servlet.jsp.jstl.i18n.basename
    </param-name>
    <param-value>messages.BookstoreMessages</param-value>
</context-param>
```

12.3.3 Filter Mappings

A Web container uses filter mapping declarations to decide which filters to apply to a request, and in what order (see Specifying Filter Mappings (page 387)). The container matches the request URI to a servlet as described in Alias Paths (page 356). To determine which filters to apply, it matches filter mapping declarations by servlet name or URL pattern. The order in which filters are invoked is the order in which filter mapping declarations that match a request URI for a servlet appear in the filter mapping list.

To specify a filter mapping you must add an `filter` and `filter-mapping` elements to the Web application deployment descriptor. Here is the element use to declare the order filter and map it to the `ReceiptServlet` discussed in Java Servlet Technology (page 367):

```
<filter>
    <filter-name>OrderFilter<filter-name>
    <filter-class>filters.OrderFilter<filter-class>
</filter>
<filter-mapping>
    <filter-name>OrderFilter</filter-name>
    <url-pattern>ReceiptServlet</url-pattern>
</filter-mapping>
```

12.3.4 Event Listeners

To add an event listener class (described in Handling Servlet Life Cycle Events (page 370)), you must add a `listener` element to the Web application deployment descriptor. Here is the element use to declare the listener class used in Java Servlet Technology (page 367) and JavaServer Pages Standard Tag Library (page 465):

```
<listener>
    <listener-class>listeners.ContextListener</listener-class>
</listener>
```

12.3.5 Alias Paths

When a request is received by Tomcat, it must determine which Web component should handle the request. It does so by mapping the URL path contained in the request to a Web component. A URL path contains the context root (described in Running Web Applications (page 360)) and an *alias* path:

```
http://<host>:8080/context root/alias path
```

Before a servlet can be accessed, the Web container must have least one alias path for the component. The alias path must start with a '/' and end with a string or a wildcard expression with an extension (`*.jsp` for example). Since Web containers automatically map an alias path that ends with `*.jsp`, you do not have to specify an alias path for a JSP page unless you wish to refer to the page by a name other than its file name. In the example discussed in Updating Web Applications (page 360), JSP pages `greeting.jsp` and `response.jsp` are referenced by their file names.

To set up the mappings for the servlet version of the Hello application you must add the following `servlet` and `servlet-mapping` elements to the Web application deployment descriptor. Note that to define an alias for a JSP page, you must replace the `servlet-class` subelement with a `jsp-file` subelement in the `servlet` element.

```
<servlet>
    <servlet-name>greeting</servlet-name>
    <display-name>greeting</display-name>
    <description>no description</description>
    <servlet-class>GreetingServlet</servlet-class>
</servlet>
<servlet>
    <servlet-name>response</servlet-name>
    <display-name>response</display-name>
    <description>no description</description>
    <servlet-class>ResponseServlet</servlet-class>
</servlet>
<servlet-mapping>
    <servlet-name>greeting</servlet-name>
    <url-pattern>/greeting</url-pattern>
</servlet-mapping>
<servlet-mapping>
    <servlet-name>response</servlet-name>
    <url-pattern>/response</url-pattern>
</servlet-mapping>
```

12.3.6 Error Mappings

You can specify a mapping between the status code returned in an HTTP response or a Java programming language exception returned by any Web component and a Web resource (see Handling Errors (page 372)). To set up the mapping, you must add an `<error-page>` element to the deployment descriptor. Here is the element use to map OrderException to the page errorpage.html used in Java Servlet Technology (page 367):

```
<error-page>
    <exception-type>exception.OrderException</exception-type>
    <location>/errorpage.html</location>
</error-page>
```

Note: You can also define error pages for a JSP page contained in a WAR. If error pages are defined for both the WAR and a JSP page, the JSP page's error page takes precedence.

12.3.7 References to Environment Entries, Resource Environment Entries, or Resources

If your Web components reference environment entries, resource environment entries, or resources such as databases, you must declare the references with <env-entry>, <resource-env-ref>, or <resource-ref> elements. Here is the element use to declare a reference to the data source used in the Web technology chapters in this tutorial:

```
<resource-ref>
    <res-ref-name>jdbc/BookDB</res-ref-name>
    <res-type>javax.sql.DataSource</res-type>
    <res-auth>Container</res-auth>
</resource-ref>
```

12.4 Deploying Web Applications

The next step after you have programmed and configured a Web application is to deploy it to Tomcat. You deploy an application to Tomcat by notifying it of a new application context. The first time you deploy a new application you must restart Tomcat. Thereafter you can reload the application as described in Reloading the Examples (xxii).

12.4.1 Specifying the Web Application Context

A *context* is a name that gets mapped to the document root of a Web application. The context of the Hello1 application is /hello1. The request URL http://localhost:8080/hello1/index.html retrieves the file index.html from the document root.

Tomcat can be notified of a new context in two ways:

- Automatically. If you copy a Web application directory or WAR to <*JWSDP_HOME*>/webapps, the context root for the application is automatically added to the Tomcat configuration. This is the approach used by the simpler applications (Hello1, Hello2, Date) discussed in the Web technology chapters.
- By adding a context entry to Tomcat's configuration. This is the approach used by the Duke's Bookstore application discussed in the Web technology chapters. For example, here is the Context entry for the application discussed in Java Servlet Technology (page 367):

```
<Context path="/bookstore1"
    docBase="../docs/tutorial/examples/web/bookstore1/build"
    debug="0">
```

There are two ways to add this entry to Tomcat's configuration:

- Edit the file <*JWSDP_HOME*>/conf/server.xml. Since this can be error prone, we recommend the next approach.
- Put an application-specific configuration file in <*JWSDP_HOME*>/webapps. The Context entry for the application discussed in Java Servlet Technology (page 367) is in the file docs/tutorial/web/bookstore1/bookstore.xml. When the application is deployed, bookstore1.xml is copied to <*JWSDP_HOME*>/webapps.

Note: Manual specification of the Context entry is a limitation of the current release of the Web Services Pack. Later releases will include an administration tool that will simplify this task.

12.4.2 Example

To deploy the Hello1 application:

1. Go to docs/tutorial/examples/hello1 and build and deploy the example by running ant. This runs the default ant target deploy which depends on the build target. The build target will spawn any necessary compilations and copy files to the docs/tutorial/examples/web/hello1/build directory. The deploy target copies the build directory to <*JWSDP_HOME*>/webapps.
2. Start or restart Tomcat.

12.5 Running Web Applications

A Web application is executed when a Web browser references a URL that is mapped to component contained in the client. Once you have deployed the Hello1 application, you can run the Web application by pointing a browser at:

```
http://<host>:8080/hello1/greeting.jsp
```

Replace <host> with the name of the host running Tomcat. If your browser is running on the same host as Tomcat, you may replace <host> with localhost.

12.6 Updating Web Applications

During development, you will often need to make changes to Web applications. To modify a servlet you modify the source file, recompile the servlet class, and redeploy the application. Except for the compilation step, you update a JSP page in the same way.

To try this feature, first build and deploy the JSP version of the Hello application:

1. Go to docs/tutorial/examples/hello2 and build and deploy the example by running ant. This runs the default ant target deploy which depends on the build target. The build target will spawn any necessary compilations and copy files to the docs/tutorial/examples/web/hello2/build directory. The deploy target copies the build directory to <JWSDP_HOME>/webapps.
2. Start or restart Tomcat.
3. Open the Hello2 URL http://localhost:8080/hello2/greeting.jsp.

Now modify one of the JSP files. For example, you could replace the contents of greeting.jsp with:

```
<h2>Hi, my name is Duke. What's yours.</h2>
```

1. Edit greeting.jsp.
2. Execute ant.
3. Reload the application as described in Reloading the Examples (xxii) by loading the URL http://localhost:8080/manager/reload?path=/hello2.
4. Reload the Hello2 URL.

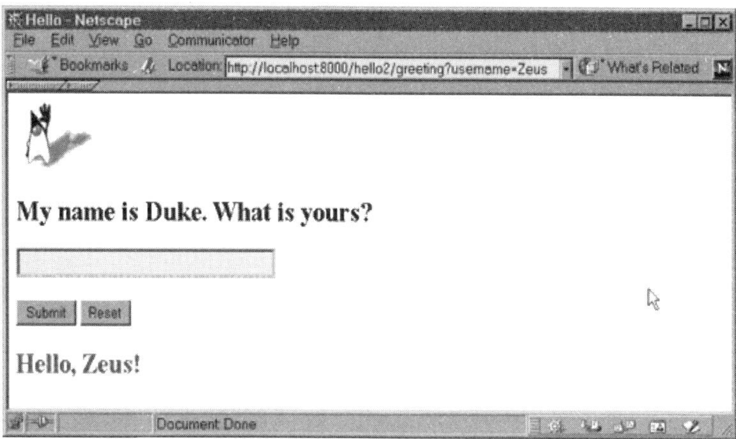

Figure 12.3 Red Response

If you make this change, the next time you execute the application, the greeting will appear as shown in Figure 12.3.

12.7 Internationalizing and Localizing Web Applications

Internationalization is the process of preparing an application to support various languages. Localization is the process of adapting an internationalized application to support a specific language or locale. While all client user interfaces should be internationalized and localized, it is particularly important for Web applications because of the far reaching nature of the Web. For a good overview of internationalization and localization see

```
http://java.sun.com/docs/books/tutorial/i18n/index.html
```

There are two approaches to internationalizing a Web application:

- Provide a version of the JSP in each of the target locales and have a controller servlet dispatch the request to the appropriate page (depending on the requested locale). This approach is useful if large amounts of data on a page or an entire Web application need to be internationalized.
- Isolate any locale-sensitive data on a page (such as error messages, string literals, or button labels) into resource bundles, and access the data so that the corresponding translated message is fetched automatically and inserted into

the page. Thus, instead of creating strings directly in your code, you create a resource bundle that contains translations and read the translations from that bundle using the corresponding key. A resource bundle can be backed by a text file (properties resource bundle) or a class (list resource bundle) containing the mappings.

In the following chapters on Web technology, the Duke's Bookstore example is internationalized and localized into English and Spanish. The key and value pairs are contained in list resource bundles named `messages.BookMessage_*.class`. To give you an idea of what the key and string pairs in a resource bundle look like, here are a few lines from the file messages.`BookMessages.java`.

```
{"TitleCashier", "Cashier"},
{"TitleBookDescription", "Book Description"},
{"Visitor", "You are visitor number "},
{"What", "What We're Reading"},
{"Talk", " talks about how Web components can transform the way you
develop applications for the Web. This is a must read for any self
respecting Web developer!"},
{"Start", "Start Shopping"},
```

To get the correct strings for a given user, a Web component retrieves the locale (set by a browser language preference) from the request, opens the resource bundle for that locale, and then saves the bundle as a session attribute (see Associating Attributes with a Session (page 394)):

```
ResourceBundle messages = (ResourceBundle)session.
    getAttribute("messages");
    if (messages == null) {
        Locale locale=request.getLocale();
        messages = ResourceBundle.getBundle("WebMessages",
            locale);
        session.setAttribute("messages", messages);
    }
```

A Web component retrieves the resource bundle from the session:

```
ResourceBundle messages =
    (ResourceBundle)session.getAttribute("messages");
```

and looks up the string associated with the key `TitleCashier` as follows:

```
messages.getString("TitleCashier");
```

This has been a very brief introduction to internationalizing Web applications. For more information on this subject see the Java BluePrints:

```
http://java.sun.com/blueprints
```

12.8 Accessing Databases from Web Applications

Data that is shared between Web components and persistent between invocations of a Web application is usually maintained by a database. Web applications use the JDBC 2.0 API to access relational databases. For information on this API, see:

```
http://java.sun.com/docs/books/tutorial/jdbc
```

12.8.1 The Examples

The examples discussed in the chapters Java Servlet Technology (page 367), JavaServer Pages Technology (page 401), Custom Tags in JSP Pages (page 431), and JavaServer Pages Standard Tag Library (page 465) require a database. For this release we have tested the examples with the Pointbase database and we provide an `ant` build file to create the database tables and populate the database. The remainder of this section describes how to install and start the Pointbase database server, set up the example tables, configure the Web application to use the database, and configure Tomcat to recognize the database.

12.8.2 Downloading and Starting the Database Server

You can download a copy of the Pointbase database from:

```
http://www.pointbase.com
```

After you have downloaded and installed the Pointbase database, you will need to do the following:

1. Set the `PB_HOME` environment variable to point to your Pointbase install directory.
2. Copy *<PB_HOME>*`/client/lib/pbclient41ev.jar` to *<JWSDP_HOME>*`/common/lib` to make the Pointbase client library available to the example applications.
3. In a terminal window, go to *<PB_HOME>*`/server`.
4. Start the Pointbase server by typing `Server`.

12.8.3 Populating the Database

1. In a terminal window, set the environment variable `PB_HOME` to point to your Pointbase installation to make the Pointbase libraries available to the `ant` task that populates the database.
2. Go to `<JWSDP_HOME>/docs/tutorial/examples/web`.
3. Execute `ant`. At the end of the processing, you should see the following output:

```
[java] ID
[java] ----------
[java] 201
[java] 202
[java] 203
[java] 204
[java] 205
[java] 206
[java] 207
[java]
[java] 7 Rows Selected.
[java]
[java] SQL>
[java]
[java] COMMIT;
[java] OK
```

12.8.4 Configuring the Web Application to Use the Database

In order to access a database from a Web application you must declare resource reference in the application's Web application deployment descriptor (see References to Environment Entries, Resource Environment Entries, or Resources (page 358)). The resource reference declares the name and type of resource and the type of authentication used when the resource is accessed.

12.8.5 Configuring the Server to Recognize the Database

Since the resource reference declared in the Web application deployment descriptor uses a JNDI name to refer to the database, you must connect the name to an actual database by providing a resource factory in the Tomcat's configuration.

Here is the resource factory used by the application discussed in all the Web technology chapters:

```
<Resource name="jdbc/BookDB" reloadable="true"
    auth="Container" type="javax.sql.DataSource"/>
<ResourceParams name="jdbc/BookDB">
    <parameter>
        <name>user</name>
        <value>public</value>
    </parameter>
    <parameter>
        <name>password</name>
        <value>public</value>
    </parameter>
    <parameter>
        <name>driverClassName</name>
        <value>com.pointbase.jdbc.jdbcUniversalDriver</value>
    </parameter>
    <parameter>
        <name>driverName</name>
        <value>jdbc:pointbase:
            server://localhost/sample</value>
    </parameter>
</ResourceParams>
```

Since the resource factory is a subentry of the `Context` entry described in Running Web Applications (page 360), you add this entry to Tomcat's configuration in the same ways that you can add the `Context` entry.

CHAPTER 13

Java Servlet Technology

Stephanie Bodoff

IN THIS CHAPTER

As soon as the Web began to be used for delivering services, service providers recognized the need for dynamic content. Applets, one of the earliest attempts towards this goal, focused on using the client platform to deliver dynamic user experiences. At the same time, developers also investigated using the server platform for this purpose. Initially, CGI scripts were the main technology used to generate dynamic content. Though widely used, CGI scripting technology has a number of shortcomings including platform-dependence and lack of scalability. To address these limitations, Java Servlet technology was created as a portable way to provide dynamic, user-oriented content.

13.1 What is a Servlet?

A *servlet* is a Java programming language class used to extend the capabilities of servers that host applications accessed via a request-response programming model. Although servlets can respond to any type of request, they are commonly used to extend the applications hosted by Web servers. For such applications, Java Servlet technology defines HTTP-specific servlet classes.

The `javax.servlet` and `javax.servlet.http` packages provide interfaces and classes for writing servlets. All servlets must implement the `Servlet` interface, which defines life cycle methods.

When implementing a generic service, you can use or extend the `GenericServlet` class provided with the Java Servlet API. The `HttpServlet` class provides methods, such as `doGet` and `doPost`, for handling HTTP-specific services.

This chapter focuses on writing servlets that generate responses to HTTP requests. Some knowledge of the HTTP protocol is assumed; if you are unfamiliar with this protocol, you can get a brief introduction to HTTP in HTTP Overview (page 491).

13.2 The Example Servlets

This chapter uses the Duke's Bookstore application to illustrate the tasks involved in programming servlets. Table 13.1 lists the servlets that handle each bookstore function. Each programming task is illustrated by one or more servlets. For example, `BookDetailsServlet` illustrates how to handle HTTP `GET` requests, `BookDetailsServlet` and `CatalogServlet` show how to construct responses, and `CatalogServlet` shows you how to track session information.

Table 13.1 Duke's Bookstore Example Servlets

Function	Servlet
Enter the bookstore	`BookStoreServlet`
Create the bookstore banner	`BannerServlet`
Browse the bookstore catalog	`CatalogServlet`
Put a book in a shopping cart	`CatalogServlet`, `BookDetailsServlet`
Get detailed information on a specific book	`BookDetailsServlet`
Display the shopping cart	`ShowCartServlet`
Remove one or more books from the shopping cart	`ShowCartServlet`

Table 13.1 Duke's Bookstore Example Servlets *(Continued)*

Function	Servlet
Buy the books in the shopping cart	`CashierServlet`
Receive an acknowledgement for the purchase	`ReceiptServlet`

The data for the bookstore application is maintained in a database and accessed through the helper class `database.BookDB`. The `database` package also contains the class `BookDetails` that represents a book. The shopping cart and shopping cart items are represented by the classes `cart.ShoppingCart` and `cart.ShoppingCartItem`.

The source for the bookstore application is located in the `docs/tutorial/examples/web/bookstore1` directory created when you unzip the tutorial bundle (see Running the Examples (page xx)). To build, deploy, and run the example:

1. Go to the bookstore1 directory and build and deploy the example by running `ant`. This runs the default ant target `deploy` which depends on the `build` target. The `build` target will spawn any necessary compilations and copy files to the `docs/tutorial/examples/web/bookstore1/build` directory. The `deploy` target copies the bookstore1 context file to `<JWSDP_HOME>/webapps` as described in Running Web Applications (page 360).
2. Start the Pointbase database server (see Accessing Databases from Web Applications (page 363)).
3. Start or restart Tomcat.
4. Open the bookstore URL `http://localhost:8080/bookstore1/enter`.

13.2.1 Troubleshooting

Common Problems and Their Solutions (page 65) lists some reasons why a Web client can fail. In addition, Duke's Bookstore returns the following exceptions:

- `BookNotFoundException`—if a book can't be located in the bookstore database. This will occur if you haven't loaded the bookstore database with data by running `ant create-web-db` or if the database server hasn't been started or it has crashed.
- `BooksNotFoundException`—if the bookstore data can't be retrieved. This will occur if you haven't loaded the bookstore database with data by running `ant create-web-db` or if the database server hasn't been started or it has crashed.

- `UnavailableException`—if a servlet can't retrieve the Web context attribute representing the bookstore. This will occur if you haven't copied the Pointbase client library *<PB_HOME>*`/client/lib/pbclient41ev.jar` to *<JWSDP_HOME>*`/common/lib`.

Since we have specified an error page, you will see the message: `The application is unavailable. Please try later.` If you don't specify an error page, the Web container generates a default page containing the message `A Servlet Exception Has Occurred` and a stack trace that can help diagnose the cause of the exception. If you use the `errorpage.html`, you will have to look in the Web container's log to determine the cause of the exception. Web log files reside in the directory *<JWSDP_HOME>*`/logs` and are named `jwsdp_log.`*<date>*`.txt`.

13.3 Servlet Life Cycle

The life cycle of a servlet is controlled by the container in which the servlet has been deployed. When a request is mapped to a servlet, the container performs the following steps.

1. If an instance of the servlet does not exist, the Web container:
   a. Loads the servlet class
   b. Creates an instance of the servlet class
   c. Initializes the servlet instance by calling the `init` method. Initialization is covered in Initializing a Servlet (page 377).
2. Invokes the `service` method, passing a request and response object. Service methods are discussed in Writing Service Methods (page 377).

If the container needs to remove the servlet, it finalizes the servlet by calling the servlet's `destroy` method. Finalization is discussed in Finalizing a Servlet (page 396).

13.3.1 Handling Servlet Life Cycle Events

You can monitor and react to events in a servlet's life cycle by defining listener objects whose methods get invoked when life cycle events occur. To use these listener objects you must

- Define the listener class
- Specify the listener class

Defining The Listener Class

You define a listener class as an implementation of a listener interface. Table 13.2 lists the events that can be monitored and the corresponding interface that must be implemented. When a listener method is invoked it is passed an event that contains information appropriate to the event. For example, the methods in the `HttpSessionListener` interface are passed an `HttpSessionEvent`, which contains an `HttpSession`.

The `listeners.ContextListener` class creates and removes the database helper and counter objects used in the Duke's Bookstore application. The methods retrieve the Web context object from `ServletContextEvent` and then store (and remove) the objects as servlet context attributes.

```
import database.BookDB;
import javax.servlet.*;
import util.Counter;

public final class ContextListener
    implements ServletContextListener {
    private ServletContext context = null;
    public void contextInitialized(ServletContextEvent event) {
        context = event.getServletContext();
        try {
            BookDB bookDB = new BookDB();
            context.setAttribute("bookDB", bookDB);
```

Table 13.2 Servlet Life Cycle Events

Object	Event	Listener Interface and Event Class
Web context (See Accessing the Web Context (page 392))	Initialization and destruction	`javax.servlet.ServletContextListener` and `ServletContextEvent`
	Attribute added, removed, or replaced	`javax.servlet.ServletContextAttributeListener` and `ServletContextAttributeEvent`
Session (See Maintaining Client State (page 393))	Creation, invalidation, and timeout	`javax.servlet.http.HttpSessionListener` and `HttpSessionEvent`
	Attribute added, removed, or replaced	`javax.servlet.http.HttpSessionAttributeListener` and `HttpSessionBindingEvent`

```
            } catch (Exception ex) {
                System.out.println(
                    "Couldn't create database: "
                    + ex.getMessage());
            }
            Counter counter = new Counter();
            context.setAttribute("hitCounter", counter);
            context.log("Created hitCounter"
                + counter.getCounter());
            counter = new Counter();
            context.setAttribute("orderCounter", counter);
            context.log("Created orderCounter"
                 + counter.getCounter());
        }

        public void contextDestroyed(ServletContextEvent event) {
            context = event.getServletContext();
            BookDB bookDB = context.getAttribute(
                "bookDB");
            bookDB.remove();
            context.removeAttribute("bookDB");
            context.removeAttribute("hitCounter");
            context.removeAttribute("orderCounter");
        }
    }
```

Specifying Event Listener Classes

To specify an event listener class, you add a `listener` element to the Web application deployment descriptor. Here is the `listener` element for the Duke's Bookstore application:

```
<listener>
    <listener-class>listeners.ContextListener</listener-class>
</listener>
```

13.3.2 Handling Errors

Any number of exceptions can occur when a servlet is executed. The Web container will generate a default page containing the message `A Servlet Exception Has Occurred` when an exception occurs, but you can also specify that the container should return a specific error page for a given exception. To specify such a page, you add an `error-page` element to the Web application deployment descriptor. These elements map the exceptions returned by the Duke's Bookstore application to `errorpage.html`:

```
<error-page>
    <exception-type>exception.BookNotFoundException</exception-type>
    <location>/errorpage.html</location>
</error-page>
<error-page>
    <exception-type>exception.BooksNotFoundException</exception-
type>
    <location>/errorpage.html</location>
</error-page>
<error-page>
    <exception-type>exception.OrderException</exception-type>
    <location>/errorpage.html</location>
</error-page>
```

13.4 Sharing Information

Web components, like most objects, usually work with other objects to accomplish their tasks. There are several ways they can do this. They can use private helper objects (for example, JavaBeans components); they can share objects that are attributes of a public scope; they can use a database; and they can invoke other Web resources. The Java Servlet technology mechanisms that allow a Web component to invoke other Web resources are described in Invoking Other Web Resources (page 389).

13.4.1 Using Scope Objects

Collaborating Web components share information via objects maintained as attributes of four scope objects. These attributes are accessed with the `[get|set]Attribute` methods of the class representing the scope. Table 13.3 lists the scope objects.

Table 13.3 Scope Objects

Scope Object	Class	Accessible From
Web context	`javax.servlet.ServletContext`	Web components within a Web context. See Accessing the Web Context (page 392).
session	`javax.servlet.http.HttpSession`	Web components handling a request that belongs to the session. See Maintaining Client State (page 393).
request	subtype of `javax.servlet.ServletRequest`	Web components handling the request.
page	`javax.servlet.jsp.PageContext`	The JSP page that creates the object. See Implicit Objects (page 410).

Figure 13.1 shows the scoped attributes maintained by the Duke's Bookstore application.

13.4.2 Controlling Concurrent Access to Shared Resources

In a multithreaded server, it is possible for shared resources to be accessed concurrently. Besides scope object attributes, shared resources include in-memory data such as instance or class variables and external objects such as files, database

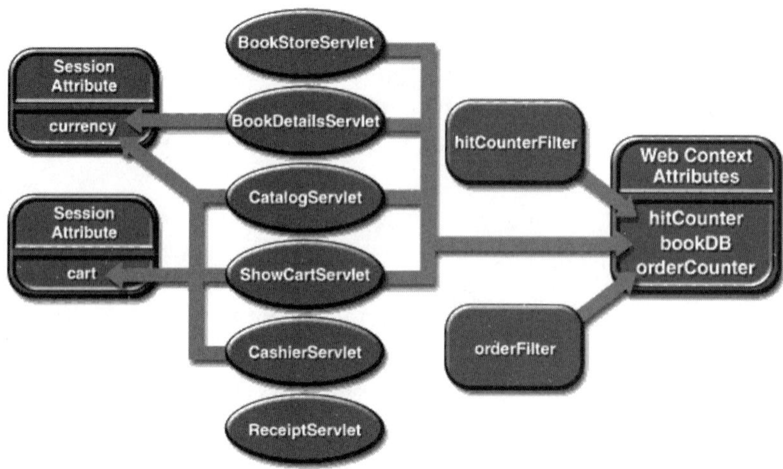

Figure 13.1 Duke's Bookstore Scoped Attributes

connections, and network connections. Concurrent access can arise in several situations:

- Multiple Web components accessing objects stored in the Web context.
- Multiple Web components accessing objects stored in a session.
- Multiple threads within a Web component accessing instance variables. A Web container will typically create a thread to handle each request. If you want to ensure that a servlet instance handles only one request at a time, a servlet can implement the `SingleThreadModel` interface. If a servlet implements this interface, you are guaranteed that no two threads will execute concurrently in the servlet's service method. A Web container can implement this guarantee by synchronizing access to a single instance of the servlet, or by maintaining a pool of Web component instances and dispatching each new request to a free instance. This interface does not prevent synchronization problems that result from Web components accessing shared resources such as static class variables or external objects.

When resources can be accessed concurrently, they can be used in an inconsistent fashion. To prevent this, you must control the access using the synchronization techniques described in the Threads Lesson in the Java Tutorial.

In the previous section we showed five scoped attributes shared by more than one servlet: `bookDB`, `cart`, `currency`, `hitCounter`, and `orderCounter`. The `bookDB` attribute is discussed in the next section. The cart, currency, and counters can be set and read by multiple multithreaded servlets. To prevent these objects from being used inconsistently, access is controlled by synchronized methods. For example, here is the `util.Counter` class:

```
public class Counter {
    private int counter;
    public Counter() {
        counter = 0;
    }
    public synchronized int getCounter() {
        return counter;
    }
    public synchronized int setCounter(int c) {
        counter = c;
        return counter;
```

```
        }
        public synchronized int incCounter() {
            return(++counter);
        }
    }
```

13.4.3 Accessing Databases

Data that is shared between Web components and persistent between invocations of a Web application is usually maintained by a database. Web components use the JDBC 2.0 API to access relational databases. The data for the bookstore application is maintained in a database and accessed through the helper class `database.BookDB`. For example, `ReceiptServlet` invokes the `BookDB.buyBooks` method to update the book inventory when a user makes a purchase. The `buyBooks` method invokes `buyBook` for each book contained in the shopping cart. To ensure the order is processed in its entirety, the calls to `buyBook` are wrapped in a single JDBC transaction. The use of the shared database connection is synchronized via the `[get|release]Connection` methods.

```
public void buyBooks(ShoppingCart cart) throws OrderException{
    Collection items = cart.getItems();
    Iterator i = items.iterator();
    try {
        getConnection();
        con.setAutoCommit(false);
        while (i.hasNext()) {
            ShoppingCartItem sci = (ShoppingCartItem)i.next();
            BookDetails bd = (BookDetails)sci.getItem();
            String id = bd.getBookId();
            int quantity = sci.getQuantity();
            buyBook(id, quantity);
        }
        con.commit();
        con.setAutoCommit(true);
        releaseConnection();
    } catch (Exception ex) {
        try {
        con.rollback();
        releaseConnection();
        throw new OrderException("Transaction failed: " +
            ex.getMessage());
```

```
        } catch (SQLException sqx) {
            releaseConnection();
            throw new OrderException("Rollback failed: " +
                sqx.getMessage());
        }
    }
}
```

13.5 Initializing a Servlet

After the Web container loads and instantiates the servlet class and before it delivers requests from clients, the Web container initializes the servlet. You can customize this process to allow the servlet to read persistent configuration data, initialize resources, and perform any other one-time activities by overriding the `init` method of the `Servlet` interface. A servlet that cannot complete its initialization process should throw `UnavailableException`.

All the servlets that access the bookstore database (`BookStoreServlet`, `CatalogServlet`, `BookDetailsServlet`, and `ShowCartServlet`) initialize a variable in their `init` method that points to the database helper object created by the Web context listener:

```
public class CatalogServlet extends HttpServlet {
    private BookDB bookDB;
    public void init() throws ServletException {
        bookDB = (BookDB)getServletContext().
            getAttribute("bookDB");
        if (bookDB == null) throw new
            UnavailableException("Couldn't get database.");
    }
}
```

13.6 Writing Service Methods

The service provided by a servlet is implemented in the `service` method of a `GenericServlet`, the `do`*`Method`* methods (where *`Method`* can take the value `Get`, `Delete`, `Options`, `Post`, `Put`, `Trace`) of an `HttpServlet`, or any other protocol-specific methods defined by a class that implements the `Servlet` interface. In the rest of this chapter, the term "service method" will be used for any method in a servlet class that provides a service to a client.

The general pattern for a service method is to extract information from the request, access external resources, and then populate the response based on that information.

For HTTP servlets, the correct procedure for populating the response is to first fill in the response headers, then retrieve an output stream from the response, and finally write any body content to the output stream. Response headers must always be set before a `PrintWriter` or `ServletOutputStream` is retrieved because the HTTP protocol expects to receive all headers before body content. The next two sections describe how to get information from requests and generate responses.

13.6.1 Getting Information From Requests

A request contains data passed between a client and the servlet. All requests implement the `ServletRequest` interface. This interface defines methods for accessing the following information:

- Parameters, which are typically used to convey information between clients and servlets
- Object-valued attributes, which are typically used to pass information between the servlet container and a servlet or between collaborating servlets
- Information about the protocol used to communicate the request and the client and server involved in the request
- Information relevant to localization

For example, in `CatalogServlet` the identifier of the book that a customer wishes to purchase is included as a parameter to the request. The following code fragment illustrates how to use the `getParameter` method to extract the identifier:

```
String bookId = request.getParameter("Add");
if (bookId != null) {
    BookDetails book = bookDB.getBookDetails(bookId);
```

You can also retrieve an input stream from the request and manually parse the data. To read character data, use the `BufferedReader` object returned by the request's `getReader` method. To read binary data, use the `ServletInputStream` returned by `getInputStream`.

HTTP servlets are passed an HTTP request object, `HttpServletRequest`, which contains the request URL, HTTP headers, query string, and so on.

An HTTP request URL contains the following parts:

```
http://[host]:[port][request path]?[query string]
```

The request path is further composed of the following elements:

- **Context path:** A concatenation of "/" with the context root of the servlet's Web application.
- **Servlet path:** The path section that corresponds to the component alias that activated this request. This path starts with a "/".
- **Path info:** The part of the request path that is not part of the context path or the servlet path.

The aliases are as listed in Table 13.4. Table 13.5 gives some examples of how the URL will be broken down if the context path is `/catalog`.

Table 13.4 Aliases

Pattern	Servlet
`/lawn/*`	`LawnServlet`
`/*.jsp`	`JSPServlet`

Table 13.5 Request Path Elements

Request Path	Servlet Path	Path Info
`/catalog/lawn/index.html`	`/lawn`	`/index.html`
`/catalog/help/feedback.jsp`	`/help/feedback.jsp`	`null`

Query strings are composed of a set of parameters and values. Individual parameters are retrieved from a request with the `getParameter` method. There are two ways to generate query strings:

- A query string can explicitly appear in a Web page. For example, an HTML page generated by the `CatalogServlet` could contain the link `<a href="/bookstore1/catalog?Add=101">Add To Cart</a>`. `CatalogServlet` extracts the parameter named `Add` as follows:

  ```
  String bookId = request.getParameter("Add");
  ```

- A query string is appended to a URL when a form with a GET HTTP method is submitted. In the Duke's Bookstore application, CashierServlet generates a form, a user name input to the form is appended to the URL that maps to ReceiptServlet, and ReceiptServlet extracts the user name using the getParameter method.

13.6.2 Constructing Responses

A response contains data passed between a server and the client. All responses implement the ServletResponse interface. This interface defines methods that allow you to:

- Retrieve an output stream to use to send data to the client. To send character data, use the PrintWriter returned by the response's getWriter method. To send binary data in a MIME body response, use the ServletOutputStream returned by getOutputStream. To mix binary and text data, for example, to create a multipart response, use a ServletOutputStream and manage the character sections manually.
- Indicate the content type (for example, text/html), being returned by the response. A registry of content type names is kept by IANA at:

  ftp://ftp.isi.edu/in-notes/iana/assignments/media-types

- Indicate whether to buffer output. By default, any content written to the output stream is immediately sent to the client. Buffering allows content to be written before anything is actually sent back to the client, thus providing the servlet with more time to set appropriate status codes and headers or forward to another Web resource.
- Set localization information.

HTTP response objects, HttpServletResponse, have fields representing HTTP headers such as

- Status codes, which are used to indicate the reason of a request is not satisfied.
- Cookies, which are used to store application-specific information at the client. Sometimes cookies are used to maintain an identifier for tracking a user's session (see Session Tracking (page 396)).

In Duke's Bookstore, BookDetailsServlet generates an HTML page that displays information about a book which the servlet retrieves from a database.

The servlet first sets response headers: the content type of the response and the buffer size. The servlet buffers the page content because the database access can generate an exception that would cause forwarding to an error page. By buffering the response, the client will not see a concatenation of part of a Duke's Bookstore page with the error page should an error occur. The `doGet` method then retrieves a `PrintWriter` from the response.

For filling in the response, the servlet first dispatches the request to `BannerServlet`, which generates a common banner for all the servlets in the application. This process is discussed in Including Other Resources in the Response (page 390). Then the servlet retrieves the book identifier from a request parameter and uses the identifier to retrieve information about the book from the bookstore database. Finally the servlet generates HTML markup that describes the book information and commits the response to the client by calling the `close` method on the `PrintWriter`.

```
public class BookDetailsServlet extends HttpServlet {
     public void doGet (HttpServletRequest request,
          HttpServletResponse response)
          throws ServletException, IOException {
        // set headers before accessing the Writer
        response.setContentType("text/html");
        response.setBufferSize(8192);
        PrintWriter out = response.getWriter();

        // then write the response
        out.println("<html>" +
        "<head><title>+
        messages.getString("TitleBookDescription")
        +</title></head>");

        // Get the dispatcher; it gets the banner to the user
        RequestDispatcher dispatcher =
            getServletContext().
            getRequestDispatcher("/banner");
        if (dispatcher != null)
            dispatcher.include(request, response);

        //Get the identifier of the book to display
        String bookId = request.getParameter("bookId");
        if (bookId != null) {
            // and the information about the book
```

```
                try {
                    BookDetails bd =
                        bookDB.getBookDetails(bookId);
                    ...
                    //Print out the information obtained
                    out.println("<h2>" + bd.getTitle() + "</h2>" +
                    ...
                } catch (BookNotFoundException ex) {
                    response.resetBuffer();
                    throw new ServletException(ex);
                }
            }
            out.println("</body></html>");
            out.close();
        }
    }
```

`BookDetailsServlet` generates a page that looks like Figure 13.2.

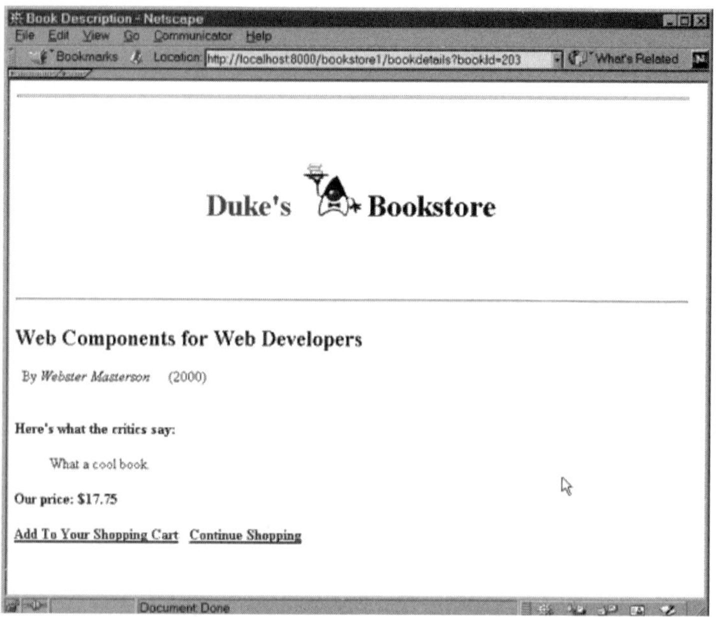

Figure 13.2 Book Details

13.7 Filtering Requests and Responses

A *filter* is an object that can transform the header and/or content of a request or response. Filters differ from Web components in that they usually do not themselves create a response. Instead, a filter provides functionality that can be "attached" to any kind of Web resource. As a consequence, a filter should not have any dependencies on a Web resource for which it is acting as a filter so that it can be composable with more than one type of Web resource. The main tasks that a filter can perform are:

- Query the request and act accordingly.
- Block the request and response pair from passing any further.
- Modify the request headers and data. You do this by providing a customized version of the request.
- Modify the response headers and data. You do this by providing a customized version of the response.
- Interact with external resources.

Applications of filters include authentication, logging, image conversion, data compression, encryption, tokenizing streams, XML transformations, and so on.

You can configure a Web resource to be filtered by a chain of zero, one, or more filters in a specific order. This chain is specified when the Web application containing the component is deployed and instantiated when a Web container loads the component.

In summary, the tasks involved in using filters include:

- Programming the filter
- Programming customized requests and responses
- Specifying the filter chain for each Web resource

13.7.1 Programming Filters

The filtering API is defined by the `Filter`, `FilterChain`, and `FilterConfig` interfaces in the `javax.servlet` package. You define a filter by implementing the `Filter` interface. The most important method in this interface is the `doFilter` method, which is passed request, response, and filter chain objects. This method can perform the following actions:

- Examine the request headers.
- Customize the request object if it wishes to modify request headers or data.
- Customize the response object if it wishes to modify response headers or data.
- Invoke the next entity in the filter chain. If the current filter is the last filter in the chain that ends with the target Web component or static resource, the next entity is the resource at the end of the chain; otherwise, it is the next filter that was configured in the WAR. It invokes the next entity by calling the `doFilter` method on the chain object (passing in the request and response it was called with, or the wrapped versions it may have created). Alternatively, it can choose to block the request by not making the call to invoke the next entity. In the latter case, the filter is responsible for filling out the response.
- Examine response headers after it has invoked the next filter in the chain.
- Throw an exception to indicate an error in processing.

In addition to `doFilter`, you must implement the `init` and `destroy` methods. The `init` method is called by the container when the filter is instantiated. If you wish to pass initialization parameters to the filter you retrieve them from the `FilterConfig` object passed to `init`.

The Duke's Bookstore application uses the filters `HitCounterFilter` and `OrderFilter` to increment and log the value of a counter when the entry and receipt servlets are accessed.

In the `doFilter` method, both filters retrieve the servlet context from the filter configuration object so that they can access the counters stored as context attributes. After the filters have completed application-specific processing, they invoke `doFilter` on the filter chain object passed into the original `doFilter` method. The elided code is discussed in the next section.

```
public final class HitCounterFilter implements Filter {
    private FilterConfig filterConfig = null;

    public void init(FilterConfig filterConfig)
        throws ServletException {
        this.filterConfig = filterConfig;
    }
    public void destroy() {
        this.filterConfig = null;
```

```
    }
    public void doFilter(ServletRequest request,
        ServletResponse response, FilterChain chain)
        throws IOException, ServletException {
        if (filterConfig == null)
            return;
        StringWriter sw = new StringWriter();
        PrintWriter writer = new PrintWriter(sw);
        Counter counter = (Counter)filterConfig.
            getServletContext().
            getAttribute("hitCounter");
        writer.println();
        writer.println("===============");
        writer.println("The number of hits is: " +
            counter.incCounter());
        writer.println("===============");
        // Log the resulting string
        writer.flush();
        filterConfig.getServletContext().
            log(sw.getBuffer().toString());
        ...
        chain.doFilter(request, wrapper);
        ...
    }
}
```

13.7.2 Programming Customized Requests and Responses

There are many ways for a filter to modify a request or response. For example, a filter could add an attribute to the request or insert data in the response. In the Duke's Bookstore example, `HitCounterFilter` inserts the value of the counter into the response.

A filter that modifies a response must usually capture the response before it is returned to the client. The way to do this is to pass the servlet that generates the response a stand-in stream. The stand-in stream prevents the servlet from closing the original response stream when it completes and allows the filter to modify the servlet's response.

In order to pass this stand-in stream to the servlet, the filter creates a response "wrapper" that overrides the `getWriter` or `getOutputStream` method to return this stand-in stream. The wrapper is passed to the `doFilter` method of the filter chain. Wrapper methods default to calling through to the wrapped request or response object. This approach follows the well-known Wrapper or Decorator pattern described in *Design Patterns: Elements of Reusable Object-Oriented Software* (Addison-Wesley, 1995). The following sections describe how the hit counter filter described earlier and other types of filters use wrappers.

To override request methods, you wrap the request in an object that extends `ServletRequestWrapper` or `HttpServletRequestWrapper`. To override response methods, you wrap the response in an object that extends `ServletResponse-Wrapper` or `HttpServletResponseWrapper`.

`HitCounterFilter` wraps the response in a `CharResponseWrapper`. The wrapped response is passed to the next object in the filter chain, which is `Book-StoreServlet`. `BookStoreServlet` writes its response into the stream created by `CharResponseWrapper`. When `chain.doFilter` returns, `HitCounterFil-ter` retrieves the servlet's response from `PrintWriter` and writes it to a buffer. The filter inserts the value of the counter into the buffer, resets the content length header of the response, and finally writes the contents of the buffer to the response stream.

```
PrintWriter out = response.getWriter();
CharResponseWrapper wrapper = new CharResponseWrapper
    ((HttpServletResponse)response);
chain.doFilter(request, wrapper);
CharArrayWriter caw = new CharArrayWriter();
caw.write(wrapper.toString().substring(0,
    wrapper.toString().indexOf("</body>")-1));
caw.write("<p>\n<center><center>" +
    messages.getString("Visitor") + "<font color='red'>" +
    counter.getCounter() + "</font><center>");
caw.write("\n</body></html>");
response.setContentLength(caw.toString().length());
out.write(caw.toString());
out.close();

public class CharResponseWrapper extends
    HttpServletResponseWrapper {
    private CharArrayWriter output;
    public String toString() {
        return output.toString();
    }
    public CharResponseWrapper(HttpServletResponse response){
        super(response);
        output = new CharArrayWriter();
```

```
    }
    public PrintWriter getWriter(){
        return new PrintWriter(output);
    }
}
```

Figure 13.3 shows the entry page for Duke's Bookstore with the hit counter.

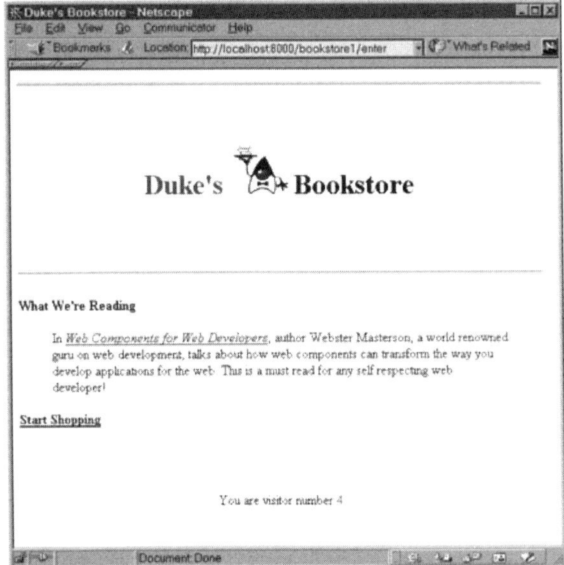

Figure 13.3 Duke's Bookstore

13.7.3 Specifying Filter Mappings

A Web container uses filter mappings to decide how to apply filters to Web resources. A filter mapping matches a filter to a Web component by name or to Web resources by URL pattern. The filters are invoked in the order that filter mappings appear in the filter mapping list of a WAR.

To map a filter to a Web resources you:

- Declare the filter using the `<filter>` element in the Web application deployment descriptor. This element creates a name for the filter and declares the filter's implementation class and initialization parameters.

- Map the filter to a Web resource by defining a <filter-mapping> element in the deployment descriptor. This element maps a filter name to a Web resource by name or by URL pattern.

The following elements show how to specify the hit counter and order filters. To define a filter you provide a name for the filter, the class that implements the filter, and optionally some initialization parameters.

```
<filter>
    <filter-name>OrderFilter</filter-name>
    <filter-class>filters.OrderFilter</filter-class>
</filter>
<filter>
    <filter-name>HitCounterFilter</filter-name>
    <filter-class>filters.HitCounterFilter</filter-class>
</filter>
```

The filter-mapping element maps the order filter to the /receipt URL. The mapping could also have specified the servlet ReceiptServlet. Note that the filter, filter-mapping, servlet, and servlet-mapping elements must appear in the Web application deployment descriptor in that order.

```
<filter-mapping>
    <filter-name>OrderFilter</filter-name>
    <url-pattern>/receipt</url-pattern>
  </filter-mapping>
  <filter-mapping>
    <filter-name>HitCounterFilter</filter-name>
    <url-pattern>/enter</url-pattern>
  </filter-mapping>
```

If you want to log every request to a Web application, you would map the hit counter filter to the URL pattern /*. Table 13.6 summarizes the filter mapping list for the Duke's Bookstore application. The filters are matched by URL pattern and each filter chain contains only one filter.

Table 13.6 Duke's Bookstore Filter Mapping List

URL	Filter
/enter	HitCounterFilter
/receipt	OrderFilter

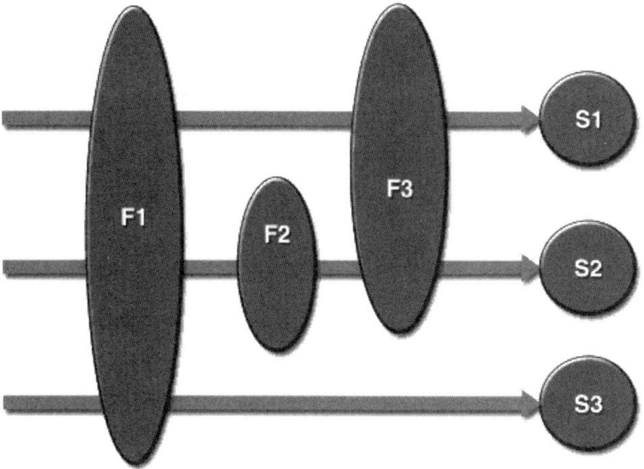

Figure 13.4 Filter to Servlet Mapping

You can map a filter to one or more Web resource and you can map more than one filter to a Web resource. This is illustrated in Figure 13.4, where filter F1 is mapped to servlets S1, S2, and S3, filter F2 is mapped to S2, and filter F3 is mapped to S1 and S2.

Recall that a filter chain is one of the objects passed to the `doFilter` method of a filter. This chain is formed indirectly via filter mappings. The order of the filters in the chain is the same as the order that filter mappings appear in the Web application deployment descriptor.

When a filter is mapped to servlet S1, the Web container invokes the `doFilter` method of F1. The `doFilter` method of each filter in S1's filter chain is invoked by the preceding filter in the chain via the `chain.doFilter` method. Since S1's filter chain contains filters F1 and F3, F1's call to `chain.doFilter` invokes the `doFilter` method of filter F3. When F3's `doFilter` method completes, control returns to F1's `doFilter` method.

13.8 Invoking Other Web Resources

Web components can invoke other Web resources in two ways: indirect and direct.

A Web component indirectly invokes another Web resource when it embeds a URL that points to another Web component in content returned to a client. In the Duke's Bookstore application, most Web components contain embedded URLs that point to other Web components. For example, `ReceiptServlet` indirectly invokes the `CatalogServlet` through the embedded URL `/bookstore1/catalog`.

A Web component can also directly invoke another resource while it is executing. There are two possibilities: it can include the content of another resource, or it can forward a request to another resource.

To invoke a resource available on the server that is running a Web component, you must first obtain a `RequestDispatcher` using the `getRequestDispatcher("URL")` method.

You can get a `RequestDispatcher` from either a request or the Web context, however, the two methods have slightly different behavior. The method takes the path to the requested resource as an argument. A request can take a relative path (that is, one that does not begin with a "/"), but the Web context requires an absolute path. If the resource is not available, or if the server has not implemented a `RequestDispatcher` object for that type of resource, `getRequestDispatcher` will return null. Your servlet should be prepared to deal with this condition.

13.8.1 Including Other Resources in the Response

It is often useful to include another Web resource, for example, banner content or copyright information, in the response returned from a Web component. To include another resource, invoke the `include` method of a `RequestDispatcher`:

```
include(request, response);
```

If the resource is static, the `include` method enables programmatic server-side includes. If the resource is a Web component, the effect of the method is to send the request to the included Web component, execute the Web component, and then include the result of the execution in the response from the containing servlet. An included Web component has access to the request object, but it is limited in what it can do with the response object:

- It can write to the body of and commit a response.
- It cannot set headers or call any method (for example, `setCookie`) that affects the headers of the response.

The banner for the Duke's Bookstore application is generated by `BannerServlet`. Note that both `doGet` and `doPost` methods are implemented because `BannerServlet` can be dispatched from either method in a calling servlet.

```
public class BannerServlet extends HttpServlet {
    public void doGet (HttpServletRequest request,
        HttpServletResponse response)
        throws ServletException, IOException {

        PrintWriter out = response.getWriter();
        out.println("<body bgcolor=\"#ffffff\">" +
        "<center>" + "<hr> <br>  " + "<h1>" +
        "<font size=\"+3\" color=\"#CC0066\">Duke's </font>" +
        <img src=\"" + request.getContextPath() +
        "/duke.books.gif\">" +
        "<font size=\"+3\" color=\"black\">Bookstore</font>" +
        "</h1>" + "</center>" + "<br>   <hr> <br> ");
    }
    public void doPost (HttpServletRequest request,
        HttpServletResponse response)
        throws ServletException, IOException {

        PrintWriter out = response.getWriter();
        out.println("<body bgcolor=\"#ffffff\">" +
        "<center>" + "<hr> <br>  " + "<h1>" +
        "<font size=\"+3\" color=\"#CC0066\">Duke's </font>" +
        <img src=\"" + request.getContextPath() +
        "/duke.books.gif\">" +
        "<font size=\"+3\" color=\"black\">Bookstore</font>" +
        "</h1>" + "</center>" + "<br>   <hr> <br> ");
    }
}
```

Each servlet in the Duke's Bookstore application includes the result from `BannerServlet` with the following code:

```
RequestDispatcher dispatcher =
    getServletContext().getRequestDispatcher("/banner");
if (dispatcher != null)
    dispatcher.include(request, response);
}
```

13.8.2 Transferring Control to Another Web Component

In some applications you might want to have one Web component do preliminary processing of a request and another component generate the response. For example, you might want to partially process a request and then transfer to another component depending on the nature of the request.

To transfer control to another Web component, you invoke the `forward` method of a `RequestDispatcher`. When a request is forwarded, the request URL is set to the path of the forwarded page. If the original URL is required for any processing you can save it as a request attribute. The `Dispatcher` servlet, used by a version of the Duke's Bookstore application described in The Example JSP Pages (page 404), saves the path information from the original URL, retrieves a `RequestDispatcher` from the request, and then forwards to the JSP page `template.jsp`.

```
public class Dispatcher extends HttpServlet {
    public void doGet(HttpServletRequest request,
        HttpServletResponse response) {
        request.setAttribute("selectedScreen",
            request.getServletPath());
        RequestDispatcher dispatcher = request.
            getRequestDispatcher("/template.jsp");
        if (dispatcher != null)
            dispatcher.forward(request, response);
    }
    public void doPost(HttpServletRequest request,
    ...
}
```

The `forward` method should be used to give another resource responsibility for replying to the user. If you have already accessed a `ServletOutputStream` or `PrintWriter` object within the servlet, you cannot use this method; it throws an `IllegalStateException`.

13.9 Accessing the Web Context

The context in which Web components execute is an object that implements the `ServletContext` interface. You retrieve the Web context with the `getServletContext` method. The Web context provides methods for accessing:

- Initialization parameters

- Resources associated with the Web context
- Object-valued attributes
- Logging capabilities

The Web context is used by the Duke's Bookstore filters `filters.HitCounterFilter` and `OrderFilter` discussed in Filtering Requests and Responses (page 383). The filters store a counter as a context attribute. Recall from Controlling Concurrent Access to Shared Resources (page 374) that the counter's access methods are synchronized to prevent incompatible operations by servlets that are running concurrently. A filter retrieves the counter object with the context's `getAttribute` method. The incremented value of the counter is recorded with the context's `log` method.

```
public final class HitCounterFilter implements Filter {
    private FilterConfig filterConfig = null;
    public void doFilter(ServletRequest request,
        ServletResponse response, FilterChain chain)
        throws IOException, ServletException {
        ...
        StringWriter sw = new StringWriter();
        PrintWriter writer = new PrintWriter(sw);
        ServletContext context = filterConfig.
            getServletContext();
        Counter counter = (Counter)context.
            getAttribute("hitCounter");
        ...
        writer.println("The number of hits is: " +
            counter.incCounter());
        ...
        context.log(sw.getBuffer().toString());
        ...
    }
}
```

13.10 Maintaining Client State

Many applications require a series of requests from a client to be associated with one another. For example, the Duke's Bookstore application saves the state of a user's shopping cart across requests. Web-based applications are responsible for maintaining such state, called a *session*, because the HTTP protocol is stateless. To support applications that need to maintain state, Java Servlet technology provides an API for managing sessions and allows several mechanisms for implementing sessions.

13.10.1 Accessing a Session

Sessions are represented by an `HttpSession` object. You access a session by calling the `getSession` method of a request object. This method returns the current session associated with this request, or, if the request does not have a session, creates one. Since `getSession` may modify the response header (if cookies are the session tracking mechanism), it needs to be called before you retrieve a `PrintWriter` or `ServletOutputStream`.

13.10.2 Associating Attributes with a Session

You can associate object-valued attributes with a session by name. Such attributes are accessible by any Web component that belongs to the same Web context *and* is handling a request that is part of the same session.

The Duke's Bookstore application stores a customer's shopping cart as a session attribute. This allows the shopping cart to be saved between requests and also allows cooperating servlets to access the cart. `CatalogServlet` adds items to the cart, `ShowCartServlet` displays, deletes items from, and clears the cart, and `CashierServlet` retrieves the total cost of the books in the cart.

```
public class CashierServlet extends HttpServlet {
    public void doGet (HttpServletRequest request,
        HttpServletResponse response)
        throws ServletException, IOException {

        // Get the user's session and shopping cart
        HttpSession session = request.getSession();
        ShoppingCart cart =
            (ShoppingCart)session.
                getAttribute("cart");
        ...
        // Determine the total price of the user's books
        double total = cart.getTotal();
```

Notifying Objects That Are Associated with a Session

Recall that your application can notify Web context and session listener objects of servlet life cycle events (Handling Servlet Life Cycle Events (page 370)). You can also notify objects of certain events related to their association with a session:

- When the object is added to or removed from a session. To receive this notification, your object must implement the `javax.http.HttpSessionBindingListener` interface.
- When the session to which the object is attached will be passivated and/or activated. A session will be passivated and activated when it is moved between virtual machines or saved to and restored from persistent storage. To receive this notification, your object must implement the `javax.http.HttpSessionActivationListener` interface.

13.10.3 Session Management

Since there is no way for an HTTP client to signal that it no longer needs a session, each session has an associated time-out so that its resources can be reclaimed. The time-out period can be accessed with a session's `[get|set]MaxInactiveInterval` methods. To ensure that an active session is not timed-out, you should periodically access the session in service methods because this resets the session's time-to-live counter.

When a particular client interaction is finished, you use the session's `invalidate` method to invalidate a session on the server side and remove any session data.

The bookstore application's `ReceiptServlet` is the last servlet to access a client's session, so it has responsibility for invalidating the session:

```
public class ReceiptServlet extends HttpServlet {
    public void doPost(HttpServletRequest request,
                HttpServletResponse response)
                throws ServletException, IOException {
        // Get the user's session and shopping cart
        HttpSession session = request.getSession();
        // Payment received -- invalidate the session
        session.invalidate();
        ...
```

13.10.4 Session Tracking

A Web container can use several methods to associate a session with a user, all of which involve passing an identifier between the client and server. The identifier can be maintained on the client as a cookie or the Web component can include the identifier in every URL that is returned to the client.

If your application makes use of session objects, you must ensure that session tracking is enabled by having the application rewrite URLs whenever the client turns off cookies. You do this by calling the response's `encodeURL(URL)` method on all URLs returned by a servlet. This method includes the session ID in the URL only if cookies are disabled; otherwise it returns the URL unchanged.

The `doGet` method of `ShowCartServlet` encodes the three URLs at the bottom of the shopping cart display page as follows:

```
out.println("<p>   <p><strong><a href=\"" +
    response.encodeURL(request.getContextPath() + "/catalog") +
        "\">" + messages.getString("ContinueShopping") +
        "</a>      " +
        "<a href=\"" +
    response.encodeURL(request.getContextPath() + "/cashier") +
        "\">" + messages.getString("Checkout") +
        "</a>      " +
        "<a href=\"" +
    response.encodeURL(request.getContextPath() +
        "/showcart?Clear=clear") +
        "\">" + messages.getString("ClearCart") +
        "</a></strong>");
```

If cookies are turned off, the session is encoded in the Check Out URL as follows:

```
http://localhost:8080/bookstore1/cashier;
    jsessionid=c0o7fszeb1
```

If cookies are turned on, the URL is simply:

```
http://localhost:8080/bookstore1/cashier
```

13.11 Finalizing a Servlet

When a servlet container determines that a servlet should be removed from service (for example, when a container wants to reclaim memory resources, or when it is being shut down) it calls the `destroy` method of the `Servlet` interface. In this method you release any resources the servlet is using and save any persistent state. The following `destroy` method releases the database object created in the `init` method described in Initializing a Servlet (page 377):

```
public void destroy() {
    bookDB = null;
}
```

All of a servlet's `service` methods should be complete when a servlet is removed. The server tries to ensure this completion by calling the `destroy` method only after all service requests have returned or after a server-specific grace period, whichever comes first.

If your servlet has potentially long-running service requests, use the techniques described below to:

- Keep track of how many threads are currently running the `service` method
- Provide a clean shutdown by having the `destroy` method notify long-running threads of the shutdown and wait for them to complete
- Have the long-running methods poll periodically to check for shutdown and, if necessary, stop working, clean up, and return

13.11.1 Tracking Service Requests

To track service requests, include in your servlet class a field that counts the number of service methods that are running. The field should have synchronized access methods to increment, decrement, and return its value.

```
public ShutdownExample extends HttpServlet {
    private int serviceCounter = 0;
    ...
    //Access methods for serviceCounter
    protected synchronized void enteringServiceMethod() {
        serviceCounter++;
    }
    protected synchronized void leavingServiceMethod() {
        serviceCounter--;
    }
    protected synchronized int numServices() {
        return serviceCounter;
    }
}
```

The `service` method should increment the service counter each time the method is entered and should decrement the counter each time the method returns. This is one of the few times that your `HttpServlet` subclass should override the `service` method. The new method should call `super.service` to preserve all of the original `service` method's functionality.

```
protected void service(HttpServletRequest req,
                    HttpServletResponse resp)
                    throws ServletException,IOException {
    enteringServiceMethod();
    try {
        super.service(req, resp);
    } finally {
        leavingServiceMethod();
    }
}
```

13.11.2 Notifying Methods to Shut Down

To ensure a clean shutdown, your `destroy` method should not release any shared resources until all of the service requests have completed. One part of doing this is to check the service counter. Another part is to notify the long-running methods that it is time to shut down. For this notification another field is required. The field should have the usual access methods:

```
public ShutdownExample extends HttpServlet {
    private boolean shuttingDown;
    ...
    //Access methods for shuttingDown
    protected setShuttingDown(boolean flag) {
        shuttingDown = flag;
    }
    protected boolean isShuttingDown() {
        return shuttingDown;
    }
}
```

An example of the `destroy` method using these fields to provide a clean shutdown follows:

```
public void destroy() {
    /* Check to see whether there are still service methods /*
```

```
    /* running, and if there are, tell them to stop. */
    if (numServices() > 0) {
        setShuttingDown(true);
    }

    /* Wait for the service methods to stop. */
    while(numServices() > 0) {
        try {
            Thread.sleep(interval);
        } catch (InterruptedException e) {
        }
    }
}
```

13.11.3 Creating Polite Long-Running Methods

The final step to provide a clean shutdown is to make any long-running methods behave politely. Methods that might run for a long time should check the value of the field that notifies them of shutdowns and should interrupt their work, if necessary.

```
public void doPost(...) {
    ...
    for(i = 0; ((i < lotsOfStuffToDo) &&
        !isShuttingDown()); i++) {
        try {
            partOfLongRunningOperation(i);
        } catch (InterruptedException e) {
            ...
        }
    }
}
```

CHAPTER 14

JavaServer Pages Technology

Stephanie Bodoff

IN THIS CHAPTER

JAVASERVER Pages (JSP) technology allows you to easily create Web content that has both static and dynamic components. JSP technology projects all the dynamic capabilities of Java Servlet technology but provides a more natural approach to creating static content. The main features of JSP technology are:

- A language for developing JSP pages, which are text-based documents that describe how to process a request and construct a response
- Constructs for accessing server-side objects
- Mechanisms for defining extensions to thc JSP language

JSP technology also contains API that is used by developers of Web containers, but this API is not covered in this chapter.

14.1 What is a JSP Page?

A *JSP page* is a text-based document that contains two types of text: static template data, that can be expressed in any text-based format such as HTML, SVG, WML, and XML, and JSP elements, that construct dynamic content. A syntax card and reference for the JSP elements is available at:

```
http://java.sun.com/products/jsp/technical.html#syntax
```

The Web page shown in Figure 14.1 is a form that allows you to select a locale and displays the date in a manner appropriate to the locale.

The source for this example is in the `docs/tutorial/examples/web/date` directory created when you unzip the tutorial bundle. The JSP page `index.jsp` used to create the form appears below; it is a typical mixture of static HTML markup and JSP elements. If you have developed Web pages, you are probably familiar with the HTML document structure statements (`<head>`, `<body>`, and so on) and the HTML statements that create a form `<form>` and a menu `<select>`. The example contains the following types of JSP constructs:

- Directives (**`<%@page ... %>`**) import classes in the `java.util` package and the `MyLocales` class, and set the content type returned by the page.
- The **`jsp:useBean`** element creates an object containing a collection of locales and initializes a variable that point to that object.

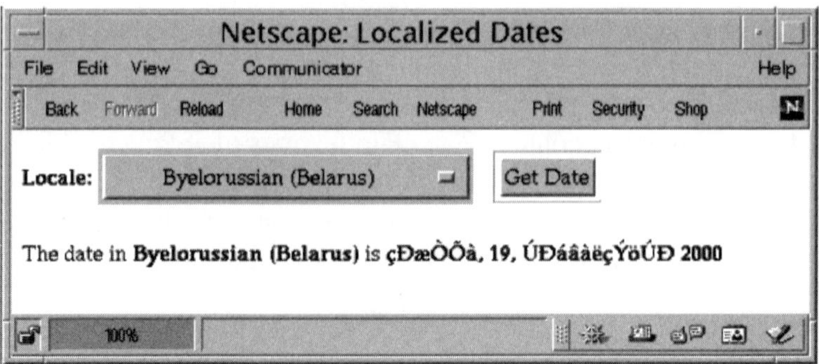

Figure 14.1 Localized Date Form

- Scriptlets (`<% ... %>`) retrieve the value of the `locale` request parameter, iterate over a collection of locale names, and conditionally insert HTML text into the output.
- Expressions (`<%= ... %>`) insert the value of the locale name into the response.
- The **`jsp:include`** element sends a request to another page (`date.jsp`) and includes the response in the response from the calling page.

```
<%@ page import="java.util.*,MyLocales" %>
<%@ page contentType="text/html; charset=ISO-8859-5" %>
<html>
<head><title>Localized Dates</title></head>
<body bgcolor="white">
<jsp:useBean id="locales" scope="application"
    class="MyLocales"/>
<form name="localeForm" action="index.jsp" method="post">
<b>Locale:</b>
<select name=locale>
<%
    String selectedLocale = request.getParameter("locale");
    Iterator i = locales.getLocaleNames().iterator();
    while (i.hasNext()) {
        String locale = (String)i.next();
        if (selectedLocale != null &&
            selectedLocale.equals(locale)) {
%>
            <option selected><%=locale%></option>
<%
        } else {
%>
            <option><%=locale%></option>
<%
        }
    }
%>
</select>
<input type="submit" name="Submit" value="Get Date">
</form>
<jsp:include page="date.jsp"/>
</body>
</html>
```

To build, deploy, and execute this JSP page:

1. Go to docs/tutorial/`examples/web/date` and build the example by executing `ant`. This runs the default ant target `deploy` that depends on the `build` target. The `build` target will spawn any necessary compilations and copy files to the `docs/tutorial/examples/web/date/build` directory. The `deploy` target copies the build directory to *<JWSDP_HOME>*`/webapps`.
2. Start or restart Tomcat.
3. Open the bookstore URL `http://localhost:8080/date`.

You will see a combo box whose entries are locales. Select a locale and click Get Date. You will see the date expressed in a manner appropriate for that locale.

14.2 The Example JSP Pages

To illustrate JSP technology, this chapter rewrites each servlet in the Duke's Bookstore application introduced in Java Servlet Technology (page 367) as a JSP page.

Table 14.1 Duke's Bookstore Example JSP Pages

Function	JSP Pages
Enter the bookstore	`bookstore.jsp`
Create the bookstore banner	`banner.jsp`
Browse the books offered for sale	`catalog.jsp`
Put a book in a shopping cart	`catalog.jsp` and `bookdetails.jsp`
Get detailed information on a specific book	`bookdetails.jsp`
Display the shopping cart	`showcart.jsp`
Remove one or more books from the shopping cart	`showcart.jsp`
Buy the books in the shopping cart	`cashier.jsp`
Receive an acknowledgement for the purchase	`receipt.jsp`

The data for the bookstore application is still maintained in a database. However, two changes are made to the database helper object `database.BookDB`:

- The database helper object is rewritten to conform to JavaBeans component design patterns as described in JavaBeans Component Design Conventions (page 424). This change is made so that JSP pages can access the helper object using JSP language elements specific to JavaBeans components.
- Instead of accessing the bookstore database directly, the helper object goes through a data access object `database.BookDAO`.

The implementation of the database helper object follows. The bean has two instance variables: the current book and a reference to the database enterprise bean.

```
public class BookDB {
    private String bookId = "0";
    private BookDBEJB database = null;

    public BookDB () throws Exception {
    }
    public void setBookId(String bookId) {
        this.bookId = bookId;
    }
    public void setDatabase(BookDBEJB database) {
        this.database = database;
    }
    public BookDetails getBookDetails()
        throws Exception {
        try {
            return (BookDetails)database.
                    getBookDetails(bookId);
        } catch (BookNotFoundException ex) {
            throw ex;
        }
    }
    ...
}
```

Finally, this version of the example contains an applet to generate a dynamic digital clock in the banner. See Including an Applet (page 418) for a description of the JSP element that generates HTML for downloading the applet.

The source for the application is located in the `docs/tutorial/examples/web/bookstore2` directory created when you unzip the tutorial bundle (see Running the Examples (page xx)). To build, deploy, and run the example:

1. Go to the bookstore2 directory and build and deploy the example by running `ant`. This runs the default ant target `deploy` that depends on the `build` target. The `build` target will spawn any necessary compilations and copy files to the `docs/tutorial/examples/web/bookstore2/build` directory. The `deploy` target copies the bookstore2 context file to `<JWSDP_HOME>/webapps` as described in Running Web Applications (page 360).
2. Start the Pointbase database server (see Accessing Databases from Web Applications (page 363)).
3. Start or restart Tomcat.
4. Open the bookstore URL `http://localhost:8080/bookstore2/enter`.

See Common Problems and Their Solutions (page 65) and Troubleshooting (page 369) for help with diagnosing common problems.

14.3 The Life Cycle of a JSP Page

A JSP page services requests as a servlet. Thus, the life cycle and many of the capabilities of JSP pages (in particular the dynamic aspects) are determined by Java Servlet technology and much of the discussion in this chapter refers to functions described in Java Servlet Technology (page 367).

When a request is mapped to a JSP page, it is handled by a special servlet that first checks whether the JSP page's servlet is older than the JSP page. If it is, it translates the JSP page into a servlet class and compiles the class. During development, one of the advantages of JSP pages over servlets is that the "build" process is performed automatically.

14.3.1 Translation and Compilation

During the translation phase each type of data in a JSP page is treated differently:

- Template data is transformed into code that will emit the data into the stream that returns data to the client.

- JSP elements are treated as follows:
  - Directives are used to control how the Web container translates and executes the JSP page.
  - Scripting elements are inserted into the JSP page's servlet class. See JSP Scripting Elements (page 412) for details.
  - Elements of the form `<jsp:XXX ... />` are converted into method calls to JavaBeans components or invocations of the Java Servlet API.

For a JSP page named *pageName*, the source for a JSP page's servlet is kept in the file:

```
<JWSDP_HOME>/work/localhost/context root/pageName$jsp.java
```

For example, the source for the index page (named `index.jsp`) for the `date` localization example discussed at the beginning the chapter would be named:

```
<JWSDP_HOME>/work/localhost/date/index$jsp.java
```

Both the translation and compilation phases can yield errors that are only observed when the page is requested for the first time. If an error occurs while the page is being translated (for example, if the translator encounters a malformed JSP element), the server will return a `ParseException` and the servlet class source file will be empty or incomplete. The last incomplete line will give a pointer to the incorrect JSP element.

If an error occurs while the JSP page is being compiled (for example, due to a syntax error in a scriptlet), the server will return a `JasperException` and a message that includes the name of the JSP page's servlet and the line where the error occurred.

Once the page has been translated and compiled, the JSP page's servlet for the most part follows the servlet life cycle described in Servlet Life Cycle (page 370):

1. If an instance of the JSP page's servlet does not exist, the container:
   a. Loads the JSP page's servlet class
   b. Instantiates an instance of the servlet class
   c. Initializes the servlet instance by calling the `jspInit` method
2. Invokes the `_jspService` method, passing a request and response object.

If the container needs to remove the JSP page's servlet, it calls the `jspDestroy` method.

14.3.2 Execution

You can control various JSP page execution parameters using `page` directives. The directives that pertain to buffering output and handling errors are discussed here. Other directives are covered in the context of specific page authoring tasks throughout the chapter.

Buffering

When a JSP page is executed, output written to the response object is automatically buffered. You can set the size of the buffer with the following page directive:

```
<%@ page buffer="none|xxxkb" %>
```

A larger buffer allows more content to be written before anything is actually sent back to the client, thus providing the JSP page with more time to set appropriate status codes and headers or forward to another Web resource. A smaller buffer decreases server memory load and allows the client to start receiving data more quickly.

Handling Errors

Any number of exceptions can arise when a JSP page is executed. To specify that the Web container should forward control to an error page if an exception occurs, include the following `page` directive at the beginning of your JSP page:

```
<%@ page errorPage="file_name" %>
```

The Duke's Bookstore application page `initdestroy.jsp` contains the following directive

```
<%@ page errorPage="errorpage.jsp"%>
```

The beginning of `errorpage.jsp` indicates that it is serving as an error page with the following page directive:

```
<%@ page isErrorPage="true|false" %>
```

This directive makes the exception object (of type `javax.servlet.jsp.JspException`) available to the error page, so that you can retrieve, interpret, and possibly display information about the cause of the exception in the error page.

Note: You can also define error pages for the WAR that contains a JSP page. If error pages are defined for both the WAR and a JSP page, the JSP page's error page takes precedence.

14.4 Initializing and Finalizing a JSP Page

You can customize the initialization process to allow the JSP page to read persistent configuration data, initialize resources, and perform any other one-time activities by overriding the `jspInit` method of the `JspPage` interface. You release resources using the `jspDestroy` method. The methods are defined using JSP declarations, discussed in Declarations (page 413).

The bookstore example page `initdestroy.jsp` defines the `jspInit` method to retrieve the object `database.BookDBAO` that accesses the bookstore database and stores a reference to the bean in `bookDBAO`.

```
private BookDBAO bookDBAO;
public void jspInit() {
bookDBAO =
    (BookDBAO)getServletContext().getAttribute("bookDB");
    if (bookDBAO == null)
        System.out.println("Couldn't get database.");
}
```

When the JSP page is removed from service, the `jspDestroy` method releases the `BookDBAO` variable.

```
public void jspDestroy() {
    bookDBAO = null;
}
```

Since the enterprise bean is shared among all the JSP pages, it should be initialized when the application is started, instead of in each JSP page. Java Servlet technology provides application life cycle events and listener classes for this purpose. As an exercise, you can move the code that manages the creation of the enterprise bean to a context listener class. See Handling Servlet Life Cycle Events (page 370) for the context listener that initializes the Java Servlet version of the bookstore application.

14.5 Creating Static Content

You create static content in a JSP page by simply writing it as if you were creating a page that consists only of that content. Static content can be expressed in any text-based format such as HTML, WML, and XML. The default format is HTML. If you want to use a format other than HTML you include a `page` directive with the `contentType` attribute set to the format type at the beginning of your JSP page. For example, if you want a page to contain data expressed in the wireless markup language (WML), you need to include the following directive:

```
<%@ page contentType="text/vnd.wap.wml"%>
```

A registry of content type names is kept by IANA at:

```
ftp://ftp.isi.edu/in-notes/iana/assignments/media-types
```

14.6 Creating Dynamic Content

You create dynamic content by accessing Java programming language objects from within scripting elements.

14.6.1 Using Objects Within JSP Pages

You can access a variety of objects, including enterprise beans and JavaBeans components, within a JSP page. JSP technology automatically makes some objects available and you can also create and access application-specific objects.

Implicit Objects

Implicit objects are created by the Web container and contain information related to a particular request, page, or application. Many of the objects are defined by the Java Servlet technology underlying JSP technology and are discussed at length in Java Servlet Technology (page 367). Table 14.2 summarizes the implicit objects.

Table 14.2 Implicit Objects

Variable	Class	Description
`application`	`javax.servlet.ServletContext`	The context for the JSP page's servlet and any Web components contained in the same application. See Accessing the Web Context (page 392).
`config`	`javax.servlet.ServletConfig`	Initialization information for the JSP page's servlet.

Table 14.2 Implicit Objects *(Continued)*

Variable	Class	Description
`exception`	`java.lang.Throwable`	Accessible only from an error page. See Handling Errors (page 408).
`out`	`javax.servlet.jsp.JspWriter`	The output stream.
`page`	`java.lang.Object`	The instance of the JSP page's servlet processing the current request. Not typically used by JSP page authors.
`pageContext`	`javax.servlet.jsp.PageContext`	The context for the JSP page. Provides a single API to manage the various scoped attributes described in Using Scope Objects (page 373). This API is used extensively when implementing tag handlers (see Tag Handlers (page 439)).
`request`	subtype of `javax.servlet.ServletRequest`	The request triggering the execution of the JSP page. See Getting Information From Requests (page 378).
`response`	subtype of `javax.servlet.ServletResponse`	The response to be returned to the client. Not typically used by JSP page authors.
`session`	`javax.servlet.http.HttpSession`	The session object for the client. See Maintaining Client State (page 393).

Application-Specific Objects

When possible, application behavior should be encapsulated in objects so that page designers can focus on presentation issues. Objects can be created by developers who are proficient in the Java programming language and accessing databases and other services. There are four ways to create and use objects within a JSP page:

- Instance and class variables of the JSP page's servlet class are created in *declarations* and accessed in *scriptlets* and *expressions*.
- Local variables of the JSP page's servlet class are created and used in *scriptlets* and *expressions*.
- Attributes of scope objects (see Using Scope Objects (page 373)) are created and used in *scriptlets* and *expressions*.

- JavaBeans components can be created and accessed using streamlined JSP elements. These elements are discussed in the chapter JavaBeans Components in JSP Pages (page 423). You can also create a JavaBeans component in a declaration or scriptlet and invoke the methods of a JavaBeans component in a scriptlet or expression.

Declarations, scriptlets, and expressions are described in JSP Scripting Elements (page 412).

Shared Objects

The conditions affecting concurrent access to shared objects described in Controlling Concurrent Access to Shared Resources (page 374) apply to objects accessed from JSP pages that run as multithreaded servlets. You can indicate how a Web container should dispatch multiple client requests with the following `page` directive:

```
<%@ page isThreadSafe="true|false" %>
```

When `isThreadSafe` is set to `true`, the Web container may choose to dispatch multiple concurrent client requests to the JSP page. This is the *default* setting. If using `true`, you must ensure that you properly synchronize access to any shared objects defined at the page level. This includes objects created within declarations, JavaBeans components with page scope, and attributes of the `page` scope object.

If `isThreadSafe` is set to `false`, requests are dispatched one at a time, in the order they were received and access to page level objects does not have to be controlled. However, you still must ensure that access to attributes of the `application` or `session` scope objects and JavaBeans components with application or session scope is properly synchronized.

14.6.2 JSP Scripting Elements

JSP scripting elements are used to create and access objects, define methods, and manage the flow of control. Since one of the goals of JSP technology is to separate static template data from the code needed to dynamically generate content, very sparing use of JSP scripting is recommended. Much of the work that requires the use of scripts can be eliminated by using custom tags, described in Custom Tags in JSP Pages (page 431).

JSP technology allows a container to support any scripting language that can call Java objects. If you wish to use a scripting language other than the default, `java`, you must specify it in a `page` directive at the beginning of a JSP page:

```
<%@ page language="scripting language" %>
```

Since scripting elements are converted to programming language statements in the JSP page's servlet class, you must import any classes and packages used by a JSP page. If the page language is `java`, you import a class or package with the `page` directive:

```
<%@ page import="packagename.*, fully_qualified_classname" %>
```

For example, bookstore example page `showcart.jsp` imports the classes needed to implement the shopping cart with the following directive:

```
<%@ page import="java.util.*, cart.*" %>
```

Declarations

A *JSP declaration* is used to declare variables and methods in a page's scripting language. The syntax for a declaration is:

```
<%! scripting language declaration %>
```

When the scripting language is the Java programming language, variables and methods in JSP declarations become declarations in the JSP page's servlet class.

The bookstore example page `initdestroy.jsp` defines an instance variable named `bookDBAO` and the initialization and finalization methods `jspInit` and `jspDestroy` discussed earlier in a declaration:

```
<%!
    private BookDBAO bookDBAO;

    public void jspInit() {
        ...
    }
    public void jspDestroy() {
        ...
    }
%>
```

Scriptlets

A *JSP scriptlet* is used to contain any code fragment that is valid for the scripting language used in a page. The syntax for a scriptlet is:

```
<%
    scripting language statements
%>
```

When the scripting language is set to java, a scriptlet is transformed into a Java programming language statement fragment and is inserted into the service method of the JSP page's servlet. A programming language variable created within a scriptlet is accessible from anywhere within the JSP page.

The JSP page showcart.jsp contains a scriptlet that retrieves an iterator from the collection of items maintained by a shopping cart and sets up a construct to loop through all the items in the cart. Inside the loop, the JSP page extracts properties of the book objects and formats them using HTML markup. Since the while loop opens a block, the HTML markup is followed by a scriptlet that closes the block.

```
<%
    Iterator i = cart.getItems().iterator();
    while (i.hasNext()) {
        ShoppingCartItem item =
            (ShoppingCartItem)i.next();
        BookDetails bd = (BookDetails)item.getItem();
%>

        <tr>
        <td align="right" bgcolor="#ffffff">
        <%=item.getQuantity()%>
        </td>
        <td bgcolor="#ffffaa">
        <strong><a href="
        <%=request.getContextPath()%>/bookdetails?bookId=
        <%=bd.getBookId()%>"><%=bd.getTitle()%></a></strong>
        </td>
        ...
<%
    // End of while
    }
%>
```

The output appears in Figure 14.2 below:

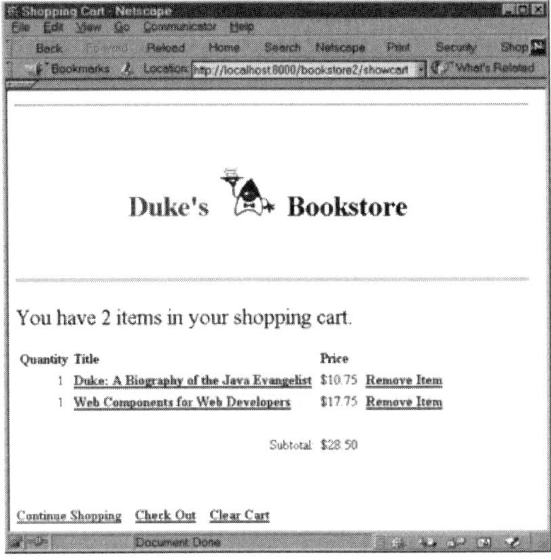

Figure 14.2 Duke's Bookstore Shopping Cart

Expressions

A *JSP expression* is used to insert the value of a scripting language expression, converted into a string, into the data stream returned to the client. When the scripting language is the Java programming language, an expression is transformed into a statement that converts the value of the expression into a `String` object and inserts it into the implicit `out` object.

The syntax for an expression is:

```
<%= scripting language expression %>
```

Note that a semicolon is not allowed within a JSP expression, even if the same expression has a semicolon when you use it within a scriptlet.

The following scriptlet retrieves the number of items in a shopping cart:

```
<%
    // Print a summary of the shopping cart
    int num = cart.getNumberOfItems();
    if (num > 0) {
%>
```

Expressions are then used to insert the value of `num` into the output stream and determine the appropriate string to include after the number:

```
<font size="+2">
<%=messages.getString("CartContents")%> <%=num%>
    <%=(num==1 ? <%=messages.getString("CartItem")%> :
    <%=messages.getString("CartItems"))%></font>
```

14.7 Including Content in a JSP Page

There are two mechanisms for including another Web resource in a JSP page: the `include` directive and the `jsp:include` element.

The `include` directive is processed when the JSP page is *translated* into a servlet class. The effect of the directive to the insert the text contained in another file, either static content or another JSP page, in the including JSP page. You would probably use the `include` directive to include banner content, copyright information, or any chunk of content that you might want to reuse in another page. The syntax for the `include` directive is:

```
<%@ include file="filename" %>
```

For example, all the bookstore application pages include the file `banner.jsp` containing the banner content with the following directive:

```
<%@ include file="banner.jsp" %>
```

In addition, the pages `bookstore.jsp`, `bookdetails.jsp`, `catalog.jsp`, and `showcart.jsp` include JSP elements that create and destroy a database bean with the element:

```
<%@ include file="initdestroy.jsp" %>
```

Because you must statically put an `include` directive in each file that reuses the resource referenced by the directive, this approach has its limitations. For a more flexible approach to building pages out of content chunks, see A Template Tag Library (page 458).

The `jsp:include` element is processed when a JSP page is *executed*. The `include` action allows you to include either a static or dynamic resource in a JSP file. The results of including static and dynamic resources are quite different. If the resource is static, its content is inserted into the calling JSP file. If the resource is dynamic, the request is sent to the included resource, the included page is executed, and then the result is included in the response from the calling JSP page. The syntax for the `jsp:include` element is:

```
<jsp:include page="includedPage" />
```

Note: Tomcat will not reload a statically included page that has been modified unless the including page is also modified.

The `date` application introduced at the beginning of this chapter includes the page that generates the display of the localized date with the following statement:

```
<jsp:include page="date.jsp"/>
```

14.8 Transferring Control to Another Web Component

The mechanism for transferring control to another Web component from a JSP page uses the functionality provided by the Java Servlet API as described in Transferring Control to Another Web Component (page 392). You access this functionality from a JSP page with the `jsp:forward` element:

```
<jsp:forward page="/main.jsp" />
```

If any data has already been returned to a client, the `jsp:forward` element will fail with an `IllegalStateException`.

14.8.1 Param Element

When an `include` or `forward` element is invoked, the original request object is provided to the target page. If you wish to provide additional data to that page, you can append parameters to the request object with the `jsp:param` element:

```
<jsp:include page="..." >
    <jsp:param name="param1" value="value1"/>
</jsp:include>
```

14.9 Including an Applet

You can include an applet or JavaBeans component in a JSP page using the `jsp:plugin` element. This element generates HTML that contains the appropriate client browser dependent constructs (`<object>` or `<embed>`) that will result in the download of the Java Plug-in software (if required) and client-side component and subsequent execution of an client-side component. The syntax for the `jsp:plugin` element follows:

```
<jsp:plugin
    type="bean|applet"
    code="objectCode"
    codebase="objectCodebase"
    { align="alignment" }
    { archive="archiveList" }
    { height="height" }
    { hspace="hspace" }
    { jreversion="jreversion" }
    { name="componentName" }
    { vspace="vspace" }
    { width="width" }
    { nspluginurl="url" }
    { iepluginurl="url" } >
    { <jsp:params>
        { <jsp:param name="paramName" value= paramValue" /> }+
    </jsp:params> }
    { <jsp:fallback> arbitrary_text </jsp:fallback> }
</jsp:plugin>
```

The `jsp:plugin` tag is replaced by either an `<object>` or `<embed>` tag, as appropriate for the requesting client. The attributes of the jsp:plugin tag provide configuration data for the presentation of the element as well as the version of the plug-in required. The `nspluginurl` and `iepluginurl` attributes specify the URL where the plug-in can be downloaded.

The `jsp:param` elements specify parameters to the applet or JavaBeans component. The `jsp:fallback` element indicates the content to be used by the client browser if the plug-in cannot be started (either because `<object>` or `<embed>` is not supported by the client or due to some other problem).

If the plug-in can start but the applet or JavaBeans component cannot be found or started, a plug-in-specific message will be presented to the user, most likely a popup window reporting a `ClassNotFoundException`.

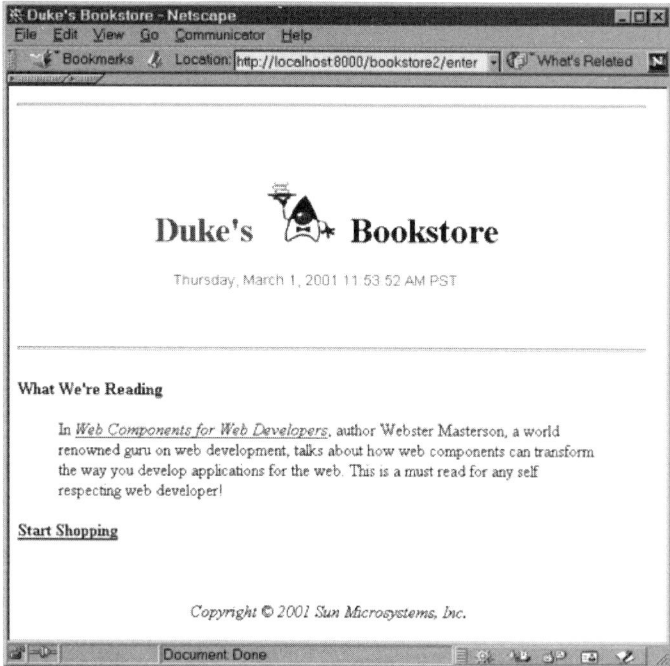

Figure 14.3 Duke's Bookstore with Applet

The Duke's Bookstore page `banner.jsp` that creates the banner displays a dynamic digital clock generated by `DigitalClock`:

The `jsp:plugin` element used to download the applet follows:

```
<jsp:plugin
    type="applet"
    code="DigitalClock.class"
    codebase="/bookstore2"
    jreversion="1.3"
    align="center" height="25" width="300"
    nspluginurl="http://java.sun.com/products/plugin/1.3.0_01
        /plugin-install.html"
    iepluginurl="http://java.sun.com/products/plugin/1.3.0_01
        /jinstall-130_01-win32.cab#Version=1,3,0,1" >
    <jsp:params>
        <jsp:param name="language"
            value="<%=request.getLocale().getLanguage()%>" />
```

```
            <jsp:param name="country"
                value="<%=request.getLocale().getCountry()%>" />
            <jsp:param name="bgcolor" value="FFFFFF" />
            <jsp:param name="fgcolor" value="CC0066" />
        </jsp:params>
            <jsp:fallback>
            <p>Unable to start plugin.</p>
        </jsp:fallback>
    </jsp:plugin>
```

14.10 Extending the JSP Language

You can perform a wide variety of dynamic processing tasks including accessing databases, using enterprise services such as e-mail and directories, and flow control with JavaBeans components in conjunction with scriptlets. One of the drawbacks of scriptlets, however, is that they tend to make JSP pages more difficult to maintain. Alternatively, JSP technology provides a mechanism, called *custom tags*, that allows you to encapsulate dynamic functionality in objects that are accessed through extensions to the JSP language. Custom tags bring the benefits of another level of componentization to JSP pages.

For example, recall the scriptlet used to loop through and display the contents of the Duke's Bookstore shopping cart:

```
<%
    Iterator i = cart.getItems().iterator();
    while (i.hasNext()) {
        ShoppingCartItem item =
            (ShoppingCartItem)i.next();
        ...
%>
        <tr>
        <td align="right" bgcolor="#ffffff">
        <%=item.getQuantity()%>
        </td>
        ...
<%
    }
%>
```

An `iterate` custom tag eliminates the code logic and manages the scripting variable `item` that references elements in the shopping cart:

```
<logic:iterate id="item"
    collection="<%=cart.getItems()%>">
    <tr>
    <td align="right" bgcolor="#ffffff">
    <%=item.getQuantity()%>
    </td>
    ...
</logic:iterate>
```

Custom tags are packaged and distributed in a unit called a *tag library*. The syntax of custom tags is the same as that used for the JSP elements, namely `<prefix:tag>`, but for custom tags, `prefix` is defined by the *user* of the tag library and `tag` is defined by the *tag developer*. Custom Tags in JSP Pages (page 431) explains how to use and develop custom tags.

CHAPTER 15

JavaBeans Components in JSP Pages

Stephanie Bodoff

IN THIS CHAPTER

JAVABEANS components are Java classes that can be easily reused and composed together into applications. Any Java class that follows certain design conventions can be a JavaBeans component.

JavaServer Pages technology directly supports using JavaBeans components with JSP language elements. You can easily create and initialize beans and get and set the values of their properties. This chapter provides basic information about JavaBeans components and the JSP language elements for accessing JavaBeans components in your JSP pages. For further information about the JavaBeans component model see `http://java.sun.com/products/javabeans`.

15.1 JavaBeans Component Design Conventions

JavaBeans component design conventions govern the properties of the class, and the public methods that give access to the properties.

A JavaBeans component property can be:

- Read/write, read-only, or write-only.
- Simple, which means it contains a single value, or indexed, which means it represents an array of values.

There is no requirement that a property be implemented by an instance variable; the property must simply be accessible using public methods that conform to certain conventions:

- For each readable property, the bean must have a method of the form: `PropertyClass getProperty() { ... }`
- For each writable property, the bean must have a method of the form:
- `setProperty(PropertyClass pc) { ... }`

In addition to the property methods, a JavaBeans component must define a constructor that takes no parameters.

The `Duke's Bookstore` application JSP pages `enter.jsp`, `bookdetails.jsp`, `catalog.jsp`, `showcart.jsp` use the `database.BookDB` and `database.BookDetails` JavaBeans components. `BookDB` provides a JavaBeans component front end to the access object `BookDBAO`. Both beans are used extensively by bean-oriented custom tags (see Custom Tags in JSP Pages (page 431)). The JSP pages `showcart.jsp` and `cashier.jsp` use `cart.ShoppingCart` to represent a user's shopping cart.

The JSP pages `catalog.jsp`, `showcart.jsp`, and `cashier.jsp` use the `util.Currency` JavaBeans component to format currency in a locale-sensitive manner. The bean has two writable properties, `locale` and `amount`, and one readable property, `format`. The `format` property does not correspond to any instance variable, but returns a function of the `locale` and `amount` properties.

```
public class Currency {
    private Locale locale;
    private double amount;
    public Currency() {
        locale = null;
        amount = 0.0;
```

```
    }
    public void setLocale(Locale l) {
        locale = l;
    }
    public void setAmount(double a) {
        amount = a;
    }
    public String getFormat() {
        NumberFormat nf =
            NumberFormat.getCurrencyInstance(locale);
        return nf.format(amount);
    }
}
```

15.2 Why Use a JavaBeans Component?

A JSP page can create and use any type of Java programming language object within a declaration or scriptlet. The following scriptlet creates the bookstore shopping cart and stores it as a session attribute:

```
<%
    ShoppingCart cart = (ShoppingCart)session.
        getAttribute("cart");
    // If the user has no cart, create a new one
    if (cart == null) {
        cart = new ShoppingCart();
        session.setAttribute("cart", cart);
    }
%>
```

If the shopping cart object conforms to JavaBeans conventions, JSP pages can use JSP elements to create and access the object. For example, the `Duke's Bookstore` pages `bookdetails.jsp`, `catalog.jsp`, and `showcart.jsp` replace the scriptlet with the much more concise JSP `useBean` element:

```
<jsp:useBean id="cart" class="cart.ShoppingCart"
    scope="session"/>
```

15.3 Creating and Using a JavaBeans Component

You declare that your JSP page will use a JavaBeans component using either one of the following formats:

```
<jsp:useBean id="beanName"
    class="fully_qualified_classname" scope="scope"/>
or
<jsp:useBean id="beanName"
    class="fully_qualified_classname" scope="scope">
    <jsp:setProperty .../>
</jsp:useBean>
```

The second format is used when you want to include `jsp:setProperty` statements, described in the next section, for initializing bean properties.

The `jsp:useBean` element declares that the page will use a bean that is stored within and accessible from the specified scope, which can be `application`, `session`, `request` or `page`. If no such bean exists, the statement creates the bean and stores it as an attribute of the scope object (see Using Scope Objects (page 373)). The value of the `id` attribute determines the *name* of the bean in the scope and the *identifier* used to reference the bean in other JSP elements and scriptlets.

Note: In JSP Scripting Elements (page 412) we mentioned that you must you must import any classes and packages used by a JSP page. This rule is slightly altered if the class is only referenced by `useBean` elements. In these cases, you must only import the class if the class is in the unnamed package. For example, in What is a JSP Page? (page 402), the page `index.jsp` imports the `MyLocales` class. However, in the Duke's Bookstore example, all classes are contained in packages, and so are not explicitly imported.

The following element creates an instance of `Currency` if none exists, stores it as an attribute of the `session` object, and makes the bean available throughout the session by the identifier `currency`:

```
<jsp:useBean id="currency" class="util.Currency"
    scope="session"/>
```

15.4 Setting JavaBeans Component Properties

There are two ways to set JavaBeans component properties in a JSP page:

- With the `jsp:setProperty` element
- With a scriptlet: `<% beanName.setPropName(value); %>`

The syntax of the `jsp:setProperty` element depends on the source of the property value. Table 15.1 summarizes the various ways to set a property of a JavaBeans component using the `jsp:setProperty` element.

Table 15.1 Setting JavaBeans Component Properties

Value Source	Element Syntax
String constant	`<jsp:setProperty name="`*`beanName`*`" property="`*`propName`*`" value="`*`string constant`*`"/>`
Request parameter	`<jsp:setProperty name="`*`beanName`*`" property="`*`propName`*`" param="`*`paramName`*`"/>`
Request parameter name matches bean property	`<jsp:setProperty name="`*`beanName`*`" property="`*`propName`*`"/>`
	`<jsp:setProperty name="`*`beanName`*`" property="*"/>`
Expression	`<jsp:setProperty name="" property="`*`propName`*`" value="<%= `*`expression`*` %>"/>`

1. *`beanName`* must be the same as that specified for the *`id`* attribute in a *`useBean`* element.
2. There must be a *`setPropName`* method in the JavaBeans component.
3. *`paramName`* must be a request parameter name.

A property set from a constant string or request parameter must have a type listed in Table 15.2. Since both a constant and request parameter are strings, the Web container automatically converts the value to the property's type; the conversion applied is shown in the table. `String` values can be used to assign values to a property that has a `PropertyEditor` class. When that is the case, the `setAsText(String)` method is used. A conversion failure arises if the method throws an `IllegalArgumentException`. The value assigned to an indexed property must be an array, and the rules just described apply to the elements.

Table 15.2 Valid Value Assignments

Property Type	Conversion on String Value
Bean Property	Uses `setAsText(`*string-literal*`)`
`boolean` or `Boolean`	As indicated in `java.lang.Boolean.valueOf(String)`
`byte` or `Byte`	As indicated in `java.lang.Byte.valueOf(String)`
`char` or `Character`	As indicated in `java.lang.String.charAt(0)`

continues

Table 15.2 Valid Value Assignments *(Continued)*

Property Type	Conversion on String Value
`double` or `Double`	As indicated in `java.lang.Double.valueOf(String)`
`int` or `Integer`	As indicated in `java.lang.Integer.valueOf(String)`
`float` or `Float`	As indicated in `java.lang.Float.valueOf(String)`
`long` or `Long`	As indicated in `java.lang.Long.valueOf(String)`
`short` or `Short`	As indicated in `java.lang.Short.valueOf(String)`
`Object`	new `String`(*string-literal*)

You would use a runtime expression to set the value of a property whose type is a compound Java programming language type. Recall from Expressions (page 415) that a JSP expression is used to insert the value of a scripting language expression, converted into a String, into the stream returned to the client. When used within a setProperty element, an expression simply returns its value; no automatic conversion is performed. As a consequence, the type returned from an expression must match or be castable to the type of the property.

The Duke's Bookstore application demonstrates how to use the `setProperty` element and a scriptlet to set the current book for the database helper bean. For example, `bookstore3/bookdetails.jsp` uses the form:

```
<jsp:setProperty name="bookDB" property="bookId"/>
```

while `bookstore2/bookdetails.jsp` uses the form:

```
<% bookDB.setBookId(bookId); %>
```

The following fragments from the page `bookstore3/showcart.jsp` illustrate how to initialize a currency bean with a `Locale` object and amount determined by evaluating request-time expressions. Because the first initialization is nested in a `useBean` element, it is only executed when the bean is created.

```
<jsp:useBean id="currency" class="util.Currency"
    scope="session">
    <jsp:setProperty name="currency" property="locale"
        value="<%= request.getLocale() %>"/>
</jsp:useBean>
<jsp:setProperty name="currency" property="amount"
    value="<%=cart.getTotal()%>"/>
```

15.5 Retrieving JavaBeans Component Properties

There are several ways to retrieve JavaBeans component properties. Two of the methods convert the value of the property into a `String` and insert the value into the current implicit `out` object: the `jsp:getProperty` element and an expression:

- `<jsp:getProperty name="beanName" property="propName"/>`
- `<%= beanName.getPropName() %>`

For both methods, *beanName* must be the same as that specified for the `id` attribute in a `useBean` element and there must be a `get`*PropName* method in the JavaBeans component.

If you need to retrieve the value of a property without converting it and inserting it into the out object, you must use a scriptlet:

```
<% Object o = beanName.getPropName(); %>
```

Note the differences between the expression and the scriptlet; the expression has an "=" after the opening "%" and does not terminate with a semicolon, as does the scriptlet.

The `Duke's Bookstore` application demonstrates how to use both forms to retrieve the formatted currency from the currency bean and insert it into the page. For example, `bookstore3/showcart.jsp` uses the form:

```
<jsp:getProperty name="currency" property="format"/>
```

while `bookstore2/showcart.jsp` uses the form:

```
<%= currency.getFormat() %>
```

The `Duke's Bookstore` application page `bookstore2/showcart.jsp` uses the following scriptlet to retrieve the number of books from the shopping cart bean and open a conditional insertion of text into the output stream:

```
<%
    // Print a summary of the shopping cart
    int num = cart.getNumberOfItems();
    if (num > 0) {
%>
```

Although scriptlets are very useful for dynamic processing, using custom tags (see Custom Tags in JSP Pages (page 431)) to access object properties and perform flow control is considered to be a better approach. For example, `bookstore3/showcart.jsp` replaces the scriptlet with the following custom tags:

```
<bean:define id="num" name="cart" property="numberOfItems" />
<logic:greaterThan name="num" value="0" >
```

Figure 15.1 summarizes where various types of objects are stored and how those objects can be accessed from a JSP page. Objects created by the `jsp:useBean` tag are stored as attributes of the scope objects and can be accessed by `jsp:[get|set]Property` tags and in scriptlets and expressions. Objects created in declarations and scriptlets are stored as variables of the JSP page's servlet class and can be accessed in scriptlets and expressions.

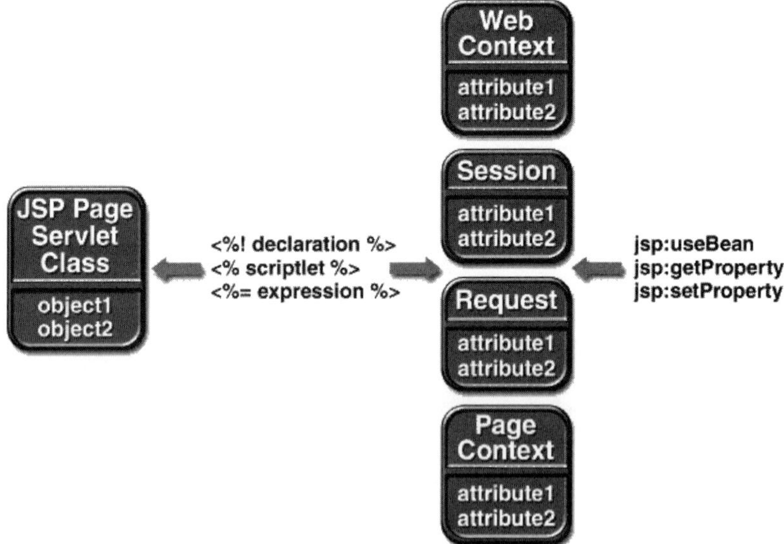

Figure 15.1 Accessing Objects from a JSP Page

CHAPTER 16

Custom Tags in JSP Pages

Stephanie Bodoff

In This Chapter

THE standard JSP tags for invoking operations on JavaBeans components and performing request dispatching simplify JSP page development and maintenance. JSP technology also provides a mechanism for encapsulating other types of dynamic functionality in *custom tags*, which are extensions to the JSP language. Custom tags are usually distributed in the form of a *tag library*, which defines a set of related custom tags and contains the objects that implement the tags.

Some examples of tasks that can be performed by custom tags include operations on implicit objects, form processing, accessing databases and other enterprise services such as e-mail and directories, and flow control. JSP tag libraries are created by developers who are proficient at the Java programming language and expert in accessing data and other services and used by Web application designers who can focus on presentation issues rather than being concerned with how to access enterprise services. As well as encouraging division of labor between library developers and library users, custom tags increase productivity by encapsulating recurring tasks so that they can be reused across more than one application.

Tag libraries are receiving a great deal of attention in the JSP technology community. For more information about tag libraries and pointers to some freely-available libraries see `http://java.sun.com/products/jsp/taglibraries.html`.

16.1 What is a Custom Tag?

A custom tag is a user-defined JSP language element. When a JSP page containing a custom tag is translated into a servlet, the tag is converted to operations on an object called a *tag handler.* The Web container then invokes those operations when the JSP page's servlet is executed.

Custom tags have a rich set of features. They can

- Be customized via attributes passed from the calling page.
- Access all the objects available to JSP pages.
- Modify the response generated by the calling page.
- Communicate with each other. You can create and initialize a JavaBeans component, create a variable that refers to that bean in one tag, and then use the bean in another tag.
- Be nested within one another, allowing for complex interactions within a JSP page.

16.2 The Example JSP Pages

This chapter describes the tasks involved in using and defining tags. The chapter illustrates the tasks with excerpts from the JSP version of the Duke's Bookstore application discussed in The Example JSP Pages (page 404) rewritten to take advantage of two tag libraries: Struts and tutorial-template. The third section in the chapter, Examples (page 453), describes two tags in detail: the `iterate` tag from Struts and the set of tags in the tutorial-template tag library.

The Struts tag library provides a framework for building internationalized Web applications that implement the Model-View-Controller design pattern. Struts includes a comprehensive set of utility custom tags for handling:

- HTML forms
- Templates

- JavaBeans components
- Logic processing

The Duke's Bookstore application uses tags from the Struts `bean` and `logic` sublibraries.

The tutorial-template tag library defines a set of tags for creating an application template. The template is a JSP page, with place holders for the parts that need to change with each screen. Each of these placeholders is referred to as a parameter of the template. For example, a simple template could include a title parameter for the top of the generated screen and a body parameter to refer to a JSP page for the custom content of the screen. The template is created with a set of nested tags—`definition`, `screen`, and `parameter`—that are used to build a table of screen definitions for Duke's Bookstore and an `insert` tag to insert parameters from the table into the screen.

Figure 16.1 shows the flow of a request through the Duke's Bookstore Web components:

- `template.jsp` which determines the structure of each screen. It uses the `insert` tag to compose a screen from subcomponents.
- `screendefinitions.jsp` which defines the subcomponents used by each screen. All screens have the same banner, but different title and body content (specified by the JSP Pages column in Table 16.1).
- `Dispatcher`, a servlet, processes requests and forwards to `template.jsp`.

The source for the Duke's Bookstore application is located in the `docs/tutorial/examples/web/bookstore3` directory created when you unzip the tutorial bundle (see Running the Examples (page xx)). To build, deploy, and run the example:

1. Download Struts version 1.0 from

    ```
    http://jakarta.apache.org/builds/jakarta-struts/
    release/v1.0/
    ```

2. Unpack Struts and copy `struts-bean.tld`, `struts-logic.tld`, and `struts.jar` from `jakarta-struts-1.0/lib` to `docs/tutorial/examples/web/bookstore3`.

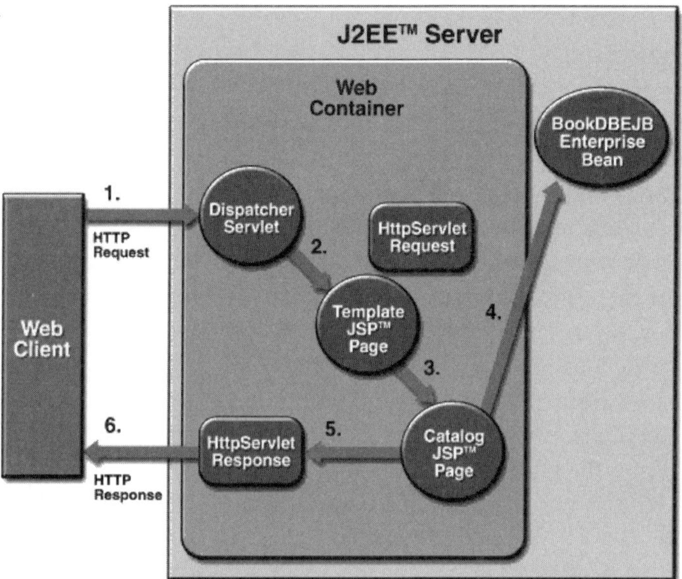

Figure 16.1 Request Flow Through Duke's Bookstore Components

3. Go to the bookstore3 directory and build and deploy the example by running `ant`. This runs the default ant target `deploy` which depends on the `build` target. The `build` target will spawn any necessary compilations and copy files to the `docs/tutorial/examples/web/bookstore3/build` directory. The `deploy` target copies the bookstore3 context file to `<JWSDP_HOME>/webapps` as described in Running Web Applications (page 360).
4. Start the Pointbase database server (see Accessing Databases from Web Applications (page 363)).
5. Start or restart Tomcat.
6. Open the bookstore URL `http://localhost:8080/bookstore3/enter`.

See Common Problems and Their Solutions (page 65) and Troubleshooting (page 369) for help with diagnosing common problems.

16.3 Using Tags

This section describes how a JSP page uses tags and introduces the different types of tags.

To use a tag, a page author must do two things:

- Declare the tag library containing the tag
- Make the tag library implementation available to the Web application

16.3.1 Declaring Tag Libraries

You declare that a JSP page will use tags defined in a tag library by including a `taglib` directive in the page before any custom tag is used:

```
<%@ taglib uri="/WEB-INF/tutorial-template.tld" prefix="tt" %>
```

The `uri` attribute refers to a URI that uniquely identifies the TLD, described in Tag Library Descriptors (page 440). This URI can be direct or indirect. The `prefix` attribute defines the prefix that distinguishes tags defined by a given tag library from those provided by other tag libraries.

Tag library descriptor filenames must have the extension `.tld`. TLD files are stored in the `WEB-INF` directory of the WAR or in a subdirectory of `WEB-INF`. You can reference a TLD directly and indirectly.

The following `taglib` directive directly references a TLD filename:

```
<%@ taglib uri="/WEB-INF/tutorial-template.tld" prefix="tt" %>
```

This `taglib` directive uses a short logical name to indirectly reference the TLD:

```
<%@ taglib uri="/tutorial-template" prefix="tt" %>
```

A logical name must be mapped to an absolute location in the Web application deployment descriptor. To map the logical name `/tutorial-template` to the absolute location `/WEB-INF/tutorial-template.tld`, you must add a `taglib` element to `web.xml`:

```
<taglib>
    <taglib-uri>/tutorial-template</taglib-uri>
    <taglib-location>
        /WEB-INF/tutorial-template.tld
    </taglib-location>
</taglib>
```

16.3.2 Making the Tag Library Implementation Available

A tag library implementation can be made available to a Web application in two basic ways. The classes implementing the tag handlers can be stored in an unpacked form in the `WEB-INF/classes` subdirectory of the Web application. Alternatively, if the library is distributed as a JAR, it is stored the `WEB-INF/lib` directory of the Web application. A tag library shared between more than one application is stored in the *<JWSDP_HOME>*`/common/lib` directory of the Java WSDP.

16.3.3 Types of Tags

JSP custom tags are written using XML syntax. They have a start tag and end tag, and possibly a body:

```
<tt:tag>
    body
</tt:tag>
```

A custom tag with no body is expressed as follows:

```
<tt:tag />
```

Simple Tags

A simple tag contains no body and no attributes:

```
<tt:simple />
```

Tags with Attributes

A custom tag can have attributes. Attributes are listed in the start tag and have the syntax `attr="value"`. Attribute values serve to customize the behavior of a custom tag just as parameters are used to customize the behavior of a method.

You specify the types of a tag's attributes in a tag library descriptor, (see Tags with Attributes (page 443)).

You can set an attribute value from a `String` constant or a runtime expression. The conversion process between the constants and runtime expressions and attribute types follows the rules described for JavaBeans component properties in Setting JavaBeans Component Properties (page 426).

The attributes of the Struts `logic:present` tag determine whether the body of the tag is evaluated. In the following example, an attribute specifies a request parameter named `Clear`:

```
<logic:present parameter="Clear">
```

The Duke's Bookstore application page catalog.jsp uses a runtime expression to set the value of the attribute that determines the collection of books over which the Struts logic:iterate tag iterates:

```
<logic:iterate collection="<%=bookDB.getBooks()%>"
    id="book" type="database.BookDetails">
```

Tags with Bodies

A custom tag can contain custom and core tags, scripting elements, HTML text, and tag-dependent body content between the start and end tag.

In the following example, the Duke's Bookstore application page showcart.jsp uses the Struts logic:present tag to clear the shopping cart and print a message if the request contains a parameter named Clear:

```
<logic:present parameter="Clear">
    <% cart.clear(); %>
    <font color="#ff0000" size="+2"><strong>
    You just cleared your shopping cart!
    </strong><br> <br></font>
</logic:present>
```

Choosing Between Passing Information As Attributes or Body

As shown in the last two sections, it is possible to pass a given piece of data as an attribute of the tag or to the tag's body. Generally speaking, any data that is a simple string or can be generated by evaluating a simple expression is best passed as an attribute.

Tags That Define Scripting Variables

A custom tag can define a variable that can be used in scripts within a page. The following example illustrates how to define and use a scripting variable that contains an object returned from a JNDI lookup. Examples of such objects include enterprise beans, transactions, databases, environment entries, and so on:

```
<tt:lookup id="tx" type="UserTransaction"
    name="java:comp/UserTransaction" />
<% tx.begin(); %>
```

In the Duke's Bookstore application, several pages use bean-oriented tags from Struts to define scripting variables. For example, bookdetails.jsp uses the bean:parameter tag to create the bookId scripting variable and set it to value of the bookId request parameter. The jsp:setProperty statement also sets the bookId property of the bookDB object to the value of the bookId request parameter. The bean:define tag retrieves the value of the bookstore database property bookDetails and defines the result as the scripting variable book:

```
<bean:parameter id="bookId" name="bookId" />
<jsp:setProperty name="bookDB" property="bookId"/>
<bean:define id="book" name="bookDB" property="bookDetails"
    type="database.BookDetails"/>
<h2><jsp:getProperty name="book" property="title"></h2>
```

Cooperating Tags

Customer tags can cooperate with each other through shared objects.

In the following example, tag1 creates an object called obj1, which is then reused by tag2.

```
<tt:tag1 attr1="obj1" value1="value" />
<tt:tag2 attr1="obj1" />
```

In the next example, an object created by the enclosing tag of a group of nested tags is available to all inner tags. Since the object is not named, the potential for naming conflicts is reduced. The following example illustrates how a set of cooperating nested tags would appear in a JSP page.

```
<tt:outerTag>
    <tt:innerTag />
</tt:outerTag>
```

The Duke's Bookstore page template.jsp uses a set of cooperating tags to define the screens of the application. These tags are described in A Template Tag Library (page 458).

16.4 Defining Tags

To define a tag, you need to:

- Develop a tag handler and helper classes for the tag
- Declare the tag in a tag library descriptor (TLD)

This section describes the properties of tag handlers and TLDs and explains how to develop tag handlers and library descriptor elements for each type of tag introduced in the previous section.

16.4.1 Tag Handlers

A *tag handler* is an object invoked by a Web container to evaluate a custom tag during the execution of the JSP page that references the tag. Tag handlers must implement either the `Tag` or `BodyTag` interface. Interfaces can be used to take an existing Java object and make it a tag handler. For newly created handlers, you can use the `TagSupport` and `BodyTagSupport` classes as base classes. These classes and interfaces are contained in the `javax.servlet.jsp.tagext` package.

Tag handler methods defined by the `Tag` and `BodyTag` interfaces are called by the JSP page's servlet at various points during the evaluation of the tag. When the start tag of a custom tag is encountered, the JSP page's servlet calls methods to initialize the appropriate handler and then invokes the handler's `doStartTag` method. When the end tag of a custom tag is encountered, the handler's `doEndTag` method is invoked. Additional methods are invoked in between when a tag handler needs to interact with the body of the tag. For further information, see Tags with Bodies (page 446). In order to provide a tag handler implementation, you must implement the methods, summarized in Table 16.1, that are invoked at various stages of processing the tag.

Table 16.1 Tag Handler Methods

Tag Handler Type	Methods
Simple	`doStartTag, doEndTag, release`
Attributes	`doStartTag, doEndTag, set/getAttribute1...N, release`
Body, Evaluation and No Interaction	`doStartTag, doEndTag, release`
Body, Iterative Evaluation	`doStartTag, doAfterBody, doEndTag, release`
Body, Interaction	`doStartTag, doEndTag, release, doInitBody, doAfterBody, release`

A tag handler has access to an API that allows it to communicate with the JSP page. The entry point to the API is the page context object (`javax.servlet.jsp.PageContext`) through which a tag handler can retrieve all the other implicit objects (request, session, and application) accessible from a JSP page.

Implicit objects can have named attributes associated with them. Such attributes are accessed using `[set|get]Attribute` methods.

If the tag is nested, a tag handler also has access to the handler (called the *parent*) associated with the enclosing tag.

A set of related tag handler classes (a tag library) is usually packaged and deployed as a JAR archive.

16.4.2 Tag Library Descriptors

A *tag library descriptor* (TLD) is an XML document that describes a tag library. A TLD contains information about a library as a whole and about each tag contained in the library. TLDs are used by a Web container to validate the tags and by JSP page development tools.

TLD filenames must have the extension `.tld`. TLD files are stored in the `WEB-INF` directory of the WAR file or a subdirectory of `WEB-INF`.

A TLD must begin with an XML document prolog that specifies the version of XML and the document type definition (DTD):

```
<?xml version="1.0" encoding="ISO-8859-1" ?>
<!DOCTYPE taglib PUBLIC "-//Sun Microsystems, Inc.//DTD JSP Tag
Library 1.2//EN"
"http://java.sun.com/dtd/web-jsptaglibrary_1_2.dtd">
```

Tomcat supports 1.1 and 1.2 version DTDs. However, this chapter documents the 1.2 version because you should use the newer version in any tag libraries that you develop. The template library TLD, `tutorial-template.tld`, conforms to the 1.2 version. The Struts library TLDs conform to the 1.1 version of the DTD, which has fewer elements and uses slightly different names for some of the elements.

The root of a TLD is the `taglib` element. The subelements of `taglib` are listed in Table 16.2.

Table 16.2 `taglib` Subelements

Element	Description
`tlib-version`	The tag library's version
`jsp-version`	The JSP specification version the tag library requires
`short-name`	Optional name that could be used by a JSP page authoring tool to create names with a mnemonic value
`uri`	A URI that uniquely identifies the tag library

Table 16.2 `taglib` Subelements *(Continued)*

Element	Description
`display-name`	Optional name intended to be displayed by tools
`small-icon`	Optional small-icon that can be used by tools
`large-icon`	Optional large-icon that can be used by tools
`description`	Optional tag-specific information
`listener`	See Listener Element (page 441)
`tag`	See Tag Element (page 441)

Listener Element

A tag library can specify some classes that are event listeners (see Handling Servlet Life Cycle Events (page 370)). The listeners are listed in the TLD as `listener` elements and the Web container will instantiate the listener classes and register them in a way analogous to listeners defined at the WAR level. Unlike WAR-level listeners, the order in which the tag library listeners are registered is undefined. The only subelement of the `listener` element is the `listener-class` element, which must contain the fully-qualified name of the listener class.

Tag Element

Each tag in the library is described by giving its name and the class of its tag handler, information on the scripting variables created by the tag, and information on the tag's attributes. Scripting variable information can be given directly in the TLD or through a tag extra info class (see Tags That Define Scripting Variables (page 437)). Each attribute declaration contains an indication of whether the attribute is required or not, whether its value can be determined by request-time expressions, and the type of the attribute (see Attribute Element (page 444)).

A tag is specified in a TLD in a `tag` element. The subelements of tag are listed in Table 16.3.

Table 16.3 `tag` Subelements

Element	Description
`name`	The unique tag name
`tag-class`	The fully-qualified name of the tag handler class
`tei-class`	Optional subclass of `javax.servlet.jsp.tagext.TagExtraInfo` See Providing Information About the Scripting Variable (page 449).

continues

Table 16.3 tag Subelements *(Continued)*

Element	Description
body-content	The body content type. See Body-Content Element (page 443) and Body-Content Element (page 447).
display-name	Optional name intended to be displayed by tools.
small-icon	Optional small-icon that can be used by tools.
large-icon	Optional large-icon that can be used by tools.
description	Optional tag-specific information.
variable	Optional scripting variable information. See Providing Information About the Scripting Variable (page 449).
attribute	Tag attribute information. See Attribute Element (page 444).

The following sections will describe the methods and TLD elements that you need to develop for each type of tag introduced in Types of Tags (page 436).

16.4.3 Simple Tags

Tag Handlers

The handler for a simple tag must implement the doStartTag and doEndTag methods of the Tag interface. The doStartTag method is invoked when the start tag is encountered. This method returns SKIP_BODY because a simple tag has no body. The doEndTag method is invoked when the end tag is encountered. The doEndTag method needs to return EVAL_PAGE if the rest of the page needs to be evaluated; otherwise, it should return SKIP_PAGE.

The simple tag discussed in the first section:

```
<tt:simple />
```

would be implemented by the following tag handler:

```
public SimpleTag extends TagSupport {
 public int doStartTag() throws JspException {
     try {
         pageContext.getOut().print("Hello.");
     } catch (Exception ex) {
         throw new JspTagException("SimpleTag: " +
             ex.getMessage());
     }
     return SKIP_BODY;
```

```
    }
    public int doEndTag() {
        return EVAL_PAGE;
    }
}
```

Body-Content Element

Tags without bodies must declare that their body content is empty using the `body-content` element:

```
<body-content>empty</body-content>
```

16.4.4 Tags with Attributes

Defining Attributes in a Tag Handler

For each tag attribute, you must define a property and get and set methods that conform to the JavaBeans architecture conventions in the tag handler. For example, the tag handler for the Struts `logic:present` tag

```
<logic:present parameter="Clear">
```

contains the following declaration and methods:

```
protected String parameter = null;
public String getParameter() {
    return (this.parameter);
}
public void setParameter(String parameter) {
    this.parameter = parameter;
}
```

Note that if your attribute is named `id`, and your tag handler inherits from the `TagSupport` class, you do not need to define the property and set and get methods as these are already defined by `TagSupport`.

A tag attribute whose value is a `String` can name an attribute of one of the implicit objects available to tag handlers. An implicit object attribute would be accessed by passing the tag attribute value to the `[set|get]Attribute` method of the implicit object. This is a good way to pass scripting variable names to a tag handler where they are associated with objects stored in the page context (See Implicit Objects (page 410)).

Attribute Element

For each tag attribute you must specify whether the attribute is required, whether the value can be determined by an expression, and optionally, the type of the attribute in an `attribute` element. For static values the type is always `java.lang.String`. If the `rtexprvalue` element is `true` or `yes`, then the `type` element defines the return type expected from any expression specified as the value of the attribute.

```
<attribute>
    <name>attr1</name>
    <required>true|false|yes|no</required>
    <rtexprvalue>true|false|yes|no</rtexprvalue>
    <type>fully-qualified_type</type>
</attribute>
```

If a tag attribute is not required, a tag handler should provide a default value.

The `tag` element for the `logic:present` tag declares that `parameter` attribute is not required (because the tag can also test for the presence of other entities such as bean properties), and that its value can be set by a runtime expression.

```
<tag>
    <name>present</name>
    <tag-class>org.apache.struts.taglib.
        logic.PresentTag</tag-class>
    <body-content>JSP</body-content>
    ...
    <attribute>
        <name>parameter</name>
        <required>false</required>
        <rtexprvalue>true</rtexprvalue>
    </attribute>
    ...
</tag>
```

Attribute Validation

The documentation for a tag library should describe valid values for tag attributes. When a JSP page is translated, a Web container will enforce any constraints contained in the TLD element for each attribute.

The attributes passed to a tag can also be validated at translation time with the `isValid` method of a class derived from `TagExtraInfo`. This class is also used to provide information about scripting variables defined by the tag (see Providing Information About the Scripting Variable (page 449)).

The `isValid` method is passed the attribute information in a `TagData` object, which contains attribute-value tuples for each of the tag's attributes. Since the validation occurs at translation time, the value of an attribute that is computed at request time will be set to `TagData.REQUEST_TIME_VALUE`.

The tag `<tt:twa attr1="value1"/>` has the following TLD `attribute` element:

```
<attribute>
    <name>attr1</name>
    <required>true</required>
    <rtexprvalue>true</a>
</attribute
```

This declaration indicates that the value of `attr1` can be determined at runtime.

The following `isValid` method checks that the value of `attr1` is a valid boolean value. Note that since the value of `attr1` can be computed at runtime, `isValid` must check whether the tag user has chosen to provide a runtime value.

```
public class TwaTEI extends TagExtraInfo {
    public boolean isValid(Tagdata data) {
        Object o = data.getAttribute("attr1");
        if (o != null && o != TagData.REQUEST_TIME_VALUE) {
            if (o.toLowerCase().equals("true") ||
                o.toLowerCase().equals("false") )
                return true;
            else
                return false;
        }
        else
            return true;
    }
}
```

16.4.5 Tags with Bodies

Tag Handlers

A tag handler for a tag with a body is implemented differently depending on whether the tag handler needs to interact with the body or not. By interact, we mean that the tag handler reads or modifies the contents of the body.

Tag Handler Does Not Interact with the Body. If the tag handler does not need to interact with the body, the tag handler should implement the `Tag` interface (or be derived from `TagSupport`). If the body of the tag needs to be evaluated, the `doStartTag` method needs to return `EVAL_BODY_INCLUDE`; otherwise, it should return `SKIP_BODY`.

If a tag handler needs to iteratively evaluate the body it should implement the `IterationTag` interface or be derived from `TagSupport`. It should return `EVAL_BODY_AGAIN` from the `doStartTag` and `doAfterBody` methods if it determines that the body needs to be evaluated again.

Tag Handler Interacts with the Body. If the tag handler needs to interact with the body, the tag handler must implement `BodyTag` (or be derived from `BodyTagSupport`). Such handlers typically implement the `doInitBody` and the `doAfterBody` methods. These methods interact with body content passed to the tag handler by the JSP page's servlet.

A body content supports several methods to read and write its contents. A tag handler can use the body content's `getString` or `getReader` methods to extract information from the body and the `writeOut(out)` method to write the body contents to an out stream. The writer supplied to the `writeOut` method is obtained using the tag handler's `getPreviousOut` method. This method is used to ensure that a tag handler's results are available to an enclosing tag handler.

If the body of the tag needs to be evaluated, the `doStartTag` method needs to return `EVAL_BODY_BUFFERED`; otherwise, it should return `SKIP_BODY`.

`doInitBody` Method

The `doInitBody` method is called after the body content is set but before it is evaluated. You generally use this method to perform any initialization that depends on the body content.

`doAfterBody` Method

The `doAfterBody` method is called *after* the body content is evaluated.

Like the `doStartTag` method, `doAfterBody` must return an indication of whether to continue evaluating the body. Thus, if the body should be evaluated again, as would be the case if you were implementing an iteration tag, doAfterBody should return EVAL_BODY_BUFFERED; otherwise doAfterBody should return SKIP_BODY.

release Method

A tag handler should reset its state and release any private resources in the release method.

The following example reads the content of the body (which contains an SQL query) and passes it to a object that executes the query. Since the body does not need to be reevaluated, doAfterBody returns SKIP_BODY.

```
public class QueryTag extends BodyTagSupport {
    public int doAfterBody() throws JspTagException {
        BodyContent bc = getBodyContent();
        // get the bc as string
        String query = bc.getString();
        // clean up
        bc.clearBody();
        try {
            Statement stmt = connection.createStatement();
            result = stmt.executeQuery(query);
        } catch (SQLException e) {
            throw new JspTagException("QueryTag: " +
                 e.getMessage());
        }
        return SKIP_BODY;
    }
}
```

Body-Content Element

For tags that have a body, you must specify the type of the body content using the body-content element:

```
<body-content>JSP|tagdependent</body-content>
```

Body content containing custom and core tags, scripting elements, and HTML text is categorized as JSP. This is the value declared for the Struts logic:present tag. All other types of body content, for example, SQL statements passed to the query tag, would be labeled tagdependent.

Note that the value of the `body-content` element does not affect the interpretation of the body by the tag handler; the element is only intended to be used by an authoring tool for rendering the body content.

16.4.6 Tags That Define Scripting Variables

Tag Handlers

A tag handler is responsible for creating and setting the object referred to by the scripting variable into a context accessible from the page. It does this by using the `pageContext.setAttribute(name, value, scope)` or `pageContext.setAttribute(name, value)` methods. Typically, an attribute passed to the custom tag specifies the `name` of the scripting variable object; this name can be retrieved by invoking the attribute's get method described in Using Scope Objects (page 373).

If the value of the scripting variable is dependent on an object present in the tag handler's context, it can retrieve the object using the `pageContext.getAttribute(name, scope)` method.

The usual procedure is that the tag handler retrieves a scripting variable, performs some processing on the object, and then sets the scripting variable's value using the `pageContext.setAttribute(name, object)` method.

The scope that an object can have is summarized in Table 16.4. The scope constrains the accessibility and lifetime of the object.

Table 16.4 Scope of Objects

Name	Accessible From	Lifetime
`page`	Current page	Until the response has been sent back to the user or the request is passed to a new page
`request`	Current page and any included or forwarded pages	Until the response has been sent back to the user
`session`	Current request and any subsequent request from the same browser (subject to session lifetime).	The life of the user's session
`application`	Current and any future request from the same Web application	The life of the application

Providing Information About the Scripting Variable

The example described in Tags That Define Scripting Variables (page 437) defines a scripting variable book that is used for accessing book information:

```
<bean:define id="book" name="bookDB" property="bookDetails"
    type="database.BookDetails"/>
<font color="red" size="+2">
    <%=messages.getString("CartRemoved")%>
    <strong><jsp:getProperty name="book"
            property="title"/></strong>
<br> <br>
</font>
```

When the JSP page containing this tag is translated, the Web container generates code to synchronize the scripting variable with the object referenced by the variable. In order to do the code generation, the Web container requires certain information about the scripting variable:

- Variable name
- Variable class
- Whether the variable refers to a new or existing object
- The availability of the variable

There are two ways to provide this information: by specifying the variable TLD subelement or by defining a tag extra info class and including the tei-class element in the TLD. Using the variable element is simpler, but slightly less flexible.

Variable Element. The variable element has the following subelements:

- name-given—The variable name as a constant
- name-from-attribute—The name of an attribute whose translation-time value will give the name of the variable.

One of name-given or name-from-attribute is required. The following subelements are optional:

- variable-class—Fully-qualified name of the class of the variable. java.lang.String is the default.

- declare—Whether the variable refers to a new object. True is the default.
- scope—The scope of the scripting variable defined. NESTED is default. Table 16.5 describes the availability of the scripting variable and the methods where the value of the variable must be set or reset.

The implementation of the Struts bean:define tag conforms to the JSP specification version 1.1, which requires you to define a tag extra info class. The JSP specification version 1.2 adds the variable element. You could define the following variable element for the bean:define tag:

```
<tag>
    <variable>
        <name-from-attribute>id</name-from-attribute>
        <variable-class>database.BookDetails</variable-class>
        <declare>true</declare>
        <scope>AT_BEGIN</scope>
    </variable>
</tag>
```

TagExtraInfo Class. You define a tag extra info class by extending the class javax.servlet.jsp.TagExtraInfo. A TagExtraInfo must implement the getVariableInfo method to return an array of VariableInfo objects containing the following information:

- Variable name
- Variable class
- Whether the variable refers to a new object
- The availability of the variable

Table 16.5 Scripting Variable Availability

Value	Availability	Methods
NESTED	Between the start tag and the end tag.	In doInitBody and doAfterBody for a tag handler implementing BodyTag; otherwise in doStartTag.
AT_BEGIN	From the start tag until the end of the page.	In doInitBody, doAfterBody, and doEndTag for a tag handler implementing BodyTag; otherwise in doStartTag and doEndTag.
AT_END	After the end tag until the end of the page.	In doEndTag.

The Web container passes a parameter called data to the getVariableInfo method that contains attribute-value tuples for each of the tag's attributes. These attributes can be used to provide the VariableInfo object with a scripting variable's name and class.

The Struts tag library provides information about the scripting variable created by the bean:define tag in the DefineTei tag extra info class. Since the name (book) and class (database.BookDetails) of the scripting variable are passed in as tag attributes, they can be retrieved with the data.getAttributeString method and used to fill in the VariableInfo constructor. To allow the scripting variable book to be used in the rest of the page, the scope of book is set to be AT_BEGIN.

```
public class DefineTei extends TagExtraInfo {
    public VariableInfo[] getVariableInfo(TagData data) {
    String type = data.getAttributeString("type");
        if (type == null)
            type = "java.lang.Object";
        return new VariableInfo[] {
            new VariableInfo(data.getAttributeString("id"),
                type,
                true,
                VariableInfo.AT_BEGIN)
        };
    }
}
```

The fully-qualified name of the tag extra info class defined for a scripting variable must be declared in the TLD in the tei-class subelement of the tag element. Thus, the tei-class element for DefineTei would be:

```
<tei-class>org.apache.struts.taglib.bean.DefineTagTei
</tei-class>
```

16.4.7 Cooperating Tags

Tags cooperate by sharing objects. JSP technology supports two styles of object sharing.

The first style requires that a shared object be named and stored in the page context (one of the implicit objects accessible to both JSP pages and tag handlers). To access objects created and named by another tag, a tag handler uses the pageContext.getAttribute(name, scope) method.

In the second style of object sharing, an object created by the enclosing tag handler of a group of nested tags is available to all inner tag handlers. This form of object sharing has the advantage that it uses a private namespace for the objects, thus reducing the potential for naming conflicts.

To access an object created by an enclosing tag, a tag handler must first obtain its enclosing tag with the static method `TagSupport.findAncestorWithClass(from, class)` or the `TagSupport.getParent` method. The former method should be used when a specific nesting of tag handlers cannot be guaranteed. Once the ancestor has been retrieved, a tag handler can access any statically or dynamically created objects. Statically created objects are members of the parent. Private objects can also be created dynamically created. Such objects can be stored in a tag handler with the `setValue` method and retrieved with the `getValue` method.

The following example illustrates a tag handler that supports both the named and private object approaches to sharing objects. In the example, the handler for a query tag checks whether an attribute named `connection` has been set in the `doStartTag` method. If the connection attribute has been set, the handler retrieves the connection object from the page context. Otherwise, the tag handler first retrieves the tag handler for the enclosing tag, and then retrieves the connection object from that handler.

```
public class QueryTag extends BodyTagSupport {
    private String connectionId;
    public int doStartTag() throws JspException {
        String cid = getConnection();
        if (cid != null) {
        // there is a connection id, use it
            connection =(Connection)pageContext.
                getAttribute(cid);
        } else {
            ConnectionTag ancestorTag =
                (ConnectionTag)findAncestorWithClass(this,
                    ConnectionTag.class);
            if (ancestorTag == null) {
                throw new JspTagException("A query without
                    a connection attribute must be nested
                    within a connection tag.");
            }
            connection = ancestorTag.getConnection();
        }
    }
}
```

The query tag implemented by this tag handler could be used in either of the following ways:

```
<tt:connection id="con01" ....> ... </tt:connection>
<tt:query id="balances" connection="con01">
    SELECT account, balance FROM acct_table
        where customer_number = <%= request.getCustno()%>
</tt:query>

<tt:connection ...>
    <x:query id="balances">
        SELECT account, balance FROM acct_table
            where customer_number = <%= request.getCustno()%>
    </x:query>
</tt:connection>
```

The TLD for the tag handler must indicate that the connection attribute is optional with the following declaration:

```
<tag>
    ...
    <attribute>
        <name>connection</name>
        <required>false</required>
    </attribute>
</tag>
```

16.5 Examples

The custom tags described in this section demonstrate solutions to two recurring problems in developing JSP applications: minimizing the amount of Java programming in JSP pages and ensuring a common look and feel across applications. In doing so, they illustrate many of the styles of tags discussed in the first section.

16.5.1 An Iteration Tag

Constructing page content that is dependent on dynamically generated data often requires the use of flow control scripting statements. By moving the flow control logic to tag handlers, flow control tags reduce the amount of scripting needed in JSP pages.

The Struts `logic:iterate` tag retrieves objects from a collection stored in a JavaBeans component and assigns them to a scripting variable. The body of the tag retrieves information from the scripting variable. While elements remain in the collection, the `iterate` tag causes the body to be reevaluated.

JSP Page

Two Duke's Bookstore application pages, `catalog.jsp` and `showcart.jsp`, use the `logic:iterate` tag to iterate over collections of objects. An excerpt from `catalog.jsp` is shown below. The JSP page initializes the `iterate` tag with a collection (named by the `property` attribute) of the `bookDB` bean. The `iterate` tag sets the `book` scripting variable on each iteration over the collection. The `bookId` property of the `book` variable is exposed as another scripting variable. Properties of both variables are used to dynamically generate a table containing links to other pages and book catalog information.

```
<logic:iterate name="bookDB" property="books"
    id="book" type="database.BookDetails">
    <bean:define id="bookId" name="book" property="bookId"
        type="java.lang.String"/>

    <tr>
    <td bgcolor="#ffffaa">
    <a href="<%=request.getContextPath()%>
        /bookdetails?bookId=<%=bookId%>">
        <strong><jsp:getProperty name="book"
        property="title"/> </strong></a></td>

    <td bgcolor="#ffffaa" rowspan=2>
    <jsp:setProperty name="currency" property="amount"
        value="<%=book.getPrice()%>"/>
    <jsp:getProperty name="currency" property="format"/>
     </td>

    <td bgcolor="#ffffaa" rowspan=2>
    <a href="<%=request.getContextPath()%>
        /catalog?Add=<%=bookId%>">
         <%=messages.getString("CartAdd")%>
         </a></td></tr>

    <tr>
    <td bgcolor="#ffffff">
```

```
          <%=messages.getString("By")%> <em>
            <jsp:getProperty name="book"
                property="firstName"/> 
            <jsp:getProperty name="book"
                property="surname"/></em></td></tr>
    </logic:iterate>
```

Tag Handler

The implementation of the Struts `logic:iterate` tag conforms to JSP version 1.1 specification capabilities, which requires you to extend the `BodyTagSupport` class. The JSP version 1.2 specification adds features (described in Tag Handler Does Not Interact with the Body (page 446)) that simplify programming tags that iteratively evaluate their body. The following discussion is based on an implementation that uses these features.

The `logic:iterate` tag supports initializing the collection in a several ways: from a collection provided as a tag attribute or from a collection that is a bean or a property of a bean. Our example uses the latter method. Most of the code in `doStartTag` is concerned with constructing an iterator over the collection object. The method first checks if the handler's collection property is set and if not, proceeds to checking the bean and property attributes. If the `bean` and `property` attributes are both set, the `doStartTag` calls a utility method that uses JavaBeans introspection methods to retrieve the collection. Once the collection object is determined, the method constructs the iterator.

If the iterator contains more elements, `doStartTag` sets the value of the scripting variable to the next element and then indicates that the body should be evaluated; otherwise it ends the iteration by returning `SKIP_BODY`.

After the body has been evaluated, the `doAfterBody` method retrieves the body content and writes it to the out stream. The body content object is then cleared in preparation for another body evaluation. If the iterator contains more elements, `doAfterBody` again sets the value of the scripting variable to the next element and returns `EVAL_BODY_AGAIN` to indicate that the body should be evaluated again. This causes the reexecution of `doAfterBody`. When there are no remaining elements, `doAfterBody` terminates the process by returning `SKIP_BODY`.

```
public class IterateTag extends TagSupport {
    protected Iterator iterator = null;
    protected Object collection = null;
    protected String id = null;
    protected String name = null;
    protected String property = null;
```

```
        protected String type = null;
        public int doStartTag() throws JspException {
            Object collection = this.collection;
            if (collection == null) {
                try {
                    Object bean = pageContext.findAttribute(name);
                    if (bean == null) {
                        ... throw an exception
                    }
                    if (property == null)
                        collection = bean;
                    else
                        collection =
                            PropertyUtils.
                                getProperty(bean, property);
                    if (collection == null) {
                        ... throw an exception
                    }
                } catch
                    ... catch exceptions thrown
                        by PropertyUtils.getProperty
                }
            }
            // Construct an iterator for this collection
            if (collection instanceof Collection)
                iterator = ((Collection) collection).iterator();
            else if (collection instanceof Iterator)
                iterator = (Iterator) collection;
                ...
            }
            // Store the first value and evaluate,
            // or skip the body if none
            if (iterator.hasNext()) {
                Object element = iterator.next();
                pageContext.setAttribute(id, element);
                return (EVAL_BODY_AGAIN);
            } else
                return (SKIP_BODY);
    }
        public int doAfterBody() throws JspException {
            if (bodyContent != null) {
```

```
<tt:definition name="bookstore"
    screen="<%= (String)request.
        getAttribute(\"selectedScreen\") %>">
    <tt:screen id="/enter">
        <tt:parameter name="title"
            value="Duke's Bookstore" direct="true"/>
        <tt:parameter name="banner"
            value="/banner.jsp" direct="false"/>
        <tt:parameter name="body"
            value="/bookstore.jsp" direct="false"/>
    </tt:screen>
    <tt:screen id="/catalog">
        <tt:parameter name="title"
        value="<%=messages.getString("TitleBookCatalog")%>"
        direct="true"/>
        ...
</tt:definition>
```

The template is instantiated by the `Dispatcher` servlet. `Dispatcher` first gets the requested screen and stores as an attribute of the request. This is necessary because when the request is forwarded to `template.jsp`, the request URL doesn't contain the original request (for example, `/bookstore3/catalog`), but instead reflects the path (`/bookstore3/template.jsp`) of the forwarded page. Finally, the servlet dispatches the request to `template.jsp`:

```
public class Dispatcher extends HttpServlet {
    public void doGet(HttpServletRequest request,
            HttpServletResponse response) {
        request.setAttribute("selectedScreen",
            request.getServletPath());
        RequestDispatcher dispatcher =
            request.getRequestDispatcher("/template.jsp");
        if (dispatcher != null)
            dispatcher.forward(request, response);
    }
    public void doPost(HttpServletRequest request,
                HttpServletResponse response) {
        request.setAttribute("selectedScreen",
            request.getServletPath());
```

```
            RequestDispatcher dispatcher =
                request.getRequestDispatcher("/template.jsp");
            if (dispatcher != null)
                dispatcher.forward(request, response);
        }
    }
```

Tag Handlers

The template tag library contains four tag handlers—`DefinitionTag`, `ScreenTag`, `ParameterTag`, and `InsertTag`—that demonstrate the use of cooperating tags. `DefinitionTag`, `ScreenTag`, and `ParameterTag` comprise a set of nested tag handlers that share public and private objects. `DefinitionTag` creates a public named object called `definition` that is used by `InsertTag`.

In `doStartTag`, `DefinitionTag` creates a public object named `screens` that contains a hash table of screen definitions. A screen definition consists of a screen identifier and a set of parameters associated with the screen.

```
public int doStartTag() {
    HashMap screens = null;
    screens = (HashMap) pageContext.getAttribute("screens",
        pageContext.APPLICATION_SCOPE);
    if (screens == null)
        pageContext.setAttribute("screens", new HashMap(),
            pageContext.APPLICATION_SCOPE);
    return EVAL_BODY_INCLUDE;
}
```

The table of screen definitions is filled in by `ScreenTag` and `ParameterTag` from text provided as attributes to these tags. Table 16.6 shows the contents of the screen definitions hash table for the Duke's Bookstore application.

Table 16.6 Screen Definitions

Screen Id	Title	Banner	Body
/enter	Duke's Bookstore	/banner.jsp	/bookstore.jsp
/catalog	Book Catalog	/banner.jsp	/catalog.jsp
/bookdetails	Book Description	/banner.jsp	/bookdetails.jsp
/showcart	Your Shopping Cart	/banner.jsp	/showcart.jsp
/cashier	Cashier	/banner.jsp	/cashier.jsp
/receipt	Receipt	/banner.jsp	/receipt.jsp

In doEndTag, DefinitionTag creates a public object of class Definition, selects a screen definition from the screens object based on the URL passed in the request, and uses it to initialize the Definition object.

```
public int doEndTag()throws JspTagException {
    try {
        Definition definition = new Definition();
        Hashtable screens = null;
        ArrayList params = null;
        TagSupport screen = null;
        screens = (HashMap)
            pageContext.getAttribute("screens",
                pageContext.APPLICATION_SCOPE);
        if (screens != null)
            params = (ArrayList) screens.get(screenId);
        else
            ...
        if (params == null)
            ...
        Iterator ir = null;
        if (params != null)
            ir = params.iterator();
        while ((ir != null) && ir.hasNext())
            definition.setParam((Parameter) ir.next());
            // put the definition in the page context
        pageContext.setAttribute(
            definitionName, definition);
    } catch (Exception ex) {
        ex.printStackTrace();
    }
    return EVAL_PAGE;
}
```

If the URL passed in the request is /enter, the Definition contains the items from the first row of Table 16.6:

Title	Banner	Body
Duke's Bookstore	/banner.jsp	/bookstore.jsp

The definition for the URL /enter is shown in Table 16.7. The definition specifies that the value of the Title parameter, Duke's Bookstore, should be inserted directly into the output stream, but the values of Banner and Body should be dynamically included.

InsertTag uses the Definition to insert parameters of the screen definition into the response. In the doStartTag method, it retrieves the definition object from the page context.

```
public int doStartTag() {
    // get the definition from the page context
    definition = (Definition) pageContext.
        getAttribute(definitionName);
    // get the parameter
    if (parameterName != null && definition != null)
        parameter = (Parameter)definition.
            getParam(parameterName);
    if (parameter != null)
        directInclude = parameter.isDirect();
    return SKIP_BODY;
}
```

The doEndTag method inserts the parameter value. If the parameter is direct, it is directly inserted into the response; otherwise, the request is sent to the parameter and the response is dynamically included into the overall response.

```
public int doEndTag()throws JspTagException {
    try {
        if (directInclude && parameter != null)
            pageContext.getOut().print(parameter.getValue());
        else {
            if ((parameter != null) &&
                (parameter.getValue() != null))
                pageContext.include(parameter.getValue());
```

Table 16.7 Screen Definition for URL /enter

Parameter Name	Parameter Value	isDirect
title	Duke's Bookstore	true
banner	/banner.jsp	false
body	/bookstore.jsp	false

```
        }
    } catch (Exception ex) {
        throw new JspTagException(ex.getMessage());
    }
    return EVAL_PAGE;
}
```

16.5.3 How Is a Tag Handler Invoked?

The Tag interface defines the basic protocol between a tag handler and JSP page's servlet. It defines the life cycle and the methods to be invoked when the start and end tags are encountered.

The JSP page's servlet invokes the setPageContext, setParent, and attribute setting methods before calling doStartTag. The JSP page's servlet also guarantees that release will be invoked on the tag handler before the end of the page.

Here is a typical tag handler method invocation sequence:

```
ATag t = new ATag();
t.setPageContext(...);
t.setParent(...);
t.setAttribute1(value1);
t.setAttribute2(value2);
t.doStartTag();
t.doEndTag();
t.release();
```

The BodyTag interface extends Tag by defining additional methods that let a tag handler access its body. The interface provides three new methods:

setBodyContent—creates body content and adds to tag handler

doInitBody—called before evaluation of tag body

doAfterBody—called after evaluation of tag body

A typical invocation sequence is:

```
t.doStartTag();
out = pageContext.pushBody();
t.setBodyContent(out);
// perform any initialization needed after body content is set
t.doInitBody();
```

```
t.doAfterBody();
// while doAfterBody returns EVAL_BODY_BUFFERED we
// iterate body evaluation
...
t.doAfterBody();
t.doEndTag();
t.pageContext.popBody();
t.release();
```

CHAPTER 17

JavaServer Pages Standard Tag Library

Stephanie Bodoff

IN THIS CHAPTER

THE JavaServer Pages Standard Tag Library ("JSTL") encapsulates core functionality common to many JSP applications. For example, instead of iterating over lists using a scriptlet or different iteration tags from numerous vendors, JSTL defines a standard tag that works the same everywhere. This standardization lets you learn a single tag and use it on multiple JSP containers. Also, when tags are standard, containers can recognize them and optimize their implementations.

JSTL has support for common, structural tasks such as iteration and conditionals, tags for manipulating XML documents, internationalization tags, and tags for accessing databases using SQL. It also introduces the concept of an expression language to simplify page development and includes several experimental languages. JSTL also provides a framework for integrating existing custom tags with JSTL tags.

For a complete description of JSTL tags, see the JSTL reference included with the Java Web Services Developer Pack (Java WSDP) at *<JSWDP_HOME>*/docs/jstl/index.html. This chapter assumes that you are familiar with the material in the Using Tags (page 434) section of Custom Tags in JSP Pages (page 431).

17.1 The Example JSP Pages

This chapter illustrates JSTL with excerpts from the JSP version of the Duke's Bookstore application discussed in Custom Tags in JSP Pages (page 431) rewritten as follows:

- Replaced the Struts logic tags with JSTL core tags.
- Replaced scriptlets accessing a message store with message formatting tags.
- Removed the JavaBeans component database helper object and replaced its function with direct calls to the database via the JSTL SQL tags. For most applications, it is better to encapsulate calls to a database in a bean. JSTL includes SQL tags for situations where a new application is being prototyped and the overhead of creating a bean may not be warranted.

The source for the Duke's Bookstore application is located in the docs/tutorial/examples/web/bookstore4 directory created when you unzip the tutorial bundle (see Running the Examples (page xx)). To build, deploy, and run the example:

1. Go to the bookstore4 directory and build and deploy the example by running ant. This runs the default ant target deploy that depends on the build target. The build target will spawn any necessary compilations and copy files to the docs/tutorial/examples/web/bookstore4/build directory. The deploy target copies the bookstore4.xml context file to *<JWSDP_HOME>*/webapps as described in Running Web Applications (page 360).
2. Start the Pointbase database server (see Accessing Databases from Web Applications (page 363)).
3. Start or restart Tomcat.
4. Open the bookstore URL http://localhost:8080/bookstore4/enter.

See Common Problems and Their Solutions (page 65) and Troubleshooting (page 369) for help with diagnosing common problems.

17.2 Using JSTL

JSTL includes a wide variety of tags that naturally fit into discrete functional areas. Therefore, JSTL is exposed via multiple TLDs to clearly show the functional areas it covers and give each area its own namespace. Table 17.1 summarizes these functional areas along with the logical TLD names and prefixes used in this chapter and Duke's Bookstore application.

To use the JSTL core tags in a JSP page, you declare the library using a `taglib` directive that references the TLD:

```
<%@ taglib uri="/jstl-core" prefix="c" %>
```

The JSTL tag libraries comes in two versions (see Twin Libraries (page 470)). The TLDs for the JSTL-EL library are named *prefix*`.tld`. The TLDs for the JSTL-RT library are named *prefix*`-rt.tld`. Since this chapter and examples use logical TLD names, we map the names to actual TLD locations with a `taglib` element in `web.xml`:

```
<taglib>
    <taglib-uri>/jstl-c</taglib-uri>
    <taglib-location>/WEB-INF/c.tld</taglib-location>
</taglib>
```

In the Java WSDP, the JSTL TLDs are stored in *<JWSDP_HOME>*`/tools/jstl`. When you build the Duke's Bookstore application these TLDs are automatically copied into `docs/tutorial/examples/web/bookstore4/build/WEB-INF`.

You can also reference a TLD in a `taglib` directive with an absolute URI:

- Core: `http://java.sun.com/jstl/ea/core`
- XML: `http://java.sun.com/jstl/ea/xml`
- Internationalization: `http://java.sun.com/jstl/ea/fmt`
- SQL: `http://java.sun.com/jstl/ea/sql`

When you use an absolute URI, you do not have to add the `taglib` element to `web.xml`; the JSP container automatically locates the TLD inside the JSTL library implementation.

Table 17.1 JSTL Tags

Area	Function	Tags	TLD	Prefix
Core	Expression Language Support	`<expr>` `<set>`	`/jstl-c`	`c`
	Flow Control	`<forEach>` `<forEachToken>` `<if>` `<choose>` `<when>` `<otherwise>`		
	Import	`<import>` `<param>` `<urlEncode>`		
XML	Core	`<parse>` `<expr>` `<set>`	`/jstl-x`	`x`
	Flow Control	`<forEach>` `<if>` `<choose>` `<when>` `<otherwise>`		
	Transformation	`<transform>` `<param>` `<transformer>`		
I18n	Locale	`<locale>`	`/jstl-fmt`	`fmt`
	Message formatting	`<bundle>` `<message>` `<messageFormat>` `<messageArg>`		
	Number and date formatting	`<formatNumber>` `<parseNumber>` `<timeZone>` `<formatDate>` `<parseDate>`		

Table 17.1 JSTL Tags *(Continued)*

Area	Function	Tags	TLD	Prefix
Database		`<driver>`	`/jstl-sql`	`sql`
	SQL	`<transaction>` `<query>` `<update>` `<param>`		

In addition to declaring the tag library, you also need to make the JSTL API and implementation available to the Web application. In the Java WSDP, these JSTL libraries are respectively `jstl.jar` and `standard.jar`, and are stored in `<JWSDP_HOME>/tools/jstl`. When you build the Duke's Bookstore application, these libraries are automatically copied into `docs/tutorial/examples/web/bookstore4/build/WEB-INF/lib`.

17.3 Expression Language Support

A primary feature of JSTL is its support for an expression language. Currently, a page author has to use an expression <%= aName %> to access the value of a system or user-defined JavaBeans component. For example:

```
<x:aTag att="<%= pageContext.getAttribute("aName") %>">
```

Furthermore, referring to nested bean properties is even more complex:

```
<%= aName.getFoo().getBar() %>
```

This makes page authoring more complex than it need be. An expression language allows a page author to access an object using a simplified syntax such as

```
<x:atag att="$aName">
```

for a simple variable or

```
<x:aTag att="$aName.foo.bar">
```

for a nested property.

Expression languages elevate JSP scoped attributes as the standard way to communicate information from business logic to JSP pages. An expression language, in concert with JSTL tags, makes it possible to easily access application data and manipulate it in simple ways without having to use scriptlets or request-time expressions. For example, this conditional tag tests whether the number of items in a session-scoped shopping cart is greater than 0.

```
<c:if test="$session:cart.numberOfItems > 0">
    ...
</c:if>
```

A goal of the next version of the JSP specification is to standardize on an expression language for all custom tag libraries. In the meantime, JSTL contains several expression languages for experimenting with, including:

- SPEL, the Simplest Possible Expression Language
- ECMAScript
- JXPath

The default expression language for the JSTL implementation is ECMAScript. However, the example discussed in this chapter uses SPEL (see Simplest Possible Expression Language (SPEL) (page 471)) because it allows you to specify the scope of objects.

17.3.1 Twin Libraries

The JSTL tag libraries comes in two versions that differ only in the way they support the use of runtime expressions for attribute values.

In the JSTL-RT tag library, expressions are specified in the page's scripting language. This is exactly how things currently work in current tag libraries.

In the JSTL-EL tag library, expressions are specified in a JSTL expression language (EL). An expression is a `String` literal in the syntax of the EL. It is the responsibility of the EL to define the metacharacter(s) used to discriminate expressions from `String` literals (for example, use `$` at the beginning of an expression).

When using the EL tag library you cannot pass a scripting language expression for the value of an attribute. This rule makes it possible to validate the syntax of an expression at translation time.

17.3.2 Specifying an Expression Language Evaluator

To use an expression language other than the default (ECMAScript) you must provide a context parameter `javax.servlet.jsp.ExpressionEvaluatorClass` in the Web application deployment descriptor. Because the Duke's Bookstore example uses SPEL, which is not the default expression language, it must convey this information to the tag library implementation. Here is the declaration from the Duke's Bookstore descriptor:

```
<context-param>
    <param-name>
        javax.servlet.jsp.jstl.temp.ExpressionEvaluatorClass
    </param-name>
    <param-value>
        org.apache.taglibs.standard.lang.spel.Evaluator
    </param-value>
</context-param>
```

It is also possible to override the default expression language setting with the `expressionLanguage` tag. For example:

```
<c:expressionLanguage class="...">
    <c:forEach items_="products/@key">
    ...
    </c:forEach>
</c:expressionLanguage>
```

The scope of the expression language specified by tag `c:expressionLanguage` is limited to its body. `c:expressionLanguage` tags can be nested, where nested occurrences shadow their ancestors.

17.3.3 Simplest Possible Expression Language (SPEL)

This is a brief summary of SPEL. For a complete syntax, see *<JWSDP_HOME>*`/docs/jstl/spel/spel.html`.

SPEL is responsible for handling both expressions and literals. The syntax of SPEL is extremely simple. Expressions begin with a `$` character. For example:

```
<c:if test="$bean1.a < 3" />
```

Any value that does not begin with `$` is treated as a literal that is parsed to the expected type using the `PropertyEditor` for the expected type:

```
<c:if test="true" />
```

Literal values that start with the $ character must be escaped using the \ character:

```
<mytags:price price="\$3.95" />
```

If a value starts with `\$`, it is treated as a literal value with the leading \ removed.

Attributes

Attributes are accessed by name, with an optional scope. Properties of attributes are accessed using the `.` operator, and may be nested arbitrarily. Indexed properties are accessed using the `[]` operator.

Attribute and property names must be Java identifiers, unless they are quoted.

If an attribute is specified with a scope of `page`, `request`, `session`, or `app`, its value is the value of that name in the given scope. If no scope is given, the value is found according to the rules of `PageContext.findAttribute(name)`.

If an attribute is specified with a scope of `header`, its value is obtained by calling `HttpServletRequest.getHeader(String)`.

If an attribute is specified with a scope of `param`, its value is obtained by calling `ServletRequest.getParameter(String)`.

If an attribute is specified with a scope of `paramvalues`, its value is obtained by calling `ServletRequest.getParameterValues(String)`.

In any of these cases, if a value is not found, the result is an `ExpressionException`, not `null`.

Relational Operators

Relational comparisons are allowed using the relational operators (==, !=, <, >, <=, >=). Comparisons may be made against other values, or against boolean, string, integer, or floating point literals.

17.3.4 Tag Collaboration

Tags usually collaborate with their environment in implicit and/or explicit ways. Implicit collaboration is done via a well-defined interface that allows nested tags to work seamlessly with the ancestor tag exposing that interface. The JSTL iterator tags support this mode of collaboration.

Explicit collaboration happens when a tag exposes information to its environment. Traditionally, this has been done by exposing a scripting variable (with a JSP scoped attribute providing the actual object). Because JSTL supports an expression language, there is less need for scripting variables. So the JSTL tags (both the EL and RT versions) expose information only as JSP scoped attributes; no scripting variables are used. The convention JSTL follows is to use the name `var` for any tag attribute that exports information about the tag. For example, the `forEach` tag exposes the current item of shopping cart it is iterating over in the following way:

```
<c:forEach var="item" items="$session:cart.items">
    ...
</c:forEach>
```

The name `var` was selected to highlight the fact that the scoped variable exposed is not a scripting variable (which is normally the case for attributes named `id`).

In situations where a tag exposes more than one piece of information, the name `var` is used for the primary piece of information being exported, and an appropriate name is selected for any other secondary piece of information exposed. For example, iteration status information is exported by the `forEach` tag via the attribute `status`.

17.4 Core Tags

The core tags include those related to expressions, flow control, and a generic way to access URL-based resources whose content can then be included and or processed within the JSP page.

Table 17.2 Core Tags

Area	Function	Tags	TLD	Prefix
Core	Expression Language Support	`<expr>` `<set>`	`/jstl-c`	`c`

	Flow Control	`<forEach>`
		`<forEachToken>`
		`<if>`
		`<choose>`
		`<when>`
		`<otherwise>`		

	Import	`<import>`
		`<param>`
		`<urlEncode>`		

17.4.1 Expression Tags

The `expr` tag evaluates an expression and outputs the result of the evaluation to the current `JspWriter` object. It is the equivalent of the JSP syntax <%= *expression* %>. For example, `showcart.jsp` displays the number of items in a shopping cart as follows:

```
<c:expr value="$session:cart.numberOfItems"/>
```

The `set` tag sets the value of an attribute in any of the JSP scopes (page, request, session, application). If the attribute does not already exist, it is created.

The JSP scoped attribute can be set either from attribute value:

```
<c:set id="foo" scope="session" value="..."/>
```

or from the body of the tag:

```
<c:set id="foo">
    ...
</c:set>
```

The JSTL expression language reduces the need for scripting. However, page authors will still have to deal with situations where some attributes of non-JSTL tags must be specified as expressions in the page's scripting language. The standard JSP element `jsp:useBean` is used to declare a scripting variable that can be used in a scripting language expression or scriptlet. For example, `showcart.jsp` removes a book from a shopping cart using a scriptlet. The ID of the book to be removed is passed as a request parameter. The value of the request parameter is first set as a page attribute (to be used later by the JSTL `sql:query` tag) and then declared as scripting variable and passed to the `cart.remove` method:

```
<c:set var="bookId" value="$param:Remove"/>
<jsp:useBean id="bookId" type="java.lang.String" />
<% cart.remove(bookId); %>
<sql:query var="books" dataSource="$bookDS">
    select * from PUBLIC.books where id = ?
    <sql:param value="$bookId" />
</sql:query>
```

17.4.2 Flow Control Tags

To execute flow control logic, a page author must generally resort to using scriptlets. For example, the following scriptlet is used to iterate through a shopping cart:

```
<%
    Iterator i = cart.getItems().iterator();
    while (i.hasNext()) {
        ShoppingCartItem item =
            (ShoppingCartItem)i.next();
        ...
%>
        <tr>
        <td align="right" bgcolor="#ffffff">
        <%=item.getQuantity()%>
        </td>
        ...
<%
    }
%>
```

Flow control tags eliminate the need for scriptlets.

Iterator Tags

The `forEach` tag allows you to iterate over a collection of objects.

Here's the iteration from the previous section using the `forEach` tag:

```
<c:forEach var="item" items="$session:cart.items">
    ...
    <tr>
        <td align="right" bgcolor="#ffffff">
        <c:expr value="$item.quantity"/>
    </td>
    ...
</c:forEach>
```

Conditional Tags

The `if` tag allows the conditional execution of its body according to value of a test attribute. The following example from `catalog.jsp` tests whether the request parameter `Add` is not empty. If the test evaluates to `true`, the page queries the database for the book record identified by the request parameter and adds the book to the shopping cart:

```
<c:if test="$param:Add != ''">
    <c:set var="bid" value="$param:Add"/>
    <c:declare id="bid"  type="java.lang.String" />
```

```
    <sql:query var="books" dataSource="$bookDS">
        select * from PUBLIC.books where id = ?
        <sql:param value="$bid" />
    </sql:query>
    <c:forEach var="bookRow" begin="0" items="$books.rows">
        <c:declare id="bookRow"
            type="javax.servlet.jsp.jstl.sql.Row" />
        <jsp:useBean id="addedBook"
            class="database.BookDetails" scope="page" />
    ...
    <% cart.add(bid, addedBook); %>
...
</c:if>
```

The `choose` tag performs conditional block execution embedded by the `when` sub tags. It renders the body of the first `when` tag whose test condition evaluates to true. If none of the test conditions of nested `when` tags evaluate to `true`, then the body of an `otherwise` tag is evaluated, if present.

17.4.3 Import Tags

The `jsp:include` element provides for the inclusion of static and dynamic resources in the same context as the current page. However, `jsp:include` cannot access resources that reside outside of the Web application and causes unnecessary buffering when the resource included is fed into another element.

In the example below, the `transform` element uses the content of the included resource as the input of its transformation. The `jsp:include` element reads the content of the response, writes it to the body content of the enclosing transform element, which then rereads the exact same content. It would be more efficient if the `transform` element could access the input source directly and avoid the buffering involved in the body content of the transform tag.

```
<acme:transform>
    <jsp:include page="/exec/employeesList"/>
<acme:transform/>
```

The `import` tag is therefore the simple, generic way to access URL based resources whose content can then be included and or processed within the JSP page. The `param` tag, analogous to the `jsp:param` tag (see Param Element (page 417)), can be used with `import` to specify request parameters.

17.5 XML Tags

A key aspect of dealing with XML documents is to be able to easily access their content. XPath, a W3C recommendation since 1999, provides an easy notation for specifying and selecting parts of an XML document. The JSTL XML tag set is based on XPath.

The XML tags use XPath as a *local* expression language; XPath expressions are always specified using attribute `select`. This means that only values specified for `select` attributes are evaluated using the XPath expression language. All other attributes are evaluated using the rules associated with the currently active global expression language.

For information on XPath see:

- Zvon XPath Tutorial
- XML in a Nutshell—XPath

This release of the tutorial summarizes the XML tags but does not illustrate their use in the Duke's Bookstore application.

Table 17.3 XML Tags

Area	Function	Tags	TLD	Prefix

XML	Core	`<parse>`
		`<expr>`
		`<set>`
			`/jstl-x`	`x`

	Flow Control	`<forEach>`
		`<if>`
		`<choose>`
		`<when>`
		`<otherwise>`		

	Transformation	`<transform>`
		`<param>`
		`<transformer>`		

17.5.1 Core Tags

The core set of XML tags provides the basic functionality to easily parse and access XML data.

The `parse` tag parses an XML document and saves the resulting object in the JSP scoped attribute specified by attribute `var`.

The `expr` and `set` tags parallel the behavior described in Expression Tags (page 474) for the XPath local expression language.

The `expr` tag evaluates an XPath expression on the current context node and outputs the result of the evaluation to the current `JspWriter` object.

The `set` tag evaluates an XPath expression and sets the result into a JSP scoped attribute specified by attribute `var`.

17.5.2 Flow Control Tags

The XML flow control tags parallel the behavior described in Flow Control Tags (page 474) for the XPath expression language.

```
<forEach>
<if>
<choose>
    <when>
    <otherwise>
```

17.5.3 Transformation Tags

The `transform` tag applies a transformation, specified by a XSLT stylesheet set by the attribute `xslt`, to an XML document, specified by the attribute `xml`. If the `xml` attribute is not specified, the input XML document is read from the tag's body content.

The `param` subtag can be used along with `transform` to set transformation parameters. The attributes `name` and `value` are used to specify the parameter. The value attribute is optional. If it is not specified the value is retrieved from the tag's body.

Sometimes the same stylesheet transformation needs to be applied multiple times to different source XML documents. Instead of processing the stylesheet on each invocation of `transform`, a more efficient approach is to process the transformation stylesheet once, and then save this transformer object for successive transformations. The `transformer` tag can be used in collaboration with the `transformer` attribute of `transform` to efficiently reuse a transformation stylesheet.

17.6 Internationalization Tags

In Internationalizing and Localizing Web Applications (page 361), we discussed the how to adapt Web applications to the language and formatting conventions of client locales. This section describes tags that support the internationalization of JSP pages.

JSTL defines two sets of tags:

- Messaging tags assist page authors with creating messages that can be adapted to any locale available in the JSP container
- Formatting tags allow various data elements such as numbers, currencies, dates and times to be formatted and parsed in a locale-sensitive or customized manner.

Table 17.4 Internationalization Tags

Area	Function	Tags	TLD	Prefix
I18n	Locale	`<locale>`	`/jstl-fmt`	`fmt`

	Message formatting	`<bundle>`
		`<message>`
		`<messageFormat>`
		`<messageArg>`		

	Number and date formatting	`<formatNumber>`
		`<parseNumber>`
		`<timeZone>`
		`<formatDate>`
		`<parseDate>`		

17.6.1 Messaging Tags

By default, browser-sensing capabilities for locales are enabled. This means that the client determines (via its browser settings) which locale to use, and allows page authors to cater to the language preferences of their clients.

The `locale` tag is used to override the client-specified locale for a page.

Specifying a Bundle

You use the `bundle` tag to specify a resource bundle for a page.

To define a resource bundle for a Web application you specify the context parameter `javax.servlet.jsp.jstl.i18n.basename` in the Web application deployment descriptor. Here is the declaration from the Duke's Bookstore descriptor:

```
<context-param>
    <param-name>
        javax.servlet.jsp.jstl.i18n.basename
    </param-name>
    <param-value>messages.BookstoreMessages</param-value>
</context-param>
```

Message Tags

The `message` tag is used to output localized strings. The following tag from `catalog.jsp`:

```
<h3><fmt:message key="Choose"/></h3>
```

is used to output a string inviting customers to choose a book from the catalog.

The `messageFormat` tag performs parametric replacement on a given pattern string, using the runtime's default locale. The pattern string may be specified via the `value` attribute; if missing, it is read from the tag's body content.

The `messageArg` tag provides a single argument (for parametric replacement) to the compound message or pattern in its parent `message` or `messageFormat` tag, respectively. One `messageArg` tag must be specified for each variable in the compound message or pattern. Parametric replacement takes place in the order of the `messageArg` tags.

17.6.2 Formatting Tags

The `formatNumber` tag is used to output localized numbers. The following tag from `showcart.jsp`:

```
<fmt:formatNumber value="$book.price" type="currency"/>
```

is used to display a localized price for a book. Note that since the price is maintained in the database in dollars, the localization is somewhat phony, because the the `formatNumber` tag is unaware of exchange rates. The tag formats currencies but does not convert them. Analogous tags for formatting dates (`formatDate`), and parsing numbers and dates (`parseNumber`, `parseDate`) are also available. The `timeZone` tag establishes the time zone (specified via the `value` attribute) to be used by any nested `formatDate` tags.

17.7 SQL Tags

The JSTL SQL tags are designed for quick prototyping and simple applications.

Table 17.5 SQL Tags

Area	Function	Tags	TLD	Prefix
Database		`<driver>`	`/jstl-sql`	`sql`

	SQL	`<transaction>`
		`<query>`
		`<update>`
		`<param>`		

The `driver` tag is provided to allow you to set driver information for the database. However, an application's business logic (for example, via a life cycle event listener or controller servlet) should normally be used to create a data source and make it available to the rest of the application. This is the approach followed by the Duke's Bookstore, which creates a data source in `listeners.ContextListener`:

```
public void contextInitialized(ServletContextEvent event) {
    context = event.getServletContext();
    try  {
        InitialContext ic = new InitialContext();
        Context envCtx = (Context) ic.lookup("java:comp/env");
        DataSource ds = (DataSource)
            envCtx.lookup("jdbc/BookDB");
        context.setAttribute("bookDS", ds);
```

The `query` tag is used to perform an SQL query that returns a result set. For parameterized SQL queries, you use a nested `param` tag inside the query tag. The `update` tag is used to update a database row. The `transaction` tag is used to perform an atomic update.

In `catalog.jsp`, the value of the `Add` request parameter determines which book information should be retrieved from in the database. This parameter is saved as the attribute name `bid` and passed to the `param` tag. Notice that the `query` tag obtains its data source from the attribute `bookDS` set in the context listener.

```
<c:set var="bid" value="$param:Add"/>
<sql:query var="books" dataSource="$bookDS">
    select * from PUBLIC.books where id = ?
    <sql:param value="$bid" />
</sql:query>
```

17.7.1 Query Tag Result-Related Interfaces

The following interfaces are used to retrieve information from objects returned from a `query` tag. For each interface we list the methods discussed in this section. For complete information about these interfaces, see the API documentation for the `javax.servlet.jsp.jstl.sql` package.

```
public interface Result
    public Row[] getRows()
public interface ResultMetaData
```

```
public interface Row
    public Column[] getColumns()
public interface ColumnMetaData
public interface Column
    public String toString()
    public Object getValue()
```

The `var` attribute set by a query is of type `Result`. The `getRows` method returns a collection of rows that can be provided to an iterator tag. The SPEL expression language converts the syntax *`result`*`.rows` to a call to *`result`*`.getRows`. The expression `$books.rows` in the following example returns a collection of rows.

When you provide a collection of rows to an iterator, the `var` attribute set by the iterator is of type `Row`. To retrieve information from a row, use the `getColumns` method of `Row` to get its columns, and the `getValue` method of `Column` to get the value. The SPEL expression language converts the syntax *`row`*`.columns[`*`i`*`]` to a call to *`row`*`.getColumns()[`*`i`*`]` which returns a `Column`. When you pass a column to `c:expr` tag, it outputs a `String` representation of the value of the column.

Thus, the Duke's Bookstore page `bookdetails.jsp` retrieves the columns from the `book` row as follows.

```
<c:forEach var="book" begin="0" items="$books.rows">
    <h2><c:expr value="$book.columns[3]"/></h2>
     <fmt:message key="By"/> <em><c:expr
    value="$book.columns[2]"/> <c:expr
    value="$book.columns[1]"/></em>  
    (<c:expr value="$book.columns[5]"/>)<br>   <br>
    <h4><fmt:message key="Critics"/></h4>
    <blockquote><c:expr value="$book.columns[6]"/>
    </blockquote>
    <h4><fmt:message key="ItemPrice"/>:
    <fmt:formatNumber value="$book.columns[4]"
        type="currency"/>
    </h4>
</c:forEach>
```

The following excerpt from `catalog.jsp` uses the `Row` and `Column` interfaces to retrieve values from the columns of a book row using scripting language expressions. First, the book row that matches a request parameter (`bid`) is retrieved from the database. Since the `bid` and `bookRow` objects are later used by tags that use scripting language expressions to set attribute values and a scriptlet that adds a book to the shopping cart, both objects are declared as scripting variables using the `jsp:useBean` tag. The page then creates a bean that describes the book and scripting language expressions are used to set the book properties from column values. Finally, the book is added to the shopping cart.

You might want to compare this version of `catalog.jsp` to the versions that use a book database JavaBeans component.

```
<sql:query var="books" dataSource="$bookDS">
    select * from PUBLIC.books where id = ?
    <sql:param value="$bid" />
</sql:query>
<c:forEach var="bookRow" begin="0" items="$books.rows">
    <jsp:useBean id="bid"  type="java.lang.String" />
    <jsp:useBean id="bookRow"
        type="javax.servlet.jsp.jstl.sql.Row" />
    <jsp:useBean id="addedBook" class="database.BookDetails"
        scope="page" />
        <jsp:setProperty name="addedBook" property="bookId"
            value="<%=bookRow.get(0).toString()%>" />
        <jsp:setProperty name="addedBook" property="surname"
            value="<%=bookRow.get(1).toString()%>" />
        <jsp:setProperty name="addedBook" property="firstName"
            value="<%=bookRow.get(2).toString()%>" />
        <jsp:setProperty name="addedBook" property="title"
            value="<%=bookRow.get(3).toString()%>" />
        <jsp:setProperty name="addedBook" property="price"
            value="<%=((Double)bookRow.get(4).getValue()).
            floatValue()%>" />
        <jsp:setProperty name="addedBook" property="year"
            value="<%=(Integer)bookRow.get(5).getValue()%>" />
        <jsp:setProperty name="addedBook"
            property="description"
            value="<%=bookRow.get(6).toString()%>" />
        <jsp:setProperty name="addedBook" property="inventory"
            value="<%=(Integer)bookRow.get(7).getValue()%>" />
    </jsp:useBean>
    <% cart.add(bid, addedBook); %>
    ...
</c:forEach>
```

CHAPTER 18

The xrpcc Tool

Dale Green

In This Chapter

PART of the JAX-RPC reference implementation, the `xrpcc` tool generates stubs, ties, and other files. Stubs and ties are class files that enable communication between a remote client and a Web service. To see how stubs and ties fit into the JAX-RPC stack, see Figure 9.1.

In addition to stubs and ties, the `xrpcc` tool can generate either Remote Method Invocation (RMI) interfaces, or Web Services Description Language (WSDL) documents. If the tool's input is a WSDL document, then it produces RMI interfaces. If the input is a set of RMI interfaces, then it creates WSDL documents. You specify the files to be generated in the `xrpcc` configuration file.

For an example of how to run the tool, see Generating the Stubs and Ties (page 311).

18.1 Syntax

The `xrpcc` tool is a command-line utility with the following syntax:

UNIX:

```
xrpcc.sh [options] config-file-name
```

Windows:

```
xrpcc.bat [options] config-file-name
```

Table 18.1 lists the tool's options. If no option is specified, the tool displays usage information.

Table 18.1 Options of xrpcc

Option	Description
`-client`	Generates client-side files: stubs, service interface, implementation classes, remote interface*
`-server`	Generates server-side files: ties, server configuration file, WSDL file*, service definition interface*
`-both`	Generates both the client-side and server-side files
`-classpath` *`classpath`*	Sets the tool's classpath
`-d` *`directory-name`*	Specifies the output directory for the generated files
`-keep`	Does not delete the generated .java files after they are compiled
-version	Displays version number of JAX-RPC

* If this file is specified in the tool's configuration file, then this file will be generated even if the command-line option is not specified.

18.2 Configuration File

The `xrpcc` tool reads an XML configuration file that specifies the files to be generated. The configuration file has two different formats, depending on whether you are starting with RMI interfaces or a WSDL document. The file can have one format or the other, but not both. The file's `<configuration>` element must have either one `<rmi>` element or one `<wsdl>` element.

Note: Although required for the reference implementation of JAX-RPC, the configuration file and `xrpcc` tool are not defined in the specifications. Their syntax and usage may change in future releases.

18.2.1 Starting with RMI Interfaces

If you are starting with RMI interfaces, the tool can generate stubs, ties, a server configuration file, and a WSDL document. In this case, the tool's configuration file must have the following form:

```
<?xml version="1.0" encoding="UTF-8"?>
 <configuration
 xmlns="http://java.sun.com/jax-rpc-ri/xrpcc-config">
   <rmi name="[1]"
        targetNamespace="[2]"
        typeNamespace="[3]">
     <service name="[4]"
              packageName="[5]">
       <interface name="[6]"
                  servantName="[7]"
                  soapAction="[8]"
                  soapActionBase="[9]"/>
     </service>
   <typeMappingRegistry>
     [10]
   </typeMappingRegistry>
   </rmi>
 </configuration>
```

The integers in the preceding syntax indicate the following:

1. Model name
2. Target namespace for the generated WSDL document
3. Target namespace for the schema portion of the generated WSDL document
4. Service name
5. Package name for the generated classes (for example, the service interface that extends `javax.xml.rpc.Service`)
6. Fully qualified name of an interface
7. Fully qualified name of a servant class that implements the interface in [6]
8. Optional—string to be used as the `SOAPAction` for all operations in the corresponding port

9. Optional—string to be used as a prefix for the SOAPAction strings for the operations in the corresponding port
10. Optional—type mapping information, see Specifying the Type Mapping (page 490)

For RMI interfaces, the <configuration> element must have just one <rmi> element. The <rmi> element may contain multiple <service> elements, which may contain multiple <interface> elements.

SOAPAction Elements

If you are an advanced user you might be interested in the following information about SOAPAction elements: If the soapAction attribute is specified, all the operations in the generated port will use that string as the SOAPAction. If the soapActionBase attribute is specified, its value will be used as a prefix for the generated SOAPAction strings. The suffix will be a unique string; in the current implementation it is the operation name. For example, if soapActionBase is set to http://hello/ and the port has two operations, opA and opB, their SOAPAction strings will be http://hello/opA and http://hello/opB, respectively. If neither soapAction nor soapActionBase are specified, the SOAPAction for all operations will be the empty string. Notice that this version of the reference implementation does not rely on the SOAPAction HTTP header for dispatching.

18.2.2 Starting with a WSDL Document

If you are starting with a WSDL document, the tool can generate stubs, ties, a server configuration file, and RMI interfaces. The tool's configuration file must have the following form:

```
<?xml version="1.0" encoding="UTF-8"?>
 <configuration
 xmlns="http://java.sun.com/jax-rpc-ri/xrpcc-config">
   <wsdl name="[1]"
         location="[2]"
         packageName="[3]">
     <typeMappingRegistry>
       [4]
     </typeMappingRegistry>
   </wsdl>
 </configuration>
```

The integers in the preceding syntax indicate the following:

1. Model name
2. URL pointing to a WSDL document
3. Fully qualified name of the package for the generated classes and interfaces
4. Optional: type mapping information, see Specifying the Type Mapping (490)

For WSDL documents, the `<configuration>` element must have just one `<wsdl>` element.

Server Configuration File

The `xrpcc` tool also generates a server configuration file for Tomcat. The name of the file is specified by the `<init-param>` element of the `web.xml` file. (The `web.xml` file is the deployment descriptor for a Web application that's packaged in a WAR file.) For example, the `web.xml` file might contain the following `<init-param>` element:

```
<init-param>
        <param-name>configuration.file</param-name>
        <param-value>/WEB-INF/config.properties</param-value>
      </init-param>
```

Here's an example of a server configuration file that is generated by the `xrpcc` tool:

```
port0.tie=hello.HelloIF_Tie
port0.servant=hello.HelloImpl
port0.name=HelloIF
port0.wsdl.targetNamespace=http://hello.org/wsdl
port0.wsdl.serviceName=HelloWorld
port0.wsdl.portName=HelloIFPort
portcount=1
```

For the `<init-param>` example shown previously, the server configuration file should be copied to the `WEB-INF/config.properties` file in the Tomcat installation.

18.2.3 Specifying the Type Mapping

Intended for advanced users, this section describes the <typeMappingRegistry> element of the tool's configuration file. Here's an example:

```
<typeMappingRegistry>
   <typeMapping
     encodingStyle="http://schemas.xmlsoap.org/soap/encoding/">
      <entry schemaType="ns1:SampleType"
         javaType="org.tempuri.WellKnownClass"
         serializerFactory=
           "org.tempuri.WellKnownClassSerializationFactory"
          deserializerFactory=
           "org.tempuri.WellKnownClassDeserializationFactory"
          xmlns:ns1="http://echoservice.org/types"/>
    </typeMapping>
 </typeMappingRegistry>
```

A type mapping registry can have multiple type mappings (for different encoding styles). Each mapping consists of multiple entries and all attributes on an entry are mandatory. For more information, see the JAX-RPC Specifications.

CHAPTER 19

HTTP Overview

Stephanie Bodoff

IN THIS CHAPTER

MOST Web clients use the HTTP protocol to communicate with a J2EE server. HTTP defines the requests that a client can send to a server and responses that the server can send in reply. Each request contains a URL, which is a string that identifies a Web component or a static object such as an HTML page or image file.

The J2EE server converts an HTTP request to an HTTP request object and delivers it to the Web component identified by the request URL. The Web component fills in an HTTP response object, which the server converts to an HTTP response and sends to the client.

This chapter provides some introductory material on the HTTP protocol. For further information on this protocol, see the Internet RFCs: HTTP/1.0 - RFC 1945, HTTP/1.1 - RFC 2616, which can be downloaded from

```
http://www.rfc-editor.org/rfc.html
```

19.1 HTTP Requests

An HTTP request consists of a request method, a request URL, header fields, and a body. HTTP 1.1 defines the following request methods:

- `GET`—retrieves the resource identified by the request URL.
- `HEAD`—returns the headers identified by the request URL.
- `POST`—sends data of unlimited length to the Web server.
- `PUT`—stores a resource under the request URL.
- `DELETE`—removes the resource identified by the request URL.
- `OPTIONS`—returns the HTTP methods the server supports.
- `TRACE`—returns the header fields sent with the TRACE request.

HTTP 1.0 includes only the GET, HEAD, and POST methods. Although J2EE servers are only required to support HTTP 1.0, in practice many servers, including the Java WSDP, support HTTP 1.1.

19.2 HTTP Responses

An HTTP response contains a result code, header fields, and a body.

The HTTP protocol expects the result code and all header fields to be returned before any body content.

Some commonly used status codes include:

- `404`—indicates that the requested resource is not available.
- `401`—indicates that the request requires HTTP authentication.
- `500`—indicates an error inside the HTTP server which prevented it from fulfilling the request.
- `503`—indicates that the HTTP server is temporarily overloaded, and unable to handle the request.

APPENDIX A

Java Encoding Schemes

This appendix describes the character-encoding schemes that are supported by the Java platform.

US-ASCII

US-ASCII is a 7-bit encoding scheme that covers the English-language alphabet. It is not large enough to cover the characters used in other languages, however, so it is not very useful for internationalization.

UTF-8

UTF-8 is an 8-bit encoding scheme. Characters from the English-language alphabet are all encoded using an 8-bit bytes. Characters for other languages are encoding using 2, 3 or even 4 bytes. UTF-8 therefore produces compact documents for the English language, but very large documents for other languages. If the majority of a document's text is in English, then UTF-8 is a good choice because it allows for internationalization while still minimizing the space required for encoding.

UTF-16

UTF-16 is a 16-bit encoding scheme. It is large enough to encode all the characters from all the alphabets in the world, with the exception of ideogram-based languages like Chinese. All characters in UTF-16 are encoded using 2 bytes. An English-language document that uses UTF-16 will be twice as large as the same document encoded using UTF-8. Documents written in other languages, however, will be far smaller using UTF-16.

About the Authors

Java API for XML Processing

Eric Armstrong has been programming and writing professionally since before there were personal computers. His production experience includes artificial intelligence (AI) programs, system libraries, real-time programs, and business applications in a variety of languages. He works as a consultant at Sun's Java Software division in the San Francisco Bay Area, and he is a contributor to JavaWorld. He wrote The *JBuilder2 Bible*, as well as Sun's Java XML programming tutorial. For a time, Eric was involved in efforts to design next-generation collaborative discussion/decision systems. His learn-by-ear, see-the-fingering music teaching program is currently on hold while he finishes a weight training book. His Web site is `http://www.treelight.com`.

Web Applications and Technology

Stephanie Bodoff is a staff writer at Sun Microsystems. She has been involved with object-oriented enterprise software since graduating from Columbia University with an M.S. in electrical engineering. For several years she worked as a software engineer on distributed computing and telecommunications systems and object-oriented software development methods. Since her conversion to technical writing, Stephanie has documented object-oriented databases, application servers, and enterprise application development methods. She is a co-author of *The J2EE™ Tutorial, Designing Enterprise Applications with the Java™ 2 Platform, Enterprise Edition*, and *Object-Oriented Software Development: The Fusion Method*.

Getting Started

Debbie Carson is a staff writer with Sun Microsystems, where she documents both the J2EE and J2SE platforms. In previous positions, she documented creating database applications using C++ and Java technologies and creating distributed applications using Java technology. She currently writes about the CORBA technologies Java IDL and Java Remote Method Invocation over Internet Inter-ORB Protocol (RMI-IIOP), Web services security, and Web services tools.

Java API for XML Messaging, Introduction to Web Services

Maydene Fisher has documented various Java APIs at Sun Microsystems for the last five years. She authored two books on the JDBC API, *JDBC™ Database Access with Java: A Tutorial and Annotated Reference* and *JDBC™ API Tutorial and Reference, Second Edition: Universal Data Access for the Java™ 2 Platform.* Before joining Sun, she helped document the object-oriented programming language ScriptX at Kaleida Labs and worked on Wall Street, where she wrote developer and user manuals for complex financial computer models written in C++. In previous lives, she has been an English teacher, a shopkeeper in Mendocino, and a financial planner.

Java API for RPC-based XML

Dale Green is a staff writer with Sun Microsystems, where he documents the J2EE platform and the Java API for RPC-based XML. In previous positions he programmed business applications, designed databases, taught technical classes, and documented RDBMS products. He wrote the Internationalization and Reflection trails for the *Java™ Tutorial Continued*, and co-authored *The J2EE™ Tutorial.*

Java API for XML Registries, Java WSDP Registry Server

Kim Haase is a staff writer with Sun Microsystems, where she documents the J2EE platform. In previous positions she has documented compilers, debuggers, and floating-point programming. She currently writes about the Java Message Service, the Java API for XML Registries, and J2EE SDK tools.

Index

A

B

F

L

M

Q

R

T

X

CD-ROM Warranty

Addison-Wesley and Sun Microsystems warrant the enclosed disc to be free of defects in materials and faulty workmanship under normal use for a period of ninety days after purchase. If a defect is discovered in the disc during this warranty period, a replacement disc can be obtained at no charge by sending the defective disc, postage prepaid, with proof of purchase to:

Editorial Department
Addison-Wesley Professional
Pearson Technology Group
75 Arlington Street, Suite 300
Boston, MA 02116
Email: AWPro@awl.com

Addison-Wesley and Sun Microsystems make no warranty or representation, either expressed or implied, with respect to this software, its quality, performance, merchantability, or fitness for a particular purpose. In no event will Addison-Wesley, Sun Microsystems, its distributors, or dealers be liable for direct, indirect, special, incidental, or consequential damages arising out of the use or inability to use the software. The exclusion of implied royalties is not permitted in some states. Therefore, the above exclusion may not apply to you. This warranty provides you with specific legal rights. There may be other rights that you may have that vary from state to state. The contents of this CD-ROM are intended for non-commercial use only.